WORLD CHANGES IN DIVORCE PATTERNS

World Changes in
Divorce Patterns

William J. Goode

YALE UNIVERSITY PRESS: NEW HAVEN AND LONDON

Designed by Sally Harris/Summer Hill Books.
Set in Meridien type by
The Composing Room of Michigan.
Printed in the United States of America by
Edwards Brothers, Inc., Ann Arbor, Michigan.

Library of Congress Cataloging-in-Publication Data

Goode, William Josiah.
    World changes in divorce patterns / William J. Goode
        p.   cm.
    Includes bibliographical references and index.
    ISBN 0-300-05537-4
    1. Divorce—Cross-cultural studies.   I. Title.
HQ814.G62   1993
306.89—dc20   92-44530
                                                          CIP

A catalogue record for this book is available
from the British Library.

The paper in this book meets the guidelines for
permanence and durability of the Committee on
Production Guidelines for Book Longevity
of the Council on Library Resources.
10   9   8   7   6   5   4   3   2   1

Contents

Preface and Acknowledgments

Although this inquiry may seem presumptuous, even in its title, my original goal was much more modest, and very different. But without my realizing it at first, this research grew over the years from my initial exploration of the relationship between class position and divorce rates in different countries over time. That inquiry had its genesis in a finding, surprising to me and others, that marital dissolution rates are higher toward the lower classes (using income or occupation as a measure) but that in the Western countries these rates had been higher toward the upper classes some generations ago. That is, only the middle and upper classes could then afford divorce or legal separation. However, as the cost of divorce was reduced—for example, in the United States—the lower classes became more likely to divorce formally than the well-to-do.[1] This seemed to be true of other countries as well, and later analysts did affirm my findings. The question then arises about the future: if divorce becomes still more widespread, will the class difference in divorce grow smaller? (Of course, if everyone does it, that will be arithmetically so.)

I did not complete that inquiry. The most important conclusion from it was that the available data could not answer my question precisely enough. By the time the work came to a halt, however, I found that I had already started on a different search. The shift was caused by my growing under-

1. For the facts and their theoretical meaning, see William J. Goode, "Problems in Postdivorce Adjustment," *Am. Soc. Rev.* 14 (1949), pp. 394–401; "Economic Factors and Marital Stability," *Am. Soc. Rev.* 15 (1951), pp. 802–12; *Women in Divorce* (New York: Free Press, 1956), chs. 4, 5; "Marital Satisfaction and Instability," *Int. Soc. Sci. J.* 14 (1962), pp. 507–26; several analyses in *World Revolution and Family Patterns* (New York: Free Press, 1963); and "Family Disorganization," in Robert K. Merton and Robert Nisbet, eds., *Contemporary Social Problems* (New York: Harcourt, Brace, Jovanovich, 1971), p. 532.

standing that the broader changes in many aspects of divorce during the past forty years were dramatic enough to deserve theoretical analysis in their own right and were also much more important. In any event, class differences seemed to play a large part in those changes, too. Thus my somewhat modest original study was gradually transformed into a more daunting one, which led eventually to larger and at times speculative conclusions.

That broader sweep required very different data. Increasing the number of countries and widening the range of topics would permit, and even require, much broader social information, not all of it easily reducible to numbers. For that matter, often the basic numbers were not available either.

The transformation would not, however, alter the need for a comparative or cross-national study, for my focus continued to be on the dynamics or causal processes that help explain changes in divorce processes over time. Only by finding out whether countries are undergoing similar experiences can we achieve a sound understanding of those processes. We can be sure, for example, that it is not some peculiarly American addiction to divorce that causes so many divorced mothers to fall into economic difficulties, when we observe a rise in mother-headed families—as well as a high poverty rate among them—not only in European nations but in many other countries throughout the world. Thus the topic itself requires a comparative approach—not merely tabulating data from many nations but actually trying to compare them within their socioeconomic context.

Of course, as a sociologist I have a bias in favor of comparative research. Scholars in this field continue, I think, to cherish the hope (now less often confessed in public) that it is possible to formulate generalizations of great scope and power, and that is more likely through a comparative study of several countries rather than from, say, a public opinion survey in a middle-sized American city. The number of such studies is doubtless increasing now (especially as the European Economic Community becomes a reality). They remain somewhat uncommon, however, especially in the United States, as may easily be seen from even a casual perusal of current book reviews in the field.

There are good reasons why most scholars avoid the hazards of comparative research, but my pleasure in it comes from early and later personal experience. When I first ventured North from Texas to begin my graduate work in sociology I was entirely unburdened with any knowledge of the field but, happily, soon found that what I was expected to study fitted neatly my intellectual tastes. In the third grade the principal of my grammar school had excited me with her summer experiences among the Eskimo, and I have remained an Eskimo buff to this day. I pored over the great "natural history" volumes in my home, full of tales, reports, and misinformation about the social patterns of wild animals as well as people. Much later, the careful pioneer field reports of animal behavior carried out by C. Ray Carpenter (one of my professors) offered new comparisons and sought to find order, and my delight in such studies and discoveries has not diminished at all. In graduate school, I was expected to study both tribal and industrial societies as well as, of course, the classical comparative studies of Emile Durkheim, Max Weber, and Vilfredo Pareto. I was encouraged there to write my first monograph, *Religion among the Primitives,* published in 1951.

My personal taste was strengthened, then, in graduate school. However, most social scientists have easily resisted such influences toward comparative analyses, and there are good reasons for this. The search for the relevant information—indeed, even finding out what that might be—is necessarily formless and frustrating, and thus time-wasting. Many of the necessary data are difficult to find or to put together. Some are entirely missing for some countries or on particular subtopics. Pressing the computer keys will not divulge them; they may not even appear in any available data base.

A second reason is that the sociologist who ventures far from his own direct experience necessarily invades the territory of regional and historical scholars, who are quick to point out how naive these interpretations are. Indeed, regional specialists typically do know the culture much better and historians have greater knowledge of a particular historical era. The comparativist who tries to intrude in their areas of special expertise is therefore truly vulnerable—as we can observe from the very bitter attacks on those who try to compare major revolutions.

Further, in addition to the likelihood of being attacked for one's boldness in comparing historical processes and/or many countries, there is a still greater risk; that of simply being wrong. After all, if our work is not subjected to such dissection, it is usually because our peers think our report is not significant enough to be read seriously. But making errors—worse yet, actually spreading them by publication—remains a nagging sore spot even after others have long ceased to read the offending error.

In fact, making such errors is especially easy in comparative analysis. That requires no special talent at all. One cannot describe everything, of course, and a comparative analysis forces one to ignore many important details. Working on many countries requires a focus on larger social processes or institutions, which are then wrenched from much of their context. Unfortunately, what is ignored may turn out to be crucial for the analysis of one country (but not for another), and none of us has been granted the wisdom of knowing in every case what can safely be left out.

In China as in Malaysia, for example, there are many subcultures as well as classes, and thus many different forms of marriage and divorce. Which of them might be important enough to transform a seemingly reasonable analysis into a foolish hypothesis? After all, this is a matter of reality. Logic cannot prove that an important factor does not exist. No rules of research design can prove that certain empirically possible data will not be found, simply because we have not yet found them.

Finally, one is plagued by cultural (and political) differences in the collection and publication of data, for they do not simply spring into being. Gathering and analyzing them was not one of the intense concerns of the statistical bureaus of many countries before the very recent surge of interest among some European countries. Thus in some nations the relevant data were never even collected, and in others, even if they were gathered they were not published. Because I once carried out demographic analyses which were not published—and which I did not even have the right to examine afterward (because they were classified data in wartime and I had no security clearance), I know there are many analyses gathering dust in unopened drawers, and that only some of these will ever be published later.

Thus we can be almost certain that what is officially published is not the entire story. Indeed, it may not even be the main story. In China, as in Eastern Europe, we know that the publication of data had a political and propagandistic aim, but we cannot know which data were correct just the same—and that may be true of those who originally authorized the publication as well. All we can do—and I have done it extensively—is to continue asking those who might know whether additional facts might be obtained. From time to time, the individual responses contain significant information.

It must also be conceded that many American scholars easily resist the allure of comparative analyses because of the barrier of languages. The unpublished paper on some aspect of divorce may well be in the writer's native language, and that is not likely to be English. Scholars in many countries may have an interest in a particular topic, such as remarriage, or religion and divorce, and they may be self-indulgent enough to write in their own tongue. They too avoid comparative inquiries, so that we can not expect them to do our work for us. Unfortunately, even the first step, of locating documents and papers in other languages, is not easy. Contrary to the celebrated new era of electronic libraries, a high but unknown number of publications in other languages on your favorite topic will probably not be found in the supposedly obvious bibliographic computer sources. Their physical location is, it hardly need be added, even more elusive.

Academics in this and other countries mostly support the polite fiction that their colleagues are respectably learned (except of course in one's own special topic), and they are careful not to ask others very closely about their languages. I think they also tend to magnify the linguistic skills of those who do cite many foreign sources. I should like to offer a personal cautionary note on this matter.

I was fortunate in my language experiences. I was introduced to German, Spanish, and Italian in high school and enjoyed them enough to continue in college. In my sophomore year my German professor set me the task of reading Paulsen on Immanuel Kant. In answer to the reader's unspoken question, I give the classic answer: Yes, I did understand a word of it; and now and then even a sentence. In graduate school, I traded German for French, using as my first text the classic work by Emile Durkheim, *Le Suicide*. With the advent of World War II, I discovered that languages were useful for a graduate student seeking a job. I sought help from my former high school debating coach and homeroom teacher, Lyndon B. Johnson (who had by then abandoned what I thought was a very promising career) and the result was a summer job in which I dictated translations of technical materials from five foreign languages. Since languages were useful to me, I continued to use them. I have lectured in both Spanish and German and wrote a book in German. In working on *World Revolution and Family Patterns*, I read books in six languages (technically seven, if one distinguishes between Afrikaans and Dutch). I "read" at least statistical tables in some others at times. Later, for a while during World War II, I also worked with the great demographer Irene Taeuber, who could do so in more than a dozen languages. Once I understood easily a Swiss radio broadcast in Romansch, and have idly read more than a few pages in Provençal.

Nevertheless, that is a far cry from a mastery of any foreign language, and I discarded (though reluctantly) that high aspiration many decades ago. I cannot quickly scan several pages in any language. In any event, it is fortunately not necessary. After all, this is social science not poetry. If the author is not singularly maladroit in his own descriptions, they are likely to be straightforward. If we perceive ambiguities, we cast our embarrassment aside, and ask someone who knows. At an extreme, we write to a foreign colleague (for example, to explain a phrase not found in any French dictionary: "divorces reduits"). If we are totally baffled by what seems to be an important text, we hire someone to read it with us. There is rarely anything mysterious in all this, and I think no great linguistic talent is required. On the other hand, a fair amount of hard work is demanded. After all, the language problem cannot be solved by simply chanting to oneself each morning, "Learn French."

The research process is one of continual searching. Those who have engaged in it know that the many pleasures of discovery outweigh by far the many necessary but tedious hours of calculating or recalculating numbers that seem reluctant to reveal their inner harmony (if it was there). That has been my experience with this work. Learning or revealing some of these social patterns was (to affirm a belief among many researchers) fun. Work is not only doing chores; it is also a joy.

The research process yields surprises, but so does writing itself. I found, as I reread these chapters, that I was expressing concern about the rise in divorce rates in many countries but more especially about the rise in mother-headed families and their disrupted lives—not only in the Western countries but almost everywhere. Perhaps that lapse in cool detachment is common in my field. Anyone who investigates in detail almost any social arrangement is likely to find situations and processes that seem deplorable. One could instead argue, correctly, that a high divorce rate shows that millions of people are now free from what they once experienced as a miserable domestic life. Nevertheless, changes in divorce patterns are creating social problems that are real, massive, and growing, and seem to require remedial action.

As I point out later, many societies have exhibited high divorce rates without generally leaving mothers and children to fend for themselves. The "modern" nations (except for Japan) will continue to be, or become, high-divorce-rate societies. Perhaps we can learn from "stable high-divorce-rate societies" how to make better programs for protecting that part of the next generation that will be involved in divorce.

Although there are numerous gaps in the data I have presented in this volume, whatever reliability and accuracy they exhibit have been a gift from the many colleagues and students who have helped me over the years. It will not be possible for me to make a complete list. Above all others, however, Noriko Iwai (now doing research in Osaka) has been foremost, not merely in digging up much material on Japan that is not easily available but—several years ago—also in organizing the many collected materials that were the beginning stage of this project. In this country, the skill of thwarting the indifferent or malevolent computer data base, which hides its best information, is rare, and Maryann Belanger at the Office of Population Research (Princeton) has used her great talent in locating data that seemed not to be listed anywhere.

But I cannot describe all who have helped me and must instead ask forgiveness for the many who will have reason to feel slighted. At the most, I can try to list as many as I can of all those who have been so generous in the periods of my need. I do so below, as a slight mark of my gratefulness.

I owe a very different kind of debt, of course, to the many friends who have patiently discussed these matters with me over the years and who have given me warm encouragement when the task became too difficult. Here again I shall commit, albeit unwillingly, the sin of omission, but I would like to mention some of them: Jerome and Arlene Skolnick, my best skiing companions; Betty Friedan; Morton Hunt; Kingsley Davis, my first mentor in sociology; Frank Furstenberg; Lenore J. Weitzman; Lillian Rubin; Gladys Topkis (yes, my editor); Cynthia F. Epstein; Nicholas Tavuchis; Angela Aidala; Erich Goode. Some will recognize former students in this list who have become original scholars. I thank all these people and many others who have granted me their friendship.

Here I record my gratefulness to: Tanya Auger, Jeremy Barnum, Nathan Keyfitz, and Susan Lehman, Harvard University; Eduardo Arriaga, U.S. Bureau of the Census; Ines Alberdi Alonso, University of Madrid; Marzio Barbagli, University of Bologna; Laura P. Bean, Mitchel LaPlante, John Meyer, and Arthur P. Wolf, Stanford University; Alicia Bercovich, Centro de Demografia, São Paolo; Maryann Belanger, Assistant Librarian, and Noreen Goldman, Office of Population Research; Larry Bumpass, Center for Demography and Ecology, University of Wisconsin; Laurel L. Cornell, University of Indiana; Dorothy Broom and Gordon C. Carmichael, Australian National University; Don Edgar, Australian Institute of Family Research; Peter McDonald, Australian Institute for Family Studies; Viola Gonzales-Díaz, Statistician, United Nations; Sten Johansson, Director, Statistics Sweden; Peter Juviler and Ward Keeler, Barnard College; Kwowk Kwan Kit, Chief Statistician, Malaysia; Inger Koch-Nielsen, Danish National Institute of Social Research; Øystein Kravdal, Central Statistical Bureau, Oslo; Gail Lapidus, University of California, Berkeley; Bernard Lewis, Center for Near Eastern Studies, Princeton University; Norma Ojeda, Colegio de la Frontera Norte; Maria Coleta Olivera, Nucleo de Estudios de Populacão, São Paolo; Julieta Quilodrán, Colegio de México; Edith Alejandra Pantelides, Centro de Estudios de Población, Buenos Aires; William L. Parish, University of Chicago; Jean Dumas, Edward T. Pryor, Director, and Gordon Priest, Census and Demography Branch, Statistics Canada; Masri Singarimbun, Population Studies Center, Gadjah Mada University, Yogyakarta; Budi Soeradji Martokoesoemo, Chief, Bureau of Family Planning and Population, Jakarta; Letitia Suarez, Centre d'Studis Demografics, University of Barcelona; Ming Tsui, State University of New York, Stony Brook; and John Western, University of Queensland.

Lenore J. Weitzman has contributed to this work in many ways, two of them of great weight. At the last stages of the manuscript she served as a dedicated, effective editor. Most of all, she never faltered in her faith that it would be important, and also possible; while I was often in doubt.

1

The Cross-National Analysis
of Changes in Divorce Patterns

The history that people remember, write about, and read is a succession of large-scale catastrophes, from the Greek defeat of Persia at Marathon to the latest famine in North Africa; and perhaps the history of the twentieth century is not much worse than that of the nineteenth. Yet without question the temper of our times through much of the world is gloomier, more anxious, more fearful and disillusioned. A century ago, decades of advancing industrialization had convinced many nations, not only those in the triumphant West, that material conditions were improving or could be bettered, that the rule of law would be extended, even that tyranny might be curbed. Today thoughtful people feel that the planet itself is threatened, that for many countries industrialization may be a large and difficult and perhaps unlikely move, that our needs—or at least our wants—will inevitably outrun our resources, that the very success of public health measures may lead to world starvation, and that introducing democracy to many nations is a much more precarious step than heretofore believed.

At the end of the nineteenth century, most enlightened leaders, East and West, thought that progress was not only possible but on the way. Now their successors have little faith in either thesis. In fact, many serious analysts view the "belief in progress" as historically naive.

The Importance of Marital Dissolution

If this pessimistic outlook has validity with respect to larger events and questions, it has even more with respect to the family. It is not merely that the traditional moralists are denouncing the hedonism and lax sexual behavior of the United States and every other country. Moralists have always done that, pointing to an idyllic period—usually in their grandparents' day—when people lived in domestic harmony, and family members dutifully and even cheerfully carried out their obligations. Some years ago I suggested a label for this illusion: "the classical family of Western nostalgia."[1]

But though the severe moralists of a century ago did prophesy doom—condemning such family changes as the easing of divorce, the rebellion of the young, the movement of (middle-class) women into the paid work force and the professions, higher education and suffrage for women, and contraception—others who were equally self-righteous saw a new and better world being born. Today it is not only the enthusiastically virtuous who envision the prospect of family dissolution. Serious social scientists, attempting rigorous and sometimes quantitative analysis, have also pointed to quite objective indices of this event.[2]

Readers may protest that the breakdown of the family, if that is indeed occurring, is surely trivial compared with the possibility of nuclear self-destruction or the devastation of the earth's natural resources. I agree. Nevertheless, an underlying thesis of any theoretically sophisticated family sociology is that the economy as well as the polity—indeed, the legal system itself—rests absolutely on the adequate functioning of the family. The family is not only a dependent variable, shaped by large economic and political forces. It is also an independent variable,[3] producing the people who must be committed to those other social institutions if they are not to fail. The fate of the family is thus the fate of the entire society.

It is a glib half-truth to respond that we must change our definition of the family and acknowledge the existence of all sorts of quasi-family arrangements, for we are now in a new era. The deeper question is whether all these new arrangements accomplish the same ends as traditional ones, or at least the necessary ends.

Surely no one could doubt the family's great significance in the past. Much of the world's great literature—the songs of all nations, the epics of the ages—was generated by and focused at length on dramatic events or marital conflict, secret alliances, fraternal hatred, and the murder of spouses. Some of these are as lighthearted as the stories of Boccaccio or the poetry of

1. William J. Goode, *After Divorce* (Glencoe, Ill.: Free Press, 1956), p. 3.
2. For an eloquent essay on this theme see Louis Roussel, *La Famille incertaine* (Paris: Editions Odile Jacob, 1989).
3. In 1963 I called attention to the family's independence as a facilitator of industrialization, and its early importance has been affirmed by MacFarlane. See William J. Goode, *World Revolution and Family Patterns* (New York: Free Press, 1963), pp. 22ff., and Alan MacFarlane, *Marriage and Love, 1300–1840* (Oxford: Blackwell, 1986).

Ovid; others are as darkly tragic, as full of heartache and violence, as the plays of Aeschylus. The tragedy of Oedipus, Helen's abduction in the *Iliad*, the tale of Genji, the Judeo-Christian Bible, the Mahabharata, and almost all bodies of folk myths tell of the turmoil that preceded or followed marital conflicts and breakups. In our time, common gossip and serious literature still focus on such events and processes.

Nor can it be said that the consequences of marital dissolution have been only personal and therefore irrelevant to larger matters. Helen's abduction led to the fall of Troy, Henry VIII's divorce led to the Protestant Reformation in England, Catherine the Great's domestic escapades (especially her relations with Orlov) led to her accession to the throne of Russia, and so on.

Marital dissolution in the modern era may have generated fewer examples of great literature, but it plays no less a part in people's imagination and emotions. If, as some have claimed, easy divorce has trivialized such events, the evidence is not widespread in contemporary fiction, whose authors paint a reality in which marital conflict is of high importance. If one could quantify so elusive a variable, perhaps the *average* divorce in the West is less explosive now than in the past, but the summed impact on the society may be even greater because the number of divorces is so much greater. What was once mostly an individual or family event, an evidence of moral failing, or a deplorably excessive response to conflict is now a social problem.

How "New" Is the Present Era?

Historians and humanists sometimes belittle our contemporary concern about some apparently startling societal change, informing us that it is but a repetition of the distant or near past, dressed in new costume. However, that correct and occasionally comforting view (a revisit of the Visigoths to modern city gates might not be comforting) is no longer valid if we take the entire world as the scope of our study. For surely the first time in history, many nations, not just Rome or Islam, show similar patterns of change: for example, the shift from collective domestic responsibility for its members to state care, a sharp and concerted rise in the divorce rate to unprecedented heights, a surge in the number of families headed by mothers, an increase in the number of children involved in divorce and living in or near poverty, and a growing administrative apparatus for handling the massive problems that result from divorce. We have no evidence that such trends were visible in so many countries in any previous historical epoch. These events create a "social problem" if only because as citizens we share at least in the tax burdens they generate, and as human beings we feel compassion for those who are so afflicted.

As divorce has become a social problem, not a curious aberration to be found in the decadent and disorganized United States, European writers have also expressed their concern about the survival of the institution of the family itself. The research literature on divorce in Western nations has also expanded greatly. This is understandable; when a country begins to define something as a social problem, it begins to offer more research grants for inquiries on that topic, and the topic no longer appears trivial.

European comments now mirror in many ways the fulminations of American moralists of the 1920s, when a new age of "looseness" in sexual and family behavior seemed to dawn. Doubtless there were reasons for this concern—moralists who cry doom *are* sometimes correct, and perhaps in the long run always so—but this is not new in Western history.

Why has divorce now become a special problem? Morally punctilious leaders are especially stimulated to action when they perceive any large changes under way, of course, but many of the nations analyzed here have permitted divorce for many generations. However, as I point out in Chapter 2, the demographics of divorce in most Western nations over the decades until the 1960s were relatively stable with respect to age structure, ages of children, and so on. On the other hand, when divorce is permitted in countries where it has not been allowed before or when continued *sharp* increases occur in the divorce rates of any country, a large number of other demographic changes occur as well, either as causes (for example, the size of the population available for remarriage) or as consequences (for example, the percentage of divorce among the older population). All these changes contribute to the recent focus on the rise of marital dissolution.

Thus I have thought it worthwhile to examine the dynamics of divorce processes over the past four decades, in many regions of the world. Our concern is not only with divorce rates of different kinds but with why they might be high or low, rising or falling. Divorce is not simply an event that happens on the day of a court appearance. It is generated by other social patterns, and in turn it sets in motion various adjustmental processes. We shall, then, be interested in such matters as the relation between divorce and many other factors such as age and class. We want to know whether the duration of marriage has changed with the increase of divorce rates, whether a higher percentage of divorcing parents are childless, and the likelihood of remarriage. How is the rise in cohabitation linked with the lessened stability of marriage? We must also consider the absence of child support by ex-husbands and the burden on the state as a consequence, and why there is a rise in mother-headed families. We shall not succeed in answering all these questions, but we are more likely to make wiser steps toward solving some of the problems of divorce if we have a better understanding of these processes.

The Selection of a Time Frame

I have chosen to focus on the period from 1950 to 1990 for several reasons. The most obvious is that this includes our own experienced lives; the most salient is that it includes the most dramatic changes in divorce patterns that the history of vital statistics affords us, and this challenges us to think anew about the processes of marital dissolution. Changes during this period have occurred at a pace and to a degree that suggest the possibility of ill effects for many other social institutions, including the economy itself.

Divorce patterns are affected greatly by major wars as well as by depressions. They are affected by periods of political turmoil, including revolutions, and by the imposition of despotic rule by a tyrant who wishes to change social patterns quickly by decree. One might argue that our intellectual strategy ought to be to seek some "normal" time period in which we can consider how family institutions change little or much when they are not under great stress.

Unfortunately, the entire twentieth century has been one of nearly constant war and revolution, with numerous serious economic depressions and large if localized famine and epidemics. If we wait for such a normal period, we may never find one. It is also possible that this same comment could be made about almost any other century in the past, but in that case we would not have the advantage of a large body of empirical data.

Whatever epoch we choose to study, we must compare family changes over a relatively long period. A mere decade is much too short. Almost every reader has, over the past two decades, encountered reports that the birth rate has risen or the divorce rate fallen. A closer look will sometimes reveal that it was not the *rate* that rose or fell but only the *number*. (For example, the number of divorces might fall in a given year simply because in the preceding year or two there had been a decline in the number of marriages, as in such Anglo countries as Canada and Australia during the 1950s.) Even if the rate had changed, in almost every instance the change was no more than a minor fluctuation up or down. During that entire period, the *secular* trend—that is, the steadier movement—of the divorce rate has been upward (just as the birthrate has been falling). Thus by using a long generation as our frame, we can feel more certainty that these changes are real. Of course, in some discussions we shall refer to still longer frames where they are relevant.

The Problem of "Causation"

Can we say anything about the "causes" of this phenomenon? This apparently simple question may not even be answerable despite the immense body of current thinking and writing about divorce.

It is a truism of historical analysis that the larger the event, the less likely it is that we can adequately specify its causes. Debates about the "causes" of industrialization, urbanization, war, the Protestant Reformation, and so on are not likely to diminish in our generation. Such events may be said to be "overcaused"; that is, we can think of numerous possible forces that moved in that direction, and after the fact the trends seem perfectly self-evident.

A second argument is much more complex, and it must be addressed on several levels: Analysts have never agreed on what "the causes of divorce" is supposed to mean. For the most part the answers have fallen into three categories: (1) the *grounds* people assert when they file divorce petitions; (2) the *reasons* people give when asked why they decided to divorce; and (3) the larger, *macro-causes* of changes in divorce patterns, such as an increase in the percentage of women in the labor force or a weakening of sexual morality.

The first type of cause may be quickly dismissed. Although the grounds that people offer for divorce have been analyzed over many decades, most researchers have come to the sensible conclusion that people choose whatever grounds are adequate for getting a divorce that are also the least costly socially or economically.[4] For example, a husband may complacently accept the legal charge of "cruelty" if it does not reflect much on his respectability and it is enough to win him his freedom. In the recent past, when the grounds for divorce were severely restricted, perjury was widely used to get over that small barrier.

The substantive meaning of such grounds, of course, changes over time, even when the law does not change at all. Thus in the United States "cruelty" moved from a charge of serious misbehavior, including physical violence, to a trivial assertion of hurt feelings. Accordingly, the analysis of

4. For a thoughtful discussion of the history of divorce law in Europe, see Mary Ann Glendon, *The Transformation of Family Law* (Chicago: University of Chicago Press, 1989), chs. 4, 5; J. DuPaquier et al., eds., *Marriage and Remarriage in Populations of the Past* (New York: Academic Press, 1981); Dirk Blasius, "Bürgerliche Rechtsgleichheit und die Ungleichheit der Geschlechter," in Ute Frevert, ed., *Bürgerinnen und Bürger* (Göttingen: Vandenhoeck und Ruprecht, 1988), pp. 67–84, as well as his "Scheidung und Scheidungsrecht im 19. Jahrhundert zur Sozialgeschichte der Familie," *Historische Zeitschrift* 241 (1985), pp. 329–60.

grounds may tell us little about the real causes of divorce, though it does tell us something about divorce *petitions*.

In the United States, moreover, all such data were typically gathered (if at all) by the agencies of the separate states, and since the legal grounds have altered so fundamentally over the past two generations, they cannot easily be compared over time. Most important, however, is the fact that it is very difficult to prove that a major change in the grounds for divorce in most Western nations has "caused" a major rise in divorce rates. For decades sociologists and legal scholars have pointed out that although a loosening of the grounds is followed by some increase in divorce rates, the change in the law often follows a change in rates as well—and the long-term trend does not seem to be affected by changes in the law. Later we shall consider this link again, in analyzing European divorce rates.

When we ask about the second category of "causes," the charges people make when researchers ask why they divorce, we mostly obtain their complaints about their spouses. If we give them the scope to do so, their complaints are likely to cover most aspects of their lives together. On the other hand, the historical form of that question would be whether these complaints have actually altered over time, in the weight or power of various types (adultery, abandonment, incompatibility, and the like) or in the percentage of various types.

Even if those complaints might lead us to the real "causes," we have no adequate *time* data to tell us what the changes have been. Few people would doubt that such changes have occurred; that is, if we had a deep understanding of causality in divorce, we would *not* find that exactly the same factors moved husbands and wives to divorce in 1900 as in 1990. At a minimum, we would suppose that much weightier complaints would have been required for marital dissolution in 1900 than today. Nevertheless, this will not tell us why a shift in "causes" or complaints would lead to the *recent* surge in the rates, or even the long-term upward movement.

Some decades ago, I pointed out that we cannot assume that the complaints of spouses are the "real" causes of divorce, since that assumes that spouses truly understand all the social, economic, or psychological factors in their own divorce process.[5] Unfortunately, that shaky assumption is the foundation of almost all research aimed at finding out why people choose to make *any* major status change—for example, choice of occupation, suicide, religious conversion, or mate choice. A wide range of variables may be relevant in such decisions, from every phase and area of the person's life.

5. *After Divorce*, ch. 10; and William J. Goode, "Family Disorganization," in Robert K. Merton and Robert Nisbet, *Contemporary Social Problems*, 4th ed. (New York: Harcourt, Brace Jovanovich, 1976), pp. 539–41.

Research on these topics has yielded diffuse answers, and researchers on divorce do not generally believe that answers to interview questions about complaints will explain the real causes of divorce.

All of the following factors (whose effect the spouse may not know very well) will probably have some weight in the decision to divorce: (1) *precipitating factors* (for example, "I fell in love with someone else"), (2) *predisposing factors* (for example, "we were never really suited for each other; we had bitter arguments for years"). Not many will say, however, that they chose their spouses or did not leave them because they had no better (3) *range of alternatives*. Nevertheless, the range of alternatives does shape choice, even if the person is not aware of it, for it can be shown that the divorce rate is higher among women who work full-time and thus have an economic alternative to remaining married. It is unlikely, however, that a high percentage of women would say that getting a job was "the cause" of their divorce. Such a large-scale decision is also shaped by (4) *social pressures from others,* as well as (5) *the individual's own norms and values.*

Each of these five sets of factors has *some* effect on all such consequential acts, whether or not the person is aware of it. Unfortunately, social researchers have not taken care to specify all of them in their attempts to ascertain the causes of divorce or other changes of status (and my own research also made these errors). It is for this reason that research on the forces that led to a particular divorce has had only modest success. If we had time data on each of these five sets of influences, I suspect we might understand better the increases in the divorce rate in our generation.[6] Since we do not really know the causes of divorce fifty or even thirty years ago, we cannot state with any certainty that the causes have changed much, or whether such changes have in turn caused the much higher rates of the present decades.

A Decline in the Centrality of the Family

With reference to our third category of causes of the recent changes, the macro-factors, some analysts put special emphasis on changes in norms and values relating to the family. This has been a primary point of accusation by moralists for generations, from the first major debates about divorce two centuries ago in France, three centuries ago in England in Milton's famous argument, four centuries ago in Germany in Luther's attack on the Church, and on through the present era.

6. This view is based, in turn, on my use of Paul F. Lazarsfeld's solutions (which we talked over at some length in the 1950s) to the methodological question of how one asks the question, "Why did you . . . ?"

Almost ten years ago I made a "prophecy" or prediction about the future that was based on present trends (published in an article entitled "Individual Investments in Family Relationships Over the Coming Decades").[7] It suggests that in our time people have been reducing their personal investments in the collectivity of the family. As its title implies, family members even in the traditional domestic unit of the distant past tried to seek their best interests, as they do now. That is, they were not merely altruistic in being loyal to the family, controling each other or working together for the common good. They did so because their best opportunities were to be found in the family. By contrast, a different structure of opportunities exists today, in which one's best self-interest is increasingly not to be found in the collectivity called the family. The unit or its kin no longer controls power or economic goods to the same extent as in the past, and so the individual member is less inclined to listen to traditional moral preachments in favor of carrying out the older family obligations. Nor does he or she have to do so. Better opportunities—for pleasure, self-enhancement, advancement, even material goods—might be found elsewhere.

If we consider decisions about marriage or fertility, relations between parents and children, cohabitation, living alone, divorce, women's work, or the ideology of egalitarianism within the family, the present trends are toward avoiding long-term emotional or economic investments in the family. It has simply become too fragile to assure payoffs that are eventually adequate or satisfactory and the lack of those investments has in turn contributed to the fragility of the family. Indeed, people have moved somewhat toward the belief that investments in oneself are likely to be more profitable over the long haul; and as they see that others share these attitudes, values, and norms, they feel more justified in their commitment to self. I do not believe this trend can continue indefinitely, for ultimately it will weaken both the economy and the polity. At present, however, people are making smaller inputs in the quality and stability of their own family life than the generation before them did.

In a parallel analysis, Louis Roussel has explored "exogenous" variables that are said to have "caused" the present fundamental changes in family behavior—effective contraception, women's employment, Easterlin's notion of the cyclical effect of large or small generational cohorts (thus facing more or less peer competition),[8] more liberal divorce legislation, the exten-

7. *The Tocqueville Review* 6:1 (1984), pp. 51–83, paper given at Arc-et-Senans, 1983.
8. See R. A. Easterlin, *Birth and Fortune* (London: Grant McIntyre, 1980), esp. pp. 19–27 and ch. 9. He also applies his notions to fertility: R. A. Easterlin and Eileen Crimmins, *The Fertility Revolution: A Supply-Demand Analysis* (Chicago: University of Chicago Press, 1985).

sion of social welfare, and so on—and concludes that these are only mediating or proximate causes. The underlying change lies in our norms, values, and goals, our very definitions of what is a desirable family life, and these changes indeed affect all social choices. Roussel stated that "The image of family life is no longer organized around the purpose of founding a stable family; and marriage is not now a primary institution, but it is becoming simply an emotional relationship."[9]

Ron Lesthaeghe has also attempted to measure directly the changes in family norms and values in Europe and he points to similar conclusions. His work presents an ingenious set of technical and methodological instruments for measuring this change and its effect on fertility and other family patterns.[10]

Similarly, after an analysis of nuptiality and divorce in Europe since the 1940s, Jean-Paul Sardon comments: "The magnitude and extension of these transformations leads one to think that we are faced with the expression, within one particular realm, the family, of the most profound mutations which affect the totality of relations and the perception of the contemporary world."[11]

To be sure, Sardon does not attempt to demonstrate that conclusion empirically, as the three preceding authors do, for he supposes that the massive changes themselves prove it. It is clear that many serious analysts are not simply expressing their moral concern but are making an attempt to measure or specify a large-scale "cause," yet none has offered a plausible *proof* of cause; indeed they have done no more than to move the question of causal process back one step: if people are now less willing to make large investments in the collectivity of the family, if family norms and values have changed radically, and if that causes a large increase in the divorce rates, what caused the initial change?

Very likely, no adequate research design can yield satisfactory proof. Divorce is a part of the family system, which has also been changing. Divorce is one of the causes of that change, but it is also one of its indices and effects. All of the candidates for "cause" are intertwined (for example, females in the labor force may be a cause of the rise in the divorce rate, but reciprocally the socioeconomic forces press women to work, and so forth). The possible

9. Louis Roussel, "Die Soziologische Bedeutung der Demographischen Erschütterung in den Industrieländern der letzten zwanzig Jahre," in Kurt Lüscher, Franz Schultheis, Michael Wehrspan, eds., *Die "Postmoderne" Familie* (Konstanz: Universitätsverlag, 1988), p. 51. See also Roussel, *La Famille Incertaine.*

10. Ron Lesthaeghe, "A Century of Demographic and Cultural Change in Western Europe: An Exploration of Underlying Dimensions," *Population and Development Review* 9 (Sept. 1983), pp. 411–35; and "Cultural Dynamic and Economic Theory of Fertility Change," unpublished working paper, 1987–89, Vrije Universiteit, pp. 1–47.

11. Jean-Paul Sardon, "Evolution de la Nuptialité et de la Divortialité en Europe Depuis la Fin des Années 1960," *Population* 41 (1986), p. 481.

factors are many, and most can be shown to be correlated with the increase, either immediately or with some time lag. Whatever links we work out, and they are many, will not answer the question of just why the sharp increase occurred at this juncture in Western history.

In so firmly denying that any of the contemporary hypotheses (including my own) about the recent surges in divorce rates can be proved as yet, I am not denying the validity of literally dozens of research findings about the many factors that are correlated with the rises or differences in the likelihood of divorce (for example, the greater likelihood of divorce among women professionals). We shall use them in our analyses. I am asserting instead that (1) several major changes do increase divorce rates, but it is not yet possible, and may not become possible, to disentangle them so as to lay bare the one or more factors that unequivocally have "caused" the sudden sharp rise in recent decades. Further, (2) many factors clearly associated with a higher propensity to divorce may not have much predictive power in explaining changes over time.

As to the first assertion, as I noted above, it is very likely that several modern social trends increase divorce rates—for example, changes in family values and in the relative priorities of family role performances, the lesser dependence of the wife on her husband's income (because of both state help and her own earnings in the labor market), the increasing importance of calculating the payoffs from investments in the collectivity of the family, the lesser relative cost of divorce in a time of general prosperity and more liberal laws, and the laws themselves—all increase the divorce rates. Unfortunately, for our hypotheses, all of them are intertwined as part of wide-ranging social and economic changes in our era; all affect one another. When so much changes, it is tempting to label our favorite cause of the lot as "the" cause, but I do not believe that any statistical technique can adequately demonstrate that choice or any other as best. Fate and history have not been kind to such global explanations.

As to the second assertion, we know that people with lower incomes experience higher rates of marital dissolution, but it does not follow that poor *countries* exhibit higher rates. It is also true that during major depressions the divorce rate has dropped, while in periods of prosperity the rates increase. If many people become well off, however, that principle cannot (very likely) be used as an explanation for higher rates—nor can the fact that the well-to-do still have a somewhat lower rate of divorce be used to predict lower rates in such a period. Rates are higher among people who marry young, but that is true relative to others in the same generation and in the same country. *That* relationship cannot be used to predict that if the age at marriage increases (as it did during these decades), the divorce rates will drop (it increased instead). Indeed, that specific, incorrect prediction was made by dozens of analysts over the past several decades. As can be seen, a correlation between variables at a specific time does not prove that either variable will rise with the other one over time.

Researchers on divorce have also studied marital happiness as a way of understanding why people divorce. Hundreds of studies of marital happiness, in many countries, have failed to yield much predictability, except in the banal sense that those who divorce are more likely to have been unhappy in their marriages than those who did not. But what causes people to feel that way? The question of marital happiness has not revealed much theoretical richness, if indeed it possesses any. Most important, it is highly unlikely that a large increase in marital unhappiness in most countries has caused the divorce rates to rise.

Some of these possible explanations fail because we cannot often apply a correlation between the traits of *individuals* to a larger unit, such as a nation or even a time period. Others fail because they apply to fluctuations in a social or economic cycle (for example, a depression) but not to a long-term trend. More broadly, they are all examples of the incorrect specification of the unit being analyzed, a seductive and widespread blunder of statistical analysis.

Although a wide array of sturdy conclusions can illuminate our understanding of divorce processes, most of them do not yield precise causal explanations why that long secular rise in divorce rates in the West suddenly made a sharp upward movement. By now it is clear that I shall not succeed in pinning the cause down either, but the data to be presented here will help us to understand better the processes that are at work.

Theories of Change in Family Dissolution

To pursue further the problems of causation and change we would have to analyze at length the theoretical and methodological issues in all large-scale theories of family change, but that would take us far afield.[12] If we apply strict standards, neither in sociology *nor in any other science* (biology, chemistry, physics) have such theories about the future achieved much precision or power, and they are not likely to do so in the future—though, to be sure, this is another such prediction. More specifically, the change we focus on here is a unique event, and science is not capable of predicting unique events. Rather it predicts a distribution or a pattern of processes and events for a *class*

12. I have done so elsewhere; see Goode, "Theories of Large-Scale Family Change," International Union for the Scientific Study of Population, Tokyo, Nov. 1988.

of phenomena. Arthur F. Stinchcombe has noted that our very best work in any science is based on the knowledge of a wide body of facts. Alas, *we do not have any facts at all about the future,* and we shall not have any until we get there.[13] The best we can do at present is to interpret the changes by using regularities that seem to apply to most current social patterns.

One of these, widely used in Western thinking since the time of Plato, was first extensively analyzed in the classic work by Ferdinand Tönnies, *Gemeinschaft und Gesellschaft,* slightly more than a century ago (1887). We continue to use those concepts today. I shall comment further on this mode of thought in a later section on declining divorce rates, but let us at least take note of it here.

It is not a theory but a rich descriptive approach which reminds us that when a broad array of social processes occur—that we generally label industrialization, urbanization, bureaucratization, and the like—social relations and social controls will also change. From face-to-face interaction, familistic patterns, interaction on the basis of our particular and special relationship with each person, agrarian property relations, and so on, the system will come to be based more on rational and universalistically applied laws, interaction based on bureaucratic rules rather than the special relations we have with each person, somewhat looser emotional ties, market controls, and so forth. Under this second group of conditions, many of the traditional rules of behavior begin to weaken, the class system is altered, and controls by elders over the younger family members will also decline. These circumstances make it likely that divorce rates will gradually rise, at least in Western countries, and that has happened over a long period of time.

On the other hand, this does not at all explain *generally* why divorce rates are very high in some systems and not in others, or why they rise suddenly in societies (such as the industrialized countries) that would *already* be called *Gesellschaften.* At best, it merely points to the likelihood that, under certain circumstances, various kinds of new social and economic opportunities will weaken traditional family controls. More important, it does not have any specific application to the recent rapid increases in divorce rates and affords no theoretical basis for predicting what a "post-modern family" would be like—*after* social life has been "modernized." If indeed we are in a post-modern era, as so many analysts proclaim, then presumably we should now be experiencing these new family patterns, but no adequate theory exists that can make those predictions.

13. Arthur F. Stinchcombe, "On Soft-Headedness on the Future," *Ethics* 93 (Oct. 1982), pp. 114–28. On the common failure of such predictions, see Seymour M. Lipset, "Predicting the Future of Post-Industrial Society in the Third Century," *America as a Post-Industrial Society* (Chicago: University of Chicago Press, 1979), pp. 135ff.

Perhaps I should comment in passing that my own work, focusing roughly on the historical period 1860–1960, attempted to offer some specific predictions, on the basis of a particular definition of industrialization as the transforming force for the family.[14] I suggested that a large number of changes in traditional family systems, including rises *and* declines in the divorce rate, begin to occur when certain specific socioeconomic patterns arise: (1) An increasing number of people earn their living from *jobs,* positions that pay wages for a particular task. They do not depend on eventually attaining a share of land or indeed any other asset that is typically under the control of family elders. (2) The need for efficiency in the economy requires that jobs and promotions be given out mainly on the basis of competence, and by people who have little stake in the familial role performance of the worker. Thus, if individuals want to defy family controls, over time their bosses become less and less concerned about that behavior. (3) Work positions in the market economy permit a person to gain a living as an *individual,* not as a member of the family. Workers receive their own wages—that is, their elders do not get those wages, and family members can spend their own wages independently of their elders.

Thus the traditional flow of rewards and punishments given to family members on the basis of conformity to family demands is interrupted or altered. It is not that these processes directly and universally work against the family. However, all family systems are under some strain, and these new processes permit far more people than before to move away from traditional family customs. I have emphasized that these processes do not arise automatically with the first factories, since family controls continue in all countries, long after factories are first built. The processes work slowly, but their corrosive effect over time is powerful.

It can be argued that the recent changes are only an intensification of such forces of family dissolution, and the payoffs from them make any large emotional, financial, or energy investments in the family collective less attractive. Nevertheless, that thesis again simply moves the inquiry back one step: What caused that intensification in our time?

The traditional assumptions about those polar types of society, *Gemeinschaft* and *Gesellschaft,* lead us to expect higher or lower rates in different countries, and thus rises over time in nations undergoing industrialization or modernization. As a consequence of such changes, many alterations in still other divorce patterns (custody, marriage duration, remarriage, families headed by mothers, and so on.) will also occur. In the long generation 1950–1990, divorce rates moved upward in Western nations, and we shall

14. See Goode, *World Revolution and Family Patterns* and *The Family,* 2d ed. (Englewood Cliffs, N.J.: Prentice-Hall, 1982), esp. chs. 10, 11.

later examine many of those other changes. The increases loom large to most readers in the West, for that has been our lifetime experience.

My own earlier theorizing, however, pointed out that some family systems may respond to the forces of industrialization and modernization with a *decline* instead of a rise in their divorce rates. This pattern deserves serious analysis, for perhaps it may offer us some suggestions for future policy in our own high-divorce-rate nations. Consequently, we shall devote much attention to it in later chapters but it merits some brief mention here as well.

Periods and Places of Declining Divorce Rates

A longer-term decline in divorce rates, though outside the experience of most Western observers, is at least conceivable. For example, many scholars have alleged that divorce rates were very high as Imperial Rome fell into decay, and this at least implies that the divorce rate in those same regions may have declined in the centuries that followed. In fact, of course, our guesses about divorce rates in the decaying Roman Empire are based on surviving gossip, attentive largely to the privileged classes; we do not know what the dissolution rate was among ordinary people. Actually, we have little or no proof that such a decline occurred after Rome fell.

Despite efforts by some of the later Roman emperors and despite the spread of Christian doctrine, after Rome fell the civil (mainly Roman) law that permitted divorce by mutual consent continued to be followed in the formerly imperial territories. It seems clear that in the centuries just prior to Charlemagne (d. 814) divorce was not difficult in the Frankish kingdom; then the Church succeeded in imposing gradually an ecclesiastical law that defined marriage as indissoluble.[15] Ecclesiastical law (as distinct from Christian doctrine), was somewhat ambiguous rather than flatly opposed. We cannot express that situation by numerical rates, but it could be claimed that until even the eleventh century casual polygamy was widespread, "with easy divorce and much concubinage."[16]

To be sure, the historical cases throughout this period are the scandals of aristocrats, but there is no reason to suppose that ordinary people were any stricter. In fact it seems much more likely that this generally permissive attitude not only existed among the British peasantry then, but persisted until very late in the modern era and possibly even into the eighteenth

15. Jo-Ann MacNamara and Suzanne F. Wemple, "Marriage and Divorce in the Frankish Kingdom," in Brenda M. Bolton et al., eds., *Women in Medieval Society* (Philadelphia: University of Pennsylvania Press, 1976), pp. 95–113.

16. Lawrence Stone, *The Family, Sex and Marriage in England, 1500–1800* (New York: Harper, 1977), p. 30; for the Elizabethan period and after, see his *Road to Divorce: England, 1530–1987* (New York: Oxford University Press, 1990), chs. 6, 7.

century, and casual unofficial divorce was fairly widespread (for example, "selling" one's wife). Such customs usually do not appear in court cases for obvious reasons, but some of them abound in the literature and especially in folklore. Certainly in the Scottish border region, "handfasting" (a handshake) as an official entry into marriage and the ease of marital dissolution that accompanied the practice ("jumping over the broom") were widespread until the eighteenth and very likely the late nineteenth century.

Westerners take the strictness of the Catholic Church so much for granted that they commonly forget that it did not succeed fully in imposing its ecclesiastical rules until 1563. Nevertheless, here at least we have what seems to be a long period (from Charlemagne to the Council of Trent) of unsteady decline in divorce rates in Europe as ecclesiastical law finally took over an area of life that had earlier been controlled by civil law, contract, and local custom.

There is no comparable case for the modern era unless it is Japan's successful attempt to impose stricter rules on its family system in the Meiji Restoration period (after 1868). I shall discuss that case later, along with other modern instances of decline in divorce rates. There I shall point out that an adequate theory of modernization does not predict that divorce rates will necessarily rise if they have generally been very high in the past. Indeed, if the prior domestic arrangements formed what I call a "stable high-divorce-rate system," that system itself may be undermined by industrialization and its accompanying forces, and thus the rates may fall at least for a while. Ultimately, I also predicted, those rates will rise again.

In the case of Japan, that prediction holds true, as it does in the special case of Taiwan. We shall also consider other instances. The example of China, a country in which divorce rates were traditionally low, reminds us of still another pattern. Contrary to Western experience, it is possible to reduce rates over a lengthy period by concerted administrative action, with no basic changes in the divorce law itself. Chinese couples who wanted to divorce found it very difficult, from the late 1950s until almost 1980, to work their way through the successive levels of rejection, from local neighborhood and factory committees, to the courts themselves.

I have suggested that stable high-divorce-rate systems have been found among both literate and nonliterate societies. They are important because they reveal a different way of "sifting" candidates for family membership. We consider them at some length because they help us to understand the Western systems that dominate the world's attention. In the final chapter I suggest another reason for their importance: Although the instability of the individual marriage was very high, the system itself could be relatively stable because—unlike our various modern high-divorce systems in the West—by following tradition and custom, they did take care of the problems created by divorce, with rules for custody, child care, support and remarriage for the mother, and so on. Indeed, I argue that we must now accept the reality of our position: Many Western countries are relatively high-divorce societies, and we must work out social customs (and not only laws on paper that generate more lawsuits) which define postdivorce care as both an individual and a collective responsibility.

As yet, no general theory of divorce rates helps us to explain how such stable high-divorce-rate systems originated or why they have continued. Nevertheless, an exploration of such patterns helps us to understand both the dynamics of divorce patterns and the wide range of possible domestic arrangements in different kinds of societies.

Catholic Countries That Now Permit Divorce

Of course, the Western nations vary greatly in their traditionalism. Some have been extremely reluctant to permit divorce at all, often taking that step only after much passionate debate and even then with severe restrictions on the conditions under which it is possible. For example, even after the 1975 "liberalization," French law remained severe. Now, almost all Western countries permit divorce; in the European region only Ireland still blocks that solution to marital breakdown.

Italy, Portugal, and Spain, all Catholic countries, have in recent years opened that door, and in Latin America, Brazil, Colombia, and Argentina have done so. These changes (which are analyzed in a separate chapter) are interesting because so many of the usual regularities found when divorce has risen slowly over decades, related to age, class, duration, and so on, are all thereby highly skewed. After all, the legal bar never prevented couples from living apart, from living together in unhappiness, from taking other partners in informal arrangements, or even from legal separation agreements (note that where divorce is not permitted at all, "legal grounds" lose some of their relevance for any understanding of marital dissolution).

Thus a handful of countries have only recently permitted divorce with the right to remarry; before, unhappy couples could only obtain a legal separation. If they could bear the scandal they might even dare to start a new union without marrying. In the last two decades, however, the scandal has diminished, and a rising percentage of couples have taken that step. In other countries, mostly in the Caribbean and Central America, divorce has been an option for many decades. Indeed, Cuba and Mexico, for example, once served as "divorce havens" for European and American citizens who found the laws of their own countries too restrictive. In this group of countries, too, cohabitation is increasing.

Thus, even though we cannot trace out a long time-curve in the divorce rates of these nations that have only recently granted a full divorce, they are of considerable interest because of the very different divorce processes they exhibit.

Data Problems

National bureaucracies have not been equally conscientious about collecting accurate divorce data, or analyzing them. Doubtless other demands loom larger. Consequently, the lack of adequate quantitative measures often plagues divorce analysis. We shall, then, take note of data problems at various points in the inquiry, but some general comments also need to be made here.

The first is that cross-national historical data on divorce rates, or even national divorce data, are a prime concern of very few statistical offices, which mostly focus instead on the classical demographic categories of births, deaths, and migration into and out of the country. India, for example, does not release divorce rates to international agencies. Divorce data in Indonesia were collected by the Department of Religion, and until a few years ago they did not appear in United Nations compilations at all. In the United States, divorces are registered at the county level, and then compiled by the state. After that step, they are transmitted to the national bureau, but coverage until recently was limited to states that maintained high standards of accuracy. At the international level, dissolution rates reported to the United Nations yearbook will vary, even for the same year, from one publication to another over a succession of years.

The former Soviet Union is a special case, of course, since it was made up of a wide diversity of cultures and subnations, with the result that some experts would argue it is not really sensible to speak of a divorce rate for the country as a whole. With its partial dissolution, of course, we are now spared the problem of interpreting such a figure.

Latin America also poses a technical problem, which I discuss more fully later on. The central informational difficulty is that the particular history of the Iberian invasion generated a very different pattern of marriage and marital dissolution. In the Caribbean and on the mainland, a considerable percentage of the population in many countries married very late, if at all, after one or more consensual unions. Thus millions of couples (mostly poorer and less educated) were never legally "divorced" because they were never legally married. And, as the reader would guess, in the past twenty years cohabitation has spread among the respectable in Latin America as it has in Europe. Consequently, their unions and their dissolution are not recorded either. It is thus a triumph of optimism rather than good sense that I have persisted in trying to interpret divorce patterns in this great region, but I believe that my interpretation of them is both surprising and reasonable.

The loyal reader will perhaps recall that in an earlier work on world changes in family patterns I excluded Latin America and Russia (because I believed the data were not robust or extensive enough). On the other hand, I then included India and Sub-Saharan Africa, which are omitted here. I have already noted the absence of Indian divorce data. I have reluctantly excluded that tier of African nations because it is difficult to get data over time. The earlier data, on which I spent perhaps thousands of happy hours, were essentially tribal, not national. The national boundaries have not respected tribal boundaries, and those historic differences in family patterns were often great. Modern data must be limited to people within the present political boundaries. Thus, although it may be possible to obtain a good anthropological report on changes in divorce patterns within a particular tribal village, changes in the nation over fifty years would be much more difficult. Analyzing divorce changes over time has not been a high priority in these nations.

Technical difficulties are also encountered in choosing which type of divorce rate to use. The figure most easily obtained in many countries is the number of divorces per 1,000 population. At a minimum, that requires an accurate census, and in many countries (in Latin America, for example) they were not a regular event until the last two decades. Equally important, it is obvious that much of the population as a whole, even of those fourteen years of age and up, is not at risk, for a large percentage is not married. This is especially true in some of the developing countries, where the age at marriage has risen substantially over the past twenty years, but the survival rate among young people has increased even more, because of public health measures. That is, an even greater percentage of the population than in the past is young and unmarried and thus cannot divorce. The basic rate of marital dissolution (among the married) may be the same or may actually increase, while the crude rate, based partly on a larger young and unmarried population, may rise slowly or not at all. Note also that this discrepancy between the divorce figures and the population at risk is especially acute in Latin American countries, for those who dissolve consensual unions do not appear in the divorce figures but are obviously part of the population.

A more valid measure is the number of divorces per 1,000 married couples, or married men or women, but that base figure is not easy to obtain in a country whose statistical office is limited in scope and effectiveness. This figure is changing from year to year, while censuses are taken at longer intervals. Thus, the population that is now married will be exactly known only if other basic population data are precise.

A third mode of calculation, the number of divorces per 100 marriages, is often scorned by demographers, for the good simple reason that only a few of those who divorce in any given year were also married in that year; indeed, especially in countries where divorce may take several years, it is likely that none came from that same population. On the other hand, in some countries those two figures were the only ones available. Under certain circumstances it may be more reliable than a figure based on a growing younger population that is unmarried (that is, divorce rates per 1,000 population). In any case, this measure does tell us something about trends if we have successive figures over time. Obviously if the number of divorces per 100 marriages continues to rise, any valid measure of the divorce rate will also show an increase.

Causes and Consequences

The widespread liberalization of divorce laws has affected the direction of modern research as well. As Glendon points out, research (especially with respect to the law itself) has moved from a concern with causes, and even causes for differences in rates, to a concern with differences in *consequences*. [17] That is to say, divorce has become so widespread, and the economic consequences have been so great, that public discussion and the changes in the law focus far more on how the legal system should help to arrange the *aftermath* of divorce, such as the prevention of injustices between divorced husbands and divorced wives, and toward children, and the problems of state support after divorce. Research has followed that general concern. These investigations have been more extensive in the Western countries and in the Anglo nations outside Europe. The changes under way were the focus of a wide-ranging symposium on "The Economic Consequences of Divorce,"[18] organized by Lenore J. Weitzman and Mavis Maclean, both of whom have done much research on the links between law and society.

Most of the contemporary studies can be characterized as "policy research." Though designed with the aim of rigorously pinning down the facts, they attempt to locate trouble points, steps in the total divorce process (including the consequences for both children and spouses) where hardship

17. Glendon, *The Transformation of Family Law,* esp. chs. 4–6.
18. Later published under the same title by Clarendon Press of Oxford University Press in 1992.

or unfairness may occur. Researchers may, for example, as in the United States and Germany, try to ascertain to what extent husbands use their influence or resources, or the threat of a custody suit, to reduce their financial obligations after divorce. Or, as in Australia and Sweden, they do not stop with a tabulation of court or administrative orders to pay or the level of state support but go on to find out how mother-headed households are faring.

Because people have strong (if contradictory) feelings about the family behavior of others, the disclosures from such studies often generate much publicity, debate, and even new legislation. Australians, like U.S. citizens, came to be indignant that so many fathers were escaping the financial burden of paternity after divorce, for that obligation is widely viewed as nearly absolute. That the burden so escaped then falls on the shoulders of the ordinary citizen only excites further disapproval. Thus the studies done by the Australian Institute of Family Studies and by Weitzman and Garfinkel (among others) in the United States have led to new laws aimed at closing that gap.

This research trend is one more change linked with the many others noted in this volume. It also suggests a widening of what is meant when we ask what has been happening to divorce over the past four decades. A half-century ago, studies focused mainly on the causes of divorce, as though it was so deviant a step that a rather searching inquiry was required to explain why anyone would take it. To ask what happened afterward was not common.[19] That focus was also in part policy-oriented: What could be done to avoid divorce, or to reduce the divorce rate?

Divorce has not come to be approved, but it is now so widespread as to be accepted as an unfortunate but expectable contingency in life. Any casual passerby can list a dozen reasons why people divorce. Thus the key policy question becomes: Now that we have high divorce rates anyway, how can we adequately cope with the large-scale consequences they generate? Since social research has become, over this same period, a widespread tool of political argument and state policy in almost all countries with adequate budgets, inquiries now seek to achieve precise analyses of those consequences.

This broad shift in the definition of divorce as a problem, and in the research agenda, is an important theme in this monograph. The comparative approach reveals that divorce becomes a problem even when the rates themselves are not extremely high by world standards, for the absolute numbers

19. To be sure, in 1946 I began a large field survey of postdivorce adjustment among a random sample of divorced mothers age 20–38 years at the time of divorce, but to my knowledge it was the first such study. See *After Divorce*.

of people involved are so much greater. Its consequences are a problem because citizens define it so, and that perception arises both because of the inevitably rising social support burden, and because more people actually know someone who has been affected by divorce. They are also a problem because more people take longer before remarriage, and there is an increase in mother-headed families. Moreover, this increase occurs in Arab countries as well as in the West.

The story of what has happened over the past generation must include, where possible, the changes in the lives of people after divorce, especially divorced mothers. We must understand those changes as a mass process. Such an account must also take note of the various responses of different nations to the many problems generated by divorce.

A Comparative Approach

A study does not automatically become comparative even when it encompasses the world. Even with so wide a scope we might simply average data on the duration of marriage for many countries or, alternatively, report on each country separately, one after the other. Many studies have selected one or the other of these choices. A comparative perspective instead seeks generalizations of greater or lesser applicability, especially within subsets of the total sample we choose.

Since every society is unique, it could be argued that no such patterns exist; on the other hand, since each is also in some respects like all others, we might be fortunate enough to find general patterns while studying only one case. Comparison, however, shows us how limited both these premises are. By considering a range of societies, we see that divorce rates do not rise or fall in an exactly parallel fashion, but here and there we can also discover why— for example, we can ascertain that in some subsets of nations divorce rates were generated by a very different kind of family system. Uncovering such a finding is less likely if we have but one case or look at many cases separately. We must *compare* in order to analyze comparatively.

As is true of any fruitful perspective, we encounter not only solutions but new mysteries. For example, even if much current analysis is correct as to some causes of the rise in divorce rates in Europe, comparative data challenge us to answer why so sharp an increase occurred in a single decade and in such a broad sample. At least we can be sure that whatever that cause may be, it cannot be unique to one country or the result of one specific law or event—a doubt that would persist if our data were confined to the United States or even the major European countries.

Comparative analysis sometimes brings surprises, as when we learn that a theoretical construct—the hypothetical possibility that when a country modernizes its divorce rate might actually fall—has a rich empirical reality, which in turn offers still another historical puzzle: How did those traditional systems actually work, and what was their origin?

Finally, a comparative approach highlights the nearly unique case. By examining common patterns, we can better see the processes at work in the unusual example. For example, we can understand how a nation *can* reduce the divorce rate under some circumstances, as China did for nearly a generation: Its leaders chose to diminish the administrative problems a rising divorce rate was already generating. Instead of making new laws, they applied both sociopolitical pressures and legal delays to lower the divorce rate, and in their public propaganda took a benignly complacent view of the domestic misery of millions of Chinese couples.

No such study can be complete, an entire inventory of numerical descriptions of divorce everywhere. It is not possible, and it will never be possible, to compare all nations with respect to all the divorce patterns we might wish to study. The necessary data have never been compiled, for obvious reasons; and for the most part they were never collected to begin with. The technically elaborate and rigorous figures from Japan cannot be calculated in China, or for that matter in most other countries. The mass of data would, in any event, be overwhelming, and it would still be necessary to study it comparatively if we want to understand divorce processes. We must always make a choice between total inclusion and our real aim of understanding the dynamics of divorce.

Thus we shall disappoint those who want to know not merely about German divorce patterns but also about those of Iceland, Monaco, or the Solomon Islands Protectorate—though Iceland has not been entirely neglected in the chapter on the Nordic countries, for I have not focused only on the great nations centered on the world stage. For example, I have included both Malaysia and Indonesia because they illuminate an important set of divorce processes—that is, stable high-divorce-rate systems. I have reluctantly excluded India because of its failure to publish the needed information and the failure of Indian scholars to conduct the research and obtain these data on their own. The comparativist is always at the mercy of the available data; one cannot make independent field surveys to fill in so many gaps.

I have also tried, in many chapters, to face the problem of individual complexity by aggregating countries into regions. This is especially useful for the Western nations, which have been most concerned about the rise in divorce. Doubtless many will object to one or another of my decisions.

Perhaps some Danes would prefer not to include Finland among the Nordic nations. Certainly some Poles do not wish to be put into any category that includes Russia, and both Hungarians and Romanians may remind us sharply that they are not Slavs. Europeanized Uruguayans may object to being grouped along with Guatemala or Paraguay.

All such groupings rest on complex criteria, different in each instance. In the chapter on the Nordic countries, I have noted the overlap of political rule among these countries over the centuries, which has led to many common patterns in divorce experiences. The Eastern European countries were not classed together because of some supposed cultural or linguistic similarities, but they have shared some decades of political oppression which I suspect has set them apart from the rest of Europe in many ways. I have not included all Arab countries, but this set of nations can be better understood together, rather than being lumped indiscriminately with all other Muslim nations.

Nevertheless, all such attempts at simplifying by making categories will do violence to the complexities of reality. They can be justified only if thereby we understand the divorce process better.

Yet no individual researcher, however gifted, can penetrate the immense complexity of each nation's divorce experience, its subtle nuances of culture, as its citizens actually live it. The meaning of marital dissolution is different from one couple to another, among different classes, among different nations. I have never understood, and thus never accepted, the first part of Tolstoy's dictum that happy families live similar lives while the unhappy are all different from one another. There is no relationship in family life so bizarre that we cannot find examples of it, often in happy families as well.

Consequently, no kind of comparative research design can make full order and sense of all such events and processes in different nations over a time of great social change. Only here and there, and often only by ignoring many complexities, can we glimpse broader patterns of some robustness. And that is my modest goal in this work.

2

Divorce in Europe: Emergence of the General Pattern

The nations we consider in this chapter—primarily Austria, Belgium, France, Germany, Netherlands, Switzerland—have all permitted divorce for many generations, unlike the Catholic nations of Spain, Portugal, and Italy we analyze in Chapter 3. Thus the demographics of divorce in most of Europe have become relatively "normal" over time with regard to age structure at divorce, ages of children, duration of marriage, and so on. As we shall see, however, when continued *sharp* increases occur in the divorce rates in any country, Catholic or not, various other shifts occur as well—for example, a rise in the number of mother-headed families and children of divorce, an increased rate of divorce among the older population, and so forth.

Although I shall make passing comments here and there about causal links, my earlier methodological cautions about causal speculations apply to the European countries as well. These nations, and especially the Nordic countries (Chapter 4), however, do seem to have moved together in an intensification of a long-term tendency for individuals to seek their own interests and happiness rather than to stay married for the sake of their children or the interests of "the family." The basic thrust of these modern research conclusions from Europe is that the contemporary changes in divorce and other family patterns are not simply the ups and downs of a trendless fluctuation or the continuation of a long-term secular trend. Instead, many measures of family behavior show strong changes, changes in the trend line itself.

European Divorce Rates

The slow rise of European divorce rates prior to the 1960s gives little hint of the sharp increases to come. In all Western countries in which divorce was legal, including the Anglo nations, the rates had been moving upward steadily since 1900.[1] The United States was the most extreme in this respect, for its divorce rate had been rising in every decade since the Civil War, well over a century ago. Nevertheless, the European curves had moved up only modestly, and though many analysts have "explained" the general upward movement they have not been able to state why the recent surge since the 1960s occurred at that specific juncture in social history. As we noted earlier, we believe that it is not likely we shall find a "cause" of that large change; its causes are many and are intertwined, and disentangling them is as unlikely as in the case of any other grand social change.

Table 2.1 shows the rise in the divorce rates in ten European countries from 1950 to the late 1980s. This is based on the population at risk—that is, those currently married. Whatever the population base used, however, all the usual modes of calculating rates yield a similar pattern in Europe: a substantial increase over these four decades.

The percentage of marriages in a given year that will *eventually* end in divorce is of course an estimate, since it will be calculated long before all those unions have ended in death or dissolution. This is a complex technique, and thus we cannot often obtain it easily on a cross-cultural basis. However, Table 2.2 shows the chances of eventual divorce for a number of European countries in recent years.

These divorce rates exhibit several standard regularities over longer periods of time: They rise with prosperity; that is, divorce is a consumer good, and people who "want" it will purchase it when they can afford it. Correspondingly, although economic problems also create marital stress, the rates fall during a long depression. It is possible, however, that the long-term negative relationship between economic depression and divorce rates is changing, although it should be remembered that in the generally prosperous period of 1950–1990 there was no recession comparable to that of the 1930s. In any event, a recent study argues persuasively that the prosperity and attitude changes of the postwar period have reduced the *relative cost* of divorce. Certainly that is correct for the social costs, and even for the monetary costs the loss from a divorce *relative* to income and expenditures may now be less. Thus if we look at the shorter rises and falls of economic well-being over the past several decades, divorce rates will rise during periods of unemployment and also during periods of rising unemployment.[2] That is, since the "cost" is now lower, a small stress will increase the rates. Whether

1. William J. Goode, *World Revolution and Family Patterns* (New York: Free Press, 1963), pp. 82ff.; Roderick Phillips, *Divorce in New Zealand* (Aukland: Oxford University Press, 1981).

2. Scott J. South, "Economic Conditions and the Divorce Rate: A Time Series Analysis of the Post-War U.S.," *J. Marr. and the Family* 42 (Feb. 1985), pp. 31–39. Since his model is general, it ought to apply to Europe as well.

Table 2.1: Divorces per 1,000 Married Females, 1950–1990

Country	1950	1960	1970	1980	1990
Austria	6.7 (1951)	5.0 (1961)	6.1 (1977)	6.8	
Belgium	2.4	2.0 (1961)	2.0 (1977)	2.6	4.9
Denmark	7.0	6.1	8.1 (1978)		11.1 (1986)
England and Wales	2.6 (1951)	2.1 (1961)	5.9 (1971)	11.6 (1978)	12.9 (1986)
Finland	4.6	4.0	6.0 (1978)	9.8	
France	5.7 (1946)	2.6	2.9		8.5 (1986)
Germany, Federal Republic of	7.7 (1961)	3.7	5.1	4.9 (1977)	8.8 (1987)
Netherlands	3.0	2.2	3.3	6.5 (1979)	8.7 (1986)
Norway	3.2	2.8	3.7	6.6 (1978)	
Switzerland	4.2	3.9	4.4		

Sources: U.N. Demographic Yearbooks and national statistics reports.

Crude divorce rates (per 1000 population) are not so valid as those based on the number of married couples, for, after all, many of them (that is, minors, unmarried, already divorced or widowed) are not at risk of divorce, but the latest figures are more up to date. The present table does show the continued upward movement, along with the evident slowing down of that rate or even—Sweden, United Kingdom—a small reversal. It seems likely that most or all of that slowdown arises because an increasing percentage of the adult population enters a union without marriage.

Crude Divorce Rates, Europe: 1950–1991

Country	1950	1960	1970	1980	1990	
Austria	1.5	1.1	1.4	1.8	2.1	(1991)
Belgium	0.6	0.5	0.7	1.5	2.0	
Denmark	1.6	1.5	1.9	2.6	2.7	
Finland	0.9	0.8	1.3	2.0	2.6	
France	0.9	0.7	0.8	1.5	1.8	
W. Germany	1.6	0.9	1.3	1.6	1.9	
Netherlands	0.6	0.5	0.8	1.8	1.9	
Norway	0.7	0.7	0.9	1.6	2.4	
Sweden	1.1	1.2	1.6	2.4	2.2	
UK	0.7	0.5	1.2	2.8	2.7	

Sources: U.N. Yearbooks and National Yearbooks.

Table 2.2: Percentage of Marriages That Will End
in Divorce, 1970–1985

Country	1970	1980	1980s	
Austria	18.2	26.2	40.0 (1983)	30.0 (1984)
Belgium	9.6	20.8		
Denmark	25.1	39.3	45.0 (1983)	
France	12.0	24.7	30.8 (1985)	
Great Britain	16.3	39.3		
Netherlands	11.0	25.1	32.0 (1983)	
Switzerland	15.5	27.3	29.0 (1984)	
W. Germany	15.9	22.7	30.0 (1985)	

Sources: Alain Monnier, "La Conjoncture Demographique:
L'Europe et Les Pays Developpés d'Outre-Mer," *Population* 40
(1985), p. 75; Jean-Paul Sardon, "Evolution de la Nuptialité et
de la Divortialité en Europe Depuis la Fin des Années 1960,"
Population 41 (1986), p. 474; and other official sources.

the older pattern would return if a major depression were to occur is not
certain.

Divorce rates drop during a long war (when so many adult males are away
from home) but rise sharply at its end. The increase after World War II came
to an end in the 1950s and thus a drop in 1960 can be seen in Table 2.1. They
may also drop briefly when laws are passed that make divorce easier and
may drop briefly when laws make divorce more costly (for example, in 1976
a German law requiring that pension rights of the husband be shared upon
divorce after a long marriage). As many analysts have shown, however,
these legal changes may themselves be a response to underlying changes in
social attitudes and behavior. Thus the long-term upward movement is not
affected much by such temporary legal shifts. On the other hand, some of
these legal changes do have specific effects: They may alter the bargaining
position of husbands and wives—as, for example, no-fault divorce laws
did—and thus can change the terms of divorce settlements, if not the gross
divorce rates themselves.[3]

A general liberalization of divorce laws did occur between 1960 and 1990 in
Europe. It is worth emphasizing, however, that some countries had changed

3. This is a major theme of Lenore J. Weitzman's *The Divorce Revolution* (New York: Free
Press, 1985).

their laws *before* the sharp upward movement of the divorce curve, while others did so when it was occurring. A recent detailed analysis suggests that it would be very difficult to prove that much of the increase was caused by the liberalization itself.[4]

One way of describing these upward curves is to ask the question, "Who will be still married at fifty years of age?" The French demographer Jean-Paul Sardon has shown that this figure is likely to be *lower* than it was even in the eighteenth century, when death rates were much higher and most dissolutions were caused by death. While people now live longer, the rates of remarriage are lower, so that remarriage does not fully replenish the ranks of the married. To be sure, his assumption (for the purpose of his computations) that no marriage ends with death is not quite realistic.

In any event, Sardon concludes that after twenty-five years of marriage, the percentage that will still be married ranges from about 35 percent for Sweden to approximately 55 percent for Great Britain and France. Finland, Denmark, and Switzerland fall between those extremes.[5] His calculations compare the divorce rates of the 1960 cohort of births with those of the 1940 cohort. In Germany the divorce rates per 10,000 existing marriages rose from 67.5 in 1950 to 87.6 in 1987, but with a sharp temporary drop when the 1976 law (noted above) was put into effect.[6] Every decennial European cohort since 1950 shows a rise, and 30 percent of the cohort of 1987 is expected to have divorced after twenty-five years of marriage.

Who Files First?

European commentators have often pointed to a rise in the percentage of divorce suits filed by women as evidence of the growing empowerment of women. Doubtless this is true in part, but who files is a somewhat ambiguous datum. This is not at all a proof of who first *wants* the divorce or who insists upon getting it. And who first "wants" the divorce tells us little about who was originally more committed to the marriage or whose acts were decisive in leading to a divorce.

Even now, when women are more likely than in the past to seize the initiative, divorce is still more commonly the outcome of what I have called a

4. Jacques Commaille et al., *Le Divorce en Europe Occidentale: La Loi et le Nombre* (Paris: Institut National d'Etudes Demographiques, 1981), esp. pp. 168–80 (by Patrick Festy) and pp. 183ff. (by P. Guibentif). This relationship was first analyzed in the United States by Max Rheinstein in *Marriage, Stability, Divorce, and the Law* (Chicago: University of Chicago Press, 1972).

5. Jean-Paul Sardon, "Evolution de la Nuptialité et de la Divortialité en Europe Depuis la Fin des Années 1960," *Population* 41 (1986), pp. 478–80.

6. *Wirtschaft und Statistik* 10 (1988), pp. 682–83: Ehescheidungen 1986–87.

"divorce strategy,"[7] in which the husband can engage in a wide ranges of acts that cause his wife to be unhappy or dissatisfied (for example, being totally involved in his work, ignoring the family, not sharing household tasks, neglecting the children, coming home late, drinking, and so on). Because such behavior may be socially acceptable, others may not criticize him much, and he may not even perceive that his wife has any right to complain. However, over time, she may come to consider divorce a better alternative than such a marriage, and even though she may take the first legal step, some might see his behavior as the "real" impetus for the divorce. "Who files," then, may mask and simplify the processes of breaking apart.

Since most charges of "fault" bear less heavily on the husband than the wife, both parties may feel it is appropriate for her to file suit. As charges of fault become less necessary for a divorce in many countries, of course, who files becomes almost irrelevant to the question of who has moved more decisively toward divorce.

In Germany, in any event, there was no large change in the percentage of women who initiate the divorce suit during the 1970s and the early 1980s; that figure had also remained steady but a bit higher (about two-thirds of all cases)[8] even *before* the 1976 law; it dropped about 10 percent after the law, to about 57–59 percent. Since divorce based on "agreement" made up 70 percent of the cases in 1986, and these were signed by both spouses, who files has become a less significant fact.

In France during roughly the same period, the percentage of all suits filed by wives (for separation as well as divorce) increased somewhat, from 65 to 74 percent. The liberalizing changes of the 1975 divorce law did not affect this trend appreciably.[9]

Grounds for Divorce

It bears repeating that grounds for divorce tell us little or nothing about the *reasons* for divorce. They are simply the legally acceptable bases for divorce. When parties decide on grounds, typically they choose those that are the least damaging socially and the least difficult procedurally for both parties. The grounds change as the law is altered. When adultery is the only acceptable ground, that charge may be made whether or not it is true, if one or both spouses want the divorce enough. If trivial or vague grounds are acceptable, either husband or wife is likely to use them instead.

In general, charges of "fault" gradually decline when less hostile grounds

7. See William J. Goode, *After Divorce* (Glencoe, Ill.: Free Press, 1956), pp. 133ff.
8. "Ehescheidung," *W. u. St.* 10 (1988), p. 684.
9. "Situation Demographique de la France," *Population* 43 (1988), p. 642.

are legally permitted. In France, for example, in the decade from 1976 to 1985, fault as grounds dropped in the adjudicated cases from 90 to 49 percent, while "mutual consent" increased from 10 percent to slightly more than 50 percent ("dissolution of marital relations" remained a small percentage of the total).[10]

These percentages for divorces *granted* are different from those for *suits filed*, in which the two main grounds are almost equal in recent years. That difference is generated by important processes in divorce negotiations. First, where a long separation is required for an easy divorce, the husband and wife may agree to use some fault charge to shorten the wait before a divorce (as has been true in England and Wales). Second, they may be unable to agree on the terms of the divorce. Then the charge of fault is likely to be resisted and the divorce delayed. After that, with the filing of a suit, the spouses are more likely to come to some agreement that can be called "consensual." Consensual divorce increased in Germany to 70 percent by 1986, and this gradual process has been repeated in other countries as laws have become liberalized.

That underlying process of negotiation can occur because, in spite of the label, "no-fault divorce," European laws remain rather strict, except in the Nordic countries. Granted, if the divorce is based on separation as "proof" of an irreconcilable breakdown of the marriage, there is no need for a fault charge. The German law that went into effect in 1977, however, requires a year's separation, consent or a joint filing, a complete statement of the spouses' financial obligations (and of course financial resources), and agreements about custody and child-support payments. If one spouse is not willing, a three-year separation is required. A spouse's refusal to accept the financial arrangements will also delay the divorce.

Thus the grounds for divorce do affect the behavior of the spouses, especially in preventing or facilitating negotiations about post-divorce arrangements in Western Europe today. The changes in such grounds over the recent decades have been analyzed in some detail by Guibentif.[11] Here, we merely summarize the main changes:

1. In 1960, only a handful of European legal systems (Belgium, Denmark, Finland, Norway, Sweden) permitted divorce by mutual consent, and most of these were the leaders in the trend toward much higher divorce rates. By 1981, almost all European nations did so, including even the Catholic countries (Spain, Portugal, Italy), with restrictive requirements for a judicial separation first (though not in Portugal).

2. In 1960 nine countries permitted divorce as a kind of "remedy" (not

10. Ibid., pp. 643–44.
11. Pierre Guibentif, "L'evolution du droit du divorce de 1960–1981," in Commaille *Le Divorce*, pp. 183–206, esp. pp. 185, 191; and Jean-Francois Perrin, "Tendances des Changements legislatifs en matière de divorce en Europe occidentale," ibid., pp. 207–21.

often used, however) for an objective problem over which the petitioner had no control (for example, a spouse's mental illness or penal incarceration, desertion for some years), and that had changed little by 1981, except for the addition of the Catholic nations.

3. The breakdown of the marriage, which has usually been translated practically into separation—and often referred to casually as "no-fault" because in fact none need be charged—was acceptable in 1960 in seven countries, most of them the "more advanced" nations (for example, Norway, Sweden, West Germany, Austria, and the like). By 1981, however, all of them had come to some acceptance of this less severe requirement. As we note later, Spain and Italy would require a *judicial* separation before a legal divorce.

4. Divorce based on the accusation of fault was used in 1961 in all countries in which divorce was possible at all, but by 1981 this charge was available in fewer countries (but in the 1980s the newly divorcing Catholic countries accepted fault grounds); and it was *used* much less where it was available. Although Belgium, Austria, Denmark, France, Switzerland, Norway, and others still allowed accusations of fault, they were used less frequently.

5. Thus by the beginning of the 1980s and following the prolonged, major restructuring of family legal systems toward "liberalization," only Sweden had instituted a total no-fault legal system of divorce—that is, either spouse can get a divorce, and neither can prevent the other from doing so (essentially, the law adopted by California in 1970). By 1987, Finland would be added to such a list.

In the 1980s in most of Western Europe it continued to be possible for one spouse to resist to some degree the other's wish to divorce. While it was unlikely that the resistance could prevent a divorce, it could delay it considerably. The delay could be used as part of a strategy for improving the financial settlement and/or custody arrangements made at divorce. The husband would usually command the greater means for that manipulation.

Duration

At first it might seem self-evident that as divorce rates rise, the average duration of marriage would be expected to decline over time, but other patterns are at least conceivable. For example, divorce rates might rise for marriages of all durations, so that the average length of marriage would remain constant; or, still less likely, divorce rates might rise, but primarily among older people with a longer duration of marriage. In fact, *divorce rates have risen among both younger and older married people in Western Europe.* The *average* duration is statistically affected very strongly by marriages of longer duration (for example, the average duration of two marriages, one lasting thirty years and one lasting two years, would be sixteen years).

Thus in Germany the average length of marriages that ended in divorce actually rose between 1970 and 1984, from 9.2 to 11.9 years.[12] Part of this increase occurred because of the 1976 divorce law, requiring one to three years of separation, and, in addition, a sometimes lengthy set of negotiations about the care and support of the wife or children. Perhaps even more important, husbands found divorce more costly after 1976 because the new law required that they share their pensions with their ex-wives and get a court approval of the whole divorce settlement. The new law thus gave older wives a degree of independence they could not have attained earlier. The net effect was an increase in divorce among older couples and a rise in the divorce rate after 1976.

But most divorces occur in the earlier years of marriage, and if the rate continues to be high or increases, that will inevitably raise the percentage of divorce among younger marriages. In turn that will eventually reduce the percentage of all marriages in the older durations and thus decrease the average duration as well.

For the contemporary period, the striking fact is that rates in Western Europe continue to rise in successive younger cohorts, and thus the average duration *for each successive cohort* continues to decrease. The increase in rates among older couples has not been so large as among younger spouses.[13] Thus as implied above, in some countries (Austria, the Netherlands, Great Britain, West Germany), the average duration has not changed much, but the duration among younger cohorts has declined just as their divorce rate has risen.[14] In summary, the overall trend in Western Europe over the forty-year period from 1950 to 1990 has been a decline in the average length of marriages that end in divorce. Up to the early 1970s the average duration of marriage among most European nations was about 13–15 years. That average dropped to about 10 years by the mid-1980s.

Children

For many decades it was asserted that children are a restraint on divorce, and certainly many spouses in conflict have stated (and very likely believed)

12. *W. u. St.* 4 (1986), pp. 108, 968; *W. u. St.* 3 (1985), p. 188.
13. C. Blayo and P. Festy, "Le divorce en France: Evolution recente et perspectives," *Population* 31 (1976), p. 620.
14. Sardon, "Evolution," p. 477.

that they were "staying together for the children." If that finding ever was correct, it does not seem to be correct in the period we are considering. That is, when other variables are held constant (such as the duration of living together and other fertility variables), the presence and number of children are not greatly different for those who divorce and those who stay married.

This conclusion seems robust. It has been validated several times and in different countries, although it seems contrary to common sense and even to the comments that divorcing couples themselves offer when they explain why they hesitated to take decisive steps toward a divorce. It becomes evident, however, when we compare not simply the total number of children born to divorced and nondivorced couples (lower of course for the divorced) but the fertility for the years the couples have actually *lived* together. (The legal duration of the marriage may, by contrast, include many years of living apart without divorce.)

With the modern trends of delayed and lower fertility and shorter marriages, divorces in the future may eventually affect a smaller percentage of couples with children, but at present the rising absolute number of divorces involving children continues to create a growing set of social and economic problems for both spouses and the society.

In most European countries, the percentage of divorces involving children has risen somewhat, although not by much. In most, a majority of divorcing couples (65–70 percent) have children.

The average *number* of children drops in all these nations because the general birth rate has continued to fall (in several, to below replacement level). And the number with three or more children has decreased since 1950, as would be expected from the lowering percentage of larger families during these years in every European country.[15]

Even in West Germany, which has a lower percentage of divorces involving children, there has been no significant change in the percentage who divorce with children (omitting those whose children are now adults) during the period we are considering (1950–1990) and indeed none since 1934.[16] In 1950, 57 percent had children; the figure is 51 percent in 1987, with a sharp drop in the two years following the 1977 law.

Because it is often supposed that the fertility of couples who divorce is low, it is assumed that these women and men have not "completed" their childbearing; thus when they remarry they may want additional children. Consequently, some researchers have asked whether those who remarry might end up with more children than couples who limit their experiments in marriage to only one. In fact, however, the total fertility of those with two or

15. *W. u. St.* 10 (1988), p. 684, "Ehescheidungen 1986/87."
16. Wolfgang Vögeli and Barbara Willenbacher, "Background Notes on Divorce in FRG," Bellaggio Conference on the Economic Consequences of Divorce, 1989.

more marriages is *lower* on average than it is among couples who marry only once. This is true for both men and women, but Heekerens offers a different explanation for the two sexes. He speculates that men who remarry are likely to have children already (and thus do not want more), while women who remarry are more likely to unite with just such men (that is, who do not want more).[17]

Remarriage

For several decades, family analysts have been reassuring the pessimists by pointing out that although divorce rates were rising (and viewed as already high) the family was not thereby weakened. After all, people seemed to be just as willing to form new families, and even if they did divorce they hastened into marriage again as soon as possible. Divorce did not seem to be spoiling their taste for marriage. The clear reasoning, toward a simple but by now obviously fragile conclusion, was that people in all the Western countries were therefore just as committed to marriage as *their* parents had ever been. Indeed, it is likely that in the period before the 1960s the rate of remarriage actually increased or remained stable.[18]

That reassurance has now disappeared. In all these countries, those who divorce have come to remarry at a slower rate, and now it seems clear that a higher percentage do not again enter the married state. We shall present some of these findings in a moment, as well as their consequences, but let us first consider the broader dynamics of this change.

In all societies, the married state has been urged upon the young as part of the natural, unquestioned progression from childhood to adulthood and a morally desirable step (in spite of ancient preachments by some Church fathers that celibacy was even finer). In the distant past, parents and elders gave their children little choice about whether and even *whom* they should marry. It was only through their children's marriage that elders could maintain their kin line and their material or power advantages. Most important, as in other institutions, those who entered that socially approved state did in fact enjoy better and even longer lives.

These gains are somewhat smaller and less likely today. The single person does not have to lead a deprived existence. More important, marriages can no longer be counted on to endure, so that the union may not last long

17. Hans-Peter Heekerens, "Generatives Verhalten Wiederverheirateter," *Z. f. Bevölkerungswissenschaft* 12 (1986), no. 4, pp. 503–17.

18. See Patrick Festy, "Formation des Familles en Europe Occidentale," *Rev. Eur. de Pop.* 1 (1985), p. 182, on Switzerland. For a broader focus, see Louis Roussel, "Le Remariage des Divorces," *Population* 36 (July 1981), pp. 765–90, and J. Dupaquier et al., eds., *Marriage and Remarriage in Populations of the Past* (New York: Academic, 1981).

enough to ensure an adequate payoff for one's emotional or work investments. Having experienced this uncertainty, both men and women divorcees are more reluctant to try marriage soon, or even again.

What is crucial for our understanding of remarriage, however, is that it is
not remarriage alone that is delayed or foregone. It is not only those who
have gone through the hurtful experiences of divorce who have moved in
this direction. People have increasingly come to feel that same wariness or
reluctance about first marriages as well.

Sardon has presented a solid array of data to show how widespread this
trend is, with only a few points at which there are reverses. With reference to
the decline in first marriages, he observed (in my translation): "This transformation of the matrimonial model, which one might have been able to
believe would be limited to the particular conditions of the Scandinavian
world, extends since the beginning of the 1970s to all of Europe. Central Europe (Switzerland, West Germany, and Austria) was first affected from the
beginning of 1970, then Western Europe (Great Britain and France) in 1972,
and finally Eastern Europe about 1975. . . . [I]n view of this similarity of
evolution, one may well ask whether the Scandinavian situation does not
predict what can only be partially observed now among all the European
nations.[19]

Contemporary marriage rates are only about 70 percent of those observed
in 1965. Monnier calculated the percentage who eventually marry in most
of the European countries from 1965 to 1983. The base year is marked by
almost "total" marriage. That is, upwards of 90 percent of the adult population would eventually marry. However, that figure steadily dropped from
1970 onward, to reach 50–60 percent in the 1980s.[20]

The period between divorce and remarriage also remained relatively stable from 1955 to 1969, with an average delay of about 2.5 years. In France,
until 1969, one-half of divorcees remarried within 2.5 years, and in most of
Europe two-thirds remarried within three to four years. (But even at that
time, less than half of those in Sweden had remarried within that period.[21])
Beginning in the 1970s. however, the rate continued to drop in Europe.
Between 1966 and the early 1980s, the drop is from about 65 remarriages in
a given year for each 100 divorces averaged over the preceding six years, to
about 40. For France, the drop from 1960 to 1984 is from 62 to 40. For
Belgium, the decrease over the same period is from 73 to 52; for Holland,

19. Sardon, "Evolution," pp. 463–72.
20. A. Monnier, "La Conjoncture Demographique: L'Europe et Les Pays Developpés d'Outre
Mer," *Population* 40 (1985), pp. 75ff.
21. Roussel, "Remariage," pp. 766–68. The earlier data are based on research reported by M.
Van Houte–Minet, "Le Remariage en Pays Industrialisés: Approche transversale et longi-
tudinale," *Recherches economiques de Louvain* (Sept. 1969), pp. 319–42.

from 75 to 39; and for Switzerland, from 63 to 40.[22] There is no reason to suppose that trend has stopped, and the estimate for France, published by the authoritative demographic journal *Population* in 1986, is 38 percent for men and 37 percent for women.[23]

In general, the ratio of men entering remarriage to women who take that step is about 3:2. Both the higher percentage of men who eventually remarry and their greater speed of remarriage were typical in past decades as well. Of course, the remarriage rate remains much higher for those who divorce in their twenties; about 80 percent will remarry.

This alteration in divorce patterns—which seems to be widespread even outside the fully industrialized countries (especially for women)—is linked with, or sets in motion, several other changes of considerable social and political importance for most nations. Some of these certainly existed in previous decades, but not in the same magnitude.

One such change is mediated through the continuing customs of the marriage market and the changing *relative* mortality of males and females. Both U.S. and European research emphasizes the overwhelming importance of *age*. Almost all those who divorce in their twenties will remarry. For example, the chance of remarriage in Germany for males aged 25 in 1960 was 99 percent, almost the same as in the years from 1979 to 1982. There is some drop for age 30: 98 percent vs. 89 percent. Even so, there is a change in the remarriage pattern: the period until remarriage was three years in 1960–62 for both age groups, but six and 6.5 years in the years between 1980 and 1983.[24]

On the other hand, women lose value in the marriage market relative to men with each year of age after thirty, and this difference is accelerated in their late thirties and early forties. In the social definitions of what is "desirable" or "marriageable," divorced men of 45 can remarry much more easily than women of the same age. Indeed, the older the man, the greater the average age difference between him and his new wife (although there is also some increase now in the number of women who remarry younger men as well). This process increases the number and the percentage of older women who do not remarry.

Second, with lower mortality rates, the usual higher life expectancy of women increases still further. It is not merely that women's lower mortality continues into the older years; their relative advantage over men *increases* in the older years. Thus the decreasing ratio of older men to older women shrinks still more the pool of older marriageable men. As a consequence,

22. Roussel, "Remariage," pp. 777–81.

23. The figures, possibly overestimates, are the ratio between the number of remarriages in a given year, relative to the average number of divorces over the preceding five years: "Situation Demographique de la France," *Population* 43 (1988), p. 739.

24. *W. u. St.* 3 (1985), pp. 110–11.

even aside from the age customs of mate choice, the number of unremarried older men is much smaller than the number of available women. As Hekeerens wryly points out, this casts doubt on the notion that older women are not inclined to marry (but men are): In simple numerical terms, even if older men on average were six times as desirous of marriage, there would still be *one* willing available older woman for every such man.[25]

Since detailed calculations of who remarries were not often made in past decades, it may not be possible to assert whether all these patterns are actually changes. For example, men with higher incomes and education are likely to remarry sooner, but that was probably true in the past as well. On the other hand, women with higher educations remarry at a slower rate, as they did in the past, because they are likely to be somewhat older and to have better incomes—so that a new marriage offers smaller advantages over independence. (In addition, even now some potential husbands may feel less than eager to unite with a well-educated mate who makes a higher income.) However, U.S. data suggest that the *drop* in the remarriage rate in recent years has been *smaller* for well-educated women.

As a trivial but thought-provoking example of pattern similarity over time, warning us against the hasty conclusion that all we see is change, it seems likely (again, contrary to most people's guesses) that women with one or two small children will remarry about as fast as women without children.[26] If one controls for age and class variables, the contemporary pattern in the United States is the same.[27]

That may not actually be a *change* in divorce patterns, for I found a similar pattern in a large random sample of divorced women in the 1940s. In that group of mothers aged thirty-eight years and under at divorce, there were few differences in social activities and attitudes toward remarriage between those who had one child and those who had more than one. However, twenty-six months after the divorce, a higher percentage of the mothers with three children than of all the rest had actually married (there were no childless ex-wives in this sample).[28]

At that time, I suggested that divorced mothers with more children were more "efficient" in their courtship behavior. That is, they wasted less time dating men who did not view such a burden as attractive. Of course, because fertility is now lower, modern samples would very likely show that three

25. See in this connection the analysis of marriage in the later years by H. P. Heekerens, "Wiederheirat im Alter," *Z. f. Gerontologie* 20 (1987), pp. 263–68.

26. Roussel, "Remariage," pp. 770–71.

27. Arthur J. Norton and Jeanne E. Moorman, "Current Trends in Marriage and Divorce among American Women," *J. Marr. and the Family* 49 (Feb. 1987), p. 11; and Paul C. Glick and Sung-Ling Lin, "Remarriage after Divorce," *Sociological Perspectives* 30 (April 1987), pp. 172–75.

28. Goode, *After Divorce*, pp. 272–73, 281–83.

children are now more of a burden than two children, but in any event there are fewer divorced mothers with more than two.

Although the rate of remarriage has slowed and the chance of remarriage may well be less than half for much of Europe, most young children eventually become part of some kind of new union. Either their mothers join with another man in some form of cohabitation or they remarry. It is, of course, especially the younger mothers, with their younger children, who will remarry. (On the other hand, as we discuss in the next section, a significant minority of children are being raised in single-parent mother-headed households.)

Thus the rising rates of divorce have many consequences for the demography of marriage. One of the most obvious is the increase in the percentage of newly married couples made up of one or more partners who have been divorced. For example, in West Germany that percentage rose from 7–8 percent in 1960 to 18 percent in 1984.[29] In France for the period from 1975 to 1984, the percentage rose from 7 percent to about 13 percent. As the pool of divorced people grows larger, more of them are available as possible mates. That trend is likely to continue.

In addition, a wider range of pairings can result: divorcees remarry divorcees, or they can marry the never-married, and of course, as traditional research has shown, the heterogamy of marriage pairings increases in these remarriages (greater age discrepancies between bride and groom, a lesser concern with religious and class differences, a wider geographical choice, and so forth).[30] Because divorce rates for the remarried continue to be higher than for the once-married, the pool of eligible new divorcees is likely to grow.

This, in turn, creates a complex of new kinship ties that greatly enlarges our conception of what a "kinship network" is and reduces the prevalence of what was once the "normal" family (once-married couple with their children, the wife staying at home to care for them)—which now may be close to a *minority* in all these countries. Today stepparenting becomes more widespread, and children have to adjust to an expanded set of parents and stepparents, stepgrandparents, and stepbrothers, plus a new set of friends through family ties. These new patterns and processes are now the subject of a growing research literature.[31]

---

29. *W. u. St.* 4 (1986), p. 108.

30. Roussel, "Remariage," pp. 769ff.

31. For a short report on these processes in Denmark, see Inger Koch-Nielsen, *New Family Patterns* (Copenhagen: Danish National Institute of Social Research, 1987); see also Irene Thery, "Die Familien nach der Scheidung: Vorstellungen, Normen, Regulieren," in *Die Postmodern Familie,* pp. 84–97; Lothar Kaufman, "Über die Verschiedenheit der Familien alleinerziehender Eltern—Aussätze zu einer Typologie," ibid., pp. 131–42; and Frank F. Furstenberg, "Die Entstehung des Verhaltensmusters 'Sukzessive Ehen,'" ibid., pp. 73–83. See also Marilyn Talmon, *Stepparent Families* (Beverly Hills, Calif.: Sage, 1990).

It should be emphasized here that although cohabitation at present may be about as likely as remarriage to succeed a marital breakup, many divorcees do not find or seek either solution. The blunt fact is that there is a steady increase of single-parent mother-headed families in these countries, and these families disproportionately bear the negative consequences of divorce.

One-Parent Households

The continued increase of one-parent households in Europe is mainly caused by divorce and a reduction in the rate of remarriage. (The rising illegitimacy ratios also create such households, but the percentages are still modest. They are much lower in Europe than in the United States.) Although a later section on postdivorce arrangements also discusses economic problems, we must take note of them here as well.

The socioeconomic position of divorced men continues to be very different from that of women, from the time of the divorce onward. The economic consequences of divorce were devastating for women in the past as well. For example, although with the new patterns of no-fault divorce and consensual agreements very few wives receive alimony, few ever received any alimony in the past either, when husbands had much greater legal control over any marital property.

In addition, men have always been reluctant to pay child support for children whom they did not see often. They have also shown very little eagerness to pay alimony to an ex-wife whom they had, after all, wished to leave. In any event, non-remarried older women generally have fewer *other* economic resources than men. At present, the absolute number of such women has increased greatly, and their percentage of the population has also increased.

The lack of financial support for divorced women has increased the welfare burden even more than it would have fifty years ago, because of a change in family norms. It is now more likely to be taken for granted that most divorced adults will not be living as dependents in the home of their parents or even of one of their grown children. Indeed, in perhaps all of these countries, independent living (where income permits) is far more common for individuals both old *and* young, than in the past.

Thus later remarriage or nonremarriage, demographic changes, changes in attitudes about sharing a home, and the weakening of traditional institutional supports have all combined to increase the number of people who live in one-parent families and thus to generate a growing set of social and economic problems in Europe. These are overwhelmingly mother-headed households, simply because in all European countries custody is given to the mother in 80–90 percent of divorces.

Thus one-parent and especially mother-headed households continue to increase. The number rose 24 percent in West Germany in the period 1972–1985. By 1981, there were about 1.1 million such family units. In the period 1970–1980 in Switzerland, the number of single one-parent households almost doubled, but the number of households with a divorced mother and children more than doubled.[32]

It is especially among such households that poverty is to be found, in Europe as in the United States. Correspondingly, a higher percentage of divorced mothers are in the labor force than of any other segment of the female population. In the early 1980s in West Germany, for example, almost half of divorced mothers with children *under* six years of age were in the labor force. That figure was higher (80 percent) for mothers with one child of eighteen years or less in 1980 but dropped to 71 percent in 1985. Comparable percentages were 41 percent and 35 percent for mothers with three or more children.[33]

As in all of these complex areas of change, it is not possible to specify which variable has contributed the most to the link between women's employment and the divorce process. Some possibilities are obvious, as we noted earlier, but disentangling cause from effect may not be possible. Certainly these factors have had some effect: (1) the growing percentage of women who remain in the labor force after they marry and after their children are born, the growing economic need for two paychecks, a social climate that increasingly encourages women to use their talents, and taking a job as a normal part of their life course; (2) the economic demand for the increasingly higher skills and education of women, which opens a bigger market for their labor and offers them greater opportunities; (3) among women who want to have a career as well as those who already work, a greater willingness to consider divorce, as well as to delay marriage or remarriage; in addition, women who want to work but do not yet work are more willing to consider divorce; (4) the fact that women who work can

32. For Germany, see Charlotte Höhn and Kurt Lüscher, "The Changing Family in the Federal Republic of Germany," *J. Fam. Issues* 9 (1988), pp. 317–33; Charlotte Höhn and Reiner Schultz, "Bericht zur demographischen Lage in der Bundesrepublik Deutschland," *Z. f. Bevölkerungswissenschaft* 13 (1987), p. 1815; Niko Keilman, "Recent Trends in the Family and Household Composition in Europe," *Eur. J. Pop.* 3 (July 1988), pp. 297, 308; and Karl Schwarz, "Eltern und Kinder in unvollständigen Familien," *Z. f. Bevölkerungswissenschaft* 1 (1984), p. 34. For Switzerland, see Olivier Blanc, "Les Ménages en Suisse," *Population* 40 (1985), p. 672.
33. Höhn and Schultz, "Bericht," p. 204.

more easily live independently than in the past, even though they may be more deprived than if they were married; and finally, and most pressingly, (5) the fact that women, especially mothers, *must* take jobs in order to survive as heads of families after divorce.

Settlements and Negotiations

As we noted earlier, most Western nations have changed their divorce laws in basic ways over the past fifteen years or so (Sweden 1973, France 1975, Germany 1976, England 1971–1973, 1984, Austria 1978, Belgium 1974–1975, for example), in addition to the normal amendments and new regulations from year to year. These share many elements. Of these, two are fundamental redirections of the law, but we shall take note of others as well.

First, divorce has become more accessible to those who wish to dissolve their marriage as the legal requirements have been broadened or "softened" in accord with people's actual divorce behavior and the courts' decisions. For example, as in the United States earlier, the designation of "cruelty" was gradually extended to a wider range of behavior. In the recent laws "the breakdown of the marriage" has become acceptable as the grounds for divorce (proved, as noted earlier, by one to three years of separation), and "mutual consent" can be legally affirmed when the spouses sign the required papers, however reluctant one of them may be.

This means that, as in marriage itself, the state has lessened its surveillance and control over the conditions people must meet in order to enter or change this status.

On the other hand, the state now shows *more* concern about the economic effects of divorce, especially about its impact on children. Although the rhetoric of the current European debate about divorce suggests that anyone can easily get out of marriage, true no-fault divorce (that is, where an unwilling spouse cannot prevent the divorce or delay it substantially) is found only in the Nordic countries. In contrast, the other European countries present various bars to divorce by mere whim. In Germany, there is a one-year wait even if there is consent; otherwise the delay may be three years or more. France permits a certain type of no-fault divorce but requires a six-year separation, and even then may refuse it on grounds of hardship. The "liberal" 1975 French divorce law is quite strict, and divorce remains somewhat difficult to get. Indeed, in perhaps most European countries, "fault" divorce remains common, because, ironically, if a fault-based claim is successful it is likely to be faster. In short, in most of these states divorce is *not* an individual's "right."

The European nations seem to follow one of two main forms:[34] (1) In the European heartland, the tendency is to retain some fault as an element in divorce but to emphasize spousal economic obligations while supplementing them with help from the state if necessary. (2) In the Nordic nations, no-fault divorce is prevalent, with the assumption that spouses will be economically self-sufficient and that both are obligated for child support, supplemented by what is viewed outside the Nordic countries as generous public benefits for children as well as mothers.

Although we shall comment separately on the Anglo countries, it is relevant in this section to note that Europe generally differs from England in that Anglo judges have much *discretionary power,* which has many consequences. Glendon has noted, for example, the administrative trend for handling child support in Europe, where child-support levels are established by formal tables that state the appropriate amounts of payments for one or many children under various conditions. These are based on socioeconomic studies and official definitions of poverty levels, which are automatically adjusted for inflation. English judges and registrars, by contrast, can and often do set very low child payments, and their decisions are often much at variance with one another. Of course, if judges have greater power, lawyers become more useful, and the spouse with more resources (typically the husband) can often manage to escape much of the spousal or child support that would simply be administratively enforced in Europe.

Another new element in European divorce patterns is the changing definition of *property.* Viewed in the past as mainly real estate or the ownership of a business, it is increasingly extended to pensions, health insurance, and other "intangible" benefits. Often the total of these assets has a fiduciary value greater than the couple's part ownership of a home. Thus negotiations come to extend to all such varieties of new property in order to arrive at an equal division if the marriage has lasted some minimum of years.

That apparent equity, on the other hand, hides many inequalities. A divorce by consensual agreement requires that the couple state how they are dividing the property or future income (another form of property), how much child support is to be paid, and so forth. Their agreement is to be evaluated by the court. In England, the division is not likely to be examined carefully. French courts will give it much more attention but courts cannot devote much time as a rule to this process.

More important, it is usually the husband who has the resources to press for greater advantages in the final agreement. In Germany, where an effort is

---

34. Especially for broad differences among nations, I have drawn upon Mary Ann Glendon, *Abortion and Divorce in Western Law* (Cambridge, Mass.: Harvard University Press, 1987).

made to equalize "marriage-dependent disadvantages," an analysis of "re-
futations" and countercharges suggests that in most cases full agreement is
not reached, even though the wife eventually signs the document.[35] Before
the 1976 law, only about 11 percent of all divorced husbands paid alimony
in West Germany, and that percentage did not change afterwards. In a recent
paper, Voegeli and Willenbacher (1991) have extensively analyzed some of
the "legal fictions" of equality in German divorce settlements.[36] In about
three-fourths of the agreements, wives give up some of their equality claims.
Alimony has not been likely in France, either. Roussel noted that in 1973, for
example, support was paid only sporadically if at all. In the Netherlands, the
mother now gets enough support or state help to stay at home with the
children, but not to get further education or part-time work.[37]

A Belgian study in the mid-1980s explored some of the factors that deter-
mine compliance with orders for child support after divorce.[38] Several of its
findings appear to apply more broadly. First, the divorced mothers who were
most in need were likely to have a lower level of education, more children, a
history of less professional activity, and to have followed a domestic pattern
of traditional housewifely roles. Thus, as in other countries, their economic
position was intrinsically weak.

Second, those who were weakest were more likely to have been involved
in a fault-based divorce, perhaps because this was the only way they could
salvage something from the marriage relationship. Third, the husbands in
such cases were likely to have lower-level jobs, lower incomes, and to have
suffered from more unemployment. Both husbands and wives in consent
divorces were more likely to be different in these sets of traits.

Mothers got custody in 80 percent of all cases, and child support was
ordered or agreed to in 80 percent of the cases of mother custody, almost
always to be paid by the father. However, a fourth pattern, again found in
other countries, was that support payments were set on average below the
subsistence minimums worked out by the Centre for Social Policy (University of Antwerp). Again the amounts set were lower for fault-based cases,

35. "Statistische Umschau: Bevölkerung," W. u. St. (12/11, 1982), pp. 6, 12–13, 45 et
passim.
36. Wolfgang Vögeli and Barbara Willenbacher, "Property Division and Splitting of Pensions
Assets in the FRG," in Lenore J. Weitzman and Mavis Maclean, eds., The Economic Consequences
of Divorce (Oxford: Oxford University Press, 1992), pp. 163–83.
37. Christine Clason, "The One-Parent Family: The Dutch Situation," J. Comp. Family Studies
11 (1980), p. 13. For further problems in applying the 1976 German law, see Doris Lucke and M.
Brater, "Eheliche Lebensverhältnisse und 'Angemessene' Erwerbstätigkeit," Soz. Welt 31
(1980), pp. 206–29.
38. Karel Maddens and Jean van Houtte, "Child Support in Belgium," in Weitzman and
Maclean, Economic Consequences, pp. 195–203. A preliminary study was carried out in two large
cities, followed by a national survey.

doubtless because the father had fewer resources, and is less likely to feel generous in fault cases.

Ironically, several factors thus interact to create even more vulnerability in the lives of divorced mothers. Those who are in the weakest position because of their own past history are more likely to be married to men with a similar history. They cannot easily be generous to one another since they have nothing to spare, and the hostility of a fault-based divorce makes them less than eager to help the other. Mothers or wives who are better off, with more education and better jobs, are less likely to be granted spousal maintenance, but their husbands are more likely to pay it if it is part of the agreement. (Only 15 percent of the most needy mothers were given "personal alimony," and only 5 percent got it regularly.)

Fathers paid regularly in 58 percent of the cases though payment problems had occurred earlier in some of these as well. The figure was much higher, 87 percent, for child support in consent divorce cases. A further regularity is found here, doubtless both cause and effect: The financially delinquent fathers were also likely to have had less contact with their children than other fathers, even during the marriage. Among all divorced fathers, about one-third do not visit their children, and that figure rises to 50 percent in cases of fault divorce.[39]

In France during this same period (mid-1980s), about 60 percent of the support payments were paid regularly,[40] an improvement over the 1970s. Again the irony appears that if the payments were set at a low figure (for example, because of the husband's resistance or low income), payments were *less* likely to be made: Only 30 percent paid regularly. If the husband was not employed at the time of the breakup, payments were even less likely (27 percent). Some 42 percent paid regularly if the spouses were in disagreement about their respective obligations. Contrary to expectation, in France as in Belgium these figures were not altered if the husband began a new relationship. In France, these figures have not changed since the 1970s.

Since Germany was the first European nation to install (under Bismarck) a broad social security system, its provisions for helping families are more developed than most. Its programs, like those of neighboring countries, have undergone sweeping changes over the past generation. Its rules for child support differ somewhat from others, however, because they begin with the *primacy* of the child support obligation. Division of property and pension yields some benefits for divorced women, but the laws make it easier for

39. Ibid., p. 199.
40. Patrick Festy and Marie-France Valetas, "Le Divorce et apres," *Population et Societes*, no. 215 (July 1987).

husbands to gain advantages in those negotiations than in their obligations toward children.

Parents are obligated for child support whether or not their own needs are being met. The child can demand maintenance through the years of vocational training or even higher level academic education if that fits his or her abilities, and for a time afterwards if the child is unemployed. In practice, this means that after divorce the noncustodial parent must make regular support payments. The custodial parent has no similar financial obligation, under the reasonable assumption that he or she will be contributing a great deal anyway.[41]

Since everyone in Germany must be registered at an address, and a junior officer of the court can garnishee wages even without holding a formal hearing, it is not easy for a father to escape this responsibility. Both before and after divorce, legal aid is given for procedures necessary to make child-support claims. Consequently, about 75 percent of divorced fathers make child-support payments in full and on time, and that percentage has been increasing since the late 1970s. Advance payments are made by the state if the father is delinquent.

The administrative rules as well as the payment schedules began in the 1969 laws which were aimed at assuring support for children born out of wedlock. They were extended to nuptial children in 1976. The parents must take the initiative, but the rules are simple, applied by junior officers, and based on standard figures, adjusted for age and number of children, income, inflation, and so on. About half of all cases are settled by private agreement, but the percentage requiring court action has been increasing, suggesting that more fathers have been resisting payments (p. 238).

Changes continue to be made in Europe with respect to the general problem of enforcing both spousal and child support payments. The spread of divorce and the greater welfare burden of mothers and children when ex-husbands do not pay has moved most nations to confront this problem, although it is safe to say that state efforts in much of Europe have had only modest success. Sweden may have the most advanced and efficient enforcement system. Even there, however, 15 percent of the (mainly) fathers pay nothing, and 25 percent pay less than 30 percent of what they owe. Thus the administrative and welfare challenge is large in all countries.

The problem continues because, as in spousal support, husbands seem to find it easier to bear the discomfort and anger of their ex-wives than the hurt of giving up part of their own incomes, and they tend to resist paying child

41. B. Willenbacher and W. Vögeli, "Child Maintenance in the FRG," in Weitzman and Maclean, *Economic Consequences*, pp. 234–35.

support for children they have sired but from whom they no longer derive any daily benefits.

A goodly handful of countries (France, Sweden, Germany, Austria, Luxembourg, and some Swiss cantons) try to fill the gap by stronger enforcement (for example, withholding wages if necessary), plus state payments of whatever cannot be collected.[42] If the single parent is an unmarried mother with two children in France, Sweden, or Germany the household will get 67–94 percent of the net average wages of a production worker. (In the United States, that figure would be closer to one-half and would be less likely to be paid.)

The Adjustment of Children

With every rise in the divorce rate, many commentators have expressed concern about the effects of divorce on children. There is also widespread agreement that those effects are bad, but well-designed research on this topic is rare. In the United States more than fifty years ago it was shown that "children of divorce" fared worse than children in a stable marriage, but those studies merely compared the two groups of children without any attempt to ascertain that they had been the same in all social and psychological traits *prior* to the divorce. That failure is crucial, since it is certain that the two groups do differ in important ways. Children of divorce engage in more acts of juvenile delinquency, and do less well in school—thus the effects seem obvious. However, more of them have younger, less educated parents living on lower incomes, and these prior factors are also associated with poorer performances of children in many areas. Children in mother-headed families are also likely to suffer downward socioeconomic mobility, another factor with negative consequences. Thus, class and poverty may play a large role in these apparent effects.

As adults, children of divorce experience a higher divorce rate, but they are also likely to marry earlier, and their parents were more likely to have reared them in poor economic circumstances, where the divorce rate was high.[43] In addition, research in the United States suggested long ago that children whose parents were in conflict but did *not* divorce had even more psychological problems. It also reports that among lower-class black families, divorce itself creates few disadvantages for their children compared with those in the same class position who do not experience divorce. That is,

42. Glendon, *Abortion*, pp. 89–90.
43. For further analysis, see Hans-Peter Heekerens, "Erhöhte Risiko der Ehescheidung," *Z. f. Soziologie* 16 (June 1987), pp. 190–203. See also notes 44–48 below.

because they already face so many difficulties in life, a mere breakup of the mother-father unit does not add much to those barriers.

It is almost certain that if we compared divorced and non-divorced children with otherwise exactly the same psychological and social backgrounds, the non-divorced children would still fare somewhat better.[44] As Maclean and Wadsworth have noted, there are both long- and short-term effects, especially for boys, with reference to school attendance, delinquency, and education. Our question here is whether there has been any *change* in this pattern over the past generation.

Of course, the absolute number of children affected by divorce has increased substantially, even though fertility has generally fallen, because a majority of divorces involve children, and the number of divorces has risen. It can also be supposed that the social stigma of the past has been reduced considerably; since the *cumulative* number of children involved in a divorce has increased greatly, they are now much less likely to be treated as a deviant group, and their parents can no longer be viewed as widely disesteemed. Most of those from middle-class families will suffer a fall in income, and these socioeconomic losses of divorce may account for many of the negative experiences such children go through. That is usual, for mothers have custody in 80–90 percent of the cases, and they suffer a loss of income in all the European countries. After the breakup, most are not able to create as comfortable a life as they formerly enjoyed.[45] Fate, then, is sometimes unfair, but we know no way of recapturing from the past a random sample of children in divorce, to see whether they suffered differently, or more, than children who suffer the burdens of divorce in modern Europe.

As Sara McLanahan notes, although there is no definitive proof that divorce itself causes lower attainment in children, there are good theoretical reasons for believing that it reduces the quantity and quality of parental investment, which would in turn reduce children's wellbeing.[46]

While reports of negative effects in children are echoed by researches in a number of countries, I have found no research that asked whether these

44. The work of Judith Wallerstein (*Second Chances* [New York: Ticknor and Fields, 1989]) expresses a somber view of the long-term effects of divorce on children, but both the sample and the measures of "effects" may have been unduly influenced by her clinical perspective. For some of the effects, see Mavis Maclean and M. E. J. Wadsworth, *Int. J. Law and the Family* 2 (1988), pp. 155–66. See also Sara McLanahan, "Intergenerational Consequences of Divorce: The United States Perspective," in Weitzman and MacLean, *Economic Consequences*, pp. 285–310; and Sara McLanahan and Larry Bumpass, "Intergenerational Consequences of Family Disruption," *Amer. J. Sociology* 94 (1988), pp. 130–52.

45. McLanahan, "Intergenerational," p. 305.

46. For an earlier discussion of this problem in causation, see Goode, *After Divorce*, pp. 307–11, as well as Paul Landis, "The Broken Home in Teenage Adjustments," *Rural Sociology Series on the Family*, no. 4 (Pullman, Washington: Institute of Agricultural Sciences, State College of Washington, 1953), pp. 10ff. His data were gathered in the 1940s.

apparent effects have changed over time. It seems reasonable to suggest that as divorce becomes more common and the stigma of divorce is reduced, and as the populations of those who divorce become more "average" in the sense that they are more like anyone else who marries, the percentage of children of divorce who do poorly in school and have other behavior problems would be likely to decline.

That question is really divisible into two very different queries. We have just considered one of them: As divorce becomes a more "normal" experience, the children of divorce might become more similar to other children, but there is another nagging question. As I have noted here and earlier (*After Divorce*, pp. 68, 308, for example), at least some part of the difference between children of divorce and others arises from class. That is, the children of divorce are more likely to be members of lower-class families and thus more likely to get lower grades in school, to do less well economically, or even to engage in juvenile delinquency. For this reason, it is not likely that the seeming difference between these groups of children will be reduced by much over time.

Moreover, a deeper question remains: It may be that most of the factors that cause these apparent differences appear not mainly at the divorce but earlier, during the marriage. Class is one of these factors, but other possibilities suggest themselves as well—the husband-wife conflict, the pervasive family conflict, personality problems of children, poverty, and so on.[47] The assumption that divorce itself is the prime agent remains steady, and much research continues to show the difference, but until very recently no one has attempted to ascertain whether the differences might have begun long *before* the divorce.

We now possess, however, relatively robust data that do compare cohorts of divorced and nondivorced children with reference to a wide variety of pre-divorce experiences. As we shall see in chapter 6, on the Anglo countries, not all those differences are caused by the divorce experience.

Unmarried Cohabitation

I have not as yet seen a serious analysis of why the large increase in unmarried cohabitation has happened during this period, nor any previous theoretical work that predicted it. It is a radical shift in European (and Anglo) family behavior. No comparable pattern appears in the past several

---

47. See Jacques Commaille, "Divorce and the Child's Status: The Evolution in France," *J. Comp. Family Studies* 14 (Spring 1983), pp. 107ff. on these points.

centuries. It is part of the changing divorce patterns of the contemporary generation, and must be considered here as well as in other chapters.

In any country, even the most restrictive sexually, there have always been some couples who lived together unmarried. Most of these were lower-class and poor individuals who could not afford the costs of marriage, or who could not get permission to marry, and whose lives were less embedded in the dominant social structure. (The Latin American pattern of "consensual marriage" has a different historical origin, but these statements apply there as well.[48])

Others were upper-class or noblemen with their mistresses. That relationship was not at all our modern "cohabitation." Typically, the couple had no publicly acknowledged common domicile. Except for the most powerful, the man could not move about in his own class with his mistress as a "couple," and others in his social circle did not accord such unions the same respect they gave to legal unions. Nor were the children of such a relationship accorded the same rights (there are some exceptions) as the issue of their fathers' legal marriages.

Now, by contrast, millions of such European couples, in all classes, expect to be given the same respect as the legally married, while, ironically, their governments have steadily moved to demand the same kinds of mutual responsibilities of such unions. It seems likely that cohabitation is most normalized in Sweden, where some assert that it is the "same as marriage," but rapid change has also occurred in Denmark and the Netherlands, while Germany lags behind France.

Roussel earlier noted the sharp rise in the percentage of those who had lived together before marriage: 17 percent of the marriage cohort of 1968–1969, 44 percent of that of 1976–1977. Now, a later full-scale study of a large sample (aged 21–44 years) in France reports that of those who had married around 1980 at the most common age of 25 years, approximately 60 percent had first lived with the subsequent spouse, or another.[49] For the marriages in the period from 1980 to 1985 that figure is 75 percent for Paris itself (p. 343). For those who are regular churchgoers, it is not much lower (50 percent) than for the sample as a whole.

At the ages of 21–24 years, when in the past most would not have been married in France, over 90 percent of these cohabiting couples are single. It

48. For a theoretical analysis of this Latin American pattern, see William J. Goode, "Illegitimacy in the Caribbean Social Structure," *Am. Soc. Rev.* 25 (Feb. 1960), pp. 21–30, and "Illegitimacy, Anomie, and Cultural Penetration," *Am. Soc. Rev.* 26 (Dec. 1961), pp. 910–25. It is analyzed in more detail in ch. 10.

49. Louis Roussel, "La cohabitation juvenile en France," *Population* 33 (1978), pp. 15–42; Henri Leridon and Catherine Villeneuve-Gokalp, "Les nouveaux Couples: Nombre, caracteristiques et attitudes," *Population* 43 (1988), p. 366.

is only after the mid-thirties that half or more have been married before (pp. 336–39). As a consequence of these changes, the rise in the prevalence of cohabitation in France compensates for the decrease in the percentage living in marital unions (for ages 21–24 years, that drop is about half since 1972) as well as for the increase in divorces until about 1981–1982.

Indeed, this is the general pattern; in Great Britain, Denmark, France, the Netherlands, and Sweden, the increase in cohabitation compensates for the drop in the likelihood of marriage.[50] In 1981–1982, in Leridon and Gokalp's view, economic factors caused many young people to stay at home for a longer period. By the early 1980s, according to an official West German study of the motivations of those who cohabit, the number cohabiting increased by 277 percent between 1972 and 1982, and the total number of persons in such unions was estimated as between 1 million and 2.5 million.[51]

Since we are considering here only changes in divorce patterns, we shall not analyze cohabitation as a form of marital union. Clearly, it is an alternative that is spreading and is less stable and fecund than legal unions. (In France, the unions of cohabitants aged 25–29 years have an average duration of three years, and those of persons aged more than 30 years have a duration of five years). It seems that this form of marriage and dissolution will become either a "normal" phase of marriage or, for a substantial minority, a substitute for it. This trend makes the future analysis of "divorce" rates very difficult, and we note some of these complexities in chapter 7, on divorce in Latin America.

It seems almost certain that the causes of this new phenomenon are to be found in the high divorce rates of the modernized nations—that is, in the transient character of modern marriage. However, the exact connection is less clear. It is almost as though marriage paradoxically becomes less desirable once it becomes easier to escape its consequences: If leaving marriage is less problematic, why enter it? Or perhaps the change is less paradoxical: Increasingly, as noted earlier, people want to enjoy the pleasures of living together, but do not wish to make a strong commitment to the union. The legal union offers more benefits, but it is perceived as a high-risk investment, with larger costs if it fails. Cohabitation yields somewhat less, but it is a lower investment, especially for the young, who still form the larger part of this population.

Cohabitation—either before marriage or after a divorce—then becomes no more than a usual phase of an extended courtship process, another step

50. Keilman, "Recent Trends," p. 311.
51. *Nichteheliche Lebensgemeinschaften in der Bundesrepublik Deutschland,* Bundesminister für Jugend, Familie u. Gesundheit (Stuttgart: Kohlhammer, 1985), p. 366.

in the search pattern, or even a substitute for a legal union. Since many do not quite find the mate they believe they want—or feel that their life circumstances are not appropriate to a long-term commitment—they remain in a nonlegal union sometimes for years, until they can reconcile themselves to what fate offers. Or they change partners again. And, of course, this trend is one more example of the desacralization of a social institution, whereby living together becomes "about the same as" marriage—but not quite—and which one is chosen is decided by weighing the perceived costs and benefits.[52]

Each of these views may be part of the reality, and all suggest a radical shift in the social definition of both marriage and divorce.

One-Person Households

The increase in divorce and the decrease in remarriage raises the percentage of one-*parent* households, but those and other social processes together also cause a rise in one-*person* households.[53] Indeed, the number of such households has been rising faster than the population. The largest part of this increase is among the never-married, who in the past mostly continued to live with their parents. With lower remarriage rates among the elderly, a group that includes both widows and the divorced, the rate of increase is also high in that age segment. And some 40 percent of all divorcees, men and women, do not have children, while another large segment (mostly men) is made up of parents who do not have custody.

This trend is fed both by divorce and by the growing social understanding that adult individuals not in cohabitation or marriage will not live with parents or other kin except when economic conditions are poor.

Both men and women are affected by it. West Germany in the period 1972–1985, the percentage of the population made up of men living alone more than doubled, from almost 5 percent to over 10 percent (the percentage among all *households* is of course higher still). The percentage made up of women living alone rose by about 50 percent, from almost 14 percent to almost 19 percent.[54] In the early to mid-1980s, the percentage of single-person households in Europe ranged from 34 percent in Germany to 25 percent in France, 26 percent in Holland, 29 percent in Switzerland, and 27

52. Jan Trost has continued to assert that in Sweden at least they are the same. Recent laws (1990) affirm that position. For his early study, see *Cohabitation* (Vasteras: International Library, 1979).

53. See Sardon, "Evolutions," p. 479; Keilman, "Recent Trends," and Olivier Blanc, "Les Ménages en Suisse. Quelques Aspects de leur Evolution de 1960 a 1989 a Travers les Statistiques de Recensement," *Population* 40 (1985), pp. 657–75.

54. Höhn and Schulz, "Bericht," pp. 185–86.

percent in Belgium. Some of these, as noted, are older people for whom living with a younger family is no longer an option, and some are younger unmarried persons who are no longer socially required to live with their parents.

The rising percentages are partially created by the new divorce regularities, however: a larger number of ex-wives who have not remarried and do not have children with them; ex-husbands; older children who do not feel welcome in stepfamilies; and so on. Here, again, we can see that changes in European divorce patterns over the past forty years have led to alterations in other areas of social life.

Many of these changes in divorce patterns have also occurred in the countries that prohibited divorce until the past fifteen years, but the changes begin from different bases and the demographics are especially distinct in the first few years of the new rules. We now turn to those nations.

3

Southern European Catholic Countries: The Recent Permission to Divorce

The Catholic Church has successfully opposed divorce in many countries in the past or pressed for a new prohibition after a period of liberalization. In recent years, divorce finally became possible in three Catholic countries of Western Europe, Italy (1970), Spain (1981), and Portugal (1974). Culturally European, Brazil could be added to this list, since divorce was made possible there in 1977, as well as in Colombia in 1976 and in Argentina in 1987, but they are treated elsewhere.

In all these countries, the new laws were accompanied by much polemic, amid fears that a flood of divorce would ensue, leading to a breakdown of the family. Women, especially older ones, opposed the new laws because they believed that their husbands would hasten to throw off their familial responsibilities. Partly as a result of widespread opposition, the resulting laws were severely restrictive—in Italy, for example, a minimum of five years of separation was made a prerequisite for divorce (reduced to three years in 1987), and in some types of cases the period was seven years.

When such laws are introduced so late in the socioeconomic development of a country, the demography of divorce is very different from that of other countries for some years afterward. Although many of the same forces that led to family dissolution in other Western countries were present in these Catholic countries over the long years when divorce was not possible (except for a dissolution "from bed and board"—that is, legal separation), they could not lead to divorce. Thus even though husbands and wives fought and separated just the same; men philandered and set up public or private relations with other women, and so on—they did so without entering the status of "divorced." For example, in Italy in the 1950s it was estimated that 40,000 couples were breaking up each year in this manner. In 1984, almost 400,000 couples were living apart.[1]

Those who were financially able to do so could go to another country, obtain citizenship, get a divorce, and then return to Italy.[2] Others could obtain a church annulment, with some difficulty and at much cost. Many legal separations, both church and civil, were obtained, but of course neither party was then free to remarry. And of those who separated, legally or informally, only men could establish a new union without much social censure.

Thus the number of "candidates" for the new divorce procedures do not represent the normal distribution of divorce-prone people in a given country. It is skewed by the accumulation over time of many people who in other countries would have obtained divorces at a much earlier age. There would of course be more divorces at older ages and thus with older or adult children. At the same time, an unknown number of older people would simply have given up. Their passions and hatreds would have cooled over time, and they would have made some adjustments to the diminished domestic and social life that a prohibition on divorce enforces.

That process operates even when divorce *becomes* possible. Thus, of those who were legally separated in 1966, who therefore *already* met the requirements of the 1970 divorce law when it became active, only 58 percent actually took the second step of actually getting a divorce, even after eight years of separation.[3]

In addition, in Italy those who could take advantage of the new law, with all its complexity, were those who had been separated for some years (and were older) since the new laws required a lengthy period of separation. They were also better educated, and somewhat better off financially. Because rural populations generally have less education as well as a lower propensity to divorce, the new divorcees would be mostly urban.

After the Italian divorce law was put into effect at the end of 1970 (in 1975 the grounds of fault were officially abolished), the number of divorces rose from 17,000 the first year (1971) to over 32,000 in the second, while legal requests in the first year numbered over 55,000.[4] Subsequently, the number of divorces dropped to 11,000 by 1975, a number that remained stable for

1. William J. Goode, *World Revolution and Family Patterns* (New York: 1963), p. 84. For 1984, see Antonio Golini, "Famille et Ménage dans l'Italie Recente," *Population* 42 (1987), p. 703.

2. Giovanni B. Gritta and Paolo Tufari, "Italy," in Robert Chester, ed., *Divorce in Europe* (Leiden: Martinus Nijhoff, 1977), p. 258.

3. Mario Greco and Leonardo Roveri Carrannante, "Separazioni e divorzi in Italia secondo l'età dei coniugi e la durata del matrimonio (1969–1978)," *Genus* 37 (July 1981), p. 134, table 3.

4. *Dati Statistici su Dieci Anni di Divorzio in Italia, Anni 1971–1980* (suppl. *Bolletino Mensile* d.d.i. Statistica, Istituto Centrale di Statistica, 1982), no. 23, p. 17.

several years, leading some analysts to suggest that previous fears about a divorce flood were groundless. As has happened so often when rates fall briefly, however, that optimism was premature. In the period 1978–1982, separations rose 30 percent to almost 38,000, and in 1980–1982 divorces rose 23 percent to over 14,000. In 1986 there were over 16,000 divorces[5]— not a flood, but a continued increase. In 1988, there were over 37,000 separations and 25,000 divorces.[6] Indeed, the steady annual rise in legal separations from the 1950s through the end of the 1970s, from just under 5,000 to about 26,000, foretold the future better.[7] And by 1988, separations had risen to more than 37,000. The crude rates, however, do show the first bulge in 1971, the drop, and then the subsequent increase (Table 3.1).

This is a rise in the absolute number of divorces in Italy from over 17,000 in 1970 to almost 31,000 in 1988. Since divorce requires a prior separation, petitions for separation thus continue to rise. Of course, this requirement adds time to the "official" marriage and thus to any calculations of the duration of marriage.

The older age skew of the new and recent divorcees also increases (a) the average age of the divorced spouses, (b) the time between separation and divorce, (c) the number of children involved as well as (d) their age, and of course (e) the total number of divorces granted in the first few years after the law. Thus all such figures are biased by the long history of *non*-divorce.

After the initial period, the supposed "grounds" usually become an existing separation "based on agreement" (over 60 percent are "consensual"), and guilt no longer had to be proved as grounds for divorce. Although the procedures are standardized now that the first big bulge has worked itself through the courts, the *procedure* alone still requires almost a year for completion. More specifically, it takes an average person with little or no education 510 days to be legally separated in the south (where there is less social approval of divorce) and 392 days in the north. To that must be added a nearly equal amount of time for the separate divorce procedure.[8] The time is almost halved if the person is a college graduate whose knowledge of the process and ability to command legal resources are greater. These procedures require less time now than in the past, and of course much less if the divorce is by mutual agreement.

As might be expected those who married in the Church are less likely to

    5. Golini, "Famille," p. 704.
    6. U.N. Demographic Yearbook 1989 (1991). Marzio Barbagli, in *Provando e Riprovando* (Bologna: Il Mulino, 1990), tables 5 and 6, gives the figure of 31,000 divorces. Later in this chapter I shall make extensive use of the analyses by Barbagli. His monograph on divorce is the best I have seen in a decade.
    7. Greco and Carrannante, "Separazioni," p. 129, table 1.
    8. Barbagli, *Provando*, tables 10, 11.

Table 3.1: Crude Rates of Marital Dissolution in Italy
per 1,000 Population, 1971–1988

	1971	1975	1980	1986	1988
Legal Separation	0.32	0.19	0.21	0.29	0.44
Divorce	0.32	0.60	0.21		0.44

Source: U.N. Demographic Yearbook, 1990.

get divorced, and the law cannot undo the religious rite. All the court can do is put an end to the civil, or legal, responsibilities of marriage. In the eyes of the Church, those who were married by religious ceremony remain married even if they get a civil divorce. The deeper commitment and the social pressures that are a part of following the religious rite thus keep their divorce rate relatively low compared with those who marry only by civil ceremony.

That difference between the two groups has continued to increase since the inauguration of the new law. On the other hand, a larger percentage of Italians are now being married in civil ceremonies, a move toward a more secular view of the union itself and thus doubtless a lower commitment.

In the contemporary cohorts, the divorce rate is almost twice as high among those who marry at less than 20 years of age, but the age distribution of Italian divorcees remains skewed toward the older years. On the other hand, as divorce has become more regularized, that skew is diminishing.[9] Over 40 percent of the women and 53 percent of the men divorcing in 1971 were aged 50 years or older, but only 27 percent of the women and 35 percent of the men were that old in the cohort of 1980. In 1988, the average age of men at divorce was 42; that of women, 39—a six-year drop in age for men, and seven for women over the period 1971–1988.

At the beginning, almost two-thirds of the requests for divorce were filed by men. We interpret this to mean that more men than women had entered upon new relationships or simply wanted to be free, and they were economically better able to support themselves. Because of women's more precarious economic position—more difficult in Italy than in other Western countries—wives were generally more reluctant to be divorced.

Nevertheless, this difference cannot be interpreted as an index of which spouse is more or less satisfied with the marriage. A rising percentage of women filing divorce petitions in a given country does not tell us unambiguously that more women than men would like to divorce. Who actually

9. Dati Statistici, 1982, p. 10, as well as Barbagli, Provando, p. 252.

files, as I noted earlier, is shaped by the existing social customs, the technical legal grounds, and the dynamics of negotiations between spouses.[10]

Husbands (very likely in almost all countries—but note the possibly exceptional cases of Malaysia and Indonesia, described in Chapters 8 and 10)—are more likely than wives to be the first to move away from approved spousal behavior and to enter into relations that estrange them from their partners. Because males are given more freedom outside the home, they engage in more acts that, while not really disapproved socially, nevertheless gradually make their wives willing to accept a divorce and even to file for it, even if they did not initially wish to take that step. Since Italian men can establish independent residence and ask for a legal separation without proving any guilt on the part of their wives (but doubtless encounter some resistance even then) it is they who more often have filed for divorce. That earlier figure has dropped, as we would expect; in 1985, 51 percent of divorce cases were filed by men.[11] In almost all cases (90 percent) the divorce will be granted eventually.

Because the divorce cohorts in the 1970s were older than is usual in Western divorces, only 20 percent of the couples had minor children. That figure later rose to 40 percent, and in 1988 it was 56 percent. The minor children of the earlier cohorts were also older: 50 percent were 15–20 years of age, reduced in recent years to 30 percent. Consequently, custody is now given to mothers in 90 percent of the cases, as against 80 percent in 1971–1974.[12]

As noted earlier, rural people have less propensity to divorce, and they have less education. It has also been alleged that those who have taken advantage of the rather stringent court procedures had more education and were in a more favorable economic position. An examination of the official statistics on this point does not confirm that supposition. A strict test requires that for every educated or economic class category we would need both the number or percent of those divorcing in that category and the total now married in that same subgroup. These data are not available.

It is at least clear that with respect to education, however, the group with only elementary schooling or none is by far the largest category among divorcees in the period 1971–1990. Similarly, although a genuine occupational breakdown is not available, the categories "independent" and "dependent" workers are noted (dependent workers are subordinates, working under a boss or manager), and in each comparison within types of each

10. I pointed out the dynamics of this process in *After Divorce* (Glencoe, Ill.: Free Press, 1956), pp. 114–15.

11. Barbagli, *Provando,* table 6.

12. *Dati Statistici,* 1982, p. 11.

activity for the same period the number of "dependent" workers is several times larger.[13] That is, lower-class workers are more numerous among those getting divorced (but they are also more numerous in the population as a whole).

A later study has reported that the two upper social strata, defined by either education or occupation, have higher divorce rates. It also outlines the historical changes that create this situation, even if it is temporary.[14] The more advantaged strata were able to get legal separations in the past because they could afford it, and the "democratization" of divorce has not proceeded very far in Italy. Suits for legal separation or divorce are still very costly in time and money. When the new law went into effect, far more well-to-do couples were already legally separated and could thus use the new opportunity more easily. If these costs are greatly reduced, doubtless the lower classes will be more prone to divorce in Italy as in other countries.

In Barbagli's analysis, Italy is distinct from the other industrialized Western countries in a number of ways, even though the same general tendencies are observable there. These differences arise because the various changes that have occurred elsewhere have been concentrated in Italy over a period of about twenty years. One difference that remains in Italy, noted previously, is that divorce is still not a substitute for separation but is simply added to separation as a legal step. Thus a divorce always requires two separate court appearances and two filings. It is only after a legal separation has been officially granted that one may file for a divorce. Moreover, about half of all couples remain at the stage of separation (as we note in Chapter 7, this is still true in Mexico), some because they have not yet accepted the idea of divorce, some because they are well on in years and are discouraged by the procedure itself, and many because the legal separation maintains a number of spousal rights—for example, that of inheritance.

The second important difference, also noted previously, is the much older ages of Italian divorcees. This has been dropping over the past two decades. One may also suppose that the long official duration of marriages (essentially unchanged for nearly two decades) may continue for a while as more older couples become accustomed to the notion of divorce. The age at *separation* has not changed fundamentally for sixty years.[15]

A third important difference is the higher divorce rate among the upper social classes, noted above, although Barbagli asserts that this difference will decline over time.

A fourth difference Barbagli reports is a definite correlation between the

13. *Anuario Statistico Italiano* (Istituto Centrale di Statistica, 1984), tables 18 and 19.
14. See Barbagli, *Provando*, pp. 60–63.
15. Ibid., p. 59.

number of children and a reluctance to divorce. In other Western countries, more rigorous and recent analysis suggests (as I noted in Chapter 2) that when other variables are controled the number of children has little relationship to a propensity to divorce—for example, when we control for age and the time actually together. But Barbagli discards several other explanations and asserts that in Italy simply having more children *is* an obstacle to divorce.[16] His data suggest indeed that this common-sense interpretation may once have been correct in Western countries too.

In the early part of the century, father custody was still fairly common in Italy, and in about a third of the cases the children (they were usually older) were given to the father after legal separation. In recent times, as noted earlier, custody has shifted almost entirely to the mother. Joint or alternate custody has remained of almost negligible importance. Similarly, although men filed more frequently than women in the first years of permissible divorce, by now the petitions are about equally divided between husband and wife.

Golini suggests another difference in Italy: he believes that 70–80 percent of the divorcees remarry, a much higher percentage than in other European countries (compared to about 50 percent in France).[17] If this is correct, presumably it would be because so many people were going through the divorce process in order to remarry. That is an unlikely conclusion in a country with such a high age at divorce, however, because remarriage after divorce is much less likely for older women. In addition, the percentages eventually entering a first marriage are not much higher than that. In a separate report, Golini limits his statement to the "newly divorced," but in the early 1980s that term would apply to all the divorced, and their average ages were still higher than in other European countries.[18] Such a high rate of remarriage would be especially unlikely for women, whose mean age at divorce has ranged from 46 years down to about 39 years. In any event, Barbagli has calculated a very different estimate (the task of working out the probability of eventual remarriage is about as difficult as that of finding a defensible figure for the chances of eventual divorce). It seems rather more likely that what is distinctive in Italy is the very large discrepancy between the chances of men and women for remarriage.

At least at the younger ages (under 30), the likelihood of remarriage in other European countries is very similar for men and women. Of course, they diverge steadily after that, and beyond age 40 they are very much different. In Italy in the late 1980s, divorced men had a probability of remar-

16. Ibid., pp. 64–67.
17. Golini, "Famille," p. 704.
18. Antonio Golini, "La Famiglia in Italia: Tendenze Recenti, Immagine, Esigenze di Ricerca," in *Annali di Statistica* anno 115, ser. IX, vol. 6 (1986), p. 22.

riage of about 50 percent, women about 27 percent.[19] Although both figures are somewhat low compared with other European countries, both Italian men and women are older at divorce than divorcees in other nations (48–42 for men in the period 1971–1988, 46–39 for women). Since until 1987 divorce required a five-year wait after a legal separation (itself a lengthy process), only a small segment of women will divorce at the most remarriageable ages. Unfortunately, age seems to be the prime variable in determining who will remarry and thus the lower figures for remarriage seem self-evident. Earlier we outlined the complex forces in the marriage market, which rapidly lower women's remarriage rates after their twenties or early thirties. Note also that the general likelihood of remarriage is lowered for both sexes when so few have been divorced, and the marriage pool is thus smaller.

The lower percentage of Italian women who remarry is also a result of attitudes—once fairly strong in other countries—that stigmatize a divorced woman, especially outside the major cities. Indeed, in all European nations, even the remarriage of a widow was once not fully approved (unless perhaps she was wealthy), and some encountered moral censure or bawdy comment. As an index of these continuing attitudes in Italy, Barbagli points out that the older "widow's mourning" law required a 300-day waiting period before a widow could remarry, and that restraint was actually incorporated into the basic divorce law as well (but modified somewhat in 1987). That restraint on divorced women further lowered their chances for remarriage by making them still older before they were allowed to remarry. Most important, the law plainly indicates their lesser value in the marriage market; their possible wishes are arbitrarily ignored. (It should be noted in passing that similar restrictions have been common elsewhere: for example, Japan, Germany, Muslim countries.)

I noted above an added element in the lesser likelihood that a divorced woman will remarry: that many women do not proceed directly to a final divorce after obtaining a legal separation and waiting the requisite period. Some of that delay occurs because in Italy (as in Spain) women see some advantages in remaining at the stage of separation. First, they correctly perceive their chances of remarriage as low, while their opportunities in the labor market have not expanded as much as in other Western countries. Second, they retain thereby some inheritance rights. This difference in the position of the two sexes may also be seen in the fact that if it is the man who files for divorce, the procedure takes a much longer period than if the woman files. That is, she cooperates much less.

19. Barbagli, *Provando*, pp. 159ff.

When only legal separation was possible, some allocation of support to the wife was frequently made by the Italian courts, for several reasons. First, both socially and legally, the couple was still "married." (We shall encounter this pattern again in Latin America.) In certain senses, the husband was still responsible for her welfare. Second, a far lower percentage of Italian wives held full-time jobs than in other Western countries, and thus many divorced Italian women would be in need. Third, it was generally the husbands who sought their freedom, and social opinion held that they should be held responsible—and perhaps punished in some fashion—for their dereliction. Finally, most of the husbands belonged to a privileged class and could afford some support to their wives, while total neglect would arouse some social criticism.

The 1970 law contained provisions for alimony or support (an "assignment of maintenance"), which was to be decided on the basis of three criteria: (1) the right of compensation, to be given to the one who has been hurt more by the breakup; (2) the economic needs of the spouse, especially if it seems likely that he or she simply does not have the means for getting out of financial difficulties; and (3) recompense for the contributions the spouse has made to family life or to the accumulation of the property or patrimony.[20]

The first criterion runs counter to the explicit rejection of "fault" in the 1975 Italian law. Technically it does not exist any longer, but judges continue to use it in some contemporary cases. The second standard, that of need, can refer to bare living expenses but also to the cases of great discrepancy between the economic circumstances of the ex-husband with a good salary and that of his former wife, with little income.

Barbagli argues that the first two criteria are traditional. That is, the first is an indemnification for damage or hurt, a kind of punishment. The second is a kind of gracious welfare, paid to the woman by her ex-husband, though of course decided on by the court. It is an extension of his obligation to care for his wife. The third criterion, recompense, is expressed in the 1987 law. It is new in Italy, Barbagli asserts, but of course it has been fiercely debated in all Western countries, with thousands of court decisions expressing some form of this principle, or rejecting it. If the couple stays together, which one "owns" the house and income, furniture and pension, salary or professional practice, is of only modest importance, for presumably all family members continue to share in their benefits. At dissolution, however, that "owner-

20. This brief analysis is based on the considerable research of Marzio Barbagli and his students *Provando*, chs. 3, 4). See also the extensive legal analysis of the rules for "assegno" in Enrico Quadri, *Rapporti Patrimoniali nel Divorzio* (Napoli: Jovene Editori, 1986), especially the "Comments," pp. 282–310. Of course, this does not include the legal changes of 1987.

ship" becomes ethically, politically, and legally crucial: Who then *really* owns it?

In most societies ownership of almost all valuable property has rested in the hands of men, both before and after marital dissolution. In Western countries, however, new doctrines have challenged that principle. For example, it is asserted that marriage is a *partnership,* and its fruits should be shared, whether or not the wife actively invested her own money or talent in the money-earning part of it. Another assertion is that wives indirectly contribute to their husbands' earning capacities by shouldering household and family tasks that free men's time. Others note the extent of women's direct contributions to their husbands' work—in their research, writing, and social life with customers or colleagues—and again they should share in the outcome. That was seen to be the basic principle expressed in the 1987 law. Another principle might be that leaving the woman to fare for herself is "changing the rules" of marriage after many years of life together.

The arguments are many, and we have noted them before. Very likely some of them seem cogent to most adults and most spouses, at least when expressed in such general terms. Indeed, I suppose that they grow from very primordial feelings about rightful sharing among or between peers and intimates. Nevertheless, at marital dissolution, very often what was once "ours" is suddenly seen as "mine," notably the accumulation of business, income-yielding property, occupational success, and pensions.

Thus it is not at all surprising that Italian ex-husbands have been somewhat less than generous in their support of ex-wives. They have, after all, many models to imitate in other modern countries. In "consensual" divorces, too, they can follow that model, for the Italian courts do not usually challenge the pretrial agreement on economic matters. Indeed, at the time of divorce they are likely to reaffirm the couple's *separation* agreement. Thus the husband can usually apply his greater power and resources to fashioning privately a set of terms, favorable to him, that the court will not scrutinize carefully.

As in the rest of Europe, basic changes have occurred. As divorce has become more common, alimony has become less likely. In the judicial separations of 1968 in Milano and Catania—the first a "modern" urban area, the second a rural area in Eastern Sicily—slightly more than half of the wives were granted support from their husbands. Thus, *before* divorce was possible, there was little difference between the two cities. By 1988, these figures had dropped considerably and diverged, to 18 percent and 34 percent, respectively; the judges in Catania remained somewhat more compassionate, or perhaps more old-fashioned.

In 1974, Bologna and Milano granted maintenance to about one-fourth of the wives in separation cases and to one-fifth in cases of divorce. By 1988, in these two modern cities of the north, 5–7 percent of ex-wives were granted support. Catania was grudging in 1975 (15 percent)—in that male-dominated world, a divorcing wife was at fault no matter what the husband had done—and had changed little by 1988 (11 percent).[21]

Clearly the percentage of women in *either* separation or divorce cases who are granted alimony or maintenance has been diminishing. It is surely of some relevance, too, that the percentage of women in divorce cases who are in the labor market has been steadily increasing over the past ten years. Doubtless both are causes and effects of each other. The decrease in such awards may also be partly due to the increasing number of marriages that have lasted only a short time. In such cases, both judges and husbands are more reluctant to be generous. By contrast, of the 1987 cohort who were housewives and who had married in 1961 or earlier, about 50 percent were awarded support in Milano, 60 percent in Catania, only 33 percent in Bologna, and 40 percent in Modena.[22] Nevertheless, for any *given* duration of marriage, whether short or long, the percentage of such allocations by judges continues to decline.[23] That pattern parallels the trend in other Western countries.

It is equally clear that whatever principles were at work in the past, their potency has been declining. An effort was made in 1987 to bolster the third standard noted above for granting maintenance—that is, to offer some compensation for the contributions of the wife to the family assets. As Barbagli points out (pp. 145–47), this principle embodies some paradoxes in the law. For example, if the wife should receive part of the husband's future earnings because of her past contributions, she should continue to receive them (as in any investment) even after entering a second marriage. However, very likely most ex-husbands would not agree to that logical inference.

In any event, the Italian courts have not explored these possible complexities because the 1987 law giving these rights has not been implemented. For example, Italian courts have so far refused to accept the wife's "ownership" of part of the husband's pension.

In the cases of the past few years, the justification for awards continues to be simply some kind of need. This is somewhat reduced in practice, since it is the settled opinion of the Italian courts (and men) that men simply have greater needs than women, and much higher expenses. Clearly, then, it is not a great discrepancy if the ex-wife lives modestly and the ex-husband does not.

21. Barbagli, *Provando,* tables 25–26, p. 264.
22. Ibid., table 28, p. 266.
23. Ibid., tables 29, 30, p. 267.

The 1987 law specified that the wife would receive, in effect, some 40 percent of the family's gains over the couple's years together. However, the law also states that she has contributed only if she was an owner, and only if she does not have adequate means of self-support or cannot rationally be expected to acquire them. In fact, the courts have continued to emphasize the weight of need while steadily reducing the percentage of wives and mothers judged needy enough to require the support of their ex-husbands.

Accompanying such changes in Italian family and divorce patterns, and inexorably following those in other European countries, is an increase in cohabiting unions, once viewed as nothing short of scandalous in Italy. An official estimate in the mid-1980s suggested there were about 200,000 couples, but Golini suggests that this figure may be only a part of the total.[24] He comments, and other data confirm, that Italian couples may not be willing to admit their status publicly, at least to interviewers from the Central Statistical Institute.

This pattern is thought to have begun in the large cities, especially where young people—in Italy until recently that meant essentially anyone not yet safely married—could live away from the supervision of their parents. As elsewhere, many observers thought it was most common among university students: unsupervised, secular, and avant-garde in thought, adult in years but without an adequate financial base for marriage.

Doubtless a large segment was and is found within that population. For example, in an unpublished study of graduates of the University of Bologna in 1989, 17 percent had been in such a union during their student years, and 29 percent of those whose families did not live in the city.[25] Among youth aged 15–24, only one-fifth expressed a negative opinion of cohabitation.[26] The national survey done by the Central Institute of Statistics in 1983 reported that 20 percent of the separated individuals aged 15–34 had experienced such a union. Only 9 percent of women under 25 years of age, however, had done so before marriage.[27]

In Italy such unions are more common among older people, and one may suppose that has been true for several decades. Some two-thirds of cohabiting couples, in contrast with other countries, are over 35 years of age.[28] Because so many married couples had broken up without being able to

24. Golini, "Famille," p. 703; as well as Antonio Santini, "Recenti Trasformazioni nella Formazione della Famiglia e della Discendenza in Italia e in Europa," in *Annali di Statistica,* 1986, pp. 131–33.

25. See Barbagli, *Provando,* pp. 40–41 n. 19.

26. The public opinion research is by A. Cavalli and A. De Lillo, *Giovani anni 80* (Bologna: Il Mulino, 1988), p. 207, to which Barbagli called my attention.

27. Santini, "Recenti Trasformazioni," p. 133.

28. Barbagli, *Provando,* p. 19; table 2, p. 249.

divorce prior to 1970 or had grown impatient with waiting through long years of separation, they had begun to live together before or instead of divorcing, or after a divorce, or they had found a new partner but were not yet willing to risk a marriage, for financial or emotional reasons. In addition—as a continuing legacy of disapproval—some couples publicly maintain separate residences, each with his or her own family or spouse, but also a third one, where they spend much of their lives together, masking their real relationship.

Attitudes about such matters have been changing generally, and not just among the young. The national inquiry into cohabitation in the mid-1980s also raised questions about divorce and the family. Although four-fifths of those interviewed (fewer men than women) favored legal marriage, only 36 percent expressed a negative attitude toward cohabitation.[29] Others were indifferent or positive. Only 10 percent believed that matrimony should be an indissoluble union, and 55 percent agreed that it could be dissolved, but only for serious reasons. Thus, although Italy began only recently to permit divorce, both actions and public attitudes are rapidly moving toward those in countries where divorce has been accepted for generations.

Spain

Spain made divorce possible only in 1981, and thus the data are even less rich and complete than for Italy, while no Barbagli has as yet appeared to do justice to its archives. In the past, marital dissolution of any kind was not given much legal or statistical recognition in Spain. The Spanish censuses from 1900 until 1940 did not even list the category of "separated."[30] In 1950 for the first time the category "legally separated and divorced" appears (although Spanish courts could not actually grant anyone a divorce at that time).

A survey carried out by the Technical Secretariat of the Supreme Court in the last three months of 1981 (apparently omitting some important cities such as Barcelona) offers a few findings. The first is that (as in Italy) the number of cases was much lower than anticipated—barely over 5,000 in the first year, as against the half-million some had feared. Commentators have offered the explanation that the Spanish are still less likely to go to court to settle problems than are people in other nations at the same level of socio-economic development. Especially in family matters they developed many informal and private modes of settling disputes because few legal procedures

29. Golini, "Famille," pp. 18ff.
30. See, for example, the tabulation in Instituto Nacional de Estadística of Madrid, *Panorama Social* (1974), p. 54.

were available to them. A Church annulment had been possible but hardly available except to the well-to-do. Legal separation, under much social disapproval, was possible but not an absolute divorce that permitted remarriage.

As a member of the Supreme Court remarked at the time of this survey: "Since this is a part of life which in high degree touches personal intimacy, it generates a logical and instinctive resistance in husbands and wives against welcoming the intervention of third parties, outside the marital relationship."[31] Later reports, as we shall note, clearly show that an increasing number of Spanish couples have nevertheless been taking advantage of this new way of getting out of their domestic conflict. Naturally, my prediction is that future data will continue to show a steady increase.

As in Italy, most of the divorcees in the earlier Spanish cohort were older than divorcees in other Western countries—among men, 73 percent over 30 years of age and 43 percent over 40 years; among women, 63 and 35 percent, respectively. The Technical Secretariat Report explained this skew by suggesting that there is an increase in the degree of domestic conflict after fifteen to twenty years of marriage, a most unlikely state of affairs. The skew toward the higher ages and durations of marriage meant, rather, that these people were already older when divorce first became possible. That is, until late in their marriages the law had simply never given them such an opportunity.

That the new generation will be different can be inferred from youth surveys done in Spain at the beginning of the law as well as more recently,[32] for younger people do not take for granted the indissolubility of marriage. In one survey, for example, only 10 percent of young adults agreed with the belief that marriage is for life, and over 40 percent asserted that the public ceremony of marriage is only a formality.[33] Thus one must suppose that the future will reveal a continuing increase in divorce.

Divorce was made less costly in Spain than in Italy, but it still requires a legal separation, by court decision, in almost all cases. Thus it is necessarily more expensive than in other countries, for couples must go through two separate court processes.

31. Santiago Borrajo Iniesta, *La Ruptura Matrimonial en España* (Madrid: Eudema, 1989), p. 21, hereafter referred to as *Ruptura*.
32. See, for example, Rosa Conde, "Tendencias de Cambio en la Estructura Familiar," *Revista Española de Investigaciones Sociales* 21 (1983), pp. 52–53; Ines Alberdi, Divorcio y Sociedad en la España Actual," *Rev. Sistema* 70 (Jan. 1986), pp. 93–112, and for Madrid, Santiago Iniesta Borrajo, "Estudio Sociológico sobre la Ruptura Matrimonial en Madrid Capital (1981–1984)," *Revista Española de Investigaciones Sociológicas* 37 (1987), pp. 113–37. On abortion and divorce, see Luis M. Rodriguez Gonzalez, "La Familia: Una Institución Que ha Cambiado?" *Documentación Social* 65 (1986), pp. 127–46.
33. Conde, "Tendencias," pp. 52–53.

Chapter 7 of the law offers several alternative bases for a judicial separation (Ley 30/81). It can be obtained on the demand of both spouses, or by
one if the other consents, and must be accompanied by a proposal specifying
what each owes to the other, how the children will be cared for, custody and
visitation rights, and so on, as in other European systems. In any case, it
cannot be filed until at least a year after the marriage.[34]

Judicial separation can also be obtained by one spouse alone, if various
faults can be proved. Among the legally adequate grounds are such grievances as infidelity, abandonment, cruelty, alcoholism, and serious or repeated failure in duties to the children. Judicial separation is also possible if
there has been a de facto separation (but the period is shorter if there is full
agreement by both). If the separation is granted, neither spouse can have any
further control over the other's property.

Legal separation presumably ends the marriage for most practical purposes, but the law requires an additional filing for divorce. By the terms of
Chapter VIII, Ley 30/81 this can be granted after one year of a judicial
separation obtained by both spouses together, or by one with the consent of
the other. It can also be obtained upon the sole request of the spouse who
had previously alleged fault as the basis of the request for separation. Divorce is also permitted if the spouses have been living in a de facto separation, agreed to by both, for two years. The two-year rule also applies to cases
in which an informal separation had begun and one of the spouses had then
committed some serious fault. Finally Article 4 provides that, if the husband
and wife have been living apart for five years, either may file for a divorce,
with or without the other's agreement.

The court also requires, as noted above, an agreement between the
spouses on a wide range of details about alimony and child maintenance,
who shall live in the marital residence, custody and visitation, and so on. If
they cannot come to an agreement, the judge will make these decisions. In
determining support, the court will consider the economic situation and
health of the spouse who will suffer a sharp economic loss upon divorce, the
likelihood of her getting a job, her professional qualifications, and her pension rights, as well as the duration of the marriage and what the couple
owns. It does not specify an equal division of marital property.

A separation requires at least one year of marriage as well as a court
procedure, and divorce itself requires a period of separation and another
procedure. Because many couples in the first cohort of 1981 had already
been separated for years, it is not surprising that they were older.

34. For an extensive exposition of both legislation and the law, see Carlos M. Entrena Klett,
Matrimonio, Separación y Divorcio (Pamplona: Aranzadi, 1990).

Although suits for either separation or divorce can be "consensual," in Spain as in other countries that phrase conceals much conflict. Some three-fourths of the separation suits and two-thirds of the divorce suits in the first cohort asserted some "cause" as well—mostly "conduct degrading or humiliating to the spouse" or "abandonment."[35] The figure for abandonment is about 20 percent but rises to almost 35 percent if other categories of separation are included. Almost all "causes" listed for divorce are equivalent to some kind of de facto separation. That is, most of these cases appear to be couples who have, for whatever reason, ceased to live together, another parallel with the situation in Italy.

Some commentators have asserted that the Spanish law is different from the Italian in one important way: it claims to allow couples with modest means and education to obtain a divorce. The first data were full of gaps, but it seems likely that most of those in this early cohort of divorcees had low incomes, in conformity with that assertion. Those with a university education were very few. On the other hand, since a large majority of the divorcing couples did not even answer the question about their incomes (and a third did not even reply about their education), I remain a bit skeptical about those findings.[36] They may have failed to answer the question about income because they believed their reply would affect the final allocation of property or support rights after the divorce. Indeed, more recent research asserts (with some contradictory data) that the lower classes do not have a higher divorce rate in Spain. If that is correct, we would predict that this class pattern will change as divorce becomes more common.

Relatively little research on divorce has been carried out in Spain. State agencies (except for the brief Technical Report by the Supreme Court noted earlier) failed to collect data. In recent years, however, additional studies have been published, as well as one monograph based on the court files— notably not based on actual interviews with the spouses. Thus we now have some basic data, even though the time period is a short one.[37]

First, the differences in rates between rural and urban areas have been diminishing. This has also occurred in other Western nations, of course, but in Spain the immediate cause is the Spanish regulations against internal migration.[38] Thus divorce-prone couples who would otherwise have migrated to urban centers for a divorce (and thus increased the apparent urban

35. Presidente del Tribunal Supremo, Secretaria técnica, "Informe sociológico y jurídico sobre la aplicación de la Ley del Divorcio," unpublished paper, p. 16.

36. Ines Alberdi, "Divorcio," pp. 104–05.

37. For example, see ibid., pp. 93–112; Borrajo, "Estudio Sociológico," pp. 113–37; Juan Nicolas, "La Familia en Europa y el Cambio Social," ibid., 21 (1983), pp. 11–31; and Conde, "Tendencias," pp. 33–60.

38. *Ruptura*, p. 116.

divorce rates) have instead remained in rural areas and increased the divorce rates where they resided.

Second, although the first large cohort of divorcees was much older than in other countries, that higher age was caused (as in Italy) by the simple fact that no one could get a divorce until then. The younger couples still form a smaller part of the divorcing population than in other Western countries, however, because now many older Spanish couples also accept, if only gradually, the possibility of divorce. In addition, the law requires a one-year or longer wait after legal separation, and the independent divorce suit will usually take as long to process as the original suit for separation. Except for special clauses in the code, it is not yet possible to make a direct petition for divorce without a legal separation.[39] The total number of both types of suits in the years 1982–1984 was about 40,000. The relative numbers over time may be worth noting (Table 3.2).

Third, there is a shift toward divorce "by consensus." In the period 1981–1984 in Madrid, the percentage of all suits filed by men dropped from 40 to 13 percent; those filed by women declined somewhat less, while the percent of consensual suits increased substantially. In addition, many suits already filed by one partner or the other were changed to "consensus." In 1984, almost half of all the suits in Madrid were consensual.[40] The rest of the country is more traditional, as we shall note later, but the trend is parallel.

This shift toward dissolution by agreement conceals a more important change. More suits were filed for separation than for divorce. In fact, in the first five years of the new law, there was a slight drop in the total number of divorce suits filed. Clearly women are agreeing to a separation on terms that put them at some disadvantage because they do not have the personal or economic resources for a long conflict and because neither party needs to charge any kind of "fault" to obtain a divorce. Thus women cannot easily refuse, but they "agree" in order to bargain later for better terms. A legal separation permits both parties to come back to the cohort for later petitions to change the earlier "agreement."

We can now examine this possibility by utilizing research data drawn from a stratified, random sample of over 1200 divorce and separation court dockets during the period 1981–1986.[41] Although we have asserted that little can be inferred about which spouse really wanted and initiated the divorce from our knowing who filed the petition, here we confront two kinds of decision, to get a legal separation and to get a divorce. At the

39. Alberdi, "Divorcio," pp. 106–08.
40. Ibid., p. 110.
41. This is the monograph by Borrajo, "Ruptura," cited above. See the description of his sample in ch. 4, pp. 43–73.

Table 3.2: Divorce and Separation Suits Filed
in Spain, 1981–1988

	1981	1985	1988
Divorce	9,483	18,291	22,449
Separation	6,880	25,046	33,240

beginning of the new law, in Spain as in Italy, a large percentage of the petitioners were men who wished to be legally free of their marriage and could now move toward that goal. Women were much less protected and therefore more reluctant. At the same time, within that accumulated cohort were many individuals and couples who wanted to legalize their separation or had to do so in order to get a divorce later.

The most basic distinction in each successive cohort is whether the suit is for separation or for divorce. The most important finding is that if it is the wife who petitions, she petitions for a separation; if it is the husband, he is more likely to petition for divorce (*Ruptura*, p. 83). Women have filed 80 percent of the separation suits, and men have filed for about half of the divorce suits (we noted earlier the much lower percentage in Madrid).

The complexities in each pattern are many, and we shall confine ourselves to only a few. They do suggest that the husband and wife are seeking very different goals. If the wife is older (45 years old or more), the husband is more likely to be the petitioner, and he is likely to be seeking a divorce. It could be supposed that younger wives, accepting the new ideas of marital freedom and mutual agreement, would be more likely to take advantage of the freedom to divorce.

The data suggest instead that the women most likely to take the initiative, to petition for separation rather than divorce, and to base the petition on some fault are those who are young, have minor children, and are *not* in the work force (*Ruptura*, Table 10, p. 78; pp. 83ff.). These are more likely to be cases in which the spouses have already separated in fact, and the wife has been forced to go to court because she and her children are in a precarious economic situation. It is only with the court's help that she can at least gain legal recognition of her right to some support from her husband. She has not been able to obtain that support on her own. To challenge him with a divorce might antagonize him further and threaten that possibility.

When divorce by mutual agreement becomes possible in a country, it does not instantly become the choice of most spouses who seek to dissolve their marriages. Some believe they can get a divorce faster by a fault procedure if the other spouse agrees not to oppose the charge. Others use charge and countercharge to delay the dissolution and/or to obtain better settlement terms. Over time, however, as legal procedures are regularized, consent does (in all countries we have considered) become more common.

This trend is observable in Spain as well (*Ruptura*, pp. 75ff.). Lumping together all cases, separations and divorces, 70 percent were filed on the basis of fault in 1981, and this dropped to 58 percent by 1986. Over 80 percent of the separation cases were based on fault in 1981, dropping to 55 percent in 1986. The change in divorce cases has been less, from 62 to 57 percent. To be sure, these figures do not suggest a high degree of domestic tranquility in Spanish cases of marital dissolution, but the trend seems clear enough.

The accumulation of broken marriages over time, with few ways open to regularize that state, meant that the "new divorcees" were rather mature and also that a simple figure for the duration of marriage is not possible. Many of the first cohort had been living apart for years, so that the *legal* duration of their marriages was long indeed. In fact, they might have actually lived together only a short time before the breakup.

The complex differences in duration as measured by the time between the wedding and (1) the dissolution of the relationship, (2) the judicial ratification of the separation, and (3) the divorce cannot all be summarized here, but some of them do help us to understand better the paths Spanish couples follow in their steps toward a new domestic life.

One dramatic contrast is found in the fact that, during the 1980s, those who asked for a divorce had been separated for an average of eight years, but those who asked for a legal separation had been apart for only about one year on the average (*Ruptura*, pp. 108–09, Table 20). Of the couples who applied on the basis of a five-year de facto separation, 94 percent sought a divorce. To be sure, those who have been married only a short time, almost no matter what the conflict is, *must* file for a separation if they wish to legalize their break, for that is nearly the only option.

Of those who file for a separation, one-third are still living with the spouse, and, of the rest, 85 percent have been separated for only one year or less. This does not mean that Spanish wives are quick to move from domestic conflict to court suit. Rather, they simply have few resources and cannot live independently for very long without the help of the law.

The legal duration of marriages that ended in divorce averaged sixteen years, but those couples had actually lived together an average of only about eight years.[42] This seemingly odd difference is caused, as already noted, by the fact that so many of the newly divorced had been living apart for a long time, adding years to their apparently enduring union. Thus, on average,

42. See *Ruptura* pp. 100ff. Indeed, those who sought a divorce had actually spent less time together than those who sought a separation. That is changing, of course.

their real time of separation was about eight years, but recent cohorts have moved to shorten the period of separation before taking the decisive step of getting either a divorce or a legal separation. As a consequence, the legal duration of marriages (ending with either of the two decisive steps) dropped from 16 years in 1981 to 11 years in 1986 (*Ruptura*, p. 103). Correspondingly, the average age of wives when they filed for a legal separation dropped from 39 years in 1981 to 33 years in 1986.

Nearly four-fifths of these divorcing couples had one or more children, and the Spanish law seems clearly to favor the mother in allocating rights to the family dwelling, but she typically cannot afford to keep it. In the first year after a de facto separation (that is, not yet legalized), slightly more than half of the wives do stay in the family house, but the percentage diminishes over time, and after nine years only one-fifth will still be there. In any event, about half choose to maintain a separate household on their own. Some 35 percent move back in with their parents (*Ruptura*, p. 141), and that figure increases for several years afterward, because so many cannot afford to keep up an independent household.

Only 35 percent of wives had been working at the time of the de facto breakup, a much lower percentage than in most European countries. Borrajo[43] suggests that at least in Spain it is not the entrance of women into the labor force that causes marital dissolution, but the reverse: They must go to work in order to survive. Of the women who had already been working when the spouses separated, 95 percent still had a job at the time of filing suit (whether for divorce or separation). Of those who had not been working earlier, 42 percent had taken a job by the time of filing. At the beginning of that decade, only 16 percent of married women in Spain were in the labor force, slightly more at the ages more likely to divorce, yet after separation 72 percent of the women were working.

I have been suggesting that Spanish women are unable to work out adequate settlements but feel it is better just the same to agree to a legal separation, in the hope that the court itself will impose more equity. That hope may be illusory, but it is clear that many spouses do attempt to improve matters in court.

In Madrid the court records for this period average 100 pages per case.[44] In 1983, there were 39,000 separation and divorce suits, but the family courts faced almost 108,000 family cases, as couples sought to move from their supposedly consensual agreements to settlements more fully under the scrutiny of the judge.

43. Ibid., pp. 149ff., 168.
44. Alberdi, "Divorcio," pp. 93–97; *Ruptura*, p. 114.

Once the law is in operation, people begin to accept divorce as a real option, and thus the Spanish disapproval of those who divorce begins to diminish. Alberdi asserts that family members are most resistant to the idea of divorce among their children and siblings, but they are also the most supportive afterward. In this as in other areas of family life, too, the opinions of the young especially are becoming more liberal.[45]

Portugal

I shall not attempt a real analysis of divorce changes in Portugal, which in any event has only recently become possible. Official data have been lacking, and little independent research has been published.[46] Nevertheless, a brief sketch seems appropriate here.

The Portuguese law of 1975 finally permitted divorce, even to couples who had married in the Church. This step was part of the widespread liberalization that took place when, six years after Salazar stepped down, his political rule was actually ended. Within two years, major changes were made in the Civil Code as well as in the Law of the Family, giving women more nearly equal family rights.

The law in Portugal was not so severe as in Italy and Spain, for divorce by mutual agreement was approved.[47] Legal separations, now unnecessary for a divorce, have become few. Although 70 percent of the first cohort of divorces were based on fault, perhaps reflecting years of bitter separation, that percentage fell rapidly, and by 1982 two-thirds were by agreement. The trend continued upward through 1989, as shown in Table 3.3. The absolute numbers rose from 1,552 in 1975 to 9,657 in 1989, a sixfold increase. The increase in the rates was almost as great although still low by European standards.

As in Spain and Italy, but to a lesser degree, the first couples who went through the process under the new law were older than couples in the years that followed, and their marriages had lasted longer. They were also more

45. Conde, "Tendencias," pp. 51–60.

46. The sole exception is the work of Marzio Barbagli, who has not only combed the available research and official statistics but has also carried out many projects on his own. See also his historical sociology of the family, *Sotto lo Stesso Tetto* (Bologna: Il Mulino, 1984).

For Portugal, however, we are able to draw upon the beginnings of such research, done by a group working in the sociology of development and headed by Franz Heimer. See Analia Torres, "Mulheres, Divórcio e Mudança Social. Divórcio: Têndencias Actuais," *Sociologia* 2 (1987), pp. 117–56. See also Analia Torres and Cristina Lobo, *Divórcio na Republica—Vidas Intimas e Historias Publicas de uma Epoca.* In the past few years, more elaborate official data have become available, in issues of *Estatisticas Demograficas* (Lisboa, Instituto Nacional de Estatistica).

47. For the law, see Jose Antonio de Franca Pitao, *Sobre O Divórcio* (Coimbra: Libreria Almedina, 1986).

Table 3.3: Divorce Rates in Portugal
per 1,000 population, 1975–1989

1975	0.16
1976	0.49
1979	0.60
1989	0.94

Sources: Official data from *Anuario Estadistico,*
various years, and *Estadisticas Demograficas,*
1978, 1989.

urban and secular than most of the population. These comparisons are sometimes shaky for the first group, since the data were not published with the necessary breakdowns. There was apparently a slight drop in the percentage of women divorcees aged 40–44 years between 1977 and 1989. I have calculated the average age of men at divorce as 40 years in 1989.

With respect to marital duration the data seem more robust. Forty percent of the marriages that ended in 1976 (the first complete year after the law took effect) had lasted for twenty years, and only 23 percent in 1989.[48] By 1989 the average duration of marriage was 14 years. Since these marriages have lasted for many years, most divorcing couples in 1975 had children, but even in 1989 two-thirds were parents.

Before these changes, divorce was rare, middle-class, urban, and restricted to those not married in the Church. It has continued to be urban. In the first full year, 65 percent of all divorces occurred in Lisbon; that percentage dropped to 50 percent in 1982,[49] yet rural divorces still made up only 26 percent of the total in 1989.

The urban-rural difference creates some technical problems in attempting to measure whether class is negatively correlated with divorce rates, and Torres is not able to surmount them with the data available. Those published in the 1989 *Estatisticas Demograficas* (beginning at page 110) do not permit such a calculation (almost all are simply listed as *"empregados,"* or employees). By education, two-thirds of the men are at the level of the "basic course" or less (Table 3.3.14, p. 111). Thirty percent of the women who divorced in 1989 were in the category "know how to read and write," and almost three-fourths had achieved the basic elementary course.[50]

Nevertheless, Torres claims that the higher the occupational level of women, the higher the rate of divorce. This is a result I would expect in a more normal divorce population, and indeed I believe it can be shown for most European countries (and the United States) if technically adequate data can be found. She also claims that divorce is least common among the

48. Torres, "Mulheres," graph 6, p. 153.
49. Ibid., pp. 119, 156.
50. I calculated this from *Estatisticas Demograficas,* 1989, table 3.3.1, p. 99.

"popular classes" and the most affluent (p. 127). Her statements about men are less systematic and seem to be based on census data about the still divorced. But it can be expected that in the first years after divorce those who took advantage of the new opportunity would be, as Torres claims, the middle classes.

Portuguese women are more likely than Spanish women to take the initiative in filing for a divorce. In both Spain and Italy, and especially Spain, women who are in an economically disadvantaged position and who do not work also take the initiative in filing. But it is not divorce they are seeking primarily. They are using a suit for legal separation to establish their marital rights. By contrast, Portuguese women are simply moving toward a divorce. As a consequence, Torres claims (p. 126) that almost no woman who does not have a job takes that initiative.

This incomplete sketch of some of the changes that have been occurring in Portugal since its 1975 divorce law affords some comparisons with the other two European countries in a similar demographic situation—that is, all three countries had a reservoir of older people who had ended their marriages informally or stayed together without wishing to do so and who were finally permitted the chance of getting a legal divorce.

Of course, in Portugal as in Spain and Italy, the young have moved away from the traditional opinions about divorce. A study of secondary students aged 16–22 years reported in the 1980s that nine-tenths were in favor of the right to divorce. And four-fifths of those who said they would marry in a civil ceremony said they would divorce if the marriage were no longer satisfying.[51]

Conclusion

Italy, Spain, and Portugal have all come to permit divorce only recently. By European standards they have been somewhat conservative in their allegiance to both Church doctrine and the ideals of traditional familism. That tradition remains evident in the fact that even after the gates to divorce were finally opened, there was no great flood of divorces or even an extremely sharp increase in marital dissolution (except in the trivial sense: from zero to thousands).

However, these countries illuminate further the dynamics of divorce in this epoch. They illustrate the difficulty of preserving older norms and family patterns by law and tight political and social controls (in Spain and Portu-

51. Antonion J. de Brito Percheiro dos Santos, "Jovens Perante a Familia," *Economia e Sociologia* 40 (1985), pp. 136–37.

gal), when in so many ways the population is experiencing the new world of mass media, high technology, the global economy, in which the dutiful fulfillment of traditional family roles may not be so rewarding as in the past. Such changes in opinion and behavior make divorce seem more desirable and the legal permission to divorce more necessary. Their effects are to be seen not in divorce alone but in other family behavior as well, such as an increasing age at marriage and delayed marriage, the spread of cohabitation, the decline in fertility and kinship activities, and the lessened sacredness of matrimony itself.

Changes, then, go on even when older laws and prohibitions stay in place. Divorce may not be legally permitted, but people are now less inclined to tolerate an unhappy marriage and so they make an exit from it one way or another. Women are affected, too, by the global call for equal rights, even when the penalties for affirming them publicly are too costly to bear. They can at least see that going to work will give them one type of independence. Since men can more easily leave them now, women also begin to understand that they should be better prepared for that contingency.

These countries also allow us to see the changes in divorce patterns when divorce finally becomes available after years of other changes. A kind of "divorce reservoir" then exists—an accumulation of people who have wanted for years to start a new domestic life. As we have noted, such a group is very much different from those who get divorced in a nation where divorce is relatively normal. I have pointed out a handful of such differences: They are older, with a much longer duration of marriage; their children are older, sometimes adult; often they have already established other unions; and of course sometimes they have given up the hope of being free. Those who could most easily take advantage of the new and long procedure were more likely to have more resources and more education. These differences at least prove that the content of the law does have powerful effects—sometimes perverse, to be sure—even when people do not want to obey its restrictions.

I have also pointed out some of the rapid changes occurring in these differences as the first bulge of divorces becomes more normal. Within those changes, however, I have given much attention to the fact that in Spain, and I think in Italy, many wives are using the legal separation not as a simple preliminary to divorce but as a status in itself, for they need to establish a legal basis for demanding support and protection under the law.

It should not be supposed that divorced mothers have fared well under these new arrangements. I have presented some evidence on this score—the likelihood that they will not be able to be economically independent, the decline in alimony, the unlikelihood of adequate child support, the necessity of returning to the shelter (however meager) of their parents' household. That evidence does not, of course, suggest that matters were better under the older system. In a traditional familistic society men were probably no more solicitous of the women they discarded than in the modern one. Indeed, perhaps they were rather less so, for the traditional husband was more certain of his male rightness than is the modern husband.

The older society, especially among the social strata where legal separations occurred, was partly made up of interlinkages among families, and it was not politically or socially wise to leave a discarded wife without sustenance. Whether a legal separation was carried out within canonical or secular law, the Church could influence the behavior of ex-spouses somewhat. Of course, a more traditional society was also more likely to take it for granted that the wife's family would step in to offer refuge to her and any children. And—since we must not forget that husbands have no monopoly over outrageous behavior—wives were not uniformly docile, and some were shrews and bullies; some husbands who were not strong enough to send their wives back also find shelter with their own families.

However, that fuller historical analysis is beyond the available data, for any modern analysis of the past two decades in these countries is handicapped by the paucity of research. Perhaps the very disapproval of divorce caused, for some time, an unwillingness to probe these matters and even some resistance to research. In any event, as divorce becomes a normal social process, research on the subject will almost certainly come to be seen, as in the rest of Europe, as potentially fruitful in its own right and a necessary foundation for confronting the social problems generated by divorce.

4

The Nordic Countries: Public Programs for Dealing with the Consequences of Divorce

In the Nordic nations—Denmark, Norway, Sweden, Finland—the overlap of legal institutions over the centuries has been profound enough to justify considering them together. For four centuries Norway was under the Danish crown, and for most of the nineteenth century its legal system was continued within a personal union with Sweden. Finland was under the Swedish crown for four centuries, and kept much of its internal autonomy and Swedish law for more than a century after it was annexed by Russia in 1809. Iceland (not analyzed here) was under Danish rule from the fourteenth century until the end of World War I. In addition, family law in all these countries was strongly shaped by the dominance of the Lutheran church.

As among other nations with closely intertwined destinies, stereotypes and counterstereotypes abound. Since Sweden has had more economic success in the outside world, its "national character" has attracted more attention from both journalists and serious students. Popenoe, for example, takes these stereotypes seriously enough to present confirming data for several of them: independence, personal privacy, social reserve, avoidance of conflict, social rationality.[1] It is widely believed in addition that Sweden has a high suicide rate while Norway does not, though in fact Sweden has a lower rate than some other European countries. Perhaps because Norway developed industrially rather late, it is sometimes thought to have a more conservative set of attitudes, especially with respect to family, but that is so only by comparison with other Nordic countries, not with other Western European countries.

1. David Popenoe, *Distributing the Nest* (New York: Aldine DeGruyter, 1988), pp. 248–53.

Even if we leave aside such stereotypes, there are many differences among these nations. Nevertheless, they do seem to be moving in a common direction as they face the problems created by modern divorce trends. Some of these differences are worth noting here, and our later analysis will present many others.

Denmark not long ago seems to have become much freer in its sexual attitudes and with Sweden led the movement toward widespread unmarried cohabitation. As to the participation of women in the labor force, which in the view of many analysts is the major factor that has increased divorce rates generally in Europe, the percentage of women in Sweden's labor force was relatively low until the 1950s. It has, however, recently risen to among the highest among Western nations (for example, over 90 percent for mothers with one child).[2] On the other hand, 60 percent of women in the Swedish labor force work part-time. By contrast, a higher percentage of all Finnish women work full-time and have done so for many decades—indeed, since the turn of the century.

Norwegian women show a very different pattern: they were less likely to be counted in the labor force, but in fact far more of them were working independently in various forms of domestic skilled or artisan labor, since so many of the husbands were away from home for long periods of time, in forestry, fishing, and shipping.

But none of those stereotypes or real differences helps us to understand why all these nations have been moving toward family institutions that seem to be guided by a very different set of goals from those of the rest of Europe— or perhaps they are simply in the vanguard.

Whatever the reasons, the shared legal and moral background of these countries combined with continued joint planning to move them more closely together over the past four decades. They have looked to one another for counsel and cooperation for many years, probably in a more intimate and effective way than the European Economic Community has done up to this date. It also seems likely that some of their common social patterns have contributed to the strong upward movement in the divorce rates over the past two decades, above those of most other European nations.

It is not entirely clear why this rise, shared with other nations, has happened exactly in this period. It does not seem likely that any of the simple explanations used so widely in causal analyses of divorce trends is adequate. And Nordic citizens do not (in contrast with those of the United States and Europe generally) seem to judge their divorce patterns as evidence of a general breakdown of the family or of moral values.

---

2. Britta Hoem and Jan M. Hoem, "The Swedish Family," *J. Fam. Issues* 9 (1988), p. 408. By U.S. standards this Swedish mode of calculation is somewhat inflationary.

Of course, all of these countries have been industrializing and urbanizing, and all show a rise in the percentage of women in the labor force, a higher educational level for women, a declining rate of marriage and fertility, and so on. As usual, Sweden is in the vanguard (though its fertility is higher than Germany's and, indeed, than that of many other European countries including Italy). But though the rise in the percentage of women in the labor force does generally correlate with an increase in the divorce rate, as early as 1910 some 39 percent of the Finnish labor force outside agriculture was female, and this appears to have had no effect on the divorce rate at all.[3] As Popenoe remarks (p. 172) of Sweden, "many of the typical U.S. explanations cannot be applied"—teenage pregnancy (it is very low), poverty, income instability, inter-ethnic marriage, or high residential mobility.

As it is too soon to be certain, I speculate that these countries are following a very different route from other Western nations, and thus the causal links seem somewhat different, though it is conceivable that other countries will also begin to move eventually toward the Nordic position. For although three trends are evident—cohabitation has risen along with divorce, the illegitimacy ratios (the percentages of births technically outside wedlock) have increased, and marriage has been postponed more and more (over one-third of Swedish women have not married by age 50)—the response to them has been unique. These countries have continued to fashion a complex set of socioeconomic supports for the inevitable problems these trends have generated. Sweden often takes the first new steps in such programs, but it should be noted that others are not far behind. For example, the 1987 Finnish Marriage Act expresses, albeit a few years later, the ideas that have shaped Swedish family programs as well.[4] By contrast, the United States especially—and other Western nations to a lesser extent—has expended far more moral indignation on these problems and far less thought and tax money on working out solutions for them.

Collective Responsibility

As noted before, all Western countries have been moving toward a less familistic set of attitudes and behaviors and toward greater individual investments in self, career, and even personal growth and goals. But in the Nordic countries this shift has been accompanied by a steady attention to a *collective*, national sense of responsibility for mothers and children, illegitimate or not,

3. Elena Haavio-Mannila and Riita Jellinoja, "Changes in the Life Patterns of Families in Finland," Vienna Center, *Current Research Reports*, vol. I, no. 1, ISSC (Vienna: European Coordination Center for Research and Documentation in Social Science, 1981), p. 6.
4. Matti Sovolainen, "Finland: The New Marriage Act Enters into Force," *J. Family Law* 27: 1 (1988–89), pp. 127–41).

divorced or not—in fact, for all citizens. They have also been more willing to accept the higher tax burden that decision necessarily creates.

If this interpretation is correct, the seemingly parallel curves in many of the family statistics of the Nordic and other Western countries conceal a very different direction of basic movement.

It is especially in these countries that cohabitation, because it is simultaneously unrecorded and so much accepted as a near-equivalent of legal marriage, creates real pitfalls for an adequate understanding of divorce data. Yet, precisely because there are so many supports for the problems that both married and unmarried couples face, their situations are very similar. We can often learn where and whether differences do exist because much research has been done on cohabiting couples.

Consequently it is often possible to de-emphasize the differences in marital status and focus instead on the dynamics of the family processes. Indeed it is one of the goals of the laws of the Nordic nations to pay less attention to family status and more to the individual's problem. For example, births out of wedlock (the illegitimacy *ratio*) comprised over 50 percent of the total births in Sweden in 1987, as they did in Iceland (in Norway, 31 percent; in Denmark, 44 percent). In almost all these cases, however, the father is publicly and socially known, and he is also held responsible. On the other hand, the *rate* of illegitimacy (the number of illegitimate births per 1000 women) among young women (including teenagers) is very low. (That is, the illegitimacy ratio is high because so many young women who bear children are not yet married, but their birth *rate* per thousand population is low.) That ratio is higher in both Denmark and Sweden than in the United States (except among Afro-Americans).

Similarly, the ratio of divorces per 100 marriages each year is high because so many in the younger years have not yet married and thus do not enter the divorce figures; but marriages are fragile. Over the two decades between the mid-1960s and the mid-1980s, the median age at first marriage rose almost five years.[5] In 1988, the official Swedish estimate of the total eventual divorce rate for that year's cohort was 41 percent, lower than that of the United States. If we add in all of the dissolutions of cohabiting couples the *total* rate was of course still higher but that step would also increase the total rate of dissolution in the United States as well, so that Popenoe's suggestion that the total Swedish rate may be the highest in the world seems unlikely.[6] To obtain such figures, of course, special surveys must be used, since neither the formation nor the dissolution of cohabiting households is officially recorded.

5. Hoem and Hoem, "Swedish Family," p. 405.
6. David Popenoe, "Family Decline in the Welfare State," *Public Interest* 102 (1991), p. 67.

In general, the public stance of the commissions that formulate Nordic legal policies for family affairs is that these decisions are private and should not affect the standing or the rights of the people who enter or leave such relationships. Correspondingly, no one is to lose any state supports, job rights, parental allowances, or other economic privileges on account of co-habitation, because all these rights are assigned to the *individual*.[7] The compassionate effort to make sure that no one suffers because of domestic events such as divorce, having a child or being a child of divorce, or living with someone without the legal protection of marriage also makes the legal bonds of marriage much less relevant and much less binding. The child is protected because the father is known and can be made responsible. If he cannot meet these responsibilities, the state fills the financial gap. It should be repeated that these protections were generally put into effect earlier in Sweden and Denmark than in Norway and Finland, but the trends are the same. The mother receives the same help whether she is legally married or not. Then why marry?

Several ironies are evident in these new patterns. For example, it seems likely that these supports were created to strengthen the family, but as a collectivity they may well have weakened it. Family decisions are judged to be private, but state policies offer a collective safety net for such decisions. This is in contrast to the United States, where the official rhetoric as well as the law asserts that the state has a right to be concerned about family matters, but in fact the government does not create adequate programs for helping those who suffer disadvantages because of private family decisions.

In all countries, the husband's wages on average are higher than the wife's, but in the Nordic countries, the state support system, coupled with a more equitable wage distribution for all, compensates for that wage differential to some extent, and at a minimum reduces the losses the wife might otherwise have to experience when a marital dissolution occurs. It seems reasonable of course that as a consequence of this lowered threat of loss the divorce rates will be higher than elsewhere.

On the other hand, although such state programs doubtless help to decrease the marriage rate and increase the dissolution rates of both divorce and cohabitation, it can also be argued that since the other Western nations showed the same trends at the same time *without* such supporting programs, the Nordic programs may be no more than a wise response to problems that were arising anyway. That is, those programs may have had at most a minor causal effect.

---

7. Hoem and Hoem, "Swedish Family," p. 897.

The Divorce Rates

Perhaps the most striking change is the apparent convergence among the divorce rates of these countries in recent years.[8] We present them in Table 4.1. All three measures are given since they yield somewhat different trends.

Table 4.1: Divorce Rates per 1,000 Mean Population, 1950–1990

	1950s	1960s	1971–1975	1981	1989
Denmark	1.49	1.51	2.61	2.82	2.95
Finland	0.84	1.06	1.87	1.98	2.93
Norway	0.74 (1950)	0.66 (1960)	0.88 (1970)	1.74	2.18
Sweden	1.18	1.32	2.38	2.42	2.22 (1990)

Divorce Rate per 1,000 Married Women

	1950s	1960s	1971–1975	1981	1988
Denmark	6.2	6.2	10.9	12.6	13.6
Finland	4.2	5.1	8.4	9.0	12.6
Norway*	2.7	3.1	4.9	7.4	9.4
Sweden	5.04	5.5	10.2	11.4	10.7

Divorces per 100 Marriages, 1960–1985†

	1960	1970	1980	1985
Denmark	19.0	25.1	39.3	42.2
Finland	11.1	17.1	27.3	30.8
Norway	9.3	13.4	25.1	31.5 (1984)
Sweden	16.5	23.4	42.2	45.5

*Patrick Festy, "Evolution Contemporaine de la Mode de Formation de Familles en Europe Occidentale," *Eur. J. Population* 1 (July 1985), pp. 180, 186.
†Alain Monnier, "La Conjoncture Demographique: L'Europe et Les Pays Developpés d'Outre-Mer," *Population* 43 (July–Oct. 1988), p. 898.

In two of them Finland shows a higher rate than Sweden, and Norway and Sweden are very close to each other in two of these measures.

By 1950, Sweden and Denmark had the highest divorce rates of these four countries, and perhaps the highest in Europe. As the table shows, all were

8. Official figures are drawn from *Kalla Nordiske Statistiske Arsbok,* 1989–90. Norway figures for 1960–70 are from Patrick Festy, "Le Divorce en Europe Occidentale," in Jacques Commaille et al., eds., *Le Divorce en Europe Occidentale, 1960–80: La Loi et le Nombre* (hereafter: *La Loi*) (Paris, INED, 1983).

soon to experience very sharp increases. These were facilitated by new laws, for (as in the rest of Europe) the laws governing divorce in these countries had changed very little in the preceding, catastrophic three decades of depression and war,[9] although people's behavior and attitudes were much altered. Moreover, the rates changed hardly at all in the period 1950–1960[10] and indeed, as generally in Europe, remained relatively stable until nearly the mid-1960s.

But though the Nordic rates overlapped with many of the other European rates at that time, it could be argued that the deeper attitudes of these countries toward divorce were different. This seems possible even if Koch-Nielsen is correct in claiming that divorce was generally disapproved well into the 1960s.[11]

Compassionate Justice: Alternatives to Strict Laws

Festy suggests a deeper divergence by grouping England and Wales with the Nordic countries, because of the larger role that judicial discretion, rather than the letter of the law, has played in the development of divorce in these countries.[12] The Nordic system was less rigid, permitting various roads toward an escape from marriage. One might even argue that it supported a secular attitude that defines divorce as less a moral dilemma than a problem to be solved.

Correspondingly, over the two centuries prior to 1950, divorce had been available in these countries by two alternative routes: in courts dominated by severe Lutheran norms, and by kingly "exemptions" (that is, personal exemptions from those norms).[13] In addition, in the nineteenth century both Swedes and Finns could obtain divorces by an accusation of "desertion" when in fact the "guilty" party had (by mutual agreement) merely crossed a convenient national border for a brief time.

More broadly, dispensations and exemptions by the monarch, in all four countries, had softened ecclesiastical and legal rigidities from the seventeenth century onward. By the end of the eighteenth century, administrative agencies for dispensing such compassionate justice had become part of the normal state apparatus.[14] Indeed, divorce decrees through this means be-

9. Festy, "Le Divorce," p. 124.
10. Ibid., fig. 11.1.
11. Inger Koch-Nielsen, *Divorces* (Copenhaven: Sozialforskningsinstutet, 1985) pub. no. 148, p. 9.
12. Festy, "Le Divorce," p. 145; the reference is to *La Loi*.
13. Torben Svenne Schmidt, "The Scandinavian Law of Procedure," in Peter Lodrup, ed., The Scandinavian Approach, Fourth World Conference on Family Law, unpublished paper, 198?, pp. 2–5.
14. Ibid., pp. 3–5.

came more numerous in Denmark than court decrees. Thus, though the statutory rules hardly changed over a period of 350 years, the attitude toward divorce was more secular and liberal at the beginning of the twentieth century than in other European nations.

By the 1920s, then, both administrative and court systems permitted divorce, and a wide variety of grounds had become available, including mutual agreement and the breakdown of marital relations.[15] Granted, the rates stayed at moderate levels for decades after that. Nevertheless, it seems probable that developments after 1950 in both law and practice were based on centuries-old customs and attitudes that defined divorce as a set of personal and social problems to be worked out, rather than a crisis in national and personal morals.

In the procession of changing laws over these decades, each set of reforms in the divorce law typically arouses much passion on both sides, but each also seems, after a decade or so, to be modest in comparison with the later reforms. The Danish law of 1948 moved the system very close to that of other Scandinavian nations.[16] At that time, all of them contained a variety of serious charges that could be made against an erring spouse, whose guilt also affected the economic consequences of divorce for both spouses.[17] All offered as well the socially less damaging route of mutual consent and the claim that the marriage relationship had broken down.

Denmark continued its practice of using both court and administrative procedures—usually the latter for mutual consent[18]—for both separation and divorce, while the normal sequence was to obtain a legal separation first. The waiting period was one and a half years, shortened in 1969 to one year. Under either system, the couple was required to try some kind of conciliation, for separation and divorce, whether the procedure was administrative or judicial. The delay in getting a final divorce led many couples to use the charge of adultery as a quicker route, and we shall later note that pattern again, in both England and Canada. During this same period, the percentage of divorces for adultery also rose in Finland (probably because it had recently decriminalized the act) to about 30 percent by 1973, and even slightly more by 1981.[19]

15. Festy, "Le Divorce," p. 145.

16. "Danemark," in *La Loi* pp. 39ff.

17. In Ibid., see pp. 39ff., 49ff., 73ff., and 97ff. See esp. Pierre Guibentif, "L'Evolution du droit du divorce de 1960 à 1981" in this volume, esp. pp. 191–93. Note also the relevant chapters in *Le Divorce en Europe Occidentale. Données statistiques et juridiques* (Paris: Collection Ministère de la Justice, Documentation Française, 1975).

18. *Le Divorce*, 1975, p. 89.

19. Kirsti Anntila, "Finland," in Robert Chester, ed., *Divorce in Europe* (Leiden: Martinus Nijhoff, 1977), p. 24; and *La Loi*, table 3, p. 54.

Thus, at the beginning of the 1950s, it could not be claimed that the laws of these countries or their attitudes were especially favorable toward divorce as compared with those of other European countries.

The Finnish law at that time was also based on the principles of guilt as well as some kind of dissolution of the marital relationship. A legal separation of two years was required for divorce, and separation required some proof of marital discord. For mutual agreement to be accepted as grounds, a conciliation procedure was required. Over the succeeding three decades, these milder claims grew to become the largest category of "legal causes."[20]

Norway, following its Danish legal roots, permitted both judicial and administrative paths to divorce. Either spouse could ask for a divorce after one year of legal separation. For grave faults, the injured spouse could demand a divorce but divorce rates continued to be low even into the 1970s, and there was no public protest against the restrictions imposed by the law. As Kristiansen remarks (writing in the mid-1970s), divorce "has—so far—been regarded as a personal rather than a social problem."[21]

From 1950 through the 1970s, some 10 percent of divorces were based on the charge of adultery, as a quicker way to divorce, but almost all the rest were preceded by one year's legal separation, based on some claim of serious marital discord. Without that legal step, a three-year wait was required. The principle of fault continued to be part of the law, however, and as in the other countries, the innocent spouse gained various advantages at divorce.[22]

The Strict No-Fault Era

It was not until 1974 that Sweden adopted the new principle of true no-fault divorce—that is, either spouse could get a divorce if he or she wanted it. That required a wait (for reflection) of six months and then a renewed application; even if both parties asked for it, a similar wait was required if they had a child less than sixteen years of age. No such delay was needed if the spouses had lived separately for at least two years.[23]

Denmark also reformulated its basic law in 1969, but without changing its principles. Its aims were to simplify and shorten the needed procedures and to focus less on fault and more on all the needs and economic capacities of the spouses, so as to lessen the problems caused by the growing divorce rate (*La Loi*, p. 40).

20. *La Loi*, table 3, p. 54.
21. Jan Erik Kristiansen, "Norway," in Chester, *Divorce in Europe*, p. 53.
22. Jan Trost, "Sweden," in ibid., pp. 35–36; and *La Loi*, table, p. 101.
23. *Le Divorce*, 1975, pp. 160–61.

As a consequence of these and other changes, almost all of them relatively modest, by 1981 all of the Nordic countries recognized the legal claim of marital breakdown as well as mutual consent, and all except Sweden still permitted some accusation of fault. Only Sweden had made fault irrelevant in effect.[24] With the 1985 and 1987 laws, Finland joined Sweden in eradicating both "fault" and the principle of the irretrievable breakdown of the marriage as a requirement for divorce.[25] In Denmark, 85–90 percent of divorces are simply processed by administrative decision if the couple has agreed on both the dissolution and its consequences, but it is still possible to obtain a divorce after a one-year separation or in case of adultery.[26] The separation requirement was abolished in Sweden in 1974. Under the present system, no actual court appearance of either party will be necessary in most cases. The filing of the appropriate papers will be enough. Of course, these new procedures also eliminate the collection of governmental data on legal grounds for divorce.

As part of the continuing effort of the Nordic countries to coordinate their domestic law, at the beginning of 1988 Finland put into effect a new set of provisions for divorce and marriage, expressing the general Nordic presumption that marriage should not have any legal effect on the personal relations between the spouses or on their property.[27] Some maintenance obligations may remain, but in actual legal practice the legal obligation for spousal maintenance within marriage or after divorce has almost ceased to exist.

This is a strict no-fault system: either spouse can get a divorce whatever the objections of the other spouse. The divorce goes into effect only six months after the proceedings are initiated, except under a few circumstances (for example, if they have already been separated for two years or more).

Duration

The relative stability (or even slight reduction) of divorce rates in these countries from 1950 until well into the 1960s could not affect the duration of marriages by much, but the very sharp increases after that did mean that many couples who might have lived out their lives together must instead have cut their marriages short. In addition, new cohorts entered marriages whose durations were to be considerably shorter. Thus, as in the rest of

24. See the charts of successive changes presented by Guibentif in *La Loi*, pp. 191, 193, 195ff.
25. Savolainen, "Finland," p. 128.
26. Koch-Nielsen, *Divorces*, p. 24; as well as Erik Manniche, *The Family in Denmark* (Helsingør: P.C. Print and Press, 1985).
27. Savolainen, "Finland," p. 132.

Europe, it was to be expected that the duration of marriage would be less over the ensuing decades.

In fact, it was not until the 1980s that a drop began to be apparent. There was a slight decrease in Norway in the period 1960–1970, and a few minor ups and downs among these countries through 1975, but the figures generally remain rather stable, hovering between 10.6 and 12.4 years. As Festy remarks: "That stability implies that the rise in the divorce rate has taken place at almost the same speed whatever the marriage duration."[28] That is, all the marriage cohorts, young and old, were affected by a widespread change of attitude toward divorce. Sweden's ratio of divorces to marriages tripled, but the distribution of the rates by duration of marriage did not change much.

Of course, as in the rest of Europe each successive cohort of marriages was to experience a greater likelihood of divorce after 1965 and thus a rising curve of divorce in the earlier years. Even if the rates increase for older durations as well, the weight of numbers in the accumulation of successive cohorts will eventually reduce the average duration. In Denmark, for example, the marriage cohort of 1975 experienced almost double the percentage of divorces registered for the cohort of 1951 within the first four years of marriage, and in that same decade the average duration had dropped by 13 percent to 8.9 years.[29] Similar patterns are found in the other countries. For example, in Sweden, the rate of divorce within the first five years of marriage almost tripled in the period 1955–1983, and the duration dropped from 14.5 to under nine years. In the Finnish marriage cohort of 1950, it took sixteen years before 10 percent had divorced, but the cohort of 1975 had done so by seven years.[30]

A final comment must be added about the demographic complexities of duration in this period. Clearly there are both *cohort* and *period* effects. That is, each new cohort of marriages will reflect a different set of experiences in its own time span, a shortened duration or earlier experience of divorce. However, the historical period is also different through the years, so that people who grew up in a period when divorce was less common may change their attitudes as they grow older, and be tempted to divorce at ages when such people would not have divorced in the past. If we add in the age at marriage, number of children, and age of the youngest child, the effect of all these variables on duration may be very complex. Moreover, they may have different effects over time. Although I have seen such an analysis only for

28. Festy, "Le Divorce," p. 129.
29. Ibid., p. 139; for other countries see figs. 11.5, 11.9, 11.10, 11.11.
30. Jarl Lindgren, "Recent Divorce Trends and Patterns in Finland," *Yearbook of Population Research in Finland* (Helsinki: Population Research Institute, 1986), p. 76.

Finland, it is very likely that these complexities would also be found in any similarly detailed calculation for other countries.[31]

Settlements Just After Divorce

At the beginning of our period, and well into the 1970s, couples could obtain a separation by mutual agreement and, after some wait, a divorce. They agreed in effect to state that marital life was intolerable. In addition, a substantial minority did so on the basis of fault. As in perhaps all Western systems of divorce in the past, a successful charge of fault yielded some advantages. For example, the innocent party in Sweden could be given somewhat more than half of the marital property instead of following the Nordic rule of equal division.[32] Similarly, the offending spouse in Finland (usually the husband) had to pay a "guilt supplement" or forgo something, as compensation.[33]

Alimony could be claimed and granted, especially if the wife's ability to earn had been reduced in her years of service as a homemaker (Norway). The spouse with the lower income might be granted some support during the separation or after the divorce (Sweden), as a lump sum or as regular payments with or without time limits.[34]

Both spouses were responsible for child support after divorce, as they were during the marriage. Since women were given custody of the children in 80 percent or more of the cases, this meant in practice that fathers were obligated to make the necessary payments. Because the Nordic countries had for decades based much of their welfare legislation and administration on continuing research, the amounts were not fixed by adversarial contests between lawyers but were more likely to be decided between spouses (with the help of court officials), with reference to known data about household and childrearing costs.

Although the foregoing statements are facts about the legal system, we have not been able to find studies of the real behavior of couples in these negotiations. This is not surprising. As Koch-Nielsen remarks, divorce rates were thought to be modest, there was not much public debate about divorce as causing large-scale social problems, and thus research on these matters was not common. Even in the United States, studies of the outcome of

31. See Wolfgang Lutz, Babette Wills, and Mauiri Nieminen, "The Demographic Dimensions of Divorce: The Case of Finland," Laxenburg, Austria: International Institute for Applied Systems Analysis, 1989, working paper 89-06, esp. pp. 1–13.

32. Trost, "Sweden," p. 36.

33. Anntila, "Finland," pp. 15, 24; and La Loi, p. 50.

34. Kristiansen, "Norway," pp. 53ff.; and Trost, "Sweden."

husband-wife negotiations about divorce settlements are still rare. Studies of whether payments and divisions actually followed the public rules became common only in the 1980s in Australia and the United States, as noted later in the chapter on the Anglo nations.

We do know that in spite of the rule in Sweden, it was not usual for small businesses and farms (that is, income-yielding property) to be divided equally at divorce.[35] Equal division under such circumstances was even less likely in Norway or Finland. Although alimony (lump-sum or regular payments) was to be awarded on the basis of need, disparity in income or private property, fault, and length of devotion to homemaking, it seems not to have been a common practice. A Finnish study of divorces in the late 1960s found that in only 4.5 percent had alimony been awarded. A few years later, a Swedish inquiry found that alimony was granted in only 6–8 percent of divorces, and usually for a limited period.[36]

Spousal freedom to negotiate toward an agreement, monitored or counseled by court or administrative officials, thus led to postmarital arrangements that were validated by an administrative staff or court. Actual conflicts in court would occur only if the spouses could not agree, for an American reader should remember that these are not litigious societies. People do not fight in court very much, perhaps not because they are more rational than elsewhere but because most people in each country know very well what the common understandings are and thus what would finally happen if they did go to court. Indeed, the counseling and advice prior to an agreement have generally taken the form of stating what the real options are. Moreover, codifications of both procedure and the expected terms of agreement are available.

Those common Nordic understandings have, however, changed substantially over the past four decades. More people came to be troubled by the growing number of lone mothers who lived in somewhat deprived circumstances and, indeed, by poverty generally. Each state, individually and sometimes in concert with others, began to make a continuing effort to reduce that poverty.

Private negotiations permit the stronger party in a divorce, usually the husband, to obtain a more advantageous settlement. State efforts and programs did not, however, take the form of giving support to the wife in her private negotiations (although legal aid was commonly available). Instead, the major steps were (1) developing a more reliable system of economic help for *all* mothers and children, in fact for all citizens; (2) making it easier for

35. Trost, "Sweden," p. 36.
36. Anntila, "Finland," p. 30; and Lars Tottie, "Matrimonial Property Disputes in Sweden," in Lodrup, "Scandinavian Approach," p. 54.

women to hold an adequate job; and (3) guaranteed payments for child support, or making these payments in advance, so that if the father defaults the mother and child will not suffer.

Since 85–90 percent of all couples use an administrative procedure or written documents rather than a court appearance to obtain the divorce and reach a settlement, they must come to an agreement, which for the most part will be accepted. For the steps toward separation and divorce in Denmark during the 1980s, for example, they would have to agree on custody, whether there will be any spousal maintenance (or lump-sum payment), who will remain in the dwelling, and the wife's right to a widow's pension. There were other questions to be decided as well—for example, the specific amount for child support or alimony, the exact terms of the division of property, and visitation rights—but the dissolution would not be delayed while those issues were being threshed out. The aim of counseling and legal advice has been to urge the couple toward compromise and agreement.[37]

Although the agreement is between the spouses, it must be emphasized that its terms will be monitored, to prevent grossly unfair allocations, to make certain that the noncustodial parent will be able to visit the child, or to assure that the child support conforms to the guidelines worked out by the state for the actual costs of childrearing.

In general, two strong trends are evident. One has already been noted, the development of standard calculations for child support depending on income, the number and age of the children, and so on. The second is the administrative move toward the position, already reached in Sweden by 1978, that in general it will be assumed that divorced spouses are not responsible for each other. There will be exceptions, of course, and even Sweden has recognized the ex-husband's obligation under some circumstances to give his former wife some financial help during the transition period.[38]

The modern Finnish code assumes joint ownership of marital property (excluding what was owned prior to the marriage or inherited afterwards), and this is the rule in the other countries as well. Under some circumstances, that rule is modified. For example, the marriage may have been very short-lived, so that full equality would be unfair; or a prenuptial contract may have created some inequity in the final sharing. That is, completely equal sharing is not to be viewed as entirely binding.

These broad changes also offer less opportunity for the negotiations com-

---

37. On these points and for comparisons with Sweden, see Schmidt, "Scandinavian Law," pp. 10–12, 18, 22–24; Noe Munck, "The Compromise as the Aim of Danish Divorce Procedures," in Lodrup, "Scandinavian Approach," pp. 36–37, 40; and Svend Danielsen, "The Economic Part of the Divorce Procedure—Three Danish Solutions," ibid., pp. 101–05.

38. On this trend in Denmark, see Danielsen, "Economic Part," p. 102.

mon in other countries, through which "divorce by agreement" is achieved. As I have noted elsewhere, that freedom to negotiate permits the stronger party (usually the husband) to use superior legal and other resources in order to press the weaker party to give consent without being willing to do so, or to make threats in order to gain property or support advantages.

For a fuller sketch of the economics of family breakup, we must again consider the situation of couples in a cohabitating union. There the rate of dissolution is higher than for legal unions, while of necessity no formal legal supervision exists. As a consequence, steps have been taken to create new rules that move the cohabiting union toward obligations or requirements that come closer to those of formal marriage.[39] In any event, it is necessary to make certain that upon dissolution each party's property interests will be protected. This usually means that the rules of protection for legal divorces should also be applied to the dissolution of cohabitation arrangements. Thus the principle that relations between any couple should be a private affair is in conflict with the need to make certain that the division of acquired possessions or valuable rights is fair to both parties in an informal union.

This is more easily accomplished in the Nordic countries, since so much of the "new property" (medical insurance, pension rights, access to child care facilities, and so on) is linked to the individual and not to the family or the head of the family. Even equal sharing, as we noted above, could be inequitable, as in fact any fixed rule might be. For example, where alternative housing is not easily available, the person who must leave may be disadvantaged. And since men still earn much more than women (this was especially so in Sweden, where a majority of women have had part-time jobs, although now full-time work is becoming more common) the sudden loss of that part of the joint income may seem unfair to the woman. In addition, as noted, a prenuptial marriage contract, seemingly entered into independently and voluntarily, may itself contain unfair provisions, which the courts or administrative agency might not be willing to approve in a dissolution.

Aside from the sharing of property, the general principle will still hold that spouses in both legal and cohabiting unions will not be responsible for the maintenance of the other. In the mid-1980s, although that legal obligation remained in Danish law, it was uncommon in practice,[40] while cohabiting couples did not owe it. However, both will be responsible for the maintenance of the children.

---

39. For an earlier comparative view of such regulations, see John Eekelaar and S. Katz, *Marriage and Cohabitation in Contemporary Societies*, (Toronto: Butterworth, 1980).

40. L. Nielsen, "Individual and Family Economic Security and the Role of the State: Changes in Denmark since 1980," in M. T. Meulders-Klein and J. Eekelaar, eds. *Family, State, and Individual Economic Security* (Brussels: Story-Scientia, 1988), p. 458.

Work and Divorce

Scandinavian women entered the labor force in increasing numbers during this long period, as women did in the rest of Europe, and they were
impelled by similar forces: a rising aspiration for more goods and services
which could not easily be obtained with only one income, a higher market
demand for labor, a lesser degree of sex discrimination in jobs. However,
state policy played a larger role than in other countries. The state actively
encouraged women to take jobs, as part of a campaign toward greater equality and also as a partial solution to the problems created by divorce. This
encouragement included programs for child daycare centers, maternity
leave with the right to return to the job without loss of benefits, and active
efforts to equalize the wages of men and women.

Finland had a long tradition of female participation in the labor force.
Norway lagged considerably. Among married Norwegian women in 1950,
only 5 percent were in the labor force. This figure rose to 10 percent in 1960
and to 20 percent a decade later. By that time, two-thirds of the married
women under 24 years of age in Finland were employed.

In Denmark 30 percent of the married women were working in the 1960s,
but that percentage had doubled by the 1980s. By the mid-1980s, for example, only about 10 percent were not in the labor force and 70 percent were
then working full-time.[41] In Sweden, the figures rose from 47 percent in
1960 to 82 percent in 1985.

Divorced women were more likely to be employed than married women,
and a higher percentage of divorced women were working full time. The
more surprising change over this period (which occurred in other Western
countries as well) was that mothers, even those with younger children,
began to appear in the labor force in percentages as high as these, or higher.
Jan Trost reports that almost nine-tenths of Swedish women with at least
one child younger than 17 years are now in the labor force (97 percent of
men are in that category).[42] To be sure, such figures were somewhat inflated
in the past, since until very recently 60 percent of the mothers were part-
time workers, many of them only a few hours a week. In addition, when
parental leave is taken in these countries, the person who stays at home to

41. See Kristiansen, "Norway," p. 59. See Koch-Nielsen, "Denmark," p. 11. On Sweden, see
Siv Gustafsson, "Labor Force Participation and Earnings of Lone Parents: A Swedish Case Study
including Comparisons with Germany," in Lone-Parent Families (Paris: OECD Social Policy
Studies, no. 8, 1990), pp. 154–55. See Koch-Nielsen, "Denmark," p. 19. For 1988, the Danish
figure was 87 percent for both married and single mothers; see Sheila Kamerman, "Gender Role
and Family Structure in the Advanced Industrialized West: Implications for Social Policy"
(Washington: Joint Center for Political and Economic Studies, 1991), table 9.

42. Jan Trost, "Scandinavian Families," Familje-Rapporter 15 (Uppsala Universitet, 1990),
p. 26.

care for the child is nearly always the mother, and she is still counted as part of the labor force during that period.

Research in both Russia and the United States suggests that this arrangement creates more husband satisfaction in marriage. This is not a surprising finding, since women then bring in additional income to the family but cannot easily escape from the responsibilities of the home. Thus men are supported in their continued reluctance to take much part in domestic tasks.

In spite of press reports about the advances in equality within the Nordic countries, it is not the sharing of domestic duties that has freed women for full-time participation in the work force. The ideologies of equality vary somewhat among these countries, but Elena Haavio-Mannila showed some time ago that men's contributions to "women's work" in the home differed very little from one Nordic country to another and indeed were not much different from many other countries where the ideology of sex equality was much weaker. And although some movement toward equal sharing has occurred and is publicly much applauded, the additional contribution often amounts to little more than a few minutes per day.[43] Both married and unmarried women have increasingly moved into full-time work in recent years. By 1986–1987, almost half of the lone mothers in Sweden and nearly two-thirds of those with older children worked full time.[44]

Both Denmark and Norway lag somewhat in pay allowances for parental leave (Denmark pays maternity benefits for 28 weeks at about 90 percent of the woman's former wages; Norway pays for 18 weeks),[45] but even in Sweden the allowance is paid at a somewhat modest rate—the income of the average factory worker. As a consequence, it is mainly women who stay at home since the loss of the man's income would be a greater hardship. It seems clear that the administrative and economic patterns that support part-time work for women and their greater contributions to domestic tasks fit the inclinations of men. It is equally clear that the greater marital satisfaction that might result has had little negative effect on the rise in the divorce rates of these countries.

Differences in Cohabitation Patterns

Trost states that in Scandinavia "there is no class difference in cohabitation, cohabitation has nothing to do with the economy, cohabitation has

43. Koch-Nielsen, "Denmark," pp. 12–13.

44. Siv Gustafsson, "Single Mothers in Sweden: Why is Poverty Less Severe?" (Washington: Joint Center for Political and Economic Studies, 1991), table 5.

45. See Rita Knudsen, "Denmark," in Alfred J. Kahn and Shiela B. Kamerman, eds., *Child Support* (Newbury Park: Sage 1987), p. 60; and Kirsti Strom-Bull, "State Support for Children in Norway," in Meulders-Klein and Eekelaar, *Economic Security,* p. 619.

nothing to do with sexuality or with childbearing." He also asserts: "The situation of today in Scandinavia is that literally almost no couples who marry, do so without having cohabited under marriage-like conditions prior to the formal marriage (first and later marriages)."[46] If the second statement is true, the first must be as well; that is, if everyone does it, then these variables cannot have any differential effect. Some interesting regional and economic differences do exist, however, and add some complexity to the divorce and dissolution patterns that are developing.

In both Sweden and Norway there were two cohabitation patterns in the past.[47] One of these was to be found in the northern territories, where it was quite common for a couple to delay marriage until after a child was born, sometimes even long afterward. Cohabitation then was a trial marriage. The other pattern was to be found in the cities, mainly in working-class neighborhoods. Both were perhaps more common even in the 1940s and 1950s than was believed. Since the 1960s, when many people openly challenged the sanctity of marriage, there has been a steady rise in the percentage of young people who entered some domestic union before marriage. Now that cohabitation has become socially acceptable, almost all couples in both Sweden and Denmark cohabit for some time before they enter a legal union, and an increasing percentage postpone that last step indefinitely. The other Nordic countries are not far behind.

Earlier research did not document systematically the rising numbers of such unions, but some figures can be presented. It seems likely that by the mid-1970s about 5–7 percent of couples in Finland, about 8 percent in Denmark, and only about 2–3 percent in Norway were currently living in a cohabiting union, though a much higher percentage would have entered one before marriage. The percentage living in a cohabiting union in Sweden rose from about 13 percent in 1975 to about 25 percent after the mid-1980s. But even by 1965, about 30 percent of all Swedish couples had lived together before marriage. That figure rose to 80 percent by 1980 and presumably now includes almost everyone.[48] However widespread, there may still

46. Trost, "Scandinavian Families," pp. 14, 19.

47. Kari Waerness, "Changes in the Life Patterns of Families in Norway," Vienna Center, *Current Research Reports*, vol. 2, no. 2 ISSC (Vienna: European Coordination Center for Research and Documentation in Social Science, 1981), pp. 60–78. Jan M. Hoem and Bo Rennermalm also report that non-marital cohabitation was much more widespread in the pre–World War II cohort than was previously known: Hoem and Rennermalm, "Modern Family Initiation in Sweden: Experience of Women Born Between 1936 and 1960," *Eur. J. Pop.* 1 (1985), pp. 81–112. See also Eva Bernhardt and Britta Hoem, "Cohabitation and Social Background: Trends Observed for Swedish Women Born Between 1936 and 1960," ibid., pp. 375–95. For the more recent period of formation of these households, see the complex analysis of categories in Thora Nilsson, "Les Ménages en Suede, 1960–1980," *Population* 40 (1985), pp. 223–48.

48. For some comparative figures, see Jan Trost, "A Renewed Social Institution: Non-Marital Cohabitation," *Acta Sociologica* 21 (1978), p. 311; and his "Cohabitation and Marriage: Transi-

be some differences in how soon couples move into marriage, or how likely they are to feel that marriage is appropriate if they wish to have a child. And, of course, there are national differences as well. For example, Danish women without previous children are twice as likely as Swedish women *not* to give birth outside of marriage, and they marry more readily.[49] The daughters of salaried employees are much less likely than those of workers to give birth in such a union.[50]

Having a child in a cohabiting union is no longer disapproved, and it should be emphasized that such an "out of wedlock" birth is not likely to be socially the same as an "illegitimate" birth in the Anglo countries, especially· the United States. By contrast with those countries, there has been no real increase in the fertility of Nordic women who are "really single." That is, as noted earlier, teenage pregnancy is uncommon, and almost all pregnancies carried to term will occur to women who are either married or in a cohabitating union. Thus, one source of American marital instability in the past—precipitate unions to avoid an illegitimacy—has little or no importance in the Nordic countries. And almost no child is born without a known father.

Nevertheless, the risk of divorce is somewhat increased if pregnancy occurs before the marriage. Kravdal has analyzed the complete register of marriages to Norwegian women who were born between 1935 and 1964 (and thus including very recent marriages) and shows that although this relationship between premarital pregnancy and divorce has weakened, it still holds. On the other hand, it be remembered that this may be again no more than a link between divorce and being in the lower classes, where both premarital pregnancy and out of wedlock births are more common.[51]

Cohabitation begins earlier today than in the past, when it was more commonly a trial marriage and thus both spouses were mature. The frequency of early cohabitation now more than makes up for the decline in formal marriage, since in the past there were few legal unions in the age

tional Pattern, Different Lifestyle, or Just Another Legal Form," in Hein Moors and Jeannette Schoore, *Lifestyles, Contraception and Parenthood* (Netherlands Interdisciplinary Demographic Institute, 1988), pp. 6–7. See also Koch-Nielsen, "Denmark," pp. 9–10; Hoem and Hoem, "Swedish Family," p. 405; and calculations from data courtesy of Dr. Sten Johannsen, National Statistics Center, Stockholm.

49. Jan M. Hoem, Bo Rennermalm, and Randi Selmer, "Restriction Biases in the Analysis of Births and Marriages to Cohabitating Women From Data on the Most Recent Conjugal Union Only," in Karl U. Mayer and Nancy B. Tuma, eds., *Applications of Event History Analysis in Life Course Research* (Berlin: Max-Planck-Institut für Bildungsforschung, 1987), p. 559.

50. Bernhardt and Hoem, "Cohabitation," p. 394.

51. Oystein Kravdal, "The Impact of First-Birth Timing on Divorce: New Evidence from a Longitudinal Analysis based on the Central Population Register of Norway," *Eur. J. Pop.* 4 (1988), pp. 247, 260ff.

period 18–24. The change in age at entering a union and in the prevalence of pregnancy may be illustrated by a comparison between the oldest and youngest cohorts in the Hoem and Home sample. In the oldest group (born 1936–1940), only one woman in five was under age 20 when she entered either type of union, but one in two of these was pregnant. In the youngest cohort (born 1956–1960), half had entered some kind of union as a teenager but only 5 percent were pregnant at that time.[52] Cohabitation at these earlier ages thus becomes more like "steady dating."

Somewhat earlier Finnish data (1969–1982) also illustrate these processes. Cohabitation began to increase there in the 1970s, later than in Sweden. As noted earlier, in the late 1970s some 8 percent of all couples were in cohabiting unions, and only 13 percent said they had "ever" been in such a union. However, a single-city survey in 1969 reported that 17 percent of all couples gave the same address before their marriage. By 1982, 11 percent of all couples were in such unions, and more than two-thirds of all marriages were preceded by cohabitation.[53]

In Finland the increase was led by a vanguard of younger people, in the cities. They were somewhat better educated than people who were married, but that is (as it is in the United States) partly because the younger generation is better educated. Very few had children in such unions, and most of the couples ultimately married. Those who did not, but who stayed together for a longer period, did not acquire as much property as married couples.

The increase in cohabitation was accompanied, as in other Nordic countries, by the postponement of marriage. That is, young men and women who enter a cohabitating union are not yet "settling down," probably have not yet established a position or career, and are still much short of the usual age at marriage in the Nordic countries, either in the recent past (25–27 years) or the present (27–29 years). For example, of the 1977 Norwegian "starters," three years later only one-third had a child.[54] These factors contribute to the lower rate of conversions to legal marriage than in the past and the higher percentage of eventual dissolutions; that is, they are younger, there is a longer period during which the couple is not yet prepared for marriage, and there is less pressure to marry formally. Thus there is a longer period in which dissolutions may occur.

In Norway, too, the first cohabitation is now less likely to be with the person one ultimately marries.[55] That is, although cohabitation is now so-

52. Hoem and Hoem, "Swedish Family," p. 401.

53. Kauko Aromaa, Ilkka Cantell, and Risto Jaakkola, *Cohabitation in Finland in the 1970s*, Research Institute of Legal Policy, pub. no. 63, pp. 3–5, 51.

54. Hoem and Hoem, "Swedish Family," p. 401.

55. Kravdal, "Impact," pp. 250–51.

cially more acceptable it is also less stable than in the past,[56] and fertility within marriage remains two to three times higher than in cohabiting unions.[57] If one considers young, childless women, 80 percent of the Swedish cohort born at the end of the 1930s married their partners within eight years, but 80 percent of the cohort born in the 1950s *did not.*[58]

Data on second unions further illuminate both regional and time differences in marriage and cohabitation. In both Norway and Sweden (as in other countries), people delay longer in entering a second union after ending a marriage than after cohabitation.[59] Of course, in both countries, the percentage who end a first cohabitation increases over time. However, Norwegian women were quicker than others to enter a second union after cohabitation. About 80 percent who ended a cohabitation after 1970 entered a second union within four years, as contrasted with 60 percent of Swedish women. In both countries, about half of those who had ended a first marriage entered a second union within the same time interval.

Time changes suggest, however, still another difference in how the sifting processes of cohabitation actually operate in the two countries. In Sweden, people who have entered a cohabiting union in recent years are *less* likely than those in Norway to marry their first partner. However, they are also *more* likely than the Norwegians to break up their first union to marry their second partner and more likely to stay in this second marriage than those Norwegians who do marry their second partner. It is as though the Swedish couples are now using cohabitation much more as a simple screening process, to attain a more stable relationship. Those Norwegians who deviate from the more common pattern of marrying their first partner may be simply "highly selected to include those who purposefully avoid marriage."[60]

A couple may decide to enter a cohabiting union, and then marry sooner than planned, later, or not at all. If marriages can be easily dissolved, cohabiting unions of course can be dissolved with even less cost. Yet if cost matters, it would be surprising if economic and class factors did not affect the couple's choice of one over the other at different life stages. And indeed the great delay in marriage grows partly out of the simple economic fact that young people who are continuing higher education or training may decide to postpone formal marriage until they have entered a better-paying occupa-

---

56. Nilsson "Les Ménages," p. 233.

57. It was once four times as high (Hoem and Rennerhalm, "Modern Family," p. 101).

58. David Popenoe, "Beyond the Nuclear Family: A Statistical Portrait of the Changing Family in Sweden," *J. Marr. and the Family* 49 (1987), p. 176. The research was done by Jan Qvist and Bo Rennermalm.

59. Ann Klimas Blanc, "The Formation and Dissolution of Second Unions: Marriage and Cohabitation in Sweden and Norway," *J. Marr. and the Family* 49 (1987), pp. 393ff.

60. Ibid., p. 398.

tion. At a different economic level they may cohabit but wait until their jobs are better or more secure before having a child. Clearly, then, the two forms of marital union and dissolution have not yet become entirely identical.

Remarriage

Although remarriage cannot solve all the problems created by divorce, it is likely to improve matters more than any other postmarital event, at least for a while. The children acquire a surrogate father or mother. The household will usually (in these countries) enjoy two incomes and is very likely to live above the zone of economic risk. Some analysts also see remarriage as an index of health in the institution of the family itself: If spouses try it again, perhaps it is not really coming apart, as so many fear.

As in the center of Europe, the general trend in the Nordic countries was a decline in both marriage and remarriage rates. Sweden's marriage rates continued to be relatively high until the mid-1960s, although it should be noted that the Swedes have generally been less tempted by marriage than other people. For example, only 75 percent of the 1945 birth cohort ever married (vs. 95 percent in the United States).[61] Norway's rates were relatively stable in the period 1950–1973, before the decrease began. In all these countries people began to marry at a slower rate, to divorce more, and to remarry more hesitantly. The Swedish remarriage rate dropped by about 30–40 percent in the eight years after 1966.[62] The remarriage rate in Finland actually began to decline in the 1950s, before the marriage rate had dropped.[63] By the late 1960s, the age at marriage in these countries had begun to rise (because of the delay in first marriages), and the time between divorce and remarriage had lengthened because fewer divorcees were embracing remarriage with the enthusiasm of a decade before. As a further consequence, the number of mother-headed households had increased.

Research in Scandinavia also confirms some of the regularities from other countries: People who divorce are more likely to remarry than single people of the same age are to marry. The young are more likely to remarry than are older people. People who have been formally married are less likely to remarry as soon as those who have left a cohabiting union. These regularities appear not to have changed in this period.

The remarriage rate in Finland dropped by two-thirds during 1950–1972 among males in the age group 20–24 years and by 58 percent in the age

---

61. Popenoe, "Nuclear Family," p. 175; the figure is from R. Schoen and J. Baj, "Twentieth Century Cohort Marriage and Divorce in England and Wales," *Population Studies* 38 (1984).
62. Trost, "Sweden," p. 51.
63. Antilla, "Finland," p. 32.

group 30–34 years.[64] Data are sparse for Norway, but by the early 1970s it was estimated that about half of the men were remarrying within three years and that 75 percent of all persons who had divorced before age 40 would eventually remarry.[65] Trost calculated for the mid-1960s that about 60 percent of divorced Swedish men and 55 percent of divorced women would remarry.

All distributions of remarriage rates by age groups since that time show steady declines. By the 1980s, however, such calculations and estimates had become confused by the rapid increase in cohabitation, especially as the first union of choice after divorce. Consequently, even when we have figures for legal remarriage, we still have only a shaky grasp of the *socially* more important datum—that is, what percentage of all divorced people have established a new marital union, whether or not formally married? Moreover, even the term "remarriage" loses some of its weight, for if it means the formation of a *new* union, a new household, that can happen after a cohabiting couple has broken up as well as after a marriage, with corresponding changes required in the figures.

I shall continue to keep these terms separate, but if we are focusing on the people who are in some kind of union (and therefore better able to care for the children, not to mention one another), the differences may be less important than tradition would assert.

In addition, cohabitation has become the *usual* type of union after divorce (in Sweden after 1970, divorcees were ten times as likely to choose cohabitation over marriage as their second union). Consequently, most older people who divorce will enter a cohabiting union in all these countries.

To illustrate the importance of economic factors here (and again the difference between marriage and cohabitation), in Sweden in 1988 a new law removed some pension disadvantages of legal marriages, again following the general principle that civil status should not affect an individual's receipt of state payments. During that year, on *every day of December* more marriages were recorded than in the usual months for marriage (beginning with the seventh week after Easter, Whitsuntide, and early summer).[66] Almost all of these couples had been married before.

Because many data about remarriage in Finland are not available, a study was made of who did remarry in one year, 1984. The researchers concluded that 34–36 percent of divorcees will remarry within ten years. About 50

---

64. Kristiansen, "Norway," p. 67; these calculations may be approximations.
65. Anntila, "Finland," p. 32.
66. Personal communication from Sten Johannsen, Director of the Swedish National Office of Statistics, to whom I am also indebted for numerous recent tables. This sudden jump is visible as well in the official statistics (unpublished).

percent of men in the young ages 20–29, 64 percent of still younger women aged 20–24, and 55 percent of all divorcees would eventually remarry.[67] Only about 11 percent of couples in some kind of union at that time were cohabiting. However, "the formation of consensual unions by divorced persons . . . was one-third greater than the number of remarried." This suggests that the percentage of those forming new unions in the first year after divorce might be as high as 30 percent.[68] The likelihood of choosing a consensual union first was greater in the 1980s because there were some tax advantages in being single.

Both before and after 1970, Swedish couples were overwhelmingly likely to enter a cohabiting union after divorce, rather than a marriage (although they might marry eventually). That choice was less one-sided in Norway, where before 1970, 20 percent would remarry within four years, and only 10 percent after that time. However, after 1970, a cohabiting union was chosen four times as frequently as marriage in all second unions. Thus, four years after divorce (after 1970), about 53 percent would enter some kind of union in Norway and about 48 percent in Sweden.[69]

A somewhat different figure for Denmark simply aggregates all who have been divorced without specifying for how long. It reports whether they are *now* living in some kind of union, whether marriage of cohabitation. In 1984 about 82 percent of the males and 67 percent of the females who had ever been divorced (of whatever age) had entered some kind of union.[70]

Lone-Parent Families

Although the foregoing figures affirm that the increase in cohabitation makes up in part for the decline in remarriage rates, the processes we analyzed earlier operate just the same. Mothers who divorce are somewhat older than divorcees without children (although in Finland mothers aged 30 and older have a higher probability of remarriage than do childless women)[71]—and thus are less likely to enter a new marital unit, the pool of eligible mates declines faster for women than for men, and the number of

67. Karl Lindgren and Mauri Nieminen, "Remarriage in Finland," *Yearbook of Population Research in Finland* (Population Research Institute, Helsinki, vol. 26, 1988), pp. 39, 42, 46.

68. Blanc, "Formation and Dissolution," pp. 394, 399, fig. 1, p. 395.

69. Inger Koch-Nielsen and Henning Transgaard, *Familienmonstre efter skilsmisse* (Copenhaven: Sozial forskningsinstitutet, 1987), pub. no. 155, fig. 4.1., p. 56.

70. Wolfgang Lutz and Douglas Wolf, "Fertility and Marital Status Changes over the Life Cycle: A Comparative Study of Finland and Austria," in *Yearbook of Population Research in Finland* (Helsinki: Population Research Institute, 1989), vol. 27, pp. 21–22.

71. Elizabeth Duskin, "Overview," in *Lone-Parent Families*, p. 15.

mother-headed households continues to grow, with all their attendant social and economic problems.

The processes that generate such a continuing rise are not new in this long generation. They have simply grown stronger, and the numbers of people affected by them are larger. Once divorce becomes permissible at all, there will be some divorced mothers who will not remarry, and they will be given custody of the children. With higher ages, and with a greater delay in remarriage, the difference between men and women in remarriage rates become still greater. And as divorce spreads, the percentage of divorces involving children also rises.

As the number of children affected by divorce increases, they become a social issue, and in almost all countries the public concern with their economic hardships and poverty grows. The problem is viewed as somehow different from ordinary poverty, more like an unfortunate accident, not caused by the children who must bear it. Most people believe that children of divorce face many life disadvantages not of their own making, while they are also the hope of their nation's future. Thus the traditional censoriousness against the divorced person seems out of place.

Although the laws and regulations in operation in the 1950s and 1960s seemed to cover this problem (alimony and child support), the evidence showed that they did not fill the income gap. Numerous studies since the 1970s have revealed that such households are more likely to suffer from poverty than other segments of the population. As one 1990 summary states: "a common observation is that most custodial parents and their children do not actually receive any support awarded or agreed upon, or, if they do initially, it does not continue over the intended period."[72] Moreover, even if for most divorced families that is a transitory phase, since most will eventually be reestablished in a household with two parents (married or not), the phase may continue for some years. It may indeed be a large part of any childhood.

It is difficult to measure exactly that rise in lone-parent households, of course, because of the increasing percentage of cohabiting unions as the first union after divorce in these countries. As a consequence, the figures may differ from one report to another. In Sweden, lone-parent households were 9 percent of all households with children in 1960, 10 percent in 1970, 11 percent in 1980, and 13 percent in 1985.[73] Popenoe gives 18 percent for

72. Constance Sorrentino's figures are from the United States Bureau of Labor Statistics compilation, in her "The Changing Family in International Perspective," *Monthly Labor Review* 113 (1990), p. 50.

73. Popenoe, "Nuclear Family," p. 178.

1980, and an estimate of 25 percent for 1986,[74] but the first set definitely excludes cohabiting mothers.

The figures for Denmark are very similar: 17 percent in 1976, 19 percent in 1983, and 20 percent in 1988. An estimate for Finland in 1988 was 13 percent. For Norway, the 1989 figure was 22 percent. Figures for the population of the United States report about 26 percent, and 17 percent for the white population in the mid-1980s, but those figures also include never-married mothers.

We should also note that these are static figures, so that even if "only" 20 percent of the children in Denmark or Norway are currently being reared in single-parent households, two or three times that number will have been reared in such households at one time or another.

The problems of such households are compounded by the unpalatable fact that those mothers who are most deprived—that is, whose husbands had little or no property or income to share and who themselves possessed few resources—are also themselves least likely to have the education and skills with which to pull themselves and their children out of that situation by getting better jobs. In any event, as more studies of divorced mothers (and lone mothers not divorced) were done, it became clear that noncustodial parents had failed in their legal duties. Both parents were responsible for the care and support of their children, and one of them shirked that task. To emphasize this view, Denmark separated the legal obligation from matrimonial law as early as 1960, making the parents liable for support no matter what were their subsequent marital careers.[75] Strom-Bull, writing in the 1980s, notes the difficulty of making Norwegian fathers pay, and the new procedures for enforcement.[76]

Of course, the amounts set as payments were often very low. In 1981, the monthly payment per child was equivalent to only forty pounds sterling, about the same as in the United Kingdom and other OECD countries.

The committees and legislators who have developed new provisions for enforcement have not supposed that divorced husbands in Scandinavian countries are likely by nature to be more virtuous than elsewhere. Instead, these countries learned over recent decades that the love of virtue or paternal solicitude did not guarantee regular payments from former husbands, espe-

74. Mavis Maclean, "Lone-Parent Families: Family Law and Income Transfers," in *Lone-Parent Families*, pp. 94–95.

75. Kirsti Strom-Bull, "State Support for Children in Norway," in Meulders-Klein and Eekelaar, *Family State*, p. 621.

76. For a description of the Norwegian system, see Odd Helge Askevold, "Support for Lone Parents in Norway," in *Lone-Parent Families*, pp. 241–52; for the Danish procedures, see Torben Svenne Schmidt, "Advance Payments by the State of Maintenance to Children," in Meulders-Klein and Eekelaar, *Family, State*, pp. 401–11.

cially when they were faced with the heady temptation to spend the money on themselves. Thus these states created enforcement provisions that were nearly automatic when a failure occurred.[77]

It also became clear over these decades that better enforcement methods, though necessary and useful, were not an adequate solution for the poverty of divorced mothers. Consequently, the Nordic countries have been aiming for a system that will attack poverty on a broad front rather than being linked to marital status.

The State's Adjustment to Divorce

The economic and social consequences of dissolution or divorce are easier to measure than the emotional hurt. They are likely to cause other personal disruptions for both spouses and children, and these are weightier for mothers and children than for fathers (whether married or unmarried).[78] Nevertheless it must not be supposed that their situation is the same in the Nordic countries as in, say, the United States or Great Britain, or even the other European countries.[79]

In the view of many conservatives in the United States, the Swedish people pay most of their income as taxes to the state, and people on welfare consume those taxes. The reality is both more complex and less dismal. To understand it, it is first necesssary to see how broadly various kinds of "welfare" or "transfer payments" are distributed in the United States. That fact is generally obscured by the rhetorical customs and political vocabulary about taxation and welfare in this country. In that discourse, a wide array of subsidies is excluded. They are not called "welfare," for example, if they are income-tax reductions because of home-mortgage interest payments, if they are government-built forest roads that yields private profits for logging companies, or if they are farm subsidies or savings and loan bailouts.

By that wider and technically more correct definition, a fairly high percentage of the population in both Sweden and the United States might be said to receive some kind of governmental "transfer payment." Indeed, in this sense it is clear that "middle-class welfare" is a large part of the total U.S. budget, in part because it is politically easier to create such subsidies than to grant welfare aid to the poor. Indeed, the total is greater than the amount given to the poor. For example, the government of the United States spent six

---

77. On the poverty of one-parent families, see H. Friis *One-Parent Families and Poverty in the EEC*, doc. V/2541/1-2, 82 (Copenhagen: EEC, 1982).

78. For a detailed comparative analysis see Lee Rainwater, Martin Rein, and Joseph Schwartz, eds., *Income Packaging in the Welfare State* (Oxford: Clarendon, 1986), esp. ch. 8.

79. Gustafsson, "Single Mothers," p. 1.

times as much money on the savings and loan bailout of the early 1990s as it did on welfare. On the other hand, in contrast with the Nordic countries, there are far fewer allowances that are given to almost everyone; the American pattern leans more toward making special grants to sub-groups.

If we narrow our focus to the usually more precarious position of solo mothers (most of whom in the Nordic countries will have experienced some kind of marital dissolution), a much smaller percentage of all the Swedish women in this category live in poverty or on welfare than in Great Britain or the United States. The most striking differences are that very few Swedish solo mothers live off welfare only; almost all work, and they earn about two-thirds of their total income. The Nordic program aims at widespread policies which, like Sweden's, "promote women's involvement in the paid work-force and encourage combining work and family rather than special policies targeted at single mothers."[80]

When lone mothers in Sweden are employed, they earn nearly 60 percent of the average male wage, in contrast to about one-third in the United States. In general, a smaller percentage of all American mothers receive transfer payments, but the amount are a larger percentage of their total income. In Sweden, most of the payments are very modest.

It should be emphasized, however, that *all* Nordic families with children receive child allowances, and all Nordic custodial mothers will receive, un-der most circumstances, child payments from the (usually noncustodial) father. If he does not pay, the state will advance the payments and try to collect from the father. And, although the state may not be making pay-ments to the custodial parent for the rent (as would occur in welfare pay-ments in the United States), the state does subsidize much housing—but not just for the poor. The aim of the total array of Nordic programs is to reduce or eliminate poverty, with much less regard to family type, while the programs in Great Britain and the United States have a special concern with solo mothers.[81] Even after taking transfer payments into account, almost one-half (45 percent) of American solo mothers, 36 percent of solo mothers in Great Britain, but only 9 percent of solo mothers in Sweden were poor.

A higher percentage of Danish than of Swedish mothers will be poor, for the payments in Denmark are lower. Norwegian as well as Danish lone mothers will not have their transfer payments reduced if they earn an ade-quate income, as occurs in the United States. Scandinavian nations do not refuse to make advance payments (when the noncustodial parent has not

80. Rainwater, Rein, and Schwartz, "Income Packaging," p. 197.

81. For details, see ibid., ch. 8; Nielsen, "Individual and Family," pp. 458ff.; Schmidt, "Scan-dinavian Law," pp. 339–411; Strom-Bull, "State Support," pp. 618–27; Knudsen, "Denmark," pp. 50–73.

paid) on the ground that the mother is living with someone or that she (or he) has an income. The main difference between Sweden and the two Anglo countries lies not in the total size of all the transfer payments but in the larger income of the Swedish women and the "floor" of minimal social supports, which most people utilize.

There have been recent cutbacks in some Nordic countries but their supports are generally more widespread than in other countries, covering more contingencies. For a very large part of the population, and in most cases all of it, this includes medical benefits, maternity (and paternity) leave and medical benefits, child allowances, advance payments when the non-custodial parent fails to pay, rent subsidies, special allowances for single mothers, home nursing, and childcare supplements for working mothers.[82] Under these circumstances, it is not surprising that so many mothers are in the labor force and that so many work full-time or more than twenty hours per week: they are encouraged to do so. Since fathers are also held responsible for their children, the state officially confirms paternity if the father seeks to evade responsibility. Since the father is not so often the object of resentment, most do continue to see their children, in strong contrast with the situation in the United States, where almost half have no contact for a year or more.[83]

None of these major changes in supports over the past generation can erase all the substantial contrasts in the structural positions of men and women, in these or any other societies. Women are the usual custodial parent; child payments are rarely equal to the costs of rearing a child; women earn less than men and a smaller percentage of them achieve as high a job rank as men; a higher percentage of women work part-time, and so on. Complete equality of the sexes after marital dissolution, even in the ideologically egalitarian Nordic countries, is about as elusive as it is during the marriage.

Since almost all divorced mothers are likely to be working, day care is of considerable importance. Sweden lags behind other Nordic nations in public day care centers, perhaps because so many mothers work part-time, but there are many private care facilities and a well-developed system of parental leave. The national plan is to have such care fully available by the early 1990s, but in the late 1980s only about 36 percent received such care. Others were cared for under some state support but by people licensed to supply day care (and still others of course were taken care of by a parent).[84] However, 84 percent of the children of lone mothers were in public child care, and "be-

82. Frank Furstenberg, "Marital Disruptions, Child Custody and Visitation," in Kahn and Kamerman, *Child Support*, pp. 277–305.

83. Popenoe, *Disturbing*, p. 321.

84. Gustafsson, "Single Mothers," p. 2.

cause day care is so universally used, the program does not stigmatize those children."[85]

Norway support patterns generally lag somewhat behind those of Sweden, while public nurseries and day care in Denmark are more fully organized. Even by the end of the 1970s in Denmark, some 50 percent of children older than 2 years were in some form of day care. It should be re-emphasized, however, that children will receive a fairly wide array of other benefits whether their parents are divorced or married and whether or not they were born out of wedlock. These are simply *children's* rights, and most are not affected very much by their parents' status or even their income. They include medical benefits, dental benefits, school lunches (in Finland), and so forth. As a consequence, many expenses that in the Anglo countries might be viewed as private burdens on the divorced mother's reduced income are met in one form or another by state support to all mothers.

Final Comment

Although we have been describing what we believe is a different route being traveled by the Nordic countries, while many of the major trends in divorce processes parallel those in other industrializing countries (rise of the divorce rate, increase in cohabitation, lowered remarriage rate, and the like) we cannot assume that these widespread supports necessarily "strengthen the family." The various aids developed by these nations seek to reduce somewhat the burdens caused by the private decisions of people to stop living together. Certainly this is an expression of a compassionate *collective concern* for spouses in a private difficulty. Nevertheless, it does seem likely just the same that these supports weaken the binding commitment between spouses, and thus what I have called personal investments in the collectivity of the family.

As noted earlier, payments are made to *individuals,* and they are made (as much as possible) without respect to people's status as family members. This is of course diametrically opposite to the patterns in all familistic societies, where so many roles, job opportunities, rights, and privileges are linked to one's performance of family role obligations. Increasingly, people seek their own destinies, and part when those destinies seem no longer to be shared. Both state supports and administrative arrangements, where they exist, increasingly pull in the same direction.

These express a widespread social concern for individuals caught in circumstances that may be immediately their own creation but are ultimately

85. Data from unpublished tables and figures sent to me by Dr. Sten Johannsen.

part of a larger set of national and even international processes. Those processes occur, that is, in other countries as well, where the divorce rates also rise, but fewer supports exist in most of them. This should not prevent us from acknowledging that these Nordic supports and administrative arrangements do not bolster the goal—much praised in the mass media—of persuading couples to live through their marital difficulties, to attempt to adjust to one another's needs, and to invest in a longer-term future, counting on the normal ups and downs of exchanges to even out what may be only temporary imbalances in a fair exchange.

Nevertheless, in spite of this persuasive set of processes in apparent support of a lessening commitment to familism, a final striking fact must be stated here. If we consider the extreme nation in this region, for which the direst predictions have been made, the Swedish data do not yet support that obvious prophecy—that is, of a total breakdown of the family. From the end of the 1970s *through* 1988, there is no important change in the Swedish divorce rate (per 1000 married population). This is also true if we consider divorce rates by age in the period 1981–1986, and it holds true for *cohabitation*, both of the never married and of the previously married, for the same years. (The dissolution rate rose a bit for the younger years, dropped for the older.) And if we calculate the probability of *eventual* divorce, there is *no real change* from 1980 through 1988. Whether these data suggest a stable plateau, or a temporary state that will be followed by a new increase, we cannot know for a few years, but they are robust enough to merit much thought. If these policies, which certainly keep many divorced mothers out of poverty, do not *strengthen* the family, at least they do not appear as yet to weaken it by much.

5

Eastern Europe: Polities as Agents of Marital Dissolution

It is not likely that we can gain an adequate understanding of the dynamics of divorce changes over the past generation in Eastern Europe for a long time to come, and perhaps it will never be possible. The kinds of detailed empirical research that have been a tradition in the West for well over a century have in the East often been blocked, hidden in fiction or poetry, or punished by imprisonment. This was especially true in the Soviet system, whose repressive patterns were generally more violent and whose dictatorship was more unremitting than elsewhere. In the 1980s, population data became even less available.[1]

Especially in Russia, reports were labeled "objective" but were written in what some have called the "indicative-prescriptive" tense; that is, they claimed to be descriptions but were really exhortations to conform. Thus a Party report could assert: "The Socialist family is harmonious because it is based on love, unlike the bourgeois family, which is exploitative and dominated by males through their control of wealth. The Socialist family, like the Socialist society, is founded on the principle of equality between the sexes." Unfortunately, such a statement expresses governmental wishfulness, not social reality. On the other hand, it must be conceded that it is less costly in effort and money to *declare* a desirable state of affairs than to accomplish it.

This chapter presents some of the available statistics for various Eastern European countries. It also suggests a somewhat radical hypothesis: that these countries (again, especially Russia) reveal a set of social patterns that may themselves have contributed to the rising rates of marital dissolution

1. On the decline in published data, see Roland Pressat, "Historical Perspective on the Population of the Soviet Union," *Population and Development Review* 11 (1985), p. 315; and, for the 1980s, his "L'appauvrissement des statistiques demographiques Sovietiques," *Population* 37 (1982), pp. 655–62.

through factors not usually considered in modern analyses of Western nations—the inability of men to protect their families, the inability of families to help individual members against the power of the state, the lack of trust, and the general failure of small social organizations to prosper. That is, in response to continued governmental repression, more people eventually sought their own interest, rather than that of their families.

Soviet Russia was a great social experiment, but like other unique experiments it has no parallel control population. Consequently, it is unlikely that we shall ever be able to decipher precisely what that experiment teaches us. Recent Russian family history is full of ironies, and I shall note a few. The years immediately after the Revolution were a period calling for freedom and equality and causing extreme social disruption. Divorce rates generally rise during such a period. Indeed, it is estimated that by 1922 there were some 9 million abandoned children in Russia, and the divorce rate in Moscow and Leningrad probably rose to levels unprecedented even in the United States and Sweden. A study made in 1929 in Moscow reported that there were four divorces for every five marriages.[2] At that time it was alleged that "postcard divorces" were easy to get, and innumerable dissolutions occurred without even that minimal civility between spouses. Marriage then was not a safe haven. In any event, though the reports may be shaky, they make such a dramatic story that they should not be examined as pitilessly as more recent facts in these less troubling times.

In the West, the steady increase of women in the work force and the sudden rise of divorce beginning in the mid-1960s seem to prove, in the view of many analysts, that when women work the divorce rate climbs; presumably, they are no longer as tolerant of their lot when they have an alternative. On the other hand, women were pressed into labor service in the Soviet Union from the very beginning, as an expression of the ideology of equality. For many years, almost all Russian women have been in the labor force, working full-time. At the present time about 50 percent of the labor force is made up of women. However, the most precipitate rise in the divorce rate occurred in recent times, in the 1960s and 1970s. Barbara A. Anderson states that the rise in 1966 occurred because a liberalizing divorce law went into effect then, making divorce easier. However, the rates continued upward.[3] In the 1980s, the rates were stable for a while. Thus the mere fact that

2. Helene Yvert-Jalu, "L'histoire du divorce en Russie Sovietique," *Population* 1 (1981), p. 51. For a description of the turmoil in the family in the immediate post-revolutionary period, see H. Kent Geiger, *The Family in Soviet Russia* (Cambridge: Harvard University Press, 1968), ch. 3.

3. Barbara A. Anderson, "Changes in Marriage and Marital Dissolution in the Soviet Union," in L. T. Ruzicka, ed., *Nuptiality and Fertility* (Liege: International Union for the Scientific Study of Population, 1979), p. 134.

women became a large part of the work force does not seem to have changed the divorce rate in any fundamental way.

On the other hand, there is much evidence that Russian women view their work as not at all a movement toward equality; it has been reported that some laugh at the notion of "feminism" as something that was tried in Russia, and it failed. In fact, as is true in other countries, equality was too daring even to be tried. Russian women have carried a much heavier burden than Western women since they were expected to work full time, shop under difficult circumstances, and do nearly all the domestic work with almost no "labor-saving" devices. Their total work load is many hours longer than that of men, they sleep less, and they have fewer hours in which to develop their own careers.[4]

Experiments in reducing women's total work hours simply gave them more time to do more housework. It is hard to believe that the experimenters thought men would leap to help more around the house, to permit their wives to use that extra time for their own education, self-improvement, and leisure. In any event, the men did not do so. As one divorced woman expressed it in a letter published in the press, "Why should I [marry again]? Having a husband is like having another baby in the apartment."[5]

At the same time, Russian women are pressed into "women's occupations" far more than Western women are, and a very high proportion of those jobs are in the low-wage sector of manual labor. Women's jobs have long included such tasks as sweeping streets, which are thought of elsewhere as the province of men. Women seem to have been especially excluded from the higher ranks of occupations. From the 1960s on, this kind of sex segregation increased.[6] The inequality is not caused by a great discrepancy in education: in the 1970s, 66 percent of all Russian women and 40 percent of those with secondary and higher education were in lower-skilled industrial jobs.[7] Consequently, the argument could equally be made that the higher divorce rates are really a way of escaping from the intolerable burden of the double job.

Western analysts have often failed to recognize that the sometimes arbitrary revisions of the Russian family codes were not an outgrowth of the heady debates of the period immediately after the revolution, when freedom was the watchword and the principle that sex was a private affair, somewhat like having a drink of water, became a widespread slogan if not a policy. The

4. E. V. Porokhniuk and M. S. Shepeleva, "How Working Women Combine Work and Household Duties," in Gail W. Lapidus, ed., *Women, Work and Family in the Soviet Union* (Armonk, N.Y.: Sharpe, 1982), pp. 270ff.

5. Quoted in Mary Ellen Fischer, "Women," in James Cracraft, ed., *The Soviet Union* (Chicago: University of Chicago Press, 1988), p. 337.

6. Ibid., pp. 333–35.

7. Gail W. Lapidus, "Introduction," in Cracraft, *Soviet Union* p. xix.

state instead was much more focused on two large goals, especially after the first several precarious years: the maintenance of a high birthrate in order to provide manpower for defense forces and industrialization, and the maintenance of a stable family unit to avoid bureaucratic anomalies and housing problems (as in China after 1953). The government failed in both goals.

More broadly, in the socialist countries the family was an area of active political policy.[8] It can be argued, of course, that even when a nation does not set a specific family program in motion, it is nevertheless engaged in some kind of "policy"—even if it claims to have none and all of these countries consciously intervened to change the family in ideologically explicit ways.

Article 53 of the 1977 Constitution under Brezhnev specifically notes that the Soviet family is under the protection of the state, which shows its concern through child-care institutions and services, child-birth allowances, privileges for large families, and other measures.[9] It is fair to say that these pronouncements and efforts were largely aimed at encouraging women to be more traditional mothers (except, of course, for the small additional obligation of holding full-time jobs as well). For Gorbachev, too, the problem has been to enable women to return to their true mission, the home.[10]

Of course, this is different from the situation in most other nations only in its arbitrariness and intensity. When nations intervene in family behavior, they generally do not aim at making the family itself work better. Instead, they aim at other goals—military, manpower, religious, and so on—and the family is seen as a mere instrument for those goals.[11] Since Russia wanted so many things from its family system, it continued to develop comprehensive programs of intervention in many arenas and used the mass media for a continual propaganda barrage aimed at eliciting conformity. It is entirely possible that the ideals presented in this propaganda were not far from the ideals of most Russians, but of course these ideals would have been very difficult to achieve under even supportive conditions, much less the deprived circumstances of Soviet families of the past generations.[12]

8. For an analysis of the relationship between political policy and the family, see Gary L. Bowen, "The Evolution of Soviet Family Policy: Female Liberation *vs.* Social Cohesion," *J. Comparative Family Studies* 14 (1983), pp. 299–313; and Helene Yvert-Jalu, "L'histoire du divorce en Russie sovietique. Les rapports avec la politique familial et les realités sociales," *Population* 36 (1981), pp. 41–61.

9. Peter H. Juviler, "The Family in the Soviet System," *Paper No. 3, Karl Beck Papers* (Pittsburgh: University of Pittsburgh Press, 1984), pp. 2–3.

10. Peter H. Juviler, "Perestroika for the Family," in Anthony Jones, Walter D. Connor, and David E. Powell, eds., *Soviet Social Problems* (Boulder: Westview, 1991), p. 199.

11. See the thoughtful analysis by Andrea S. Sanjian, "Social Development, Social Deviance and the Socialist Family: Recent Family Policy in the USSR," *Studies in Comparative Communism* 20 (Autumn/Winter 1987), pp. 304–06.

12. For an analysis of both the modest feminist dissent and the difficulties of achieving state goals for the family, see Andrea S. Sanjian, "Social Problems, Political Issues: Marriage and Divorce in the USSR," *Soviet Studies* 43 (1991), pp. 629–49.

Laws can control the divorce rate simply by making divorce difficult without at all affecting the forces that press toward dissolution. Thus, after the more restrictive legislation of 1936, the divorce rate was cut in half in Moscow in the period 1936–1937, and in 1936–1938 in European Russia there was a drop of 37 percent in the number of divorces, but the decline was brief.

In 1944, faced with appalling losses from World War II and concerned with future manpower needs, Stalin issued a much stricter family reform, aimed at increasing the stability of the family. Only official marriages would be recognized, and no paternity would be accepted except within a legal marriage. Divorces had to be processed by two court levels independently, both of which were to examine carefully the possibility of reconciliation. Divorce was made both expensive and lengthy. Like nearly all such efforts, however, this had no long-term effect; the divorce rate went up after a brief setback. The effort certainly reduced domestic stability among people in unregistered marriages since a man could then simply walk out. Under the new law, he owed nothing to his wife or to their children.

The social costs of those restrictions were great, and the defects of the law were widely discussed, even before Stalin's death.[13] By 1955 they had eased somewhat in some jurisdictions and under some judges. By the end of that decade, a movement was under way to reform the law. The law passed in 1965 eliminated the large fee for divorce and essentially moved the final hearing from the higher court to the lower People's Court. Understandably, the divorce rates were higher in 1960 and still higher in 1970.[14]

Although one might concede that the ideologically conceived controls on divorce had some temporary effect, it could equally be asserted that the scanty figures on divorce suggest a contrary thesis: that from the very beginning, just after the Revolution, there was a large amount of existing domestic conflict that found easy expression in the new legal freedom, and this could be checked only partially and briefly by later and stricter divorce laws.

The divorce restrictions were eased in 1965, and these changes went into effect in 1966. They were revised in 1968, and the later decrees of 1980, amended somewhat in 1987, reaffirm some of the principles of the 1968 revisions.

The major features of these laws are as follows: First, no fault need be asserted if the marriage can be dissolved by the agency for registering changes in civil status. That is, under many conditions, if couples can agree upon getting a divorce and there is no property, they need not go through a court proceeding at all. Second, a court proceeding is required if the spouses

13. Geiger, *Family*, p. 261.
14. Juviler, "Family," p. 5; and his "The Urban Family and the Soviet State: Emerging Contours of a Demographic Policy," in Henry W. Morton and Robert C. Stuart, eds., *The Contemporary Soviet City* (Armonk: Sharpe, 1984), pp. 95–96.

have minor children, if one spouse does not consent, or if they continue to dispute about the division of property or the payment of alimony or child support. In addition, the husband may not file for divorce without his wife's consent while she is pregnant or within one year after childbirth. These more complex instances are prevalent enough to make domestic disputes the largest category of civil cases in Russian law.[15] Most deal with custody and child support.

If there is no court proceeding but only a civil registration, then a fee must be paid and three more months must pass before the registration is final (at which time a further fee is required).[16] The fee was raised in 1985, and the 1968 requirement of an attempt at reconciliation if the case proceeds to court was reaffirmed in 1987. Individual courts, however, vary greatly with respect to how much delay they will impose and, indeed, whether they will permit the divorce to go through at all.[17]

The freedom and the turmoil of the 1920s led to innumerable unregistered unions and to millions of children who had no parents to be responsible for them. The failure to register unions and dissolutions continued through the decades. Thus the relatively high divorce rates reported in Russia, now and in the past, are only the official dissolutions. Because of the difficulties of getting a divorce or the shortage of housing, large numbers of Russian men and women have lived together without being officially married, dissolved their unions without registration, established new unions (again without registration), shifted housing without official permission, and so on. Thus the published data, including the figures offered below, may hide complexities of a large quantitative order, which we cannot now even estimate.[18]

Tables 5.1 and 5.2 present the available official divorce rates and a technically more sophisticated set of figures based on the population actually at risk (that is, those in the married status). Comparable figure are about 20–25 percent higher for the Russian Republic (RSFSR), which comprises about half the Russian population, and generally in the more developed western areas.

Under the general program of centralization, Soviet policy largely ignored regional and rural-urban differences in customs, and thus the periods of easy divorce had less effect on the rural patterns. These were much more set against divorce, whether it was legally easy or difficult. Consequently, large differences have always shown up between great urban centers and the rural countryside. For example, in 1982, the USSR rate was 3.3 per 1,000 popula-

15. Peter B. Maggs, "Law," in Cracraft, *Soviet Union*, p. 342.

16. *Izvestia*, April 20, 1984 (*Current Digest of Soviet Press*).

17. W. E. Butler, "USSR: Divorce in Soviet Courts," *J. of Family Law* 27 (1988–89), pp. 317–18. On regional variations in reconciliation patterns, see William Moskoff, "Divorce in the USSR," *J. Marr. and the Family* (May 1983), pp. 421–22.

18. For a discussion of these patterns see Wesley A. Fisher, *The Soviet Marriage Market* (New York: Praeger, 1980), pp. 36ff.

Table 5.1: Divorce Rates in Russia,
1950–1990

Year	Per 1,000 Population	Per 1,000 Marriages
1950	0.4	32
1960	1.3	104
1970	2.6	269
1980	3.5	341
1985	3.4	342
1990	3.4	

tion but 6.2 in Riga (Latvia), 5.7 in Leningrad, and 5.3 in Moscow.[19] Indeed, Viktor Perevedentsev stated in an interview in 1985 (without explaining how the figures were calculated) that half of all marriages in the urban areas of Russia ended in divorce.[20]

As to the duration of marriage, Russian analysts have frequently cited Perevedentsev's remark that "one third of all divorces take place in families less than one year old, another third in families one to five years old,"[21] but the actual distributions are somewhat less dramatic. In recent years, about 36 percent occurred in the first four years of marriage.[22]

Russian analysts have reported both a large rise in the divorce rates and a decline in marriage rates (as in the West). In fact the marriage rates have dropped only modestly since 1950, and there was no drop at all between 1970 and 1983 and only a small decrease in the succeeding years.[23] In 1987, there were roughly 2.8 million marriages in Soviet Russia and somewhat over 950,000 divorces.

The continued rise in the divorce rate increases the percentage of people who enter the status of divorced, while the relatively high (but falling) rate of remarriage absorbs many but not all of them; the consequence is that the percentage of those who were in the status of divorced in the 1985 census rose modestly over 1979. That means, of course, that a fairly high percentage of those who marry are entering marriage again. In 1986 divorced men made up 23 percent of the men who entered the nearly 1.5 million marriages in the Russian Republic; the figure for women is 22 percent.[24]

Here we note a small discrepancy in the data on remarriage. It is generally understood that because of the enormous losses during World War II there

19. Sanjian, "Social Problems," p. 634.

20. *Molodoi Kommunist,* June 1984, pp. 51–57 (*Current Digest of Soviet Press*).

21. A. G. Kharchev and M. S. Matskovski, "Family Roles and Marital Stability," in Gail W. Lapidus, *Women in Soviet Society,* (Berkeley: University of California Press, 1978), pp. 198–99.

22. Sanjian, "Social Development," p. 316; cf. Sanjian, "Social Problems," p. 635.

23. *Nase'leniie SSSR 1987* Statisticheskii Sbornik (Moscow: Finansi i statistika, 1989), p. 190 (translation courtesy of Susan Lehman).

24. Ibid., p. 204.

Table 5.2: Divorces in Russia per 1,000
Married Couples, 1958–1985

1958–1959	5.3
1969–1970	11.5
1978–1979	15.2
1984–1985	14.1

Sources: A. B. Kharchev and M. S. Matskovski,
"Family Roles and Marital Instability," in Lapidus, *Women in Soviet Society* (Berkeley: University
of California Press, 1978) p. 193; and *Nase'leniie
SSSR* 1987: Stasticheskii Sbornik (Moscow: Finansi I Statistika, 1989), p. 190 (translation courtesy of Susan Lehman).

was a shortage of eligible men, and women have faced a more restricted set
of choices in the marriage market.[25] It is also generally understood that the
rate of remarriage has been dropping somewhat. However, recent data suggest a more complex pattern. World War II created a sharp skew in the sex
ratios of Russian people in the marriageable ages. Millions of men were
killed, and other millions were missing or confined for shorter or longer
periods of time in other countries. Thus that period was one in which the
available men had an unprecedented choice in the marriage market. Some
"married" more than once or shifted mates informally, and women had to
offer special inducements to obtain a spouse, frequently through public
advertisements. Although analysts continue to refer to the sex ratio as a
cause of some current anomalies in marriage and divorce patterns, whatever
biases exist are likely to be small at the present time. More than a generation
has passed since that period of a "man shortage."

In any event, if we consider a time frame of five years after divorce or
widowhood (the official Soviet data often do not disaggregate these two, but
most of these cases will be divorces), since 1950 there has been a continued
drop in the percentage of men who enter a subsequent marriage, but during
the same period there has been a continued *rise* in the percentage of women
who eventually reenter marriage. For example, five years after divorce or
widowhood, 550 per 1,000 Russian men entered into another marriage
during the period 1950–1954, but 449 in 1975–1979. For women the corresponding figures are a rise from 136 per 1,000 in 1950–1954 (when men
were very scarce) to 194 in 1975–1979.

Nevertheless, these data reveal a very large difference in the remarriage
rates for men and women after divorce. By comparison with Western figures, these male-female differences are huge.

25. For a full-scale analysis of the dynamics of these social market processes, see Fisher, *Soviet
Marriage Market,* esp. chs. 3, 4.

If we enlarge our time frame to a ten-year period, the same trends are visible for both men and women, although of course the most recent ones (1975–1979) cannot be obtained as yet. *Pravda* reported in December 1985 that 80 percent of men and 40 percent of women remarried but did not state how those figures were calculated.

Kharchev and Matkovski make the ambiguous statement that "no more than 12 percent of the divorced men remarry each year,"[26] but of course over a five-year period that might be in harmony with the figures we noted above.

Nevertheless, the great discrepancy in the basic remarriage rate between men and women means that an increasing number of once-married women are without husbands. Since 56 percent of divorces involve minor children (Butler, 1988–89, pp. 318–19, reports 70% for the mid-1980s) and custody is overwhelmingly (98 percent) given to women,[27] they are likely to face considerable financial difficulty after divorce. Of course, the father is supposed to provide child support (presumably one-fourth of his income for one child, one-third for two, one-half for three),[28] but alimony has never been a serious part of the divorce system, since it is assumed that all women will be working.

As against the Western view of Russia as maintaining complete control over private life, many fathers do not pay for child support. To remedy this problem, a 1984 decree announced that when fathers did not pay, the state would pay the child support and obtain repayment from the evading father when he was located. The amounts themselves were small: 20 rubles for one child, 30 for two, 40 for three. To pay for this program, a new tax on divorce was imposed.[29] Thus, as in the West, divorced women and their children comprise a growing percentage of those who live in poverty.

These mothers are also less likely to get help from their own mothers than in the past, yet one study reported that 50 percent of newlyweds think that their parents will look after the children.[30] A study of the "babushka shortage" reported that most older women now continue to work past retirement age and are simply less available to take care of their grandchildren.[31] Unfortunately, the state still takes it for granted that most women

26. Kharchev and Matskovski, "Family Roles," p. 199.

27. Sanjian, "Social Problems," p. 637.

28. Viktor Perevedentsev, in *Literaturnaya Gazeta*, June 13, 1984, p. 13 (*Current Digest of Soviet Press*).

29. Sanjian, "Social Development," p. 317; and *Izvestia*, April 20, 1985 (*Current Digest of Soviet Press*).

30. *Molodoi Kommunist*, June 1984, pp. 51–57 (*Current Digest of Soviet Press*).

31. Sanjian, "Social Developments," p. 318.

will have some help from their mothers. Similarly, though an equal division of property at divorce is presumed, typically there is no property that is income-producing, and in fact it is the court that decides on its division. In the special case of a long marriage in which the wife is within five years of retirement age, however, the husband is required to pay alimony, and the division (as may also occur under some accusations of fault) can give more than half to her.[32]

Of course, lone mothers do receive state support. If they are very poor and also have three children—the Soviet Union was resolutely pro-natalist until the breakup—their children received school uniforms, free breakfasts, and other amenities.[33] If the mother received child support from the father of less than 20 rubles per month, the local soviets could supplement that amount by as much as 20 rubles for each child until the age of 16, or 18 if he or she is a student.[34] The mother is also entitled to ten days of paid sick leave to care for a sick child.[35]

These provisions are part of a larger system aimed at helping children and mothers. A mother who decides to stay home to care for her child is entitled to 16 months' leave with full pay, 35 rubles monthly, from the fifth month of pregnancy until the child is one year old. She also receives leave to take care of a sick child. If her income is less than 60 rubles per month, her children receive free kindergarten or daycare.[36]

It can be objected that these amounts are small, and in the economic disorder after the breakup of the Soviet regime they lost whatever value they once had. On the other hand, the country was poor, and many of the basic necessities—rent, bread—were highly subsidized. Nevertheless, there can be no doubt that divorced women and their children were in a relatively disadvantaged economic position in the former Soviet Union, as they are elsewhere. The state provisions are meager (and allocated to a restricted pool of families that must be very poor and must have three or more children), and the lack of child support and alimony, when coupled with women's lower wages, leave many divorced mothers and their children in real poverty.

In summary, we have noted four major themes in the divorce patterns in the former Soviet Union. First, we have observed a continuing increase in

32. Juviler, "Family," p. 12.
33. *Pravda*, Sept. 27, 1985; and *Izvestia*, Oct. 21, 1985 (*Current Digest of Soviet Press*).
34. *Argumenty i Fakty*, no. 37, Sept. 10, 1985 (*Current Digest of Soviet Press*).
35. Juviler, in A. Jones, W. D. Connor, D. E. Powell, eds., *Soviet Social Problems* (Boulder, Westview, 1991), p. 209.
36. *Argumenti i Fakty*, no. 37, Sept. 10, 1985 (*Current Digest of Soviet Press*).

divorce rates—often in spite of explicit policies to increase family stability by restricting divorce—from the period immediately after the Revolution, when divorce rates were the most permissive and divorce rates soared, to the restrictive laws of 1936 and 1944, through which divorces continued to climb (despite temporary setbacks), to the more liberal reforms of 1965, which permitted a civil registration for divorce by agreement. Since the 1965 reforms the divorce rates have continued to rise in the 1970s and 1980s. Although we lack precise data on the formation of informal unions, those figures would only sharpen the upward trend of marital dissolution.

Second, we observed high marriage and remarriage rates throughout these decades, although the remarriage rate for men is much higher—almost double the rate for women, according to some estimates.

Third, the discrepancy in the remarriage rates and the fact that women get custody in 98 percent of the divorces lead to a large number (and percentage) of divorced women who are rearing children in one-parent families.

Finally, many of these mother-child families are poor and face economic hardships after divorce because:

1. There is virtually no alimony or other forms of income support from former husbands;

2. Divorced fathers often do not pay child support;

3. State-provided child support (when fathers do not pay) is meager;

4. Single mothers face a child-care crisis because they can no longer count on their own mothers ("the babushka shortage") for help;

5. Most important, although virtually all women are in the labor force, because of severe occupational segregation and large disparities in both wages and occupational status, women earn much less income. For single mothers this means fewer resources at the very point at which they most need additional help to shoulder the financial responsibility for their children (as well as for themselves);

6. Finally, the state has been generally unresponsive to the plight of these mother-headed families. Its safety net is both limited (to sick leave, meager child-care subsidies) and often restricted to the very poor.

Thus divorce patterns in the former Soviet Union reveal a continuing disparity between the official policy of supporting the family and the underlying reality of little social or economic support for the most vulnerable members of the family—women and children. Despite the official pronouncements and the continued Soviet focus on the "stable family" (and its importance for the desired high birthrate), the government was blind to the real poverty that was generated by inadequate support for lone mothers and insensitive to the privileged position of men relative to women.

Poland

Poland is one of the two Eastern European countries (Bulgaria is another) with relatively low divorce rates, which have risen over the period we consider. A Catholic country, Poland first permitted divorce in 1946. Since the 1940s, the divorce rates have more than doubled or tripled, depending on which measure is used. For example, the divorce rate per 1,000 married couples rose from 2.1 in 1950, to 3.4 in 1965, to 4.6 in 1970. Although it may have risen further in the mid-1970s, it appears to have leveled off at 4.6 during the 1980s. Most of the change seems to have occurred in the 1960s and 1970s. The basic pattern of change is presented in Table 5.3.

The views expressed in the earliest postwar legal formulations in Poland emphasized the importance of marital stability. Dissolution should occur only if there was total disintegration of family life and if the divorce would not undermine the child's welfare. The code assumed that someone was guilty, and the guilty person could not apply for a divorce.

The code of 1950 continued this position but developed further the notion of the socialist marriage, affirming equal rights for women, support for various needs of mother and child (for example, protection of pregnant women, child-care centers, and so forth), and the secular character of matrimony. The simultaneous emphasis on marital stability, the right to divorce, children's welfare, and equality made, as Lobodzinska remarks drily, "a difficult combination from a legal point of view."[37] During the subsequent period, divorce procedures often took a long time, and courts in the 1960s rejected 10–40 percent of the cases before them (or they were withdrawn). For most of the period 1960–1982 the fault of the husband was alleged in 25–30 percent of the cases. That figure rose a bit in the 1980s, but only because judges were requiring more "proof" that the marriage was really over.[38]

The 1964 Code attempted to address some of the controversies and problems that seem to have arisen from earlier formulations of family policy: the problem of who is guilty, the child's welfare, the very high rate of divorce among the young, and the conception of marriage in a socialist country. As usual in such controversies, no solution could be found for all of these issues. The new Code attempted to affirm the equality of rights and duties in marriage and also raised the age of marriage for men (presumably to assure their maturity). While the code implicitly conceded the possibility of a "no-fault divorce," since either mate could demand the dissolution of a marriage if it

37. Barbara Lobodzinska, "Divorce in Poland: Its Legislation, Distribution and Social Context," *J. Marriage and the Family* 45 (1983), p. 929.
38. Ibid., p. 935.

Table 5.3: Divorce Rates in Poland, 1950–1990

Year	Per 1,000 Population	Per 100 Marriages	Per 1,000 Married Couples
1950	0.4		2.1
1960	0.5	6.1	2.3
1965	0.8		3.4
1969		12.2	
1970	1.1		4.6
1975		12.5	5.1
1979	1.1	12.6	
1980		13.0	4.6
1981	1.6		4.6
1982		20.7	
1990	1.1		

Sources: Barbara Lobodzinska, "Divorce in Poland: Its Legislation, Distribution and Social Context," *J. Marr. and the Family*
(Nov. 1983), pp. 932–34; Ewa Les, "La Dislocation de La Famille en Pologne: Le Problème du Divorce," *Revue D'études Comparatives Est-Ouest* 16 (1985), pp. 147–57. The 1990 figure is
from the U.N. Demographic Yearbook.

had already broken down, that clause was weakened by proclaiming that
divorce was inadmissible if the welfare of children would suffer or some
other hardship might arise. The code also reaffirmed the principle that the
guilty spouse could not demand the divorce, although this provision was
also qualified. In practice, following this new code, guilt was used much less
as a basis for divorce, and indeed no-fault divorce has come to be viewed as
"proper behavior."[39]

In turn, critics came to feel that the 1964 code made divorce too easy, and
the Supreme Court subsequently issued some amendments aimed at lowering the divorce rate: every divorce case must henceforth be subjected to a
reconciliation procedure; where children were involved, witnesses for both
parties would be asked to offer evidence. These recommendations also attempted to specify, in a time of severe housing shortage, who should get the
dwelling after a divorce. That recommendation apparently was not fully put
into effect.

Aside from the rise in the divorce rate over this period of some thirty years,
and a slowdown at the end of it, various other changes are evident. Divorce
has become easier, both procedurally and socially. Poland remains more
conservative in its familial attitudes than Hungary or Russia, but divorce has
become at least accepted as an action that should not be harshly condemned.

The duration of marriage has also increased somewhat, although the
apparent changes were partly created by a new statistical definition of dura-

39. Ibid., p. 391.

tion. In the 1950s a very high percentage of divorces occurred in the early years of marriage. In 1951, 31 percent of divorces occurred in the first year. That dropped to 6 percent in 1960, and it was still lower in the 1970s. By 1982, only 2.5 percent of marriages lasted less than one year. The figures for marriages of two years and less show corresponding decreases. Recent figures do not permit an exact calculation, but roughly 50 percent of the marriages dissolved in 1951 had ended within two years, and that figure can be no more than approximately 15–20 percent in the 1980s.[40]

That increase in duration, as in the Western countries, cannot be interpreted as a stabilization of marriage, for even by the 1970s it was clear that more divorces had begun to occur among the older population as well. The evidence shows, however, that the divorce procedure is by no means "easy" by the standards of other countries. It remains true that nearly half of the cases coming before the court are turned down or sent back for further consideration, even though one study has shown that 90 percent of those couples do not renew their conjugal relations.

In the past, men were more likely to file for divorce than women. That has changed; now some 60 percent of cases are filed by women. It is possible, as Les asserts, that this change is associated with the greater economic independence of women.[41] In addition, since in divorce settlements housing is supposed to go with the children, the father may lose his right to that privilege.

Needless to say, custody is overwhelmingly given to women (90 percent), and children are involved in some 60 percent of the divorces. That figure is a slight increase since 1960, when 45 percent of divorces involved no children at all.[42] Here, as in Russia, analysts assume that the presence of children reduces the propensity to divorce, but I have seen no technically adequate calculations that would prove that point. The apparent change since the 1950s very likely appears because a much higher percentage of marriages were then of short duration and thus without children. (It has been generally easier to get a divorce swiftly if no children are involved, and thus the *apparent* duration of the marriage, from the date of the wedding ceremony to the final court action, will be somewhat shorter in such cases.)

Modern cohabitation is different from that in the past in several ways. The fact that it is no longer hidden and makes some claim to social acceptance has given rise to legal confrontations and an increase in court decisions or specific legislation about the property rights of the two parties. This is true even in Catholic Poland, which is more conservative than most European

40. Ibid., p. 936; Ewa Les, "La dislocation de la famille en Pologne: Le probleme du divorce," *Revue d'etudes comparatives Est-Ouest* 16 (1985), p. 151.
41. Ewa Les, "La Dislocation."
42. Hungarian Central Statistical Office, *Statistical Yearbook, 1983*, table 4.11.

countries and whose rates of cohabitation are much lower. By the end of the 1980s, the Polish Supreme Court had made a number of decisions about the possible claims each partner might make on the other, or on other organizations.[43] It continued to resist the claims of cohabitants to enjoy the rights of the legally married status, but conceded some rights under the notion of "dissolution of joint partnership." Among these is the right to continue to use the home and furnishings if a partner dies (but not the pension rights of a partner whose husband dies of a work accident).[44] On the whole, however, the court continued to disapprove of this mode of domestic life by restricting those claims. It can be assumed that under the new political regime the rights of cohabiting couples will continue to move toward those of married couples.

Hungary[45]

The increase in divorce rates in Hungary has not been so spectacular (by some measures) as in some other East European countries because they were always higher, but it is still substantial. Table 5.4 presents three measures of this increase.

In Hungary the divorce rate increased from the turn of the century, following the usual pattern of fluctuation—that is, dropping during an extended war period and a depression, rising during periods of extreme social dislocation (for example, after World War I and II). Since the war period, the rates have gone up, although some rises and falls appear here and there, possibly due to other events—such as the Hungarian revolution in 1956—and to changes in administrative or legal rules. For example, a 1945 government decree made it easier to dissolve marriages, and in 1946 the number of divorced increased by four times.

In 1952 a law was passed that seemed to depart from the notion of specific fault and permitted either party to make a request for divorce,[46] but it required that dissolution be based on "a serious and profound cause" and that the court decide whether the divorce was justified. Doubtless this was a signal to the courts to be somewhat more severe in their decisions. The

43. Wanda Stojanowska, "Poland: Cohabitation," *J. Family Law* 27:1 (1988–89), pp. 275–79.

44. Ibid.

45. Much of this discussion is based on the findings of Andras Klinger, submitted to the Bellaggio Conference on the Economics of Divorce, 1989, and cited in table 18.1 in Weitzman and Maclean, *Economic Consequences*, pp. 350–51; hereafter cited as Klinger, 1989. See also Pal Löcsei, "Probleme der Eheauflösung in Ungarn," *Kölner Z. f. Soz. u. Sozialpsychologie* 31 (March 1979), pp. 79–96.

46. Klinger, 1989, p. 4.

Table 5.4: Divorce Rates in Hungary, 1948–1990

Year	Per 1,000 Population	Per 1,000 Married Couples	Per 1,000 Marriages
1948	1.2	5.3	113
1960	1.7	6.5	187
1970	2.2	8.4	236
1980	2.6	9.9	346
1985	2.8	10.9	400
1990	2.4	11.3	452

Source: Andreas Klinger, paper presented at a conference on the Economic Consequences of Divorce, Bellaggio, April 1989. Data from the National Statistical Bureau.

following year, divorces dropped by one third,[47] and rates by an equal amount.

But although such fluctuations do appear (as in most series of divorce figures), a steady upward movement from midcentury to 1990 is evident. The number of divorces per 1000 married couples, for example, more than doubled in that period. At 11.3, that rate is higher in 1990 than those of Sweden and Norway in 1988. The number of divorces per 1000 marriages— to be sure, always a somewhat ambiguous rate—is nearly one half, attesting to at least a widespread fragility.

But that fragility has been evident for some time. At the beginning of the 1950s, the number of people in nonlegal dissolutions or separations was in fact *greater* than the number in the status of legally divorced.[48] That is, a large proportion of all couples involved in some kind of marital breakup were simply separating without divorce, because the Hungarians viewed the law as rather strict. After that period, the somewhat less restrictive divorce laws reduced that ratio, but the absolute number of people still married but separated continued to grow. In the 1960s and 1970s, several special surveys of communities showed this growth, and in 1972 in many rural areas (where Catholic allegiance to the divorce bar was stronger) the two categories were close to the same size. In urban areas it was mainly the working class that separated rather than getting a divorce.

Löcsei's analysis of more than a decade ago asserted that much of Hungarian society had moved from "unequivocal condemnation of divorce" to "acceptance of divorce as a not especially agreeable but often unavoidable solution."[49] Among the forces driving that change he notes these: More people moved to the cities, away from the land, and into factories. Women

47. Löcsei, "Probleme," p. 82.
48. For an analysis of these changes see ibid., pp. 83–85.
49. Ibid., p. 79.

became a much larger part of the work force—indeed, almost half by 1975. Couples became more nearly equal in their marital relations. During these stressful decades there was much upward and downward mobility, altering the balance between husband and wife that held when they married. Finally, he argues that young people especially seek their own personal interests, not those of the family.[50]

A 1964 law permitted dissolution on the grounds that were becoming more common in other European countries—the "breakdown of the marriage," attested by the agreement of the couple. No great change in the rate occurred in the following year. This was also true of the 1974 law, which at least offered either spouse the right to a divorce if married life had "completely and irreversibly" broken down.[51] By contrast, the law of 1986, which went into effect in 1987, did have a short-term immediate effect: a drop in the number of divorces in 1988. That law introduced a compulsory reconciliation effort by the court, a pre-divorce hearing. It also imposed additional costs for the hearing and required an elaborate agreement between the spouses on the placement of the children, support and maintenance, the use of the home, and the like.[52] Thus getting a divorce would take a longer period of time; yet the divorce rate continued to rise again in 1989 and through 1990.

Official resistance to this general trend, however, is evident throughout these four decades. In contrast to Löcsi's judgment, noted above, public opinion surveys of the 1980s reported a general disapproval of divorce, among younger as well as older people. Courts could and did inquire whether an "irremediable breakdown" of the marriage had really occurred and could try to reconcile the parties. In 1984 it was claimed that almost half of the divorce petitions were "withdrawn" as a consequence.[53] Although such assertions may be classed as propaganda, they do show that an effort was made to stem the divorce tide. Assuming that these actions had some effect, we can perceive how strong were the forces toward divorce during this long generation.

The official data on the duration of marriage suggest no real trend over these decades but possibly a slight increase in marriages of ten years or more.[54] Since cohabitation of one form or another has been fairly common

50. Ibid., pp. 91–94.
51. Klinger, 1989, p. 4.
52. Ibid., pp. 4–6.
53. Marta Soltesz, "Hungary: Toward a Strengthening of Marriage," *J. Family Law* 26:1 (1987), pp. 112, 116.
54. *Hungarian Central Statistical Office. Statistical Yearbook 1983*, tables 4.5, 4.10.

during this entire period (we noted above the importance of informal unions and disunions), these small differences may not be robust.

On the other hand, divorces with children form an increasing percentage of the total (almost three-fourths at this writing), and in the 1960–1983 period there was an increasing number of children per divorce.[55] The total number of minor children affected by divorce also increased in the period 1980–1987.[56]

Because the divorce suit requires that an agreement between the spouses be filed on the important matters of custody, residence, child support, visitation rights, and alimony, most divorces (about 70 percent) are at least nominally consensual. The basic principle of property division is like Russia's— that is, joint marital property. The theory is that spouses form a partnership, and almost all property is joint, including intellectual work, such as publications. Whatever has been jointly or separately acquired during the marriage is to be divided equally upon divorce. Spouses can modify that arrangement through a marriage contract. Property owned before marriage or acquired through inheritance can be excluded as well.

The second principle of division is, as in other joint-property jurisdictions, to prevent either spouse from gaining any unfair advantage. The court will also make decisions with respect to dwelling rights. For example, it may affirm the right of the minor child to use the home (and thus, typically, the right of the mother, as custodial parent, to continue living there). That provision increases in importance as the number of children involved in divorce rises. With reference to the general division of property, in slightly more than half of the cases the law itself was not invoked, which I take to mean that a division was reached without the intervention of the court. With respect to the use of the joint family home, just under half of the cases did require a court decision; and in some 44 percent of those cases the decision was made to the advantage of the wife, while in 37 percent of the cases some other type of division was ordered.[57]

All these are major legal changes that have taken place over the last several decades. Hungary makes a more explicit provision for alimony than other Eastern European countries do, but in practice it is rare that a divorcee claims (or gets) any support from the other spouse. On the other hand, a woman raising a child alone is entitled to receive a child-care allowance from the state irrespective of whether she is divorced, widowed, or never married. In addition, in 1987, all the children in divorce cases were awarded some

55. Ibid., table 4.11, p. 46.
56. Klinger, 1989, p. 13.
57. On these points, see ibid., pp. 6–13.

support, but less than 1 percent of the wives and a still smaller percentage of the husbands were granted alimony. That is, because it is assumed that both spouses are workers, the only support claims that are warranted are for minor children.

If the custodial mother is rearing her child alone, she is entitled to a greater family allowance from the state than a still married wife. Indeed, under modern family provisions, in some circumstances the divorced mother may receive a pregnancy allowance, child-care pay or allowances, a family allowance, and (rarely) alimony.[58]

The higher divorce rates in Hungary may be driven higher yet if the usual factors at work in rising divorce rates have their usual effect. During the past several decades the nation became more industrialized and more urbanized, while the percentage of the labor force that is female rose from 29 percent in 1949 to 44 percent in 1975—that is, to almost half the labor force. As Löcsei points out, all these variables are associated with higher divorce rates.[59] However, he argues that a major factor is that Hungarian life has become increasingly individualized, both husband and wife finding their best interest outside the family. While I have pointed to this phenomenon as a world-wide trend, I believe that these processes have probably been exacerbated by the stressful lives that men and women who have lived in the authoritarian states in Eastern Europe have experienced, especially those who lived in the Soviet Union, and I shall comment on it later.

Cohabitation has become more common in Hungary, especially among previously married people.[60] As in other Western countries, it is more common in urban than in rural areas and among people with less education. More than one-third of all cohabiting women are divorced mothers, who are more likely to cohabit than nonmothers. Such mothers may have a greater need for a partner, and doubtless they are also more attractive because they are likely to have the right to some housing. Of course, in the older age groups men are more likely to be cohabiting than women, just as they are more likely to be remarried.

Although I have not been able to obtain adequate numerical data, in all of the East European countries the rise of unmarried cohabitation has been widely observed. As in the West, it is not easy to measure the exact increase because we do not have defensible figures for even the fairly recent past, such as forty or fifty years ago. This situation is more complex in the East because there has been a very severe housing shortage, while housing has

58. Ibid., tables 9–12.
59. Löcsei, "Probleme," table 7, pp. 87–89.
60. E. Carlson and A. Klinger, "Partners in Life: Unmarried Couples in Hungary," *Eur. J. Pop.* 3 (1987), pp. 85–89.

Table 5.5: Crude Divorce Rates per 1,000 Population, 1950–1990

Country	1950	1960	1970	1980	1987–1990
Bulgaria	0.6	0.9	1.2		1.4 (1987)
Czechoslovakia	1.1	1.1	1.7		2.6 (1990)
East Germany	2.5	1.4	1.6		3.0 (1989)
Yugoslavia	1.1	1.2	1.0		0.8 (1990)

Source: U.N. Demographic Yearbook.

been almost completely controlled by the state bureaucracy. For various reasons, noted earlier and also described by many who have experienced the repressive regimes in Eastern Europe since World War II, many people who have shifted their marital status and residence have had good reason to try to avoid bureaucratic notice. In addition, the administrative rulings permitted some exploitation. As a consequence a large but unknown number of people have lived together without a formally registered marriage.

In these countries as in the West, the administrative rules with respect to pensions have also persuaded many elderly pensioners to avoid marriage though living together, for fear that they would lose some of their pension rights.[61] The exact component of these various forms of cohabitation cannot at present be disentangled in the case of Hungary or other East European countries, and of course this means that we cannot disentangle their effect on the total rate of dissolution among all kinds of unions.

Other East European Countries

Our information on other East European nations—Bulgaria, Romania, and what were formerly East Germany, Czechoslovakia, and Yugoslavia—is even less satisfactory, for obvious reasons. However, let us consider them briefly, beginning with the basic changes in the divorce rates (Tables 5.5, 5.6, and 5.7).

In presenting data from each of these countries, I have used the name and geographical entity that existed between 1950 and 1990 because the data, though scarce, were collected for those nation states.

While one can point to an overall rise in the divorce rates in Eastern Europe in this period, the rates in several countries do not show a continuous rise. For example, both Yugoslavia and Romania show considerable irregularities—the latter because of sudden administrative or political decisions under Ceauçescu that restricted the flow of divorce.

61. See, for example, ibid., p. 89.

Table 5.6: Number of Divorces per 100 Marriages

Country	1965	1970	1975	1980	1985
Bulgaria	10.3	14.8	15.4	18.5	19.1 (1984)
Romania	20.4	4.8	20.2		
Czechoslovakia	16.8	21.8	27.3	26.6	30.9

Source: Alain Monnier, "La Conjoncture Demographique: L'Europe et Les Pays Developpés d'Outre-Mer," Population 43 (July–Oct. 1988), p. 899.

As we noted above, the data in these tables are affected by both marriage and cohabitation rates and are therefore—especially during this period of uncertain political consequences—rather poor indicators of the rate of family dissolution. Nevertheless, many of the other patterns of divorce in Eastern Europe are similar to those we have been analyzing. For example, most divorces involve younger children now. Marriages between younger spouses are also more likely to end in divorce. (It should be remembered that "younger" means relative to the usual age in that nation. In general, people in the Eastern European countries have married somewhat earlier than in the West, but their divorce rates were nevertheless lower than in the West, for those younger ages were "normal" for the East.)

An increasing percentage of all couples are cohabiting before or instead of legally marrying, with the expectable complex and obscure results for the official divorce rates. Custody is overwhelmingly given to the mother. Since women in these countries are even less likely to remarry (or to remarry soon) than in the West, the number of single-parent households continues to increase. For the most part they are made up divorced mothers and their children. (The illegitimacy rates remain low compared to the West.) For example, the one-parent (mostly divorcees) household forms 20 percent of

Table 5.7: Number of Divorces per 1,000 Married Couples, 1950–1971

Country	1950	1960	1970
Bulgaria	3.2 (1946)		
Czechoslovakia	3.9 (1947)	4.9 (1961)	5.6 (1967)
German Democratic Republic (GDR)	11.7		7.3 (1971)
Yugoslavia	7.6 (1948)	5.1 (1961)	4.3 (1971)

all households with children in Hungary and 14 percent in Poland. In most of these countries the percentage of widows in such households is modest.[62] The rates still show substantial differences between rural and urban regions and are especially high in industrialized areas, but the rural and urban rates gradually begin to converge as both the stresses and the social patterns of rural life become more like those in the cities.

Conclusion

These changes in divorce curves reflect many other fundamental changes in the social and attitudinal patterns of these countries. They show, for example, the erosion of the line that Hajnal drew a generation ago between the countries of the West and those of Eastern and Southern Europe.[63] Simultaneously, because of the long-term high participation of women in the work force, they suggest a challenging hypothesis about what has caused these major family changes.

For nearly half a century, the nations of East and West have been focused on each other's military and political intentions. The enormous number of studies of the Eastern countries have mainly weighed their possible threat to peace, and even the modest number of studies devoted to social or family life have mostly analyzed its effects on the political arena. This bias has greatly limited our understanding of family life in that great region—and of course that limitation was apparent among scholars in those countries, too. However, as we have seen, family patterns have not simply remained static during this period while the military drama has been playing. These countries have experienced both an intensive effort at industrialization and an overwhelming economic failure in moving toward that goal. Almost certainly the divorce rates reflect the political and economic stresses of this period.

Earlier chapters have considered a central shift in the complex of family attitudes and behaviors of Western peoples. Specifically, as I and others have argued, a steadily increasing percentage of individuals has become less willing to make long-term investments in the collectivity of the family. In the cartoons of the 1980s, people were seen as greedier. At present that is a self-reinforcing process, for as family investments seem to pay off less and less,

62. See Dirk J. van de Kaa, "Europe's Second Demographic Transition," *Population Bulletin* 42 (1987), p. 35.

63. John Hajnal, "European Marriage Patterns in Perspective," in D. V. Glass and D. E. C. Eversley, eds., *Population in History* (London: E. Arnold, 1965), pp. 101–43.

people also become less willing to put as much time, energy, material goods, or emotion into them and thereby they further increase the likelihood that they will not benefit from the family.

What has been overlooked is that this shift might also be occurring in some of the less "successful" countries—those that experienced a widespread breakdown in social services, economic productivity and allocation, trust in the fairness of rewards, political allegiance, and medical and public health facilities. Under those circumstances people also come to feel that their foremost concern should be for their own welfare, not that of the larger social collectivity or even the smaller one of the family. It has been widely believed that such processes occur under long-term conditions of epidemic or famine, but not that they could grow from a longer-term decline in political trust.

Without attempting the massive study that would be needed to test this far-reaching hypothesis, at least a few of the relevant data can be adduced here.

Russia was the first country to legalize abortion (1920) but banned it in 1936 and in 1955 it was reinstated. Most of the Eastern European countries have generally permitted it since the late 1950s or mid-1960s. Although each relaxation was eventually followed by restrictions, these in turn have not generally been successful (for example, Romania 1966–1983). Even the highly controlled nation of Bulgaria reported almost as many abortions as live births in 1984, while Yugoslavia and Romania reported still higher numbers. The data for Russia show a rate of that same order of magnitude, but some observers estimate that abortions may number two to three times the live births.[64]

Many would argue that easy abortion is a mark of some compassion. A very high rate, however, suggests other factors: the failure of the political, economic, and social processes to make contraception available, and a widespread unwillingness to bear more children under difficult social conditions. Thus I am not surprised (although Hajnal might have been) that the total number of lifetime births per woman in the East European countries was generally *lower* than in the West in 1965. That figure has continued to drop (not so fast as in the West), and by 1985 Hungary and the German Democratic Republic had net reproduction rates less than replacement, Czechoslovakia about the level of replacement, and Poland just above it.[65] In spite of their strong pronatalist propaganda, these countries experienced a continuing drop in the birthrate. Whenever the ban on abortions was eased or dropped, the rates of abortions increased sharply; that is, contraceptives

64. Sanjian, "Social Developments," p. 313. The figures are from R. Pressat.
65. Van de Kaa, "Transition," pp. 23, 27, 31.

were not generally available, and many did not want children. In 1985, for example, the rate of abortion per 1,000 women in the reproductive ages was 102 in the Soviet Union and 123 in Russia proper as compared with 6 in West Germany and 11 in England.[66]

From the immediate postwar period until 1984, mortality rates fell for both men and women in the West. By contrast, in the period 1970–1984, male mortality rates rose and life expectancy dropped in Bulgaria, Czechoslovakia, Hungary, the Soviet, and Romania, and stayed the same in Poland.[67] Marriage rates fell in the West, but they fell in the East too. These patterns and many others seem to reflect a lessened commitment not merely to the stability of marriage, as evidenced by higher divorce rates, but to the whole complex of family life.

It is obvious that the conservative moralist cannot ascribe these changes in Eastern Europe, as he or she might in the West, to a superfluity of material goods, to women being in the labor force (since they were there long before divorce rates began their spectacular rise), or to the hedonism of daily life that comes from a rising standard of living—this last factor a bitter joke. I might instead venture the hypothesis that 1) the continuing violation of socialist ideals, 2) the harshness of political and economic life that refuted the state's official, resolutely unreal, roseate view of reality, 3) a widespread and growing feeling that the individual could not trust either the state or other persons, and 4) a general difficulty in achieving what most viewed as a "normal" family life created a feeling of deprivation and malaise. These changes have led to a movement away from the family collectivity, which after all seemed to offer few of its traditional payoffs or advantages but instead a great deal of stress.

My statements apply especially to women, who may have felt in addition that their husbands, who should have protected them, instead bowed to the system. They could not invest heavily in a relationship that in reality failed them again and again. As Nadezhda Mandelstam documents so poignantly in *Hope against Hope*, people had good reason not to trust each other over the long haul, as friends or family members. Or, in words that were actually applied to a despotic African regime, eventually "the paranoia of the people matches the paranoia of their government."[68] Small collectivities wither in such a system because they require continual inputs, which will be forthcoming only if members trust each other to carry out their duties.

66. Juviler, "Perestroika."
67. Van de Kaa, "Transition," p. 37.
68. This is Caroline Alexander's comment on Banda's rule in Nyasaland, in *The New Yorker* (Dec. 16, 1991, p. 64), but it applies to the Soviet Union and to all of the East European countries for much of the period after World War II until recently.

Francine du Plessix Gray has offered a still more radical, but conforming, thesis. She reports (on the basis of her interviews and other sources) that Russian women try to invest as much of their energies and commitment as possible in their children and their networks of women friends and kin rather than in their relations with their men. They feel they are stronger than their men: Whether husbands or lovers, their men could not adequately lead them, protect them, or even support them, and actually added to their burdens rather than lightening them.[69] They show an ironic parallel with the attitudes and feelings that many Afro-American women in the lower classes have expressed about their men. For Russian women, to leave such a relationship was a loss, but not a great one. From Siberia to Moscow, Francine du Plessix Gray describes similar patterns. They suggest a family dynamics from which little stability could be expected.

How far such patterns might apply to other East European countries is not clear. Nevertheless, it seems certain that the repressive state systems generated personal distrust, increased the difficulties of living normal family lives, made it impossible or difficult for many men to be adequate heads of families, tried to persuade family members of norms and "official facts" that were belied by ordinary observation, and did not allow the family to protect and support its members. That is not surprising, since it is a central aim of such a mass society to force the individual to live face to face with state power, without any independent social organization as a buffer.

Under such circumstances, more people would see less advantage in putting all their energies into the collectivity of the family. A likely consequence is that the family is becoming less stable. Correspondingly, it will be most interesting to see how these various curves of change will alter over the next two decades, as the citizens of these countries achieve more control over their own social, economic, and political destinies. With more reason to have faith that personal investments in any self-chosen collectivities, including their families, will not be destroyed by external and arbitrary power, possibly the family itself might become stronger in the future.

69. Francine du Plessix Gray, *Soviet Women: Walking the Tightrope* (New York: Doubleday, 1990).

6

The Anglo Countries:
The Common-Law
Tradition in Different Settings

England and the four nations whose early settlers were almost entirely from the British Isles—New Zealand, Canada, Australia, and the United States—exhibit many of the trends that have been occurring in Western Europe. A separate analysis of these countries may be useful, however, since their divorce patterns emerged from very different historical roots, and they have pioneered in social science research on key facets of the divorce process.

Roman law was imposed on or accepted by both Europe and England for several centuries. But that imposition was never so complete in England as on the continent. Neither the Roman nor the Norman conquest succeeded in erasing a robust and rich set of legal patterns based on ancient customs. The reassertion of those customs and beliefs in the Magna Carta, about a century and a half after William's invasion, attests to that strength, especially if we remember that in that era there were comparable expressions of resistance to kingly power on the Continent that did not enjoy a similar sturdiness.

The Roman legal system and the European ones that grew from it were much more likely than Anglo legal procedure to be stated as general principles, to aim at "rationality," to leave less room for local custom, just as modern European marital law is more likely to be expressed as administrative rules. Legal procedure in England by contrast more often took the form of ascertaining what the ancient local customs were and being guided by them through specific cases, which were decided by an adversarial procedure, frequently a jury system. Eventually, lawyers and judges played a larger role, and "the" law became the accumulated decisions that were remembered and annotated over the years.

The incorporation of Catholic ecclesiastical law into secular family law occurred in England, as well as on the Continent, until Henry VIII (1509–1547) and to a large extent continued after that, since the Anglican Church remained part of the national legal system. The break with the Church when Henry insisted on his right to divorce was, however, in harmony with the Anglo pattern of viewing each case as having its own peculiarities, to be weighed in its own right. Even that spectacular case was not seen as a *general* principle. For though divorce could be said to be possible, on the basis of that kingly example, in the period 1670–1857 there were only 375 divorces in all of England, about two a year.[1] Almost all of them involved great families and were thus "special cases." Even the 1857 law merely permitted divorce through court proceedings rather than an Act of Parliament while stipulating, or continuing, rather serious grounds for it.

Because the other countries we consider here were all English colonies, we might expect that the earlier developments in their family laws would have been shaped by frontier life (as in some of the western states of the United States, which usually gave more freedom to women). However, the British rulers simply imposed the Anglo common law in each of them. That was hardly a controversial step, since the settlers had taken it for granted throughout their lives. Nor did the American Revolution seek a new, rationally chosen legal path. The leading lawyers of its first generation were mostly trained in London, and the authorities they cited were British.

Of course, that very tradition, based on a respect for local customs, specific cases, and the accumulation of decisions, ultimately guarantees a divergence from the rules followed in the mother country. In the sphere of political and social patterns, for example, the differences are striking, as Lipset has pointed out in great detail, among Great Britain, the United States, Canada, and Australia.[2] U.S. citizens have had a long history of resistance to governmental institutions; Australians are even more inclined to be disrespectful of authority; while Canadians seem somewhat more conservative and more willing to trust their officials.

Thus until 1968 Canada did not grant a divorce unless one spouse could be proved to have committed adultery; and even then the "proof" of marital breakdown remained stringent until 1985. Indeed, adultery continued to be cited in about one-third of all divorces.[3] Similarly, in New Zealand, although

1. Roderick Phillips, *Divorce in New Zealand* (Auckland: Oxford University Press, 1981), p. 17.

2. S. M. Lipset, *The First New Nation,* rev. ed. (New York: Norton, 1979), and *Revolution and Counter-Revolution,* rev. ed. (New Brunswick: Transaction, 1988).

3. D. C. McKie et al., *Divorce* (Ottawa: Statistics Canada, 1983), p. 141; and John F. Peters, "Divorce and Remarriage," in G. N. Ramu, ed., *Marriage and the Family in Canada Today* (Scarborough, Ontario: Prentice-Hall Canada, 1989), p. 220.

the 1968 Marital Proceedings Act did reduce the waiting period from three years to two in the case of desertion, no major liberalization of divorce occurred until the Marital Proceedings Act of 1980.[4] Until recently New Zealand was seen as a model of agrarian middle-class life, and in the late nineteenth century every proposed modification of divorce law was strongly protested.

More strikingly, the three Anglo countries still linked with Great Britain delayed major changes in their divorce laws until fairly recently (1980 in New Zealand; 1975 in Australia; 1985 in Canada) and only then took the major step of using "marital breakdown" rather than grave fault as the central ground for divorce. All continue to require some waiting period before permitting divorce, but essentially "fault" does not have to be proved now. All continue an adversarial system with judges and lawyers, and in all of them (with the recent, emerging exception of Australia) the "agreement" between husband and wife is likely to be a package agreed upon between lawyers rather than imposed by administrative rules.

On the other hand, the United States is the only major industrial nation that has no general allowance program for families with children, and no national medical insurance system.[5] In contrast with that pattern of "libertarianism," leaving every person to fend for himself, Canada has a strong state, bent toward communitarianism and group solidarity, elite leadership, many church-controlled schools supported by most provinces, more welfare, and a higher rate of taxation than the United States. Thus, among these nations, so far-flung geographically, there are many shared traits, but also many divergences.

Rates of Divorce

Canada began the decade of the 1950s with the lowest divorce rate of any of these countries, and remained in that position until 1969, one year after its first hesitant step toward a "modern" view of divorce, when irretrievable marital breakdown became acceptable grounds for divorce. In that year, its rate more than doubled, rising above that of any other Anglo country (except of course that of the United States).

In all of them, the rates declined in the 1950s, falling from the peaks they had attained just after World War II. At that time, as after other large-scale wars, marriages that had dissolved informally during the war were legally

4. Gordon A. Carmichael, "Remarriage among Divorced Persons in New Zealand," *Australian Journal of Social Issues*, 20(1985), pp. 87–104.
5. On this discrepancy see J. Palmer, T. Smeeding, and B. B. Torry, *The Vulnerable* (Washington, D.C.: Urban Institute, 1988).

ended, reunited couples decided their relationships had worsened, and marriages were begun precipitately, only to be quickly terminated.

Over the long generation 1950–1990, the rates paralleled the increases in other Western countries, including the especially strong surges at the end of the 1960s and the early 1970s. Some of the jumps, of course, coincided with new legislation, but not all of them. For example, in the years 1968–1969 in the United States the rise was almost 50 percent, though of course no national legislation caused that rise. Canada's rate over these decades rose the most, to nearly ten times the 1950 level, the rate in England and Wales rose by almost five times, in Australia and New Zealand by almost three times—while the United States experienced the slowest increase, for its rates rose only to about twice the 1950 rates. Table 6.1 shows these changes in simplified form.

In the 1980s, some small slackening of the official crude rates occurred, and at the end of this period several countries showed a tiny decrease. Many commentators suggested that this might be the end of the rise and that divorces would fall again. It is also possible, though, that the lowering of the rate during this period is merely a result of the decline in marriage rates and the simultaneous increase in cohabitation in all these countries. Both of these changes effectively remove millions of couples from the risk of official divorce, though not of course from informal dissolutions, with higher rates than among legal unions.

The rates per 1,000 married women, shown in Table 6.2, give a more precise figure than the crude rates. Note that with these more refined figures we can still observe a slackening of rates, even a slight decline, at the end of the 1980s. Of course, these figures do not include the dissolutions among cohabiting unions.

Table 6.1 traces these changes in simplified form; it begins with the peak divorce rates of 1950 (as expected, after a major war) and shows the declines in the 1960s. From those low rates we see a sharp increase in the divorce rates from 1960 to 1970 to 1980. By 1980 the crude divorce rates had reached a high of 5.2 in the United States.

Table 6.1: Crude Divorce Rates per 1,000 Population, 1950–1990

	1950	1960	1970	1980	1980s
Australia	.90	.65	.97	2.7	2.5 (1989)
Canada	.39	.39	1.4	2.6	3.0 (1987)
New Zealand	.85	.69	1.1	2.1	2.6 (1989)
United States	2.6	2.2	3.4	5.2	4.7 (1990)
England and Wales	.69	.51	1.2	3.0	2.9 (1989)

Sources: U.N. Demographic Yearbook, 1958, 1969, 1984, 1988, 1990 and other official statistical publications.

Table 6.2: Divorces per 1,000 Married Women, 1950–1990

	1950	1960	1970	1980	1980s
Australia	3.6 (1954)	3.9 (1961)	4.3 (1971)	12.1 (1981)	10.8 (1989)
Canada	1.7 (1951)	1.6 (1961)	5.5 (1971)	11.3 (1981)	12.4 (1986)
New Zealand	3.6 (1951)	3.2 (1961)	5.1 (1971)	12.1 (1981)	12.0 (1990)
United States	1.3	8.3	14.9	22.5	21.0 (1988)
England and Wales	2.7 (1951)	2.0	4.6	12.0	12.7 (1989)

Sources: Official Yearbook of Australia; Official Yearbook 1985 and Census 1971, 1961, and 1951; New Zealand Official Yearbook (and Paul Brown, Department of Statistics); Statistical Abstract of the United States; Annual Abstract of Statistics; and other governmental publications.

In the 1980s, some slackening of the official crude rates occurred, and at the end of this period several countries showed a tiny decrease. Many commentators suggested that this might be the end of the rise and that divorces would fall again. It is also possible, however, that the lowering of the rate during this period is merely a result of the decline in marriage rates and the simultaneous increase in cohabitation in all these countries. Both of these changes effectively remove millions of couples from the risk of official divorce, though not of course from informal dissolutions (and, as we noted, cohabitants have higher dissolution rates than legal unions).

Table 6.1 also shows the current crude divorce rates in each of the Anglo countries. The United States, as we noted, still have the highest divorce rates (4.7 per 1000 population in 1990), followed by Canada (3.7 in 1987) and England and Wales (2.9 in 1989). The lowest divorce rates among these roughly similar countries were in Australia (2.5 in 1989) and New Zealand (2.6 in 1989).

The divorce rates per 1,000 married women, which are more precise than the crude rates, are shown in Table 6.2. Here too we see the highest current rates in the United States (21 divorces per 1,000 married women in 1988). The other Anglo countries have considerably lower rates and are closely grouped together: 12.7 in England, 12.4 in Canada, 12 in New Zealand, and 10.8 in Australia between 1986 and 1989. Note that with these more refined figures we can still observe a slackening of rates, even a slight decline, at the end of the 1980s. (Of course, all these figures also exclude the dissolutions among cohabiting unions.)

Changes in Grounds for Divorce

A systematic coverage of the grounds in all these countries cannot be done within a small compass, since in both Canada and the United States (and Australia until the 1959 divorce law) the states and provinces all applied somewhat different rules. Nevertheless some brief description should be useful.

Although Canada seemed to be leading the way with its 1968 recognition of irreconcilable marital breakdown as sufficient grounds for divorce (adopted by Australia in 1976; England and Wales in 1973; and New Zealand in 1980) that law also continued the option of using matrimonial offenses (cruelty, adultery, drunkenness, and the like) as did other Anglo countries. Indeed, in the period 1973–1985, there was little change in the grounds used by Canadians. "Marital breakdown," as we see in China and Europe, may not be an easy road to divorce, if stringent proof for it is required. Three years of separation or five years' desertion were still a requisite in Canada for that proof. Thus over that period, only one-third of the couples followed that seemingly easier course; many viewed the charge of matrimonial offenses as a quicker solution, while others reared in a fault framework viewed it as more appropriate. Still others used fault charges to gain some advantages in the settlement. Even the 1986 law still permitted such offenses to be used, but today, if the couple can reach an agreement they can get a divorce almost immediately. That is, if they petition before the year of waiting is over they might be divorced when the period is completed.[6] Thus by 1987–1988, about 80 percent of all divorces were based on a separation of one year or more.

In New Zealand, there was no major liberalization of divorce until 1980, when it followed the Canada 1968 law and reduced the waiting period before a petition could be made to two years in cases of desertion and formal separation, and to 4–7 years without that formality.[7] A more important step was also taken in 1968, however,—the Domestic Purposes Benefit Act. Even women who had been separated from their husbands, not only those who were widowed or deserted, could receive state assistance if necessary. By the time of the 1980 act, which (like the 1975 Act in Australia) simply accepted a single ground, the irreconcilable breakdown of marriage, divorce had become common in New Zealand. Living apart for two years is all that is legally required for the purpose, and the other party cannot prevent it. It is, in effect, a slow "no-fault" divorce.

In Australia the effect of the new law in 1976 was a rise from 7.3 divorces per 1,000 married women to 19.2 in the following year when it took effect.[8] Since the law required only a waiting period, the jump was made up largely of people who had already completed that wait; after that the rate fell until the early 1980s,[9] when it began to rise once more.

In England and Wales, the Marital Proceedings Act of 1969 began a series of changes embodied in subsequent legislation (effective in 1973), which wee stimulated by and in turn caused much public debate and family research. This sociolegal debate continued through the 1980s. The trend was toward less stringent grounds for divorce, and increasing attention to the problems of economic settlements after divorce. The 1969 law permitted divorce on the basis of separation, but it did not lead to amicable proceedings, and fault continued to be alleged even after the Matrimonial Act of

6. *Health Reports,* supplement no. 17, 1990, vol. 2, no. 1, "Divorces 1987–1988," (Ottawa: Statistics Canada), pp. 34–37. On these points, see John F. Peters, "Divorce and Remarriage," pp. 220, 221.

7. Carmichael, "Remarriage," p. 88.

8. Phillips, *Divorce,* p. 47.

9. Carmichael, "Remarriage," p. 102.

1984: in 1987, some three-quarters of all divorce petitions alleged the faults of adultery, "behavior" (in effect, "cruelty"), or desertion.[10]

Indeed, from 1950 to 1971, when most of the new provisions were finally in place, the charge of adultery was made in 50–70 percent of the cases filed by husbands and 37–47 percent of those filed by the wife. Charges of desertion continued to be high until the end of the 1960s (one-half to one-fourth of the cases). By the 1970s, desertion as a charge by either spouse dropped to very low percentages.[11] By contrast, allegations of cruelty ("behavior") rose threefold between 1950 and 1986, to include about half of all cases.

While some people who charge their spouses with adultery or cruel behavior may in fact believe that their spouses are guilty of such marital misconduct, the large number of fault-based divorces may also be explained by the fact that this is the quickest route to getting a divorce in England and Wales. A fault charge may be heard as soon as a hearing can be scheduled— in contrast to divorces by agreement, which require a two-year separation, and those without an agreement, which require a five-year separation.

From the 1950s on, legal aid from the state was used by English wives in about 70 percent of their petitions (Stone, pp. 437–88). A similar program was begun in the United States in the 1970s, as part of an expanding poverty-law program. It was thought that the poor most needed help in problems relating to landlords and business debts, but instead the greatest demand was from wives who wanted legal help in getting out of a marriage, or relief from a difficult husband. The American response was to make some effort to restrict the number of cases (for example, to those in which there was physical violence), since otherwise the government would be charged with aiding the dissolution of marriage.

The basic ground in England and Wales is the same in all cases. The breakdown of the marriage is "proved" by (1) any of the three older faults (adultery, desertion, or "behavior"); (2) two years' separation with an agreement between the spouses; or (3) five years' separation without such an agreement. These grounds do not require, however, and in practice discourage, a court fight or even an appearance. Most divorces occur instead through a "special procedure." One party fills in a form stating the presumed facts, and this is considered by a judicial officer. The other party can legally resist the petition, but lawyers will advise against it. The state will only rarely give any financial support for such a fight, and as a practical matter it would be useless in the long run.[12]

10. On these points see the "Background Materials" by Mavis Maclean and John Eekelaar, Bellaggio Conference, 1990.

11. Lawrence Stone, *Road to Divorce* (New York: Oxford University Press, 1990), pp. 440–41.

12. Maclean and Eekelaar, 1990.; see also G. C. Davis and M. Murch, *Grounds for Divorce* (New York: Oxford University Press, 1988).

Thus, though in a formal sense some fault may still be charged, in the usual course of events the allegation now is no more than a clerical necessity. Moreover, except in extreme cases, courts will not consider fault in cases of custody or support for wives and children. Nevertheless, in 1985, only about 22 percent of all divorce cases were based simply on separation with mutual consent.[13]

Canada, too, moved toward less severe rules for divorce through the introduction in 1968 of marital breakdown as grounds,[14] in addition to the usual marital offenses. Breakdown was to be shown by a separation for three years, desertion for five years, or addiction to alcohol. It was not until 1986 that a Canadian variety of no-fault divorce was possible—that is, one year of separation, or a separation with agreement, which could presumably be granted as soon as the year was over. Legally, the couple might apply together and get a divorce as soon as the court convened.

Matrimonial offense may still be used for divorce in Canada, however, as in England and Wales. Indeed, in the period 1973–1985, divorces granted on the grounds of separation alone remained steady at about one-third of all cases. (Again, this process was slower and took at least three years.) The effect of the 1985–1986 law was quick and decisive: once separation for only one year was the basis for divorce, it became the choice of four-fifths of the couples obtaining a divorce between 1987 and 1988.[15]

Although liberalization of divorce law occurred still later in New Zealand, in the Family Proceedings Act of 1980, important steps toward it took place in 1968. One was an act that reduced the waiting period, as noted earlier.[16] The more significant change was the Domestic Purposes Benefits Act, which granted financial support from the state to all women in need, whether widowed, divorced, deserted, or separated. The number who sought that help increased fourteenfold in ten years. The possibility of state support and the increasing number of wives taking jobs probably led more women to utilize the available legal grounds and also assured husbands that very likely they would not have to bear the full financial consequences of divorce. Thus the political pressure to ease the laws increased. The 1980 act was the first major liberalization of divorce, in effect making irreconcilable breakdown of the marriage the only ground: living apart for two years with legal dissolution an automatic procedure.[17]

13. Divorce Series FM2, no. 12, *1985 Marriage and Divorce Statistics* (London: Office of Censuses and Surveys), p. 99, table 4.6.

14. Peters, "Divorce," pp. 210–11.

15. *Health Reports*, "Divorces 1987–1988," pp. 34–37; and Owen Adams, "Divorce in Canada, 1988," ibid, p. 57.

16. Carmichael, 1985, "Remarriage," pp. 87–90.

17. Phillips, *Divorce*, p. 47.

In the United States the individual states have maintained separate family laws even more than the separate states of Canada or Australia. In 1969, for example, when California became the first state to pass a "pure" no-fault law (either partner could get the divorce, and the other spouse could not refuse it even if "innocent"), New York and South Carolina still permitted divorce only for adultery. All the states form part of a distinctive "modern high-divorce-rate culture" and march in a common direction even though some lag at times far behind the others.

Of all Western nations the United States has had the highest divorce rate, and now competes only with Sweden (and probably Russia) for preeminence in this dubious achievement. Still, its legal acceptance of divorce was reluctant, too, until after the 1950s. The new laws began to appear in various states in the late 1960s, paralleling changes in other Western countries.

By 1990, 14 states had accepted irreconcilable differences or breakdown as "a sole ground," 22 accepted that plus additional grounds, and a majority required some period of separation (often with some additional requirement).[18] In all these states, it seems clear that the legislative changes followed alterations in marital behavior and the actual practices of courts. That is, successive interpretations by courts had already weakened the laws, and the real behavior of couples often simply evaded the laws—for example, by establishing a false residence in a "quick-divorce" state or fabricating an "adultery" case in the states with severe laws. Thus, when the laws were made to conform more closely with real practice, they had only modest effects on the rates.

On the other hand, it seems equally obvious that the laws have always opened the door for some couples who would not have taken that step without the new liberalization; and the laws have also helped to create a set of social understandings as to how easy it is to become divorced if married life seems irksome.

Nevertheless, despite the persistent diversity of the divorce laws in the fifty U.S. states, there appears to be a legal consensus emerging: most people believe that individuals who are unhappy in their marriage have a "right" to get a divorce and that it is unfair and inappropriate for the state to erect legal obstacles to prevent them from exercising that right. Thus most states have adopted some form of no-fault divorce law, which makes it relatively easy to get a divorce with mutual consent and, in many states, only slightly more difficult to get a divorce if only one party wants it. (The difficulties in the legal process, which help lawyers earn a living, vary from state to state and de-

---

18. Doris Jonas Freed and Timothy B. Walker, "Family Law in the Fifty States: An Overview," *Family Law Review* 23 (Winter 1990), pp. 515–16.

pend on the "formal" grounds, filing procedures, waiting periods, costs, and requirements for legal separations and separation agreements.)

While there is increased freedom to end a marriage, there is also an increased concern about the economic aspects and effects of divorce and a feeling that it is appropriate for the state to oversee and regulate such matters. Courts therefore spend more time today on valuing and dividing marital property and establishing orders for child support (and, less frequently, alimony). As a result, as Lenore Weitzman observed in *The Divorce Revolution*, the focus of the legal process has shifted from moral questions of fault and responsibility to the economic issues of the ability to pay and financial need. Today fewer husbands and wives fight about who did what to whom: they are more likely to argue about the value of marital property, what she can earn, and what he can pay.[19]

Divorce laws among the six Australian states were independent until the Marital Causes Act of 1959, which enacted a uniform law for the nation as a unit.[20] The existing separate grounds for divorce were kept, but standards for proof were set for all. Thereafter, anyone could obtain a divorce on the grounds of separation for five years. So long a duration did not seem appealing to many, and thus the most common grounds remained adultery or desertion (two years) until the mid-1970s. The act came into effect in 1961, and was part of a series passed during the years from 1959 to 1966.[21]

The Australian Family Law Act of 1975 went into effect the succeeding year, and the divorce rate per 1,000 married women rose almost threefold, from 7.3 to 19.2, though it fell sharply after that.[22] Essentially the act reduced the grounds to a "continued separation for one year." It required no proof of fault, as fault is no longer relevant. Thus a divorce is possible even if only one party wants it.[23]

Duration of Marriage and Chances of Eventual Divorce

As in many European countries, the average duration of marriages in the Anglo nations has decreased only little over the past four decades, in spite of the strong rise in divorce rates. Often durations are reported as medians (the

19. Lenore J. Weitzman, *The Divorce Revolution: The Unexpected Social and Economic Consequences for Women and Children in America* (New York: Free Press, 1985), p. x.

20. Gordon A. Carmichael and Peter F. McDonald, "The Rise and Fall (?) of Divorce in Australia, 1968–1985," San Francisco: Population Association, 1988, unpublished paper.

21. See *Yearbook Australia 1985* (Canberra: Australian Bureau of Statistics), p. 92.

22. Gordon A. Carmichael, "The Changing Structure of Australian Families," *Australian Quarterly* 57 (1985), p. 102.

23. See also Kate Funder and Richard Ingleby, "The Economic Impact of Divorce: The Australian Perspective," in Weitzman and Maclean.

midpoint of all durations in a given year) rather than averages (all durations divided by the number of divorces) because a few very long durations may give a false impression of what is typical. Thus, in the period 1984–1999, the *average* duration in Australia stayed in the range of 10.1–10.6 years, but the median was 7.3–7.8 years.

In any event, it must be kept in mind that duration is calculated from all divorces in a given year. Some of these unions began decades ago, under very different social conditions, and thus give little hint of the duration that is likely for a couple marrying *now*. For example, in 1988 the average duration of Canadian marriages ending in divorce was 12.5 years,[24] but the likely duration for contemporary marriages is less than six years.[25]

In each of these countries, the average or median duration from 1950 to 1980 changed but little, varying between 12 and 14 years (except in the United States), and only in the last decade is there a real drop. In the United States, too, the figure varies little, remaining close to an average of nine years (and a median of about seven). Indeed, the stability of the latter figure, in this most divorcing of Western nations, is even more startling: This figure has hardly changed for a century. During that entire period, U.S. marriages that ended in divorce lasted only seven or eight years.[26] However, the curves of dissolution for each successive cohort move upward more sharply over recent decades, so that the expected duration drops in all these countries, just as is happening in Europe. Thus between 1951 and 1985 in England and Wales the durations 0–4 years rose from 10 percent to 27 percent of the total number of divorces, in spite of the fact that during most of this period (through the legal changes of 1969–1973) divorces were generally barred any earlier than three years after marriage.[27] By 1982, 20 percent of divorces in Australia had a duration of five years, but 36 percent of divorcing couples had already separated by that time.[28] By 1982, 60 percent of all dissolutions were occurring in less than ten years.

The laws that lowered the required separation period before filing have also reduced the likely duration for the recent cohorts. That is, the average durations into the 1970s and even the 1980s were artificially high, because of these restrictions. Until the 1971–1973 laws in England, couples who wanted to use the grounds of desertion required a three-year wait. Until the

24. *Health Reports*, "Divorces 1987–1988," p. 57.

25. Jean Dumas, *Report on the Demographic Situation in Canada, 1990* (Ottawa: Statistics Canada), p. 12.

26. *One Hundred Years of Marriage and Divorce Statistics: United States, 1867–1967*, p. 52, table 22.

27. Stone, *Road*, pp. 411, 442; Robert Chester, "England and Wales," in Robert Chester, *Divorce in Europe* (Leiden: Martinus Nijhoff, 1977), p. 70.

28. *Social Indicators*, no. 4, (Australian Bureau of Statistics, 1984), p. 27.

introduction of the Australian Family Law in 1976, a five-year separation was required, or charges of fault. In New Zealand, the liberalizing act of 1968 still demanded 4–7 years of informal separation, or three years with a legal separation.

Many couples in each of these countries shortened that time by privately agreeing to allow one party to initiate a fault-based divorce (which often involved fabricating various charges including adultery). Nevertheless, the time restrictions for divorces based on separation did lengthen the average duration of marriage and still do to some extent. That effect cannot be measured precisely, but it can at least be estimated by noting that in England and Wales the average duration of marriage cohorts born between 1900 and 1945, when such severe restrictions were in place (or only grave faults were acceptable), dropped only from 35 to 31 years as divorce became more common; as a consequence, these couples spent over half their lifetimes in the married state, whether or not they were actually living together all that time.[29]

A more hypothetical figure is sometimes calculated to describe the changes in divorce patterns: the likelihood that marriages in a given year will end in divorce. The *perceived* likelihood, even without a specific figure, certainly makes prospective spouses somewhat wary of how much they are willing to invest in the union. As to the figure itself, people can read such estimates—often overestimates—in the popular press, where they often appear as a symbol of modern family breakdown. Of course, the real chances will vary with an array of background experiences and traits—for example, marriage at younger ages, premarital pregnancy, lack of religious affiliation, husband's unemployment, and lower socioeconomic status all increase the propensity to divorce. When divorce rates themselves are stable over a long period, they also yield a rough estimate of those chances fairly well, but we have experienced no such stable period for some time.

Such calculation of one's chance of eventual divorce is really a prediction about the future, but it must be based on past data. Consequently, each analyst will come to somewhat different conclusions depending on which forces are thought to drive future events. Preston and McDonald have used U.S. data from the long period since the Civil War (in 1870 the likelihood was only 7 percent) and report that for the cohort that married in 1950, the chance of a divorce by 1970 would be 17–27 percent, depending on the assumptions followed.[30] However, Martin and Bumpass triple that predic-

29. R. Schoen and J. Baj, "Twentieth-Century Cohort Marriage and Divorce in England and Wales," *Population Studies* 38 (1984), p. 442.
30. Samuel H. Preston and John McDonald, "The Incidence of Divorce within Cohorts of American Marriages Contracted since the Civil War," *Demography* 16 (1979), pp. 3–4, 11.

tion: using a large 1985 sample, they conclude that in spite of the apparent recent decline in the U.S. crude divorce rates, it seems likely that 64 percent of recent marriages will end in separation or divorce.[31]

In the 1950s, only about 9–12 percent of Australian marriages ended in divorce, but that figure was likely to be about 30 percent in 1987–1988. McDonald has reported a slightly different figure—40 percent—for the period 1980–1982.[32] Dumas has calculated the duration-specific divorce rates for the Canadian marriage cohorts of 1943–1944 to 1987–1988 over twenty-five years.[33] The total divorce index for the cohort of 1943–1944 was 14 percent (observed in 1969), rising to 37 percent by 1988.[34] The only figure we have found for New Zealand is 27 percent, based on 1980 data (calculated by Carmichael).[35]

In England and Wales, within the cohort born in 1945 (and thus mostly marrying in the mid-1960s to mid-1970s) some 27 percent were divorced.[36] The chances of eventual divorce rose to 38 percent by 1980–1981.[37] Such data cannot be surprising, since all the basic divorce rates (except those of the United States) have risen several-fold over these four decades. They are nonetheless dramatic, if only because they transform the relatively low numbers for rates *per year* into a cumulative total over a lifetime. Simultaneously they become *personal* data, for they describe our own chances of becoming divorced over the course of one or more marital careers. In addition, they point to a growing social problem for the future, since they ignore the low rates of older couples and focus on the fate of the new marriage cohorts, whose rates are higher and whose marital durations are shorter.

Finally, it is important to note that all of these projections underestimate the total incidence of intimate relationships that dissolve because they ig-

---

31. Teresa Castro Martin and Larry Bumpass, "Recent Trends in Marital Disruption," *Demography* 25 (1989), pp. 37, 40; but see later comment on this larger study in the section on U.S. patterns.

32. Peter McDonald, "What Percentage of Australian Marriages End in Divorce?" *AIFS Newsletter*, no. 8 (Dec. 1983), pp. 5–6; Ruth Weston, "After Separation," *Family Matters* 26 (April 1990), p. 48.

33. Dumas, *Canada, 1990*, pp. 14–15.

34. These figures may be compared with the 25-percent estimate by Basavarajappa, calculated over the longer time interval from 1970–1972 until the eightieth birthday; an estimate for 1975 of one-third and another of 40 percent for the period 1984–1986. See Owen Adams, *Health Reports* (1988), pp. 64–65, and bibliographical notes at p. 66, as well as T. R. Balakrishnan et al., "A Hazard Model Analysis of the Covariates of Marriage Dissolution in Canada," *Demography* 24 (1987), pp. 395–406.

35. Gordon M. Carmichael, "Children and Divorce in New Zealand," *J. Marr. and the Family* 47 (1985).

36. Schoen and Baj, "Cohort Marriage," p. 440. However, the figures for the later years in this cohort are based on 1975 rates.

37. John Haskey, "The Proportions of Marriages Ending in Divorce," *Population Trends* 22 (1982).

nore dissolutions among the growing number of couples in cohabiting unions.

Divorces with Children

In Europe, as noted earlier, the percentage of divorces involving at least one child increased over the period 1950–1990. The absolute number of children also continued to grow, in spite of the widespread drop in birthrates. The Anglo countries show no such increase in the percentage of divorces with children, but the absolute number of children in most cases remains unchanged or rises because the drop in the total number of divorces (where it occurs) is not great. Also, for part of this period in some countries (for example, New Zealand) when older people move toward divorce their marriages have lasted long enough to produce more than one child. That is, a further increase appears here and there (for example, Canada, New Zealand, and Australia) because the average number of children per divorce may rise a bit.

Specifically, over these decades the percentage of divorces with one or more children rises slightly in the period 1950–1970 to a bit more than 70 percent in England and Wales, then drops off slightly, remaining in the range of 66–72 percent through 1989. In the period 1970–1985, the figures for Canada stay the same, 52–53 percent. Those for New Zealand rise from 70 to 78 percent between 1950 and 1975, then drop sharply to 53 percent in 1990. In Australia, the figure remains within the range of 60–66 percent through the early 1980s, then drops to 55 percent in 1989.

Thus, by 1990, we find a convergence among these countries. Slightly more than half (about 53 percent) of the divorcing couples in Canada, New Zealand, and Australia have one or more children at the point of divorce. The percentage is slightly higher in England (66–72 percent). The United States falls in between (around 60 percent).

I am somewhat puzzled by these apparently simple data. At first their narrow range of relative stability suggests a clear pattern, but since several seemingly official sources present somewhat different figures, I wonder whether the "correct" numbers would yield a more orderly pattern, or at least one that would suggest an interesting interpretation. In addition, it seems unlikely that during a period of rapid changes in divorce patterns the percentage of divorces with no children would not also change substantially.

An increase in the percentage with children at the time of divorce might be expected when a larger part of the married population moves toward divorce, affecting more couples who had for some years supposed they enjoyed a stable marital life. That did happen in Europe. Similarly, Carmichael argues that in New Zealand, "older couples with mature families led the trend toward more widespread divorce."[38]

On the other hand, as the birthrate falls, as more young spouses are both working and thus delay the first birth, and as the duration of marriage shortens with each new marriage cohort, it seems likely that a drop might occur in the percentage of divorcing couples with one child or more. This interpretation does apply to Australia, and the pattern is also found in the United States.[39] In any event, a drop in the absolute number of children occurs in Australia only with the drop in the total divorces in the past decade. In the other countries, during most of this recent period, the total number of children in divorce rose or remained steady, with a drop at the very end of the period.[40]

Remarriage

In all these countries, almost nine-tenths of those who enjoyed a normal lifespan married eventually, a total rate that was higher than in Europe and almost as high as in Japan or China. During much of the past forty years, they seemed to lose little of their enthusiasm for marriage even after the daunting experience of divorce. Indeed, a divorcee was more likely to marry than a single person of the same age, in part because some in the latter group were simply less inclined to marry at all.

Glick and Lin report that in 1980, of all people aged 65–74 years who had ever divorced (most of whose marriages must have occurred in the 1930–1945 period), some 80 percent had remarried at some time.[41] In the 1950s, over 90 percent of divorced U.S. women aged 30 and under entered a new marriage eventually (although, as we note below, those over 30 had a different experience). In the 1960s, almost all New Zealand divorcees eventually remarried.[42] Thus the pattern of high remarriage rates was common in the Anglo countries.

Despite this difference, many of the patterns of remarriage that we observed in Europe have also appeared in these countries: (1) an increasing

38. Carmichael, "Children and Divorce," p. 225.
39. *Social Indicators* 4 (1984), pp. 28, 36. There was no change in the average number of children per marriage, 1984–1989 (*Divorces Australia* (cat. 3307.0) (Canberra: Australian Bureau of Statistics, 1989); see also James A. Sweet and Larry Bumpass, *American Families and Households* (New York: Russell Sage, 1987), p. 136.
40. Canada: *Health Reports,* "Divorces, 1987–1988," p. 63; England and Wales: *Annual Abstract of Statistics,* no. 127 (London: HMC Central Statistical Office, 1991), p. 25.
41. Paul C. Glick and Sung-Ling Lin, "Remarriage after Divorce," *Sociological Perspectives* (April 1987), pp. 165–66.
42. Carmichael, "Remarriage," p. 96.

percentage of all marriages contain at least one divorced partner; (2) the rates of both remarriage and first marriage have been dropping; (3) the delay in remarriage has lengthened, and thus the number of people who divorce but do not remarry continues to grow; and (4) the increase in cohabitation, before or after marriage, makes any interpretation of the trends less clear.

Of course, divorced persons are a larger component of the total of new marriages, because they are a larger part of the total pool of eligible partners. Thus divorcees made up about 7–8 percent of all New Zealand brides and grooms in 1950, but 14–16 percent by 1980.[43] In 14 percent of Australian marriages in the 1960s and 1970s, at least one partner had been married before, but that rose to one-third by the mid-1980s.[44] In Canada in 1985, that figure was only slightly lower, 27 percent.[45] The figures are higher in the United States (about one-half in recent cohorts) and England, but the trends are parallel, a several-fold increase.

Such increases do not describe the chances of remarriage after divorce, however, which have fallen for both men and women, though more for women. Through most of the 1960s in the United States, the rate of remarriage actually rose, but it peaked in the early 1970s and has continued downward ever since. A similar pattern occurs in New Zealand, although the later decline was obscured for a while by the very young age composition of the population (who were of course more likely to remarry). A decline also shows up in England after 1972, in all but the oldest age groups.[46]

The decline has been most evident in the age groups where remarriage was most common—for example, 25–39 years—and somewhat less for men than for women. In Australia, the remarriage rate in the 1960s was 473 per 1,000 divorced men aged 25–29 years. That figure dropped to 357 in 1971 and to 249 in 1981. Similar breakdowns by civil status may not be available for later years, but the remarriage rates for the *combined* statuses of widowers and divorced men of the same age dropped steadily from 342 per 1,000 in 1976 to 138 in 1988.[47] Between 1971 and 1986, in the larger age group of 25–39 years, the drop was 35 percent for men and 42 percent for women. For all age groups, the figures drop from 201 per 1,000 divorced men in 1976 to 88 in 1989; and from 146 to 66 for women in the same years.[48] The remarriage rate of Canada was 216 for divorced women and

43. Ibid., p. 91, table 2.

44. *Social Indicators* 4 (1984), p. 28.

45. *Marrying and Divorcing*, p. 10.

46. John Haskey, "Remarriage of the Divorced in England and Wales—A Contemporary Phenomenon," *J. Biosoc. Science* 15 (1983), pp. 256–57, tables 2, 3.

47. *Social Indicators* 4 (1984), p. 28, *Marriages Australia* (Canberra: Australian Bureau of Statistics, 1991), p. 6.

48. *Yearbook Australia 1990*, p. 137.

332 for men in 1951, and dropped to 77 for women and 117 for men in 1986, a decline of almost 65 percent for both sexes.[49]

The percentage ever remarrying—this is of course an estimate, and makes some assumptions about the future—does not drop so sharply, since many who do not take that step in a given year may eventually marry. Afro-Americans in the United States delay remarriage much longer than whites do, but their eventual totals are very close. If we consider the brief period between the mid-1970s and the mid-1980s, that percentage drops in Canada (1975–1977 to 1984–1986) from 75 percent to 64 percent; in the United States (1975–1983) from 83 percent to 76 percent; and in England and Wales (1975 to 1980–1982) from 81 percent to 74 percent.[50]

In the preceding chapters, we analyzed the socio-demographic processes that create the differences between the sexes in remarriage, and those apply of course to the Anglo countries as well. In general, men are much more likely to remarry, and the difference between the sexes in this regard increases with age. Thus, while 75 percent of the divorced women under 30 will remarry, that percentage drops to 50 percent for women 30–40 and to only 28 percent for women over 40.[51] Most women who are 40 or older at divorce will not remarry. Most men of that age, in contrast, are still likely to remarry.

Causal Patterns in U.S. Divorce

In this section I present a brief array of findings from the United States. I believe that many of them may be relevant to other countries as well, although in most cases we do not have comparable data. The U.S. data are enlightening for several reasons. First, although it is unlikely that any European nations, with the possible exceptions of Denmark and Sweden, will ever experience the high level of divorce rates in the United States, they move in the same directions. In many obvious ways, U.S. patterns in the past were harbingers of the future, though not always welcome ones, in other developed countries.

Second, these findings are based on large samples that permit complex analysis of the possible causal factors in divorce changes. For that reason, they can be viewed as relationships that may already exist in other countries

49. Bali Ram, *Current Demographic Analysis: New Trends in the Family* (Ottawa: Statistics Canada, 1990), pp. 16–17, table 2.5.

50. *Marrying and Divorcing*, pp. 14–15.

51. See generally National Center for Health Statistics, U.S. Department of Health, *Monthly Vital Statistics Reports*, Sept. 1980.

but have not yet been reported. Thus they suggest fruitful sociological questions that may be answered elsewhere in the future.

Third, we include some data on Afro-American divorce patterns, which are important for several reasons. They are often given little or no attention in national samples because they make up only a modest percentage (12.5) of the population. On the other hand, because of the great political and social discrimination blacks have suffered and the violent struggles the United States has gone through to come to terms with what Myrdal called the "American dilemma"—the conflict between the goal of equality and the unwillingness of many whites to accept Afro-Americans as equals—literally thousands of studies of this population have been carried out over the generations.[52]

The importance of this group has another dimension: there are parallels with other Anglo and European countries. Because the United States is the only one of these countries to have had a full-fledged slavery system, and engaged in a civil war partly to eliminate it, and because through most of its history it encouraged immigration, the nation has been much more aware of its racial and ethnic divisions than other countries are. European intellectuals, predominantly Marxist, have devoted some decades of attention to the oppression of Afro-Americans, but only very recently have they been forced to accept the awkward social fact that every major country contains some large and small blocs of racial and ethnic peoples that it has systematically discriminated against—the *burakumin*, Ainu, and Koreans in Japan, Algerians and other Africans in France, Gypsies throughout Europe, Indians and Afro-colonials in England, and so on. It is likely that the family and divorce patterns in most of these groups exhibit many parallels with those of similar groups in the United States, and very likely for similar reasons. Thus the patterns of the Afro-Americans in the United States may illuminate those of other racial and ethnic groups in other developed countries, especially when (as is typical) those groups are predominantly in the poorer strata.

In this section we mostly analyze some of the factors that increase or decrease the likelihood of marital dissolution. As will be seen, not all of these are *changes*. Some are differences that have persisted over time, while some of the apparent differences themselves have either changed or been revealed to be less robust than once believed.

The divorce rate in the United States is probably higher than that of any other nation, although it has not risen as much as the rates of other Anglo or European countries over the past four decades. (In fact, the U.S. divorce rate

52. A century ago, for example, Willcox compared the divorce rates of whites and Afro-Americans. See Walter F. Willcox, *The Divorce Problem* (New York: Columbia University Studies in History 1891).

has been relatively stable in the most recent decade.) At the present time, according to Castro and Bumpass,[53] "Perhaps two-thirds of all recent marriages are likely to end in separation or divorce" within thirty years.[54] It should be kept in mind that this estimate does not distinguish between divorce and separation since different groups delay more or less in getting a divorce after separation (Afro-Americans delay more).

Most of those who separate in the United States will divorce eventually. Almost half of all children, and about four-fifths of Afro-American children, will thus spend some of their lives in a one-parent family. A further characteristic of American familial life is that "a majority of persons cohabit outside of marriage at one time or another."[55]

If we first focus on family background variables, the most striking fact is that disruption rates (including separation) are 58 percent higher among Afro-Americans than among whites and Hispanics, whose rates, in turn, are about the same.[56] That differential appears to be rising, but there are technical problems in the sample that make such a conclusion less than secure.

It is now more than thirty years since I first analyzed the relationship between divorce rates and social class.[57] At that time people were surprised by the higher divorce rates among people of lower socioeconomic status. The inverse relationship between divorce and social class has remained strong over the decades, irrespective of the measure of social class. Thus

53. Teresa Castro Martin and Larry Bumpass, "Recent Trends and Differentials in Marital Disruption," Madison: Center for Demography and Ecology, June 1987, unpublished paper. These data are for 1985 and are part of a sample of more than 15,000 women, made up of about 1,000 women from each of the preceding 15 years' cohort of marriages. The women's marital histories were gathered in the June 1985 U.S. Current Population Survey and analyzed at the University of Wisconsin. Much of this section of findings was published by Castro Martin and Bumpass under the same title in *Demography* 25 (1989), pp. 37–51, but my citations are to their larger analysis and to other papers from their group, noted below.

54. Castro and Bumpass project one of the highest estimates of the proportion of recent marriages that will end in divorce. At the lower end is Robert Schoen's estimate of 44.1 percent for married women and 43.9 percent for married men, and James Weed's projection that 51 percent of the 1985 marriages will end in divorce. For further discussion of these projections see Andrew Cherlin, *Marriage, Divorce, Remarriage,* rev. ed. (Cambridge: Harvard University Press, 1992), pp. 20–27.

55. Larry Bumpass, Teresa Castro Martin, and James Sweet, "Background and Early Marital Factors in Marital Disruption," Madison: Center for Demography and Ecology, 1990, unpublished paper. This study is based on a similarly large but different sample. See also Larry L. Bumpass and James A. Sweet, "Preliminary Evidence on Cohabitation," Madison: Center for Demography and Ecology, 1988, unpublished paper, pp. 7ff.

56. Castro Martin and Bumpass, "Recent Trends," pp. 8–9.

57. See generally William J. Goode, "Problems in Postdivorce Adjustment," *Am. Soc. Rev.* 14 (1949), pp. 394–401; "Economic Factors and Marital Stability," *Am. Soc. Rev.* 15 (1951), pp. 802–812; *Women in Divorce* (New York: Free Press, 1956), chs. 4, 5; "Marital Satisfaction and Instability," *Int. Soc. Sci. J.* 14 (1962), pp. 507–26; several analyses in *World Revolution and Family Patterns* (New York: Free Press, 1963); and "Family Disorganization," in Robert K. Merton and Robert Nisbet, eds., *Contemporary Social Problems* (New York: Harcourt, Brace, Jovanovich, 4th ed., 1976), pp. 531–36.

professional men continue to have lower divorce rates than blue-collar workers; women with college educations continue to have lower divorce rates than those with high-school educations: and families with middle and upper incomes continue to have lower divorce rates than poor families.[58] (It is very likely that these factors operate in part by altering the age at marriage.)

That U.S. Catholics are less prone to divorce than are members of other religious groups has often been assumed but not proved, since governmental agencies were forbidden to use this variable in censuses or official records. My own data (recorded in 1946 and published in *Women in Divorce* in 1956,[59] found only a minute difference. In any event, if there was once a lower rate, that has changed. At present, those reared as Catholics have a slightly higher rate of divorce, though largely because of the much higher dissolution rate among those who marry non-Catholics.[60]

It has sometimes been argued that just as marrying early is associated with a greater likelihood of divorce, so might be marrying late, for both are "deviant." On similar grounds, one might also expect a larger chance of divorce if the wife is older than the husband. Within this larger sample, however, neither hypothesis is correct. Indeed, for spurious reasons, the last of these is reversed: when the wife is older the dissolution rate is 42 percent *lower.* That is, the "discrepant" age does not increase stability; rather, if the wife is older then both partners are likely to be older, and such unions are more stable.

By contrast, some "traditional" unions are associated with stability, just as folk wisdom asserted in the past. For example, if the husband is in a higher educational category than his wife, the rate of dissolution is one-third lower. If instead the woman's education is in a higher category, the divorce rate is one-third higher. On the other hand, if the husband is "unemployed at any time during the first year of marriage the risk of disruption is two-thirds higher than if neither was unemployed."[61] This may not be purely the effect of economic problems. It is also more likely that a man will be unemployed if he is in a lower-class occupation. (Since I believe that the *relative* resources of husband and wife alter the chances of divorce, I shall take note of this pattern later on).

Some of the differences in these comparisons arise, I think, because in contrast with men, higher incomes and (especially postgraduate) education among women are *positively* associated with divorce.

58. Castro Martin and Bumpass, "Recent Trends," pp. 9–10.
59. William J. Goode, *After Divorce* (Glencoe, Ill.: Free Press. 1958), pp. 34–36.
60. Bumpass, Castro Martin, and Sweet, "Background," pp. 10, 16.
61. Ibid., pp. 15–16, 18.

Since people who divorce are more likely to divorce again, it could be supposed that even in a first marriage a woman would run a higher risk of divorce if she married a divorced man. However, that higher risk is found only when the husband did not have children in his previous marriage, in which case it is twice as high as in a union with a never-married male. As Bumpass, Martin, and Sweet comment, "a selection with reference to family values is likely to be involved."[62]

I have pointed out more than once that marriages at young ages are more prone to break up, but what is "young" is a cultural definition, varying with what is the "normal" age at marriage in the group. Thus the increase in the average age at marriage in the last two decades may have no general effect on divorce; it merely changes the "young" ages in which divorce rates are higher. Correspondingly, during the past decade in which the total divorce rate has risen only modestly, the rate among women in the age group 20–22 years (no longer teenagers, but young by the new standards) rose by nearly 40 percent.[63]

The general effect of age on divorce rates appears to have dropped or disappeared during this period. This change is difficult to interpret, in part because the variable itself is associated with numerous other factors, such as class, education, job level, geographical mobility (those who marry early are less likely to be mobile), and heterogamy (those who marry early are more likely to find a spouse in the same church, class, or ethnic group). Until we understand that change better, I remain a bit skeptical of its robustness.

Like other Western countries, the United States has witnessed a rise in illegitimacy ratios, and that in turn has also affected divorce rates. By the late 1980s, one in seven U.S. women who entered a first marriage (and 44 percent of Afro-American women) had already borne a child.[64] The rate of divorce among these women is higher, as it is in Europe: They are more likely to be younger, to be lower-class, and at least some have married without as much commitment, if only to avoid the stigma of illegitimacy.

Moreover, that effect, of increasing somewhat the likelihood of divorce, has been increasing over the three five-year cohorts between 1970 and 1985.[65] However, these patterns contain some interesting questions. Some of these unions were formerly cohabiting couples, and the marriage is in fact a stabilizing move. In addition, illegitimacy is not so widely disapproved as formerly, so that precipitate, "forced" marriages are much less common.

62. Ibid., p. 17.
63. Castro Martin and Bumpass, "Recent Trends," p. 13.
64. Sweet and Bumpass, 1987, p. 33, table 2.7.
65. Castro Martin and Bumpass, 1987, "Recent Trends," table 2 and p. 15.

More important, the increasing effect has occurred primarily among *whites,* not Afro-Americans. Moreover, Bumpass, Castro Martin, and Sweet have used a multivariate analysis to show that if such variables as education and age at marriage are controlled (that is, if "class" is held constant), there is "no significant direct effect" of either premarital pregnancy or birth.[66]

This complex pattern shows again the elusive but pervasive effects of class. Among the Afro-Americans who are at lower-class levels, the additional problems of beginning a marriage with a child born out of wedlock do not, it would seem, add much additional strain.[67] The gross disadvantage of entering a marriage with a child can be shown, but the effects may actually arise because such couples are also more likely to be working-class, to be younger and less educated, and to live in neighborhoods where marital stability is not generally high to begin with. Thus, if we "control for class" completely, we may simply erase a complex intellectual problem.

In the three five-year marriage cohorts between 1970 and 1985, both Hispanics and Afro-Americans seemingly experienced substantially greater increases in divorce rates than whites, in a period of slowly rising rates[68] (the rates among the less educated rose even more). In fact, the seeming increase in the difference may be caused by better data.

As is known, on average Afro-Americans are poorer and less educated than U.S. whites; they have less rewarding jobs and higher rates of unemployment. At least some of the difference in rates can be explained by such factors, but Castro and Bumpass have presented a thought-provoking comparison: If we consider only the *low-risk* women (marriage at a mature age, no premarital birth, college education, and so forth), the chance of a disruption within 15 years of marriage would be only 18 percent among whites but more than twice that among Afro-Americans. In contrast, at the high-risk end of the distribution, the two groups are very close: almost 80 percent of the whites and 90 percent of the Afro-Americans would divorce or separate in 15 years.[69]

Without controling for education, occupation, and so on, the rates for Afro-Americans have for some years been about 50 percent higher than for whites. Since so many live under social conditions that cannot be easily captured by such bland indicators as education or occupation, attempts to "hold constant" all the divorce-associated factors will not be completely successful. Needless to say, this also applies when comparing divorce rates by class.

66. Bumpass, Castro Martin, and Sweet, "Background," p. 12.
67. Castro Martin and Bumpass, "Recent Trends," pp. 15–16.
68. Bumpass, Castro Martin, and Sweet, "Background," p. 5.
69. Castro Martin and Bumpass, "Recent Trends," pp. 17–18.

Remarriage

Since the United States excels among nations in the sheer exuberance of its flow of divorces and marriages, many second and third marriages occur in this country, in spite of the decline in remarriage rates. By utilizing large samples, it is now possible to clarify a finding that once seemed self-evident. Even a generation ago it was clear that there was a higher divorce rate among second marriages. They were more fragile. This "common sense" finding was to be expected, since it was thought that people who divorced were different from others to begin with: their personalities, however varied, were ill-suited for marriage; they had experienced divorce once, and thus it would not seem so forbidding the next time; they were already stigmatized and so had little to lose; and so on.

That finding has been affirmed in other countries as well.[70] Thus it is not surprising that in recent U.S. cohorts such remarriages were 25 percent more likely to be dissolved than first marriages.[71] However, that seemingly firm conclusion is now transformed into a surprise. If education is held constant (remarrying women have less education on average) and so is age at marriage, "there would be no difference at all in the dissolution risks." We cannot suppose that this is a *change* over time, although that is possible. For example, I would assert (with no numerical proof) that second marriages in traditional high-divorcing societies may well be as stable as all first marriages. In any event, the fact is that until now, these calculations had not been made in prior research.

To put this differently, but more dramatically, 62 percent of remarriages are unions in which the woman first married as a teenager, and disruption rates are higher in such age groups. When such couples divorce, they are still relatively young in the marriage market, and so are very likely to remarry, but they still have all the traits that were linked with divorce the first time: neighborhood, education, income, and so on. But this conclusion, though enlightening, is not a sociological "explanation." If, when we hold education constant, age alone accounts for *all* the excess of divorces among second marriages compared with first marriages, we still do not know what causal factors are hidden within age. Indeed, the divorce effect of this trait, as with class and race, could almost be said to be overdetermined, for it covers so

70. However, an Australian study reports an apparent exception, for divorce rates of first marriages and remarriages in 1982 seemed not to be very different. Peter McDonald uses the 1982 rates to create a synthetic cohort for this purpose, in "What Percentage of Australian Marriages End in Divorce?" *Newsletter*, Institute of Family Studies (Melbourne), no. 8, Dec. 1983, p. 7.
71. Castro Martin and Bumpass, "Recent Trends," pp. 21–24.

many other underlying forces. It is nevertheless striking that age continues to have an effect in second marriages as well.

Cohabitation

By now, the place of cohabitation in the changing patterns of modern domestic life seems clear enough, though we have no data to suggest what the future might be. People can enter into cohabitation both before and after marriage, can leave it to marry their present partner or a different one, and can decide to stay within the cohabiting relationship indefinitely.

What is clear is that it is now a socially acceptable—though mostly temporary—alternative to marriage or singlehood, even if it is not fully approved in all social networks. In the period 1950–1970 it was seen as a quasi-clandestine union, or a temporary substitute for marriage when partners were not yet free to marry, or perhaps as a common arrangement among the lower classes. Now, by contrast, traditional parents may learn that their offspring take for granted the right to live in a union without a formal ceremony.

I give such prominence to cohabitation in this inquiry because many cohabitors are living in intimate relationships that are similar to legal unions. Although cohabitors tend to be younger, and their unions tend to be shorter than legal marriages, many of these relationships are similar to the short-term marriages—and divorces—of younger couples (where there are no children and little property to divide). But because the dissolutions of cohabiting unions are not recorded, they do not appear in any official statistics and are not included in the divorce rate. Nevertheless, the ending of these unions is part of the larger pattern of the formation and dissolution of intimate unions in these societies at the present time.

While the problems arising from the dissolution of a cohabiting union are like those of formal divorce, neither the laws nor customs fully guide the parties adequately. Cohabitation also affects the apparent illegitimacy rates, for some couples do have children while cohabiting, but the social position of the child is very different from that of a child born to a single mother. Of course, it affects the "remarriage" rates, for many people seriously enter new unions but are not counted among the remarried.

The main regularities in Anglo cohabitation patterns may be summarized here.

1. In each of these nations, as far as can be guessed from imperfect data, the prevalence of cohabitation did not change much in the period 1950–1970 but has been rising ever since. By various indices, it has risen to several

times its level in the earlier period. Census data cannot easily be used to measure the trend, and most of these figures are estimates, but occasional special studies and surveys have been made, always lagging behind contemporary reality.

2. The few attitude data we have confirm what most adults now feel is a significant change: That most people now feel or express little disapproval of cohabitation.

3. The age distribution of people in such unions is somewhat bimodal, since they include those who have not yet married as well as those who have divorced, as well as some in the older years who may be concerned about the effect of marriage on their pensions or property. Nevertheless, in the Anglo countries as in Europe (but perhaps not in Italy), most cohabiters are younger than couples in formal marriages.

4. Being young, they are likely to have less education or training than the legally married, less steady or high-ranking jobs, and both partners are more likely to be working.

5. The rate of dissolution is much higher than for legal unions. To be sure, the figures must be carefully examined, since (as in Latin America) researchers have sometimes counted all endings as dissolutions though in fact many cohabiting unions "end" simply because the partners marry each other. Nevertheless, these relationships are much less stable than legal marriages. Marriages that occur after cohabitation are also less stable than other marriages.

6. This last point is of great importance, because one of the changes in the past twenty years is the increasing percentage of all marriages that are preceded by cohabitation. Until that period began, we know that a substantial fraction of all partners who planned to marry engaged in some intimate relations before the ceremony. The evidence is that in many countries some 20–25 percent of all marriages were preceded by pregnancy, and that pattern can be traced in Europe for literally hundreds of years in the past. By contrast, couples today are less likely to be pregnant before marriage, and more likely to have shared a household. Nevertheless, although at present it is likely that most Anglo couples will live together first, most people who live together at some time will not marry each other.

7. Finally, in all these countries, the prevalence of these relationships and the problems that arise from their dissolution have led to a growing body of law that seeks to treat them more like marriages.

In reading published data on this change, especially in the popular media, several cautions are in order. First, the data are obtained from personal interviews, and some unknown part of the answers will not be correct. Because it is common for people to say they are legally married even though they are not, the surveys may have missed some proportion of cohabitors. Second, the phrasing of the questions may impose a specific definition of cohabitation. For example, the 1984 Canadian Family History Survey question spoke of "common law marriage" or "living as husband and wife," which would eliminate many short-term unions. Third, the percentage of very young people in such unions seems very large because the report may be phrased "of all people aged 15–19 years living together, x percent are not married," but it must be remembered that most people that young would not be married either; if they are living together they are still not likely to be married. Similarly, it is much more likely for women aged 15–19 to be cohabiting (or to be married) than for men of this age, since such women will be living with older men.

The rise in the percentage of cohabiting couples among all couples has been relatively modest during the past four decades, and it is still small in the United States, because the numbers in the new cohorts cannot as yet loom large against the cumulative totality of the married population and because most people do not remain in a cohabiting relationship for a long time.

The rise may be seen best by noting differences in age as well as phase of the life course. In the mid-1980s, only 4 percent of U.S. couples were in cohabiting unions, but 16 percent (of all ages) had cohabited before their first marriage, and 25 percent had ever done so (this includes remarried couples). However, half of the married population aged 30–34 had done so at some time, in contrast to only 6 percent of those over 60 years of age.[72] Some 34–38 percent of cohabiting New Zealanders are in the age group 25–34 years.[73]

Similarly, a Canadian study done in the 1980s reported that 90 percent of all cohabiting unions had begun in 1970 or later.[74] In the period 1970–1974, 7 percent of English first marriages were preceded by cohabitation, and that figure had risen to 26 percent by 1980–1983. If we include all marriages (including remarriages), comparable figures are 42 percent to 79 percent.[75] Using census data, Glick states that in the period 1960–1980 the percentage of cohabiting couples increased more than threefold in the United States, and four-fifths of the rise occurred after 1970.[76] In the decade

72. Bumpass and Sweet, "Cohabitation," p. 6.

73. Anastasia Greenebaum, "Divorce and Associated Factors in Anglo Countries," Harvard University unpublished honors thesis, 1990, p. 44. Data courtesy of H. Bick, Victoria, Australia.

74. Thomas K. Burch and Ashok K. Madan, *Union Formation and Dissolution* (Ottawa: Housing, Family and Social Statistics Division, 1986), p. 19.

75. Kathleen E. Kiernan, "Age at Marriage: Inter- and Intra-Cohort Variation," *Brit. J. Sociology* 38 (1987), p. 60; and "The British Family: Contemporary Trends and Issues," *J. Social Issues,* 9 (1988), pp. 301–02.

76. Paul C. Glick, "Married and Unmarried Cohabitation in the United States," *J. Marr. and the Family* 42 (1980), pp. 21, 29–30; and "American Household Structure in Transition," *Family Planning Perspectives* 16 (1984), pp. 206–07.

1965–1974, 11 percent of married couples had cohabited before marriage, and that figure rose to 44 percent by 1980–1984. By the mid-1980s, it was 60 percent for second marriages.[77] Comparable figures have been reported for Australia, although for sampling reasons they seem less robust.[78]

Bumpass and Sweet suggest an interesting, if partial, explanation for this change in behavior. With the widespread availability of effective contraceptives, there is wider and earlier participation in sexual activity. Before the 1970s, the society disapproved of living together unmarried, because the couple was under suspicion of at least engaging in sex. Now, however, since "everybody is doing it"—that is, sex—the disapproval of both sex and cohabitation has dropped.[79] It is also possible that the AIDS epidemic has made a cohabiting relationship seem "safer" and more "moral" than a sexually active single lifestyle. Because of the fear of AIDS, parents may even be "thankful" when their unmarried children are in a cohabiting relationship, and, ironically, some may view cohabitation as the more stable and "conservative" prelude to marriage.

At present, it is likely that a substantial majority of all people of all ages in all of the Anglo countries would express little or no disapproval of cohabitation. For example, even at the beginning of the 1980s, most young Australians expressed an acceptance of couples living together with no plans to marry.[80]

Since most of these cohabiting couples are young, they are likely to be less educated and to have a somewhat lower socioeconomic position. In the Bumpass and Sweet sample, if they have recently married for the first time and also had cohabited before marriage, almost all of them (93 percent) had cohabited with the marriage partner (p. 7). If they did not cohabit with a first marriage partner, they did not cohabit with anyone else either.

As we noted for Europe, such unions (between young people, of less education and job attainment) are somewhat unstable, just as marriages are in the earlier years. In the Glick sample, 40 percent did not last a year. In Canada, the median duration was three years.[81] About 60 percent of first cohabitations end in marriage. Moreover, although the percentage ever cohabiting before marriage is rising so rapidly that soon a majority will have done so before marriage, those who do marry will experience higher divorce rates as well. That may still be linked to their younger ages, lesser education, and the fact that more of them come from divorced families, for all these

77. Bumpass and Sweet, "Cohabitation," p. 7.
78. Siew-Ean Khoo, *Living Together* (Melbourne: AIFS, 1982), pp. 1–2, 5–7.
79. Bumpass and Sweet, "Cohabitation," pp. 6–7.
80. Carmichael, "Changing Structure," pp. 99–100.
81. Burch and Madan, *Union Formation* p. 19.

factors are associated with higher divorce rates. On the other hand, in the United States, Afro-Americans are less likely than whites to be in such unions.

Thus, the additional knowledge gained from living together before marriage does not increase the stability of the formal union, although common-sense (and some economic theory) would have it so. After the dissolution, however, there is still likely to be a difference between the legal and the cohabiting union. The latter is less likely to produce a child, both partners are likely to be working, the accumulated property is likely to be minimal, and thus the difficulties in rearranging their lives after a breakup are not likely to be so severe. Still, problems do arise, and the need to protect the rights of each person has led to legislation aiming at that goal.

Before ending this section, I want to add a note of caution. It is clear that cohabitation is not the equivalent of legal marriage in any of these societies, and systematic differences are observable between those who cohabit and those who marry. While young cohabiting couples are most similar to young married couples in that they typically have less education and less income when they marry, and are also most similar to young married couples when they divorce in that they are poorer and have less property to divide, even in this most comparable group there are clear differences: those who marry are more likely to have had a child and more likely to have some financial assets. Thus dissolution for young married couples is likely to involve more substantial legal and social issues.

The differences between the two groups are even greater if we compare the breakup of all cohabiting couples with that of all divorcing couples. Married couples who divorce are much more likely to have lived together longer, to have one or more children, and to have accumulated more property. In addition, wives in legal marriage are much more likely to have invested in their families by reducing or altering their employment while women cohabitors are more likely to maintain continuous full-time employment. Partners in a legal marriage are also less likely to maintain their independence in other spheres as well and are more likely to merge their friendship and kinship networks. They are also more likely to co-mingle their assets and money and to share responsibility for each other's parents and children. Finally, in the Anglo countries there are still substantial differences in their legal entitlements to property (such as the family home or apartment) and to the "new property" (such as medical benefits, insurance, pensions).

We emphasize these differences here because a number of researchers have carelessly "combined" data on cohabiting couples who have separated with data on married couples who have divorced to study the "economic consequences of divorce." (See, for example, Duncan and Hoffman.[82]) But it is clear that any analysis that co-mingles these two groups with the aim of reporting the economic effects of divorce on women will erroneously show that "divorcing" women have experienced a much smaller loss in income than in fact occurs.

Post-Divorce Arrangements

The changes that now seem most important to most people in the Anglo nations are not the small but cumulative rises in the divorce rates, or even the "causes" of these rises, but the consequences of divorce and the new policies aimed at its effects. The problems are not new, but they have become "social" problems because they have expanded greatly in magnitude. In turn, the proposed "solutions" of the last decade or so are a major part of the changes in divorce patterns in our time.

The central problem is the increase (here as in other countries) in the sheer number of mother-headed households, and the successful efforts of ex-husbands to evade paying for the support of their children or former wives, together with the simple inability of some of them to pay enough. This is coupled with a second issue: which wives if any should be given support? Two contradictory principles seem to be at work here: 1) the notion that divorce should accomplish a "clean break," and 2) the fact that women, especially those who have spent years at homemaking, are at a structural disadvantage when they try to work in an economy where their average wages will be 35–45 percent lower than those of men. A further issue is how the resources of the family should be split at divorce, especially future earnings and the "new property" such as education, future earning capacity, pensions, medical and other insurance rights.

Because of the political tradition in all these countries, a wide array of lobbies and pressure groups continues to work actively to rewrite the rules and change each other's attitudes, while every change may be challenged in the courts. Men's organizations have publicly deplored "alimony drones," women supported by their financially strapped ex-husbands; legislators have proclaimed that welfare was supporting the new "boyfriends" of ex-wives; and women's groups have argued that mothers and children have been abandoned by men on an erotic whim.

Several important new factors are weighty in this conflict. One is a growing feeling of indignation, however labeled, among women in all these

82. See the discussion of Duncan and Hoffman in note 89 below.

countries, at their structural, normative, and even legal disadvantages, and their increased political effectiveness in fighting for greater equality.

A second factor is the vastly increased reliance on social research, which sometimes even achieves that political miracle, the replacement of rhetoric with fact, often disproving some of the earlier allegations. The tears shed for the thousands of men who must support parasitical ex-wives are revealed as false when it is demonstrated that only a tiny minority of wives are granted alimony by courts, and a still smaller percentage ever receive it.[83]

In the past decade several important studies have not only revealed the appalling reality behind some of these myths but have—to the surprise of the academic researchers—been taken seriously by policymakers and used to reform the laws. When research by Mavis Maclean and John Eekelaar of Oxford University[84] and Margaret Harrison, Kate Funder, and Peter McDonald in Australia[85] showed that the average child-support payment was about $20 a week per child, most people responded with sympathy for the custodial parent and disapproval of the nonsupporting parent, usually the ex-husband. When the ordinary citizen hears that his or her tax burden is higher because the state is paying for the child support that ex-husbands evade, speeches defending the right of the divorced father to "spend his own money" seem hypocritical. Australia has been a leader in confronting those dismaying problems and responding to the research results by reforming its system of setting and collecting child support. And even England, which had been somewhat laggard in the past, moved in that direction after the publication of Maclean and Eekelaar's research.

Similarly, when Lenore Weitzman's research on no-fault divorce law showed that the unintended effect of California's pioneering law was increased economic hardship for women and children,[86] the California Senate established a Task Force to recommend new legislation, and that state eventually passed fourteen new laws to reform the standards and procedures for alimony and child support (along with measures to provide continuing education for family law judges on the economic difficulties that women and children face at divorce).[87]

A third new factor is the response to what in the United States is called

83. Lenore J. Weitzman and Ruth B. Dixon, "The Alimony Myth," *Family Law Quarterly* 14:3 (Fall 1980), pp. 141–81.

84. Mavis Maclean and John Eekelaar, *Children and Divorce: Economic Factors* (Oxford: Oxford University Press, 1983).

85. See, generally, the papers in Peter McDonald, ed., *Settling Up* (Melbourne: Prentice-Hall, 1986).

86. Lenore J. Weitzman, *The Divorce Revolution: The Unexpected Social and Economic Consequences for Women and Children in America* (New York: Free Press, 1985).

87. California Senate, *Final Report of the Task Force on Family Equity* (Sacramento, Calif.: State of California, June 1987).

"the welfare burden," a sense that a large part of the tax revenues goes to help those near or below the poverty level. That has led to calls for a reduction of the "burden," of course, but also to a search for its causes. The most striking finding has been the close connection between the post-divorce mother-headed family and poverty.[88] And the most dramatic link is that fathers are generally better off after divorce, for they can now spend most of their money on one person, themselves, while mothers and their children at best must divide a smaller share among several people.[89] Meanwhile, the taxpayer foots the bill.

In the United States as in Great Britain, there was much debate as to whether mothers should "neglect" their children in order to go to work. It was also ascertained that the poorest of these women would not earn very much in the labor market if they did go to work, since their skills are worth little at current wages. Much more striking, in both Australia and the United States it became clear that there was little connection between actual child-support payments and the husband's income. In New Zealand, that connection had been severed by the 1968 Domestic Purposes Benefit Act, in which the state agreed in effect to take on the burden of support after divorce, with the ex-husband's payments often serving only as a supplement.

In the Anglo countries, welfare policies also discouraged mothers from working, by reducing support payments in tandem with their earned wages, but the public (except in Australia, and in the late 1980s) has not seized on that issue. The focus has rather been on the simpler fact that fathers were avoiding their "natural parental obligation" while taxpayers were reluctantly being forced to shoulder it for them.

Whether viewed as a tax issue, an issue of fairness in allocating the burdens of divorce, or simply meeting the needs of children, support for children and ex-spouses remains a complex political problem.

There are actually three distinct economic decisions that the courts are empowered to make at the time of the divorce: (1) the division of marital property; (2) what used to be called alimony but is now more often referred

88. For a "semi-official" report from Europe, but including the main Anglo countries, see *Lone-Parent Families*, OECD Social Policy Series no. 8, (Paris: OECD, 1990). This volume also contains summaries of enforcement procedures used in various countries.

89. Weitzman, *Divorce Revolution*, chs. 6, 10, has extensive data on this point for every income group and every marital duration. Although G. J. Duncan and S. D. Hoffman have attacked her summary statistics (in "A Reconsideration of the Economic Consequences of Marital Dissolution," *Demography* 22 [1985], pp. 485–98, and "What Are the Economic Consequences of Divorce?" *Demography* 25 [1988], pp. 641–45), the discrepancy between men's and women's standard of living after divorce shows up in every study of divorce in the United States and other countries. In fact, Duncan and Hoffman's own data reveal wide discrepancies between the income of the ex-husband and that of the members of the post-divorce mother-headed family.

to as spousal maintenance after divorce; and (3) the determination of child support. Although these issues are intertwined, we may gain some conceptual clarity by considering them separately.

Marital Property: Its Definition and Division

Marital property—the property acquired by the spouses during marriage—was traditionally considered the husband's property because he was typically the family breadwinner and, under the common law rules of forty-two states, "owned" the property purchased with his wages, especially if it was "titled" in his name. In fact, under the traditional common law rules, the courts were *prohibited* from awarding any property or any share of the property to which the husband held title (even if it was the "family farm") to his wife at divorce.[90] As these strict title rules were revised in the 1970s and 1980s, divorce courts began to award a share of the marital property to the wife, depending on her virtue and his fault.[91] Nevertheless, the basic premise in the 42 common law states was that they were awarding her a share of "his" property. (In contrast, in the eight community-property states, the traditional law regarded wives as equal owners of all property acquired during marriage.)

The differences between the two legal systems have faded in recent years, and the current trend throughout the United States is to divide the marital property equally at divorce.[92] While the principle of an equal division is important symbolically, researchers have found that most divorcing couples do not have very much property to divide. According to Weitzman, the average divorcing couple had less than $20,000 in net assets.[93] If this property is divided equally, each spouse receives $10,000, which is not much of an economic cushion to weather the economic dislocations and expenses of divorce. In addition, a strictly equal division of the marital property may lead to the sale of the family home, which is often the family's only major asset. That not only causes disruption in the lives of minor children but is also

90. See generally Lenore J. Weitzman, "Marital Property: Its Transformation and Division in the United States," in Weitzman and Maclean, eds., *The Economic Consequences of Divorce: The International Perspective*, (Oxford: Oxford University Press, 1992), especially pp. 89–91.

91. Herma Hill Kay, "Beyond No-Fault: New Directions in Divorce Reform," in S. D. Sugarman and H. H. Kay, eds., *Divorce Reform at the Crossroads* (New Haven: Yale University Press, 1990) p. 12.

92. Grace Blumberg, "Marital Property Treatment of Pensions, Disability Pay, Workers' Compensation, and Other Wage Substitutes," *UCLA Law Review* 33 (1986), p. 1251 n. 4. For the ongoing debate over whether an "equal division rule" is preferable to an "equitable division rule," see also Martha Fineman, "Societal Factors Affecting the Creation of Legal Rules for Distribution of Property at Divorce," *Family Law Q.* 23:2 (1989), pp. 279–99.

93. For a review of this research in the United States see Weitzman, "Marital Property," pp. 91–97.

linked to the economic hardships that women and children experience after divorce.

Weitzman asserts, however, that divorce courts are not really dividing marital property equally because they are defining property too narrowly and leaving out the most significant assets acquired during marriage—what she calls career assets, including the spouses' earning capacities and the benefits and entitlements of their jobs (such as their pensions and medical insurance).[94] These assets, she argues, are as valuable or more valuable than traditional property, and for many couples they are the major fruits of the marital partnership. If they are not divided at divorce, the courts are allowing one spouse, typically the husband, to leave the marriage with the principal assets of the marriage.

Weitzman, a sociologist, draws on her interviews with divorced men and women in California to show that married couples consider investments in the career of the major wage-earner joint investments in the marital partnership. As a fifty-one-year-old housewife put it, "It was supposed to be a partnership. . . . It isn't fair that he gets to keep it. It isn't fair for the courts to treat it as his. I earned it just as much as he did" (p. 193).

In the past five years U.S. courts have begun to recognize these career assets and to divide them at divorce.[95] For example, divorce courts in almost every state now recognize pension and retirement benefits as valuable marital assets and divide them at divorce. (As we noted in chapter 2, the former West Germany pioneered in this trend and established a nationwide system for calculating and dividing pension entitlements at divorce.)

The basic theories governing the division of these assets in the United States form an interesting contrast to those in Australia. In the United States, the theory is that marriage is an economic partnership and the "fruits of the partnership" are shared at divorce. In Australia, according to Kate Funder, a psychologist at the Australian Institute of Family Studies, the theory focuses on "sharing the debts."[96] Funder outlines the disadvantages that accrue to women who are mothers and homemakers during marriage and notes that Australians feel that it is fair to divide these "costs of marriage" between the husband and wife. Putting aside the income disparity between men and women that is due to the gender gap in earnings, she calculates the differing effects of marriage, child-bearing, and child-rearing upon the post-divorce earning capacities of women. It is these disadvantages that Australians wish to divide when a divorce occurs.

94. Weitzman, *Divorce Revolution*.
95. Weitzman, "Marital Property."
96. Kathleen Funder, "Australia: A Proposal for Reform" in Weitzman and Maclean, *Economic Consequences*, pp. 143–62.

Alimony and Spousal Maintenance after Divorce

The second major economic decision divorce courts face is whether to award any income support for the wife after divorce. Despite the widespread belief that divorced women in the United States have been the beneficiaries of generous alimony awards (a belief that is probably based on a few widely publicized awards), the vast majority of divorced wives, 80–90 percent, have not been awarded any alimony at all.[97] It was not until the hard data from research reports began to emerge and the process of divorce negotiations was described more fully that we became award of the extent to which divorced men had been able to avoid alimony. But we now know that because men typically had greater economic resources, better legal representation, and more power in the divorce negotiations, they were able to avoid paying alimony to a degree that was surprising to most people.

The question of whether ex-husbands should be responsible for supporting their ex-wives after divorce has continued to be a somewhat ambiguous issue for a number of reasons. First, since women were increasingly moving into the labor market, many people (including some feminists) felt that wives should not expect financial support after divorce. As we have noted, the Nordic countries generally have followed the notion that spouses should live independent lives after a divorce, with no obligations to each other. (However, that belief is easier to hold in a society with extensive public benefits and guaranteed income support.) Moreover, the attitude is widespread that a divorce should somehow end the relationship completely, except for the possibility that wives might receive some temporary help while they prepared themselves for making a living on a full-time basis.

On the other hand, several studies, notably those by Weitzman,[98] argued that a genuine cutoff in financial help from former husband to former wife was not practical under current social conditions.[99] First of all, it is mostly women who become the custodial parent, which sharply limits their possible success in the economic world. In addition, the cost of rearing children is likely to be about twice as much as most child payments. Moreover, a large number of wives are in effect being told that the rules of marriage have suddenly been changed. They had been led to believe that if they did not go into the labor market but took care of their home, children, and spouse, that would in effect be their contribution to an ongoing partnership. Now, after having done so, they are told that they should expect no help at all.

In addition, it is impossible for the break to be complete. *Some* kind of

---

97. Lenore J. Weitzman and Ruth B. Dixon, "The Alimony Myth."

98. Weitzman, *Economic Consequences*, ch. 11.

99. For more details on England, see John Eekelaar and Mavis Maclean, *Maintenance after Divorce* (Oxford: Clarendon Press, 1986).

relationship between father and children—and thus between former spouses—will continue for many years. A simple division of the property accumulated during marriage (if any) and a clean break would not recognize that fact.

Finally, women's earnings continue to be much lower than those of men, even when we hold all other factors constant. Women are more likely to have low-paying jobs, fewer benefits, and less likelihood of promotion. It is rare for a woman who has been out of the labor market for a number of years to be able to step back in and get a job as lucrative as that of a woman who has been in the work force without any interruption.

In light of these continuing difficulties that divorced women face, it is not surprising that feminists are asserting the need for alimony—or some form of post-divorce payment—for three groups of divorced women: older women who have been homemakers and mothers in marriages of long duration; middle-aged women who need to invest in their job skills and enhance their earning capacities so that they can maximize their employment potential; and women who retain major custodial responsibilities.[100] While we have continued to use the term "alimony" in this discussion, a number of states in the United States have begun to use lump sum and periodic payments (variously called "compensatory alimony," "retraining alimony," "maintenance," "spousal support," and so on) as a more general means of adjusting "equities" at divorce.[101]

Some ex-wives will need only modest subsidies for retraining, others need almost total support for full-time studies but for only one or two years, while still others—especially those who have been "career homemakers"—will need support for a longer duration, perhaps for the rest of their lives.

The strongest claims for continued sharing of the husband's income come from this last group of women, who, to use Weitzman's terms, have built their husbands' career and earning potential as the major asset of their marital partnership. In response to their claims, the California Senate Task Force on Family Equity (which was established in response to Weitzman's book) urged the reformulation of alimony to ensure the sharing of all assets built during the marital partnership, including the enhanced earning capacity of the major wage-earning spouse. As they wrote: "The assumption of "self-sufficiency" [behind alimony awards] ignores the fact that many of these wives have sacrificed their own career opportunities and earning potential because of tacit or express marital partnership agreements. Adequate support awards . . . reflect societal perceptions of the importance and value

100. See generally Lenore J. Weitzman, "Alimony: Its Premature Demise and Recent Resurgence in the United States," in Weitzman and Maclean, *Economic Consequences*, pp. 247–62.
101. Ibid.

of homemaking and child-rearing contributions and sacrifices made during marriage."[102]

The Task Force went on to propose that the law be changed to create a presumption of permanent support after a marriage of long duration "to meet the economic crisis of the displaced homemaker and other dependent spouses . . . [to be] viewed as a form of legal insurance, protection or pension for the spouse who has given priority to the other spouse's career and to child rearing instead of developing his or her own career to marketable skills."[103] That recommendation was adopted by the California legislature in 1987 and is now the law.

California has also pioneered in new legislation for using spousal support to assist women in becoming self-sufficient by requiring payment of retraining expenses. Thus, although the issue of spousal support has not been as much in the limelight as child support, it will not disappear soon,[104] because the fundamental structural position of women, especially divorced mothers, in the labor force continues to be less advantageous than that of men.

Australia has also confronted these difficulties. Its social scientists created a large body of research that has made political leaders as well as citizens more aware of the sources and dimensions of the problems. As a consequence, the country inaugurated an elaborate program to solve these problems (which is discussed further below).

Child Support and Poverty in Mother-Headed Families

Researchers in the United States, Australia, and England have found a close relationship between the economics of divorce and poverty among women and children.

In the United States almost one-quarter of all children live in a single-parent family, most of these in a family headed by a divorced or separated mother. (Only 7 percent of single-parent families are headed by widows or never-married mothers.)[105] These single-parent mother-headed families are the fastest growing segment of the American poor. In 1985 the poverty rate for children in female-headed families was 54 percent in contrast to the 12 percent rate for children in all other families.[106] Even when these mothers work—and most of them are in the labor force today—their

---

102. California Senate, *Final Report* p. V–5.
103. Ibid., p. V-4.
104. Weitzman, "Alimony: Its Premature Demise."
105. Alfred J. Kahn and Sheila B. Kamerman, *Child Support: From Debt Collection to Social Policy* (Newbury Park, Calif.:, Sage, 1988) p. 10.
106. Ibid.

earnings may not be adequate to bring the family income above the poverty level. Women working full-time at a minimum-wage job still end up with incomes below the poverty level for a family of three—a mother and two children—the typical mother-headed family of the 1980s.[107] This means that the lack of financial support from the absent parent, usually the divorced father, is the major factor in child poverty today.[108]

There are two major problems with child support awards in the United States. The first is the inadequate sums the courts award. The second is the widespread lack of compliance with even those minimal court orders. Of all children in the United States who were supposed to receive child support from an absent parent, less than half received it. In fact, one-quarter of the children received nothing.[109] Despite an increasing array of federal and state laws, as of the end of 1989, more than $18 billion in accumulated unpaid child support was owed to 16 million children.[110] in the United States.

Since the enactment of the Family Support Act of 1988, the states have become more aggressively involved in collecting court-ordered child-support awards, taking in a record $6 billion in 1990. New mechanisms include garnisheeing the wages of parents who owe child support, using the records of the Internal Revenue Service to locate absent parents, and intercepting their tax refunds for past-due child support. All states must now report delinquent parents to credit agencies. In addition, the National Council of State Child Support Enforcement issues a list and wanted posters for the nation's "22 Most Wanted Deadbeat Dads," who collectively owed $661,000 in unpaid child support in 1991.[111] Most states have started issuing their own lists of "most-wanted deadbeat dads" and staging roundups to arrest parents who fail to pay. These tactics not only generate publicity and public support for stronger enforcement; they also produce payments from fathers who wish to avoid negative publicity. But there is still a long way to go before children receive the support they were promised from their noncustodial parents.

The statistics in Australia are strikingly similar. However, that country has created a much more aggressive centralized effort to deal with the problem. Public concern about the growing poverty among children of divorce and the welfare burden they created was initially stimulated by Australian re-

107. Ibid.
108. Ibid.
109. Ibid.
110. Tamar Lewin, "New Tools for States Bolster Collection of Child Support," *New York Times,* June 15, 1991.
111. Karen Timmons, "Child Support Enforcement: A National Disgrace," UPI wire from Washington, D.C., July 17, 1991.

search demonstrating a close relationship between poverty and mother-headed families. The welfare budget rose after the institution of the 1975 Family Law Act, and there was much anger at the ease with which the non-custodial partner avoided financial responsibility.

Some part of the close relationship between poverty and mother-headed families grew from a provision of the Act which permitted the welfare entitlement to be taken into account when child support was being adjudicated, so that support payments were lowered. As a consequence, welfare was treated (as in New Zealand) as the major support for most mother-headed households, and the father was not required to do more than add whatever small amount was necessary to bring the total child support up to some minimal poverty level. Many escaped or ignored even that obligation. By 1985, almost 90 percent of all custodial parents were on some type of social-welfare program, and less than 20 percent received any income at all beyond the absolute minimum.[112] This arrangement also reduced the economic motivation of women to enter the labor force, since if they did so their welfare support would then be reduced.

In addition, and much less open to solid research, the negotiations behind the scenes gave much greater weight to the pressures from men to avoid such payments or reduce them substantially. As Margaret Harrison has emphasized: "Very few property disputes are actually determined by a judge. . . . The vast majority of people bargain in the shadow of the law, receiving advice from lawyers who, from their knowledge of the legislation and the case law, advise clients of the parameters of any dispute, and of its possible outcome."[113] As a consequence, the welfare burden continued to rise and there was much public indignation at the disclosure that a very high proportion of mother-headed families are living at or near the poverty line, while their former husbands are doing very well indeed.

In the late 1970s and early 1980s, then, the issues increasingly focused on child support, in part because the fact that children were suffering from neglect aroused public indignation at the fathers' failure to fulfill a parental role.[114] Australian studies also found that some 40 percent of all parents who were supposed to be receiving maintenance of some kind received no payments at all, and no more than about 40 percent of all support orders were fully complied with.

112. Margaret Harrison, "Child Maintenance in Australia: The New Era," in Weitzman and Maclean, *Economic Consequences*, pp. 219–32.
113. Peter McDonald, "Introduction," in McDonald, *Settling Up*, p. 9.
114. More extensive comments on these issues are found in Mavis Maclean and Lenore Weitzman, "Introduction," in Weitzman and Maclean, *Economic Consequences*, pp. 187–94, and Weitzman, "Alimony: Its Premature Demise," pp. 247–62; and in Maclean and Eekelaar, *Children and Divorce*.

Wherever these questions have been raised in any of the Anglo countries, the research findings are similar. The "going rate" in the mid-1980s in Australia (as in England, the equivalent of $20 per week) would have been higher in the United States, but the pattern of non-payment of either alimony or child support was general: When 50 percent of the divorced fathers do not comply with court orders to pay child support it is not surprising that men's economic status improves after divorce while that of mothers and children worsens.[115]

Australia's program has moved in the direction of European systems in attempting to work out an administrative procedure rather than force women to rely on success in repeated conflicts in court. The plan envisioned a two-step program. In the first stage, efforts would be made to insure collection of the maintenance specified in existing court orders, especially by making the system a part of the Australian Taxation Office.

It should be noted that this arrangement violates the common law tradition. In all the Anglo countries in the past the court made an order for payment, and generally husbands did not comply. To force compliance, wives had to go to court again. They had to hire a lawyer, which many women could not afford when they were not receiving support. In addition, pursuing the case in court meant they had to take time off from work (another economic hardship) to appear in court. With overcrowded courts, lenient judges, and permissible delays, the price of "justice" was high. And even if they succeeded in getting a new court order, the husband was typically required to make payments that were *already* due. He could still avoid making the next payment, thus forcing the wife to try again. Most women soon gave up the struggle.

In the second stage of the new Australian plan the amounts themselves would be set by administrative assessments, using a formula based on the actual costs of rearing children in Australia. This step was put into effect by late 1989 for the newly divorced. Provisions were included to permit women to work without reducing their total income from maintenance or welfare payments by the amount of their earnings. Payments by the non-custodial parent can be made directly to the Child Support Agency or will be collected directly at the source by the payer's employer and then transferred to the Agency. There is very little discretion in all of this and these arrangements do not require a court fight of any kind—again a major shift from Anglo legal tradition.

115. Annemette Sorensen has analyzed the complexity of this relationship in "Estimating the Economic Consequences of Separation and Divorce: A Cautionary Tale from the United States," in Weitzman and Maclean, *Economic Consequences*, pp. 263–82.

A study done just before his plan was put into effect found that the situation of a mother-headed household was worse than had been understood earlier: Only 34 percent of custodial parents were receiving regular payments; 12 percent had once received it but no longer did so, and 23 percent had never managed to obtain an order or agreement to make regular payments.[116] When the maintenance *had* been paid it was only about $24 per child per week. Needless to say, the newer procedures have created both resentment and satisfaction, and coverage has been very incomplete, but the system does appear to be improving conditions for the custodial parent.

The Stage Two system will apply only to dissolutions after 1989, and thus there has been little opportunity to test it as yet.[117] The payments will be based on the taxable income of mainly the non-custodial parent and on the number of children eligible for support. In addition, if the non-custodial parent has a new set of children, the principle being followed is that neither the first nor the second family should benefit at the expense of the other.

The core of the system, however, is that fairly clear guidelines are applied, based on studies of the actual costs of rearing children, not on negotiations between lawyers, or conflicts in court. They are much closer to the arrangements in Belgium, Germany, and the Nordic countries, which take it for granted that the basic costs of childrearing under different circumstances can be assessed, and that children must receive at least that much.

Only in rare cases will the non-custodial parent be able to escape the net. For example, in the past, many New Zealand fathers took advantage of free entry to Australia. In effect, the Australian government now accepts the harsh fact that the usual social pressures of modern society will not force a father to pay for his children; the government must make that demand so that it has the same legal weight as the requirement that the individual pay taxes. Moreover, the payments will be collected at the source—that is, taken out by the employer before the ex-husband receives his wages.

It is anticipated, of course, that there will be many court challenges to these arrangements, for they go against the usual patterns of domestic law in Australia, as in other Anglo countries. On the other hand, precisely because these new formulas for assessment are based upon rather robust social research, and since Australian indignation at the combined failure of fathers to pay for their own children and the cost of welfare support is high, it is very unlikely this new system will be abandoned soon.

116. Harrison, "Child Maintenance," pp. 224–25.
117. A preliminary study of the successes and difficulties of the new plan is reported in Margaret Harrison et al., *Who Pays for the Children?* (Melbourne: Australian Institute of Family Studies [AIFS monograph n. 29], 1990).

As we noted above, efforts in the United States have relied more on the individual states, but some changes have occurred here as well. If states do not make efforts to track down delinquent fathers, they will lose federal support for welfare systems. Michigan has made the experiment, a success to the surprise of many, of threatening delinquent fathers with jail—and of actually jailing them to enforce compliance. Wisconsin does so too, and five other states have also focused more efforts on making fathers pay directly to an agency of the courts, so that they can be better monitored. In some states with less vigorous governmental program, private collection agencies have arisen to aid in enforcing payments. However, since all such systems vary widely from state to state, the development of an effective system of requiring fathers to pay regularly and adequately has been relatively slow and sporadic.[118]

Such efforts are a response to the processes we have been analyzing. New Zealand, Canada, and Great Britain are moving toward the Australian example, but haltingly, that is, strong enforcement of payments that have been set administratively, based on the actual cost of rearing children. Perhaps the United States is most laggard in this area. Total state payments to children are several times as large as private support payments but in only a few states are the husband's payments based on systematic data, and by and large the welfare system discourages divorced and single mothers from working. Since the United States is lacking in much of the general social support for children found in other major countries, its children of divorce fare somewhat less well. As Garfinkel remarks about the families receiving state benefits, "Close to 90 percent are on welfare because the fathers are absent from home." They are absent, and they also fail to pay.[119]

In summary, then, we can see a convergence taking place in the programs being adopted in the Anglo countries to assure more effective enforcement of child-support awards. Essentially, these programs have several main elements:

1. The amount of child support to be paid is not set by a judge or in an adversary court case, but by administrative boards or agencies, based on research data on the *actual* costs of rearing a child and specific data on the spouses' incomes, the ages of children, the level and type of education, whether the children will continue to occupy the family residence, and so on.

2. Support typically will be collected directly from the source of the father's income, usually through payroll deductions.

118. For a review of such programs in the United States see Irwin Garfinkel "Child Support Trends in the U.S.," in Weitzman and Maclean, *Economic Consequences*, pp. 206–15.
119. Ibid., p. 206.

3. The custodial parent does not have the burden of locating or pursuing the parent who is delinquent in paying. Instead of lawsuits, crowded legal calendars, and unenforced court orders there are administrative agencies with sufficient personnel to locate absent parents and enforce their compliance.

4. When the noncustodial parent fails to meet his or her obligation, the state will fill the gap and the delinquent parent will have to reimburse the state. (As we noted above, this is still rare in the United States but is part of the experimental program in Wisconsin.[120])

5. In turn, the state assumes more responsibility for enforcing compliance; where necessary it will track down delinquent parents and use state resources to collect the money due. This is more difficult in Anglo countries, where there is no system for the registration of residence and no identity cards. Nevertheless, even in the United States, federal procedures—including the use of Internal Revenue Service and Social Security records—are now available to track down fathers who have tried to escape their parental obligations.

The Effects of Divorce on Children

In the public consciousness, one problem seems large but does not appear as an issue because no one has any sensible solution for it: the effects of divorce on children, in these or any other countries. Since those effects are thought to be substantial, the rise in the number of children involved seems alarming. However, recent research has questioned whether the problem is as imposing as is commonly believed.

Earlier I noted that research has generally confirmed the commonsense belief that children are hurt by divorce. They have lost one parent, and thus either a gender model to emulate or an opposite gender role to interact with; it is a period of trauma and sometimes social disapproval. Usually they suffer some economic deprivation and often must move to a different neighborhood and school. It is thus not surprising that studies report a wide variety of post-divorce problems in children, from emotional troubles and poor school work to delinquency.

However, the comparisons on which these findings rest are almost always presented as a contrast between children of divorce and those in intact families. Often the research simply describes the troubled lives of divorced children, without any comparison data at all.

120. Ibid., pp. 214–15. The state of Wisconsin is implementing the child-support assurance system in stages. The assured benefit was scheduled to be piloted in 1990 in two counties but was postponed.

If some of these problems arise from social disapproval, then over the decades they should diminish as divorce becomes "normal." On the other hand because divorce is more common among the lower classes (and in the United States among Afro-Americans), and because many childhood problems are also more common among families with fewer economic resources, perhaps the differences are no more than we could expect among children in those classes—that is, lower school performance, poorer health, somewhat higher rates of delinquency, and so on. In any event, until recently no one has followed a set of families over time to see whether the problems reports had existed *before* the divorce. In short, were the child's experiences and family life different before the breakup occurred?

Such a study has now been done.[121] It does not report that changes have also taken place over time; we have no comparable data about the past. I feel certain that the data would also be confirmed in other countries, but again we lack such data. However, if these findings are correct, it seems likely that the negative effects on children do not come primarily from the divorce itself and the difficulties subsequent to it.

The work was done by two teams. The British team studied a complete birth cohort of one week in 1958. They obtained an array of data on the children in 1965, from teachers, health visitors, mothers, and tests. A further round of data gathering was completed in 1969, when the children were aged eleven.

The U.S. team focused on a random sample of children who were surveyed at ages 7–11 in 1976. The published analysis was based only on those who were in intact families at that date. The information, largely from mothers, describes various social and psychological patterns. In addition, married parents answered many questions about family and social life. In 1981, when the children were aged 11–16, further interviewing was done. The U.S. team also interviewed a sample of intact, low-conflict families in 1976. In both studies the children were followed over the years whether or not a divorce occurred.

The analysts attempted to hold constant a large number of factors in an effort to develop adequate causal models. In both studies crude differences were apparent between children of divorce and others, but they diminished as one or another item was controlled. However, even after controlling for class, race, and (in the U.S.) mother's working outside the home, the differences diminished but did not disappear.

On the other hand, when the *pre-existing* problems of family and child were held constant, the differences between boys who experienced divorce

121. Andrew J. Cherlin et al., "Longitudinal Studies of the Effects of Divorce on Children in Great Britain and the United States," *Science* 252 (June 7, 1991), pp. 1386–89.

and those who did not were reduced to statistical nonsignificance. For girls the results differ. In Great Britain on half of the four main measures some small differences remained; that is, even after controlling for pre-existing difficulties the girls in intact families showed fewer problems. However, although these differences among U.S. girls also become smaller, they are reversed: the girls who experienced divorce show *fewer* problems.

The U.S. authors express some doubt about the firmness of that last result, and it should be kept in mind that when many factors are controlled properly the number of people actually being compared gets smaller, so that the results are not always so robust as we would wish. However, at a minimum the research demonstrates what some earlier analysts had suggested, that a crude comparison of children of divorce and children in intact families misses a crucial causal factor: Many if not most of the problems exhibited by children of divorce were visible in their families long before the legal dissolution took place. Their class deprivations, their neighborhoods, their schooling, the conflict between parents, the children's own psychological traits will affect their life course and would do so even if the parents did decide to "live together for the sake of the children."

This very important study may be ignored for some time because of the fixed opinion that divorce itself causes all the apparent difficulties that children of divorce experience. However, the research literature (including my own work) has continued to report data that challenge this morally satisfying conclusion. In fact, the research not only shows that many of the so-called effects of divorce were present before the divorce but suggests an even more radical hypothesis: in at least a sizable number of families, the problems that *children* generate may create parental conflict and thereby increase the likelihood of divorce.

Conclusion

Of course it is not possible to summarize the content of a chapter so swollen with detailed data, but a commentary may be useful here. One of the several ways in which this group of nations is distinct from the other regions we are considering is that it is made up of a mother country and its former colonies, all speaking the same language (and each contesting that very statement) and sharing a common source of family law. On the other hand, their social institutions, and even more their daily social practices, have diverged with the years.

However, all followed the common law tradition of viewing family disputes, and thus the problems of divorce, as adversarial proceedings in which the rights of the two parties were to be decided on the basis of an accumulating body of individual cases, guided by folk principles. Thus the written law changed not only by judicial fiat but by legislatures, and came to be gradually transformed by the particular histories of each nation. This was, as we noted, in contrast to the Roman law that was the dominant pattern in Europe. There, family law was more likely to be written by jurists, by reference to settled rules and principles, logically developed, and ideally shaped to fit all possible cases—that is, closer to administration than to adversary adjudication.

Nevertheless, it is clear from our review that all the broad changes in family and divorce patterns throughout Europe have been occurring in the Anglo countries as well: sharp increases in the divorce rates (less in the United States), and decreases in marriage and remarriage rates, among peoples whose eventual marriage rates were formerly very high among Western nations; increases in illegitimacy ratios, in mother-headed families, and in the percentage of women who remain in the divorced status; an increased number of children involved in divorce, and apparently a rise in the number of divorces with children (fertility remains relatively high in the Anglo countries, compared with Europe). Cohabitation has not become so common as in some European nations, but these countries are catching up; in the United States, very likely two-thirds of marriages are preceded by living together.

Perhaps more striking, the divorce rates among the rest of these countries have not caught up with those of the United States, but their rates have converged; in the 1950s their rates were very different. Several puzzles exist here, with no easy answers.

European intellectuals have often claimed that much of the world's ills came from the United States, as other countries fell victim to its "modernization," or "Coca Cola–ization." However, these changes in divorce patterns seem too pervasive, too indigenous, to be merely impositions from an outside leviathan. Rather, each country seems to take part in and contribute to a kind of vanguard world culture, which shapes us as we create it, meanwhile deploring its many consequences. Since all these countries were changing at about the same time, but with different legal changes along the way in different years, it is difficult to locate some large outside stimulus at work.

Even the case of "U.S. exceptionalism" is not clear. All these countries permitted divorce, and all but the United States had low rates until half a generation ago. In that country, the rates have risen in every decade since the Civil War. It is almost impossible to single out some key factor that caused this long trend. One might almost suggest that the culprit has been the incorrigible romanticism of this population, cherishing the dream of romantic life in marriage, believing in the individual's right to pursue happiness, so that the grubby reality of daily married life seems to many a personal defeat. During the past twenty years a keener alertness to self-interest and a lowered commitment to the family is also observable.

The research on divorce in these countries, as in Europe, has increased greatly. It has also shifted over the past fifteen years away from an emphasis on why people divorce—as though that was a deviance to be explained—to a focus on the consequences of divorce, which have widened and grown to become a serious social and taxation problem. This is an intellectual shift, toward practical research. It also creates both difficulties and opportunities for social science.

The opportunities are obvious, and to be seen in the increased budgets for social science research in all the Anglo countries (although the last Thatcher years do form a temporary exception). The difficulties are less obvious, and deserve note. They arise because social science has done best at social analysis, not social engineering: We are better at finding out how a social system or pattern operates than at repairing it, better at proving that a plan is unlikely to succeed than at demonstrating that it will work. There are sound methodological reasons for this, among them the notorious difficulty in real social life of "holding all the variables constant but one."

The larger difficulty is that the *core* of all social problems cannot be solved by social science, because basically each is an arena of conflict among values and norms, not to mention passionate self-interests. No science has worked out a method for proving empirically that cleanliness really is next to godliness, or that it is evil to divorce, or not to pay support to one's ex-spouse or children.

However, social science—especially sociology—has been of immense help in measuring trends and numbers empirically, in finding out how many divorced husbands pay how much for support, whether ex-husbands and fathers with higher incomes are any more devoted to this duty than those with lesser incomes, or what are the effects of poverty on family and divorce behavior. Almost no one, and especially legislators, can know these facts from personal experience.

In all these countries, with Canada and New Zealand perhaps lagging behind a bit, the contribution of social science knowledge, gathered for practical purposes, and carried out by both national statistical bureaus and independent researchers, has been immense. It has created a basic framework of fact. Within it, these problems have been confronted and debated in the press as well as in state and national parliaments. It is with these carefully researched data that special commissions have deliberated and proposed new laws for coping with these problems in the Anglo countries.

We have reviewed the main alterations in the laws during our historical period, noting once again the pull and haul of law and divorce behavior in these nations. The law seems at times to lag, and at others to lead. In general, in the Anglo countries the laws have been rewritten only after a long period of high ingenuity and energy in slipping past their restrictions.

Nevertheless, at times the laws do make a clear difference in the Anglo countries. A true no-fault divorce law certainly makes it difficult for a reluctant spouse to force the other to offer better terms of settlement, by withholding consent. More effective enforcement procedures, especially requiring the father to pay for a child's support directly to the state, without question reduce the percentage of delinquent fathers.

I have included in this chapter a special section of data on divorce in the United States, for I believe they will help to illuminate these processes in the other Anglo countries, as well as in Europe. Not all are genuine trends; some even suggest that a supposed trend or pattern may be doubted. They are based on large samples, analyzed with some technical sophistication, and thus they reveal patterns that had not been clear before—for example, the very high percentage of women in a second marriage (and thus possibly heading for a second divorce) who had entered their first marriage as teenagers.

These data also shed light on divorce patterns among Afro-Americans, often neglected because they make up only a small fraction of the whole population. The findings are important in their own right but also have a wider significance because various ethnic groups, typically discriminated against and often suffering economic disadvantages, exist in perhaps every nation of even moderate size, and their family and divorce patterns may be different as a consequence.

I have considered at some length the many efforts these countries have made to respond adequately to the poverty so often found among divorced mothers and their children. They have been somewhat handicapped by a long reliance on adversary court proceedings in which the ex-husband usually has the advantage. As we have emphasized, however, they have also been aided politically by the increasing amount of useful social science knowledge that shows how inadequate the system was to cope with the magnitude of the problem and offers sound data on which to build effective programs for enforcement of child support orders. Whether any of them will follow the Australian example in moving toward a simpler administrative model is not clear as yet. It does not seem likely as yet that any will move firmly toward the Swedish system, with its broad support for the whole population of mothers and children.

7

Latin America: A Regional System of Formal and Informal Divorce

Most great conquests have ultimately failed. In spite of overwhelming force and even generations of stable administration, the victors did not succeed in imposing their own traditions, languages, and culture on the conquered. The Dutch ruled Indonesia for almost four centuries, the Manchus held sway over the Chinese for over three hundred years, the British were overlords in India for over two centuries, and so on, but in each case the rulers were eventually either swept aside or swallowed up. The grand exceptions are few: Rome, Islam, and the Iberian conquest of Latin America.[1] This vast region is culturally Western in spite of the many remaining pockets of indigenous peoples, and the ethnic sentimentalizing of many writers. Nevertheless, its family arrangements do not entirely conform to those of the West nor, for that matter, do they conform to those of the indigenous cultures either, so that it is nearly impossible to obtain a valid contemporary analysis of changes in divorce patterns at present.

The central problem is not merely the lesser sophistication of statistical agencies, or the recency of the permission to divorce in some countries, but the baffling misfit between the bureaucratic system and the existing familial traditions. Specifically, in many of these countries a large minority of all adults, and in some subregions a majority, have at some time entered a consensual or informal union. Since they have not married legally, their separations do not appear in the divorce figures either. In several Central American countries, such as El Salvador, the Dominican Republic, Guatemala, Honduras, and Panama, such unions may well be a majority of all beginning unions and the dissolution rates are probably three to seven times

1. I do not include the Anglo conquests of Australia, New Zealand, Canada, and the U.S. mainland because their system (if not their intention) was to destroy the indigenous people.

higher than those of legal unions. In Argentina, Brazil, and Chile, on the other hand, only about 5 percent of existing first unions are not legal. Thus when we read that the Venezuelan divorce rate in 1981 was 3.7 per 1,000 married men (as high as in many European countries) but only 0.36 per 1,000 population (very low by the same standard), we must remember that in 1976–1977, 38 percent of all women who entered some type of union began with a consensual union; if that ended the breakup would not be included in the official divorce rate.

In spite of the technical difficulties in the data, I propose here a hypothesis which (to my knowledge) has not been offered in the research literature up to this date: I shall try to prove that informal marital dissolutions in Latin America as a whole outnumber formal ones. It is likely that this pattern has been in existence for some time in this extensive Catholic region.

Since the difference is class-based, any officially reported divorce rate is mostly the dissolution rate of the middle or upper social strata—and that population base is essentially unknown to the statistical agency. That statement, too, is no more than a general, non-quantitative, and individually unspecifiable assertion, since some unknown percentage of the lower strata will also marry legally in their first union, and in the rural regions of some countries (Mexico, Peru, Costa Rica, and Colombia) half or more will legalize one of their unions at some time.

Are there any adequate solutions for this problem? The World Fertility Survey of 1976–1977 interviewed members of both kinds of union, calculating dissolution rates for each. They did not, however, integrate their findings with official data. Most important for our purposes, they could not calculate trends, since their figures applied of course only to the sample populations interviewed at that one time. To be sure, they attempted to create artificial cohorts by tabulating their sample into age groups, but one does not capture an actual trend with that procedure.

In addition, any efforts, by the World Fertility Survey or a governmental agency, to ascertain dissolution rates separately for the two types of unions will always be frustrated by the fact that an unknown percentage of both men and women have vested interests in giving erroneous answers to questions about their marital status. Many women, especially if the consensual union has lasted for some time, claim the legal status; many men will deny it. That pattern is found in other countries, of course; it is simply more common in Latin America. We cannot correct the figure by using superior field surveys because the field surveys themselves report incorrect information.

I believe that there is nevertheless at least some merit in presenting some curves of change despite their real weaknesses. For example, if the number of divorces in a given country triples over several decades, that is likely to be a robust trend even if we cannot be sure to what percentage of the population it really applies. After all, it is unlikely that the population has tripled during the same period.

Further problems arise when we consider these rates over time, which are similar to those found in the Arab data discussed in Chapter 8. The *base* population has grown rapidly as health measures have lowered the rate of deaths, especially those of infants, while the reduction of the birthrate (if any) has been modest. Simultaneously, the age at marriage has risen. For example, at the end of the 1970s, the average age of women at first union was about 23 years in Argentina, Chile, and Brazil. Consequently, an *increasingly* large percentage of the population is young, not married, and therefore not exposed to the risk of divorce.

Thus, whatever may be happening to the real divorce rate, the official rate must be calculated on a population base that is to a large extent not really in the "divorcing pool." This would tend to lower or slow down the official rate even if the underlying rate is rising. It then follows, that if the official rates are *nevertheless* rising (as they are in Latin America), the real crude divorce rate is actually increasing faster than official figures show.

Where we can obtain divorce rates based only on the married population, we can ignore the problem of interpretation, though we must keep in mind that those who are married are often not an adequate sample of all who live in some kind of marital union. As we noted earlier, if the rise of cohabitation in Europe continues, some of these same problems will become more acute there as well. (One difference, however, is that in some of the European countries with a large number of unwed unions, such as Sweden, respondents are likely to affirm their nonmarried status in response to field surveys, and more of these surveys are conducted and analyzed.) The figure for the married population in Latin America is not, however, always available since the base population figure changes each year, and its calculation is necessarily an estimate.

We can also resort to the divorce rate demographers disdain—the ratio of divorces to marriages in any given year—because, they say, the divorces in a given year occur mostly *not* to the marriages of that same year, but marriages of previous years. That is correct, but it can be answered in part, as I indicated earlier. First, a higher percentage of divorces in Latin America than in Europe do occur in the first few years of marriage. Second, all those who marry in a specific year are at least at risk for divorce in that year. And third, I believe it can be shown arithmetically that over time this ratio will exhibit a curve as close to reality as the estimates made of the percentage of marriages that eventually end in divorce.

We must keep in mind, nevertheless, that the general problem is not diminishing at the present time because the percentages of consensual unions in the major countries are probably rising. We also do not know whether the dissolution rates of consensual unions in Latin America are exactly parallel to the curves of legal unions over the same period, although I suppose that is so. I would assume that, as in legal unions, the dissolution rates would go down during periods of depression and rise during periods of prosperity, on the reasonable assumption that there are at least some real costs to any dissolution, and they are more easily met during periods of comparative affluence. The changes over a long period may or may not be driven by the same time variables, but I do suppose they are.

Cohabitation and Consensual Unions

Although the widespread pattern of consensual unions in the New World and the continuing rise of cohabitation in industrial nations create similar problems for divorce analysis, their roots and their position in the social structure have been very different. Let us consider these differences for a moment.

First, even the delay of formal marriage among Swedish or Norwegian farmers in the past was different from the Latin American pattern, since cohabitation in the Nordic countries was seen as a kind of trial marriage, to be followed almost certainly by a formal, church benediction as soon as some expected event occurred, such as the gathering of the harvest, a transfer of property, or the birth of a child. In the Latin American village, by contrast, the initiating union *was* the marriage.

Consensual unions have very likely been widespread in rural, poor Latin American populations for several hundred years, spreading and continuing after the major destruction of cultural and social patterns that began in the sixteenth century among the indigenous peoples. Such unions were not confined to the deviant or to those whose marital status was somewhat ambiguous or to those who elected to brave social disapproval by leaving their spouses and living together. Among many rural populations in Latin America, almost all the poor peasants took it for granted that they would enter such a union. Among some groups a church wedding would have seen as socially pretentious. It would also have been prohibitively expensive because socially it required a village *fiesta*.

To be sure, such unions enjoyed less social approval than legal marriages, but even that simple statement is not quite correct in the Latin American context because most couples who entered consensual unions would have had to elevate their social status somewhat in order to enter a legal union.[2] While the spouses in such unions were of course young, for young unions were customary, they were not like those of Western nations, who are not yet ready or willing to take on adult responsibilities or have not yet achieved career stability. They intended to start a "normal" family and had already acquired the kinds of skills they needed for their anticipated adult life.

Thus cohabitation was the common, ordinary union among the poor, and especially among peasants. By contrast, until the 1960s, it was uncommon in Europe and had something of the clandestine about it. Now that is *has* become common in Western countries, it is taken for granted that respectable middle-class couples may choose to do it. In Latin America until the 1970s, however, when middle-class people entered an informal union, they were more likely to do so in order to evade the many problems widespread in countries with repressive divorce laws. It was not then acceptable as a *first* union among those classes.

Since such unions among peasants and the urban proletariat involved little or no property, laws were not usually created in the various Latin American nations to specify the rights of those who entered them. Correspondingly, although children of legal unions enjoyed more social respect than children born of consensual unions, that is also in part caused by the simple fact that people who were legally united usually enjoyed a somewhat higher status anyway.

With such deep roots in the fractures of social and cultural life caused by the Conquest, consensual unions might be expected to diminish as each nation modernized. After all, some civic rights are linked with marital status, documents are required in a bureaucratic society, the pension rights of survivors may be linked to marital status, and new regimes may, as Mexico did in the past, attempt to organize large-scale weddings in which dozens of couples participate.

That speculation is incorrect. In fact, in perhaps most Latin American countries, consensual unions have been *increasing*. "Respectable" classes have begun to engage in it, just as their peers in Europe have done. In addition, the net reproduction rate among the lower classes has been high, thus breeding more of the poor who will enter similar unions. When those with more advantages enter such unions—whether they are spouses of professionals escaping severe divorce laws or younger middle-class couples who are not yet ready to marry formally—that union has the same legal

2. For a broad, specific, theoretical interpretation of these processes, with some empirical tests, see William J. Goode, "Illegitimacy in the Caribbean Social Structure," *Amer. Soc. Rev.* 25 (Feb. 1960), pp. 21–30; and "Illegitimacy, Anomie, and Cultural Penetration," *Amer. Soc. Rev.* 26 (Dec. 1961), pp. 910–25.

standing as any peasant's *de facto* union and will be counted as "consensual" in the census.

Many of these "new" consensual unions have occurred in such countries as Argentina and Brazil, where real divorce was not permitted until recently, but marital conflict and dissolution continued just the same. Similar patterns occurred, as we noted before, in Spain and Italy. Nevertheless, while the age at marriage increases and a higher percentage of young people become educated, and while the "new morality" of Europe becomes the culture of urban life, still more young people in Latin America have entered *de facto* unions.

Whether "new" or traditional, such unions are less stable than legal ones. I shall later estimate just how much weight should be given to them, in assessing the total number of marital dissolutions in all of Latin America.

Major Changes in the Divorce Laws

In considering divorce rates in Latin America, it is important to distinguish between the countries lying south of the United States to the northern coast of South America, including several islands in the Caribbean, and the main continent of South America. In the former, divorce has long been common and the rates relatively high; in most of the latter, divorce is relatively recent and the rates continue to be low (except in Venezuela). It seems likely that in all of them the rates have been rising. We shall first take note of South America.

Perhaps the most easily visible important change in divorce in South America over the past four decades is the establishment of the right to divorce in all of the major countries except Chile. Several countries had briefly permitted it at one time or another, but it seems likely that this change will now be a firm part of the future.

Colombia in 1977, Brazil in 1978, and Argentina in 1987 joined Peru, which had had divorce since 1936. Each had followed Church doctrine in permitting only legal separation, usually requiring rather serious allegations of fault. This continues to be available in modern divorce law, and in commentaries and analyses until recently, a legal separation was frequently called "divorce" although of course it did not permit remarriage. On the other hand, over the past several decades, a growing number of informal unions began between couples who were barred from a new legal marriage by the existing laws.

As of 1991, Chile remains the only major nation in South America without legal divorce. Although the term "divorce" is used in the law of civil matrimony of 1984 (with subsequent modifications), it requires one or more of some thirteen allegations to establish the grounds for legal separation.[3] As an interesting exceptional case, Chile has evolved a widely understood body of procedures for *annulment,* remarkably akin in their ingeniousness to the elaborate grounds for annulment in Church courts in Europe over the several centuries after the indissolubility of marriage was finally imposed (in 1563).[4] They were then, as they are now in Chile, most easily utilized by families with adequate means to pursue their goals with the aid of lawyers.

Since a legal marriage in Chile can go forward only after a number of official facts are filed, it follows that any proof that the official record contains errors could become the grounds for annulment. This can be as trivial as the claim that the addresses of the prospective spouses were not correct. Needless to say, this possibility is not written explicitly into the law. On the other hand, it can only be done with the collusion of the couples as well as the court judges. Because an annulment does permit remarriage, it is, then, the Chilean "substitute" for a real divorce. (Annulment does not apply to consensual unions, which legally are not marriages.)

These changes over time in both the law itself and the actual adjustments that couples and the law courts have made to their domestic lives once more point to the ambiguities in the official and, until recently, miniscule crude rates of divorce. In the Central American countries, perhaps the legal changes have been less dramatic, since they had permitted divorce before the recent period, and the rates have been relatively high compared with those of South America.

Brazil's 1977 law required a prior constitutional amendment and did not make divorce easy.[5] It required three years after a judicial separation, or five years of de facto separation. In 1988, these requirements were reduced to one year and two years, respectively.[6] Otherwise, the marriage could be dissolved only on traditional grounds, which may be "any act that is a grave violation of matrimonial obligations."

Although Venezuela has experienced high rates relative to other South American countries, its laws were also restrictive, offering a long list of rather serious faults as possible grounds (from the prosaic one of alcoholism to the scandalous act of offering one's children for prostitution). A partial revision

---

3. Ley de Matrimonio Civil, *Apéndice del Código Civil,* paragraph 5, article 21.

4. Ibid., ch. 6, esp. article 31).

5. Jose Abreu, *O Divorcio No Direito Brasileiro* (Rio de Janeiro: Forense, 1985), pp. 195ff.; Sebastião Luiz Amorim, *Teoria e practica da separaçao e do divórcio* (São Paulo: Livraria e editora universitaria de direito limitada, 1987); and Paulo Lucio Nogueira, *Alimentos, Divórcio, Separaçao* (São Paulo: Editora Saraiva, 1987).

6. Joao Baptista Villela, "Brazilian Family Law from 1988–1991: Toward Equality and Social Rights," *J. Family Law* 30 (1991–92), pp. 275–76.

in 1982 shortened the time required after a judicial separation before a legal divorce, from two years to one year. It also contains a provision (as do the laws of Brazil, France, and Spain) that permits divorce after five years of separation if the spouse who has left appears in court to affirm the end of the marriage.[7] Whether so elusive a spouse, after such a time, is easily brought to court I have been unable to ascertain. But this is also the only route to divorce for someone married to an "innocent" spouse who will not agree to a judicial separation or divorce.

Uruguay has long been considered "more European" than its neighbors, and its divorce laws have been less restrictive. In addition to the traditional menu of severe grounds, it has permitted divorce after three years of de facto separation. It also permits divorce in unions "where there may be no hope of re-establishing the joint spiritual and material life" although this type of dissolution does require three separate court hearings.[8] This is of course a kind of divorce by agreement and need not charge any fault.

The Argentine law that was put into effect in 1987 also permitted divorce by agreement,[9] and that is the direction in which other systems have been moving. As I shall note in considering what happens after divorce, the court requires the couple making such a petition to present a complete plan for the allocation of resources and support after divorce.

The Rise in Dissolution Rates

Let us first consider the rise in the crude *numbers* of divorces during this period. Although even crude rates are more useful than crude numbers, such rates are only as accurate as the base population figure. In Central America and the Latin American islands, that base may at times be less than robust. There are many technical difficulties (including geography, transportation, and communication) in the way of a valid census in this region, as well as the nearly constant political turmoil over the past several decades (except in Costa Rica).

That problem is intensified here because in most of these countries the percentage of consensual unions is higher than in the rest of Latin America, and thus even the answers to census questions are open to much doubt. Whatever the real rate may be however, the crude numbers have gone up

7. Jesus Esparza, "Venezuela: A New Approach to Family Law," *J. Family Law* 29:2 (1991), pp. 492–93.

8. Eduardo Vaz Ferreira, "Uruguay: Novel Thoughts on Divorce and Legitimization," ibid., pp. 481–82.

9. For the full text of the law, see *Divorcio vincular ley 23.515* (Buenos Aires: AG ediciones, Facultad de derecho y ciencias sociales, Universidad de Buenos Aires, n.d.).

Table 7.1: Percentage Increase in the Numbers of Divorces,
1950–1985

Costa Rica		1437 percent
Cuba	(1960–1985)	848 percent
Dominican Republic	(1950–1976)	1094 percent
El Salvador	(to 1984)	481 percent
Guatemala	(to 1985)	569 percent
Honduras	(1951–1983)	1206 percent
Panama	(1952–1985)	481 percent

steadily since 1950. Table 7.1 presents the percentage increase in the numbers of divorces recorded officially from the 1950s to the 1980s. It shows a rise of 1437 percent in Costa Rica, a rise of 1206 percent in Honduras, 1094 percent in the Dominican Republic, 848 percent in Cuba, 569 percent in Guatemala, and 481 percent in El Salvador and Panama. (The reader will recognize the irony that the South American countries with more advanced statistical capacity yield much less understanding of trends, simply because divorce has not even been available until recently.)

Before we examine the next set of figures, the crude divorce rates, we should bear in mind why they are so minute (until the last few years). They are, as noted above, calculated on the base figure of the total population, most of whom are young and therefore unmarried. This group is proportionately much larger than in Europe because the birthrates are higher and public health and medical measures have reduced mortality. The rates of divorce, in turn, are about one half to one fifth those of Europe because registered dissolutions in Latin America occur only to the *legally* married, who form a smaller percentage of the total adult population. Finally, several of the important South American nations in which divorce is now permitted have not yet published analyses of their divorce rates. For Brazil (not shown) we can give a figure that includes "desquites" as well as "divorcios" (that is, any form of legal dissolution including legal separation: 0.08 per 1,000 population in 1960, 0.17 in 1970, 0.61 in 1980, and 1.3 in 1985.

However, Table 7.2 shows a clear increase in the rates in the past fifteen years, in parallel with those in Europe, in many cases just as sharply. As in Europe, it is not clear just why this has happened at this particular time. Indeed, this great region is instructive, since it would be difficult to show how the various social changes adduced in Europe to explain these alterations—the independence of women, feminist ideology, being more concerned about one's own self interest, and so on—should have had so large an impact in Latin America at the same time, or indeed whether those social changes are so rapid in this hemisphere. (Those same charges *are*

Table 7.2: Crude Divorce Rate per 1,000 Population, 1950–1989

	1950	1960	1970	1980	1982–1989	
Costa Rica	0.1	0.15	0.13	0.77	1.02	(1982)
Cuba		0.51	2.89	2.52	3.15*	(1989)
Dominican Republic	0.39	0.29	0.92	1.7	1.22	(1985)
				(1979)		
Ecuador			0.22	0.33	0.41	(1987)
El Salvador	0.19	0.18	0.24	0.33	0.41	(1985)
Guatemala	0.12	0.15	0.13	0.15	0.18	(1987)
Honduras		0.10	0.13	0.17	0.19	(1979)
Mexico			0.22	0.31	0.33	(1985)
			(1972)			
Panama	0.44	0.38	0.42	8.59	0.79	(1988)
Uruguay	0.64	0.68	1.04	1.48	1.38	(1987)
Venezuela	0.15	0.25	0.24	0.39	1.24	(1987)
				(1979)		

Source: *Boletin Estadistico de Cuba; all other data: U.N. Demographic Yearbooks.

made in Latin America, for the moralists are equally active there, but the data to prove any link are less easily available.)

Countries such as Peru and Colombia, which do not appear in the table, also have relatively low rates, because the grounds required continue to be restrictive.[10] Mexico did have higher official rates in the past, which then dropped with a 1971 law that revoked the easy "fly in–fly out" one-day divorces once granted to foreigners (mainly U.S. citizens). Cuba, too, was once a haven for non-citizens who sought divorces outside their own restrictive jurisdictions, but its rates continue to be high. These and other complexities do not alter the fact that the rates in Latin America have generally been rising.

A divorce rate calculated on the basis of the total married population is more valid than a crude rate, but in Latin America that figure is (with few exceptions) obtainable only in a censal year. In some cases (Ecuador 1982 and Costa Rica 1984) years may pass before the final population figure is achieved. These censuses also contain many errors and gaps. Again, this rate refers only to those who claim to be legally married; many who do so will never appear in the divorce register because in fact that claim rests on shaky ground. Table 7.3 shows the divorces per 1,000 married females in Latin

10. Olga H. Helo and Marta B. Guerra, *El Divorcio en Colombia* (Bogotá: Ministerio de Justicia, 1977), pp. 15ff., and Carmine J. Cabello, *Cincuenta años de Divorcio en el Perú* (Lima: Pontificia Universidad Catolica Peru, 1987), pp. 22ff. Although "rupture of family life" is permitted in Brazil, until 1988 the main grounds continued to be de facto separation of five years, legal separation plus three years, absence for four years, and other serious grounds. See Abreu, *O Divorcio*, pp. 195ff.

Table 7.3: Divorces per 1,000 Married Females, 1950–1988

	1950	1960	1970	1980s
Brazil (divorcios and desquites)	0.08	0.17	0.61	1.3 (1985)
Chile (Nulidades)				1.6 (1982)
Costa Rica	1.6	0.8 (1963)	1.74 (1974)	
Cuba		22.2		
Dominican Republic	5.3	3.8	11.9	
Ecuador		2.3 (1965)	2.0 (1974)	
El Salvador	2.3	2.3 (1961)	3.5 (1971)	
Guatemala	1.6	1.7 (1964)	1.8 (1973)	
Honduras	1.4 (1951)	1.8 (1961)	3.4 (1974)	
Mexico	1.72	3.01	4.18	
Panama	5.7 (1952)	4.3	5.3	7.9 (1988)
Uruguay		5.1 (1963)	6.2 (1975)	
Venezuela	1.7	2.5 (1961)	2.8 (1971)	3.6 (1981)

Sources: U.N. Demographic Yearbooks and James W. Wilkie, ed., *Statistical Abstract of Latin America* (Los Angeles: UCLA Latin American Center, 1980).

America. Of course these numbers are higher than the crude rates, but the trend is the same: a steady increase, though perhaps less spectacular than we encounter in the crude rates. Since the base population is (mainly) the one at risk, and mostly in the classes in which people are more likely to be counted in an official census, the rise appears to be statistically robust.

I have also calculated the ratio of divorces per 100 legal marriages for a number of countries, a figure in Latin America that may be a better index of real change than the crude rates, but both only mirror the underlying patterns.

They contain some noteworthy differences, however. Since they need not wait for a censal year they may be a fair index of what is coming, perhaps even in some cases a closer approximation to a figure that is rather difficult to obtain in Latin America: the eventual likelihood of divorce (that is, if the ratio continues steady). From modest beginnings in 1950 (2–5 divorces per 100 marriages), several rates had risen to European dimensions toward the end of the 1980s: Cuba at 44 divorces per 100 marriages (1989), Uruguay, 19.3 (1986), and Venezuela, 21.6 (1987). The figure for Brazil remained low at 3.3 in 1987.

I noted earlier the impossibility of obtaining technically adequate *trends* of marital dissolution rates among consensual unions, for they escape the official registration agencies. Since the rates are three to seven times higher than those for legal marriages, we must consider them seriously. I wish here to consider what may seem a startling hypothesis: *A majority of the total Latin*

American dissolutions are breakdowns of consensual (or cohabiting) unions. The few data we have on which to base a guess about *trends* (the World Fertility Survey and related surveys) also suggest the likelihood that these rates will at least keep up with those among legal marriages. And, as already noted, the percentage of consensual unions among all unions has been increasing.

The most basic problem inherent in any such analysis was noted before: We do not have sound statistical data on the percentage of people in consensual unions in two respects. First, the data we do have come from responses to census questions that are potentially problematic because some of the people in consensual unions will claim to be legally married. Second, census surveys are infrequent—often only once in ten years—and capture only one point in time. Nevertheless, these are the data we have available, and even these less-than-perfect data reveal a consistent pattern of change: the percentage of the population in consensual unions is rising consistently and dramatically.

As to the dissolution rates, the only data available are from several surveys done by the World Fertility Survey in 1976–1978 and other similar surveys. These also give some basis for inferring *changes* in rates, which appear to be rising at least as much as legal divorce rates.

Next, we can summarize the larger patterns that lead to my broad conclusion that the total number of marital dissolutions among consensual unions is probably greater than that of legal unions. I offer this strong conclusion even though two of the larger countries (Brazil and Argentina) report only moderate percentages of consensual unions on rather firm data, but without any great precision in the exact numbers. If this conclusion is correct, on the other hand, consensual unions must be given far more weight in any understanding of Latin American family systems and their history.

The conclusion rests on the following main elements in the system as a whole:

1. In some countries the percentage *now* in a consensual union is substantial (for example, Venezuela, 18 percent; Peru, 14 percent; Guatemala, 16 percent; Honduras, 16 percent).

2. But there is a substantial *turnover*, three to seven times higher than that of legal unions; up to 50 percent of such unions eventually dissolve, and the rate of *legalization* is also high (again, up to 50 percent, and even 65 percent in Peru). As a consequence, the percentage of those who have *ever* entered a consensual union is several times higher than the percentage who are now in that status, and in many countries it is much higher than the current percentage of the legally married.

3. Surveys assert that the censal percentages of people *now* in this type of union are *underestimated* by about one-third, a further support for the nu-

merical weight of consensual union dissolutions in the total of all dissolutions in Latin America.[11]

4. As noted above, Brazil is a large nation and has a modest percentage of consensual unions, but in some regions (northeast) very likely two-thirds of all couples entering a union follow that pattern. There are many other regions in Latin America in which a majority of first unions and a still higher percentage of second or higher-order unions are also consensual.

Successive censuses try to count the total population in each of the major socially recognized statuses (single, married, widowed, divorced). In Latin American countries, it has been typical also to count those in consensual unions. As a first part of our earlier argument, to confirm the large weight of dissolutions occurring to such unions, we wish to present this basic datum.

In published reports, however, the percentage of consensual unions is much diminished by the fact that it is typically presented as a percentage of the *whole* population, or sometimes of those aged 12 or 14 years of age and over. That younger group is a very large part of the population in Latin America, and therefore it is more fruitful to focus only on that part of the population that is now *in some type of union*.

Table 7.4 presents the answer to this question. It looks at those who are now in a union and shows what percentage are in a consensual union. As can be seen, when we ask the question in this way we find that a very substantial part of the population in some type of domestic union is in a consensual union. In some countries, almost half of all unions are consensual. El Salvador and the Dominican Republic (not shown) would also fall in that category. In another four countries (Colombia, Ecuador, Peru, and Venezuela), one quarter to one third are currently in consensual unions. Table 7.4 also shows an increase in consensual unions, sometimes a substantial one, from 1970–1975 to 1980–1985, except for two countries in Central America.

We must keep in mind, however, that this figure is only for those who are in that status *at present*. Since people move into and out of these statuses, it is important to gain some information about what percentage of people *ever* enter a consensual union.[12] That figure would of course be much higher,

11. Noreen Goldman, "Dissolution of First Unions in Colombia, Panama, and Peru," *Demography* 18 (Nov. 1981), p. 660. See also C. E. Florez and N. Goldman, "An Analysis of Nuptiality Data in the Colombia National Fertility Survey," *Scientific Reports*, no. 11, World Fertility Survey, 1980. For Argentina, see the painstaking work by Edith A. Pantelides, "Análisis y Propuesta de Corrección de la Información Sobre Estado Civil en los Cuatro Primeros Censos Nacionales Argentinos," unpublished paper Buenos Aires: Centro de Estudios de Población, 1984.

12. Noreen Goldman "Dissolution," citing the work of Z. Camisa, notes that the frequency of informal unions may exceed that of formal marriages in Guatemala, Honduras, Panama, El Salvador, and the Dominican Republic in 1970 (p. 659). Doubtless Guyana should be added to that list.

Table 7.4: Of Those in Some Type of Union, What Percentage
Is in a Consensual Union?

	% Consensual 1980–1985	% Consensual 1970–1975	% Change
Brazil	10.5	6.5	62
Chile	6.3	4.5	40
Colombia	28.6	18.3	56
Costa Rica	20.7	15.4	34
Ecuador	29.4	24.9	18
Guatemala	44.6	52.3	−17
Honduras	53.5	45.7	17
Mexico	13.6	15.3	−12
Panama	49.5	49.5	—
Peru	28.0	27.3	2.6
Uruguay	10.6	7.8	28
Venezuela	33.4	31.3	6.7

just as the percentage who ever get divorced in the United States is much
higher than the percentage who are *now* in the status of "divorced." For example, the percentage of those in any union in Mexico who were in a consensual union in 1980 was about 14 percent, but the 1982 National Demographic Survey found that some 25 percent of all people who had entered
some type of union had entered a consensual union as their first one.[13]

Thus we ask the question, of those ever in any union, what percentage
enters a consensual union at some time in the age group with the highest
percentages (not cumulative)? Here, as noted before, we are forced to rely
upon the various investigations related to the World Fertility Survey, including the Mexican survey in 1969. These figures date from 1976–1978, and of
course they are, like censuses, based on information from one particular
time period. They did, however, contain information on ages, which permitted the construction of artificial cohorts. In Table 7.5 we present data based
on these reports and estimates. In most of these countries, the percentage is
even higher (Venezuela, 60 percent; Costa Rica, 40 percent; Mexico, 47
percent). If we look only at the young age group of 15–19 years, where the
consensual union is much more common, and legal marriage is in turn less
common because of the general higher ages for legal unions, the figures are
still higher. (I do not present such a table because that age skew biases the
data in favor of my conclusion.)

I have not been able to find a comparable figure for Brazil—that is, the
percentage of unions that are consensual of those who have ever been in any
domestic union. Every datum shows an increase in the percentage who

13. Norma Ojeda, "La Importancia de las Uniones Consensuales," *Demos* (México: Instituto
Nacional de Estadística Geografía e Informática, 1988), p. 21.

Table 7.5: Of Those Ever in Any Union,
What Percentage Has Ever Entered
a Consensual Union, in the Age Group
with the Highest Percentage?
(Not Cumulative)

Colombia	32–38
Panama	54–59
Peru	31–41
Dominican Republic	78
Costa Rica	24
Ecuador	40
Mexico	18–28
Paraguay	36

Sources: The first figure in the sets of figures for
Colombia, Panama, and Peru are from Noreen
Goldman, "Dissolution," p. 670; it applies to the
age at the time of interview, about 25–39 years.
The second figure in these three sets is from Ju-
lieta Quilodran, "Modalités de la Formation et
Evolution des Unions en Amerique Latine," *Inter-
national Population Conference,* vol. 3 (Liège 1985),
pp. 274–75. The remaining figures are also from
Quilodran, except for the higher figure of 28 per-
cent for Mexico, which is from Anne R. Pebley
and Noreen Goldman, "Legalización de Uniones
Consensuales en México," *Estudios Demográficos y
Urbanos* 1 (1985), p. 279.

enter such unions, and for particular age groups the figure is rather high and
has been increasing from 1960 to 1980. Thus, for Sao Paulo, for the male
population 15–19, that figure rose from 9 percent to 38 percent between
1970 and 1980; for women of the same age, it rose from 9 percent to 23
percent. During the same period, civil and religious marriages dropped
somewhat. Similarly, Recife in the Northeast has generally had high levels of
consensual unions, rising from 43 percent in unions begun before 1970 to
61 percent between 1971 and 1976.[14]

Since, however, our aim is to understand these processes that generate
high rates of total dissolution and not simply to make the case for the larger
importance of consensual dissolutions, we now introduce a dynamic that
reduces their importance. As I emphasized several decades ago in two articles

14. For these and related data, see Maria Coleta Oliveira, "The Family in Brazil: Demographic
Analysis and Recent Trends," International Union for the Scientific Study of Population, Tokyo
Conference, 1988, unpublished paper, pp. 13–17. For further data on the "non-traditional"
domestic arrangements, see Elza Berquo, Maria Coleta Oliveira, and Suzana M. Cavenaghi,
"Arranjos Familiares 'Não Canónicos' No brasil," São Paulo: Nucleo de Estudos de População,
1988(?), unpublished paper.

on illegitimacy in the New World,[15] many people move from the civil status of consensual to the status of married. Some of the rates of "dissolution" are therefore *lower* than those recorded in some surveys because those studies counted some unions as "dissolved" that did not actually break apart but were united legally. This is more likely to occur early in the relationship if it happens at all, more likely in a first union, and I believe more likely if the woman possesses some advantage such as education, property, or status.

There is some disagreement as to whether being a practicing Catholic affects this likelihood. In Mexico, the likelihood that a legal marriage would occur within ten years after the beginning of cohabitation was 38 percent for practicing Catholics versus 22 percent for other women, but in Colombia, Costa Rica, and Peru that factor seems to make little difference.[16]

Legalization does, however, substantially reduce the real importance of consensual unions and their dissolutions.[17] Within ten years of the beginning of cohabitation, the percentage of consensual unions that were later legalized was 22 percent in Mexico, 19 percent in Colombia, 18 percent in Costa Rica, and 35 percent in Peru. After the first few years of a consensual union, the rate of legalization drops, but of course some marriages do occur just the same. In Peru, for example, 50–65 percent of those who enter a consensual union will eventually enter *some* legal union (though probably not with the same person). The figure for Costa Rica is about half that.[18] If such events are widespread, it is clear that this dynamic would reduce the real rate of dissolution among consensual unions.

As noted earlier, although divorce rates among the legally married have risen for some two decades or more, they have remained low. From the cohort data in the various fertility studies already noted, they are also rising among consensual unions, but they have in addition been considerably higher as well.

In a 1985 Mexican study,[19] the cumulative probability of dissolution for a first consensual union (the rate for later unions is of course higher) was 46 percent, but only 19 percent for marriages that begin with a civil ceremony alone and 6.4 percent for marriages that were solemnized by both a civil and a church ceremony. In a separate study, in the period 1973–1982 in Mexico, the specific divorce rate was 22 per 1,000 women in consensual unions

15. *Amer. Soc. Rev.*, February 1960 and December 1961.

16. Anne R. Pebley and Noreen Goldman, "Legalization of Consensual Unions in Mexico," *Social Biology* 33 (1986), p. 201.

17. See Norma Ojeda de la Pena, "Separación y Divorcio en México: Una Perspectiva Demográfica," *Estudios Demográficos y Urbanos* 1 (1985), pp. 243ff.; Pebley and Goldman, "Legalization," pp. 205–12; and Quilodran, "Modalités," pp. 274–77.

18. Noreen Goldman and Anne R. Pebley, "Consensual Unions in Latin America," *Social Biology* 28 (1981), pp. 53–54.

19. Ojeda, "Separación," table 2, p. 240.

Table 7.6: Probability of Dissolution Within Five Years
After the Date of Union Among Women Aged 15–19 Years
at the Time of the Union

	% Legal Marriage	% Consensual Union
Colombia	3	32
Costa Rica	4	22
Dominican Republic	10	41
Ecuador	4	28
Mexico	4	27
Panama	10	33
Paraguay	2	39
Peru	3	30
Venezuela	9	33

Source: Quilodran, "Modalités de la Formation."

versus 2.98 per 1000 in a civil union alone and merely 1.1 among those married by both a civil and a religious ceremony.[20] The comparisons in other countries are just as striking. After twenty years, 63 percent of first unions are dissolved in Colombia, 56 percent in Panama, and 53 percent in Peru, as contrasted with 13 percent, 23 percent, and 7 percent for legal unions in those countries.[21] Quilodran uses a somewhat different mode of calculation, with a broader perspective, as shown in Table 7.6.

All these forms of comparison point to the same conclusion: the rate of dissolution among consensual unions is high. Together with the data presented earlier on the large population involved at some time in consensual unions, this suggests, again, that of the total number of all marital dissolutions in Latin America, the total number occurring to consensual unions are very likely higher than those occurring to legal marriages. Thus, to understand fully the processes of divorce change, these data must be given greater weight than they have been in the past.

Duration has been shorter in consensual unions, and in the artificial cohorts created by several World Fertility Survey studies the time appears to be shorter in the more recent unions. However, they are also relatively shorter among legal unions than in Europe, though the trend is not clear. For legal unions, the modal (that is, most frequent) duration of marriage before divorce is about three years in Mexico, Cuba, and the Dominican Republic. If instead we consider the median, the duration at which about half of all divorces will occur, then about half of all marriages that end in divorce last

20. Norma Ojeda and Raul Gonzalez, "Niveles y Tendencias del Divorcio y la Separación Conyugal en el Norte de México," (Tijuana: Colegio de Frontera Norte, 1990), p. 19, table 3. The rates are also rising for the marriage generations 1943–1952 and 1953–1967 (ibid., table 4, p. 20).
21. Goldman, "Dissolution," p. 671.

about five years or less in Cuba, six years or less in Mexico, seven years or less in Venezuela, nine years in Ecuador, and ten years or less in Uruguay.

Since data are not consistently available for the past decades, these figures are not entirely reliable (some are from the 1970s), and thus no definite trends seems to be visible. It should be kept in mind, however, that in several European countries there is no clear trend in these gross averages either, because an increasing number of older couples are getting divorced as well. It is possible that this process has been occurring in Argentina and Brazil, where divorce was introduced only recently, during a period in which many de facto dissolutions had been occurring just the same. Thus the backlog of new divorces will include many who are somewhat older and thus have a longer duration of marriage.

Children

Most of the available long-term data on the percentage of divorces with children come from Central America, since that region has permitted divorce for a longer period. Fertility is relatively high, as it is generally in Latin America, and consequently, most unions have produced children by that time even though the duration of marriage is relatively short. The data may show a slight rise in the percentage of divorces with children, but since the figures move somewhat erratically from one year to the next, that trend is not at all clear. In any event, from two-thirds to four-fifths of all marriages that end in divorce report at least one child.

After Divorce

It is not possible to make an adequate analysis of what happens after divorce in Latin America, primarily because studies of actual behavior, as distinct from the official laws, have not been carried out (except in Argentina). Aside from final divorces, a very high proportion of all dissolutions occurring to legal marriages result in short- or long-term legal or de facto separations before divorce or (as in Italy and Spain) in separations that are never transformed into divorce. These patterns of living have not been studied either, and of course post-divorce arrangements have not been studied over time.

With respect to consensual unions, there is a very small body of law. Mexico has had some laws relating to consensual unions since 1928. Though numerous clauses relate to property, mutual support, inheritance, and other rights, "neither in the Federal District nor in the other states are there provisions for the dissolution of the union."[22] Provisions for inheritance in the case of death do exist, but these focus on the exercise of parental authority over the children the couple had in common. The laws do not make any provisions for support in case of dissolution. Nevertheless, the 1983 reforms (in the Federal District) at least did recognize that each partner owes support to the other. Whether that can be used to enforce support payments after a breakup is not clear.[23]

In Mexico special regulations provide for the division of the common property of those in consensual unions, and in one state a former consensual wife can lay claim to a deceased man's property. With reference to inheritance generally, there are no distinctions between the children of consensual unions and those of later legal marriages, if all are recognized by the father. This is a common provision in Latin America.

Court judgments in Uruguay have affirmed the general rights of cohabiting women to assets acquired by the man.[24] There are also laws with reference to consensual dissolution in Ecuador, Guatemala, and Honduras. These, however, have to do only with cases in which there is a one-sided demand for dissolution and in such cases a court judgment can be required.[25]

In Argentina, if a consensual wife has been in a stable union, she can inherit from her deceased spouse. Consensual husbands are now lobbying for that right as well.[26]

If one is legally married, in contrast, a much more elaborate body of laws becomes relevant, much of it based on the large corpus of past Argentinian court decisions as well as on the new legislation of 1987. First, it is still possible to obtain either a judicial separation or a final divorce, and many of the grounds remain the same. As in France, there is still a "divorce for cause," based on grave faults such as adultery or injury. Then there are new provisions as a "remedy" for the breakdown of the marriage, as proved by some presentation of evidence, usually a de facto separation (two years for a judicial separation, three years for a divorce), or a joint petition after two

22. Karl August Prinz von Sachsen-Gessaphe, *Das Konkubinat in der Mexikanischen Civilrechtsordnung* (Tubingen: J. C. B. Mohr [P. Siebeck], 1990), p. 47.

23. Alicia E. Perez Duarte y Norona, *La Obligación Alimentaria* (Mexico: Editorial Porrúa, 1989), pp. 133–34.

24. Eduardo Vaz Ferreira, "Uruguay: Novel Thoughts on Divorce and Legitimization," *J. Family Law* 29:2 (1991), p. 483. For additional legal rules in Colombia, see Arturo Valencia Zea, *Derecho Civil,* vol. 5, *La Familia,* 6th ed. (Bogota: Temis, 1988), pp. 411–27.

25. Sachsen-Gessaphe, "Konkubinat," p. 80.

26. Personal communication from Edith A. Pantelides, Centro de Estudios de Población, Argentina.

years of marriage, for separation (two years of de facto living apart) or divorce (three years). Neither spouse then charges the other with fault.

Both judicial separation and divorce have similar effects on a range of post-separation relations between spouses.[27] The reforms of 1987 focus more on the consequences of divorce than on who is at fault. However, the innocent spouse has the right to alimony at a level that would preserve the living standards of the marriage. If there is no question of who was at fault, either spouse has the right to support if he or she lacks adequate resources.[28] Even if the home is the personal property of one spouse, the law protects the family dwelling, presumably to give shelter to the children. Custody is given to the mother, and child support is the responsibility of both, though of course it will usually be the husband who actually has the resources to make those payments. The law also gives the noncustodial parent the right to communicate with the children and a voice in other matters that concern them.[29] Laws similar to these are common in other Latin American countries.

Several broad conclusions about the rules for settlements after legal divorces are worth noting. The first is that the philosophy of law that has gradually been incorporated into Latin American family codes over the past several decades reflects the continuing egalitarian bias of these legal systems. Whatever the actual power of men in this great region, the laws themselves assert implicitly or explicity the legal equality of men and women. This implies, at least in legal stipulations, to matrimonial property. In most countries such property is to be divided equally, except, apparently, in Ecuador.[30] Correspondingly, both husband and wife are responsible for the support of their children. Indeed, in many countries, under some circumstances, they continue to be responsible for each other even after divorce.

But despite these legal proscriptions, it is my firm belief, based on the few published data and on my personal experience in Latin America, that in none of these countries is the legal stipulation of equal division of property actually put into effect.

This broad principle of equality has altered the traditional legal presumption or stipulation that husbands command the authority of the household, including the decision as to where the couple will live. With reference to a

27. Cecilia P. Grosman, "Argentina: Recent Reforms in Family Law," *J. Family Law,* 30 (1991–92), p. 243; see also Mario Bendersky, "Argentina: Divorce at Last!" *J. Family Law* 27 (1988–89), pp. 1–5.

28. Grosman, "Argentina," p. 244.

29. Ibid., p. 245.

30. Luis Parraguez, *Manuel de Derecho Civil Ecuatoriano,* vol. 1, 2nd ed. (Quito: Gráficas Mediaville, 1983), p. 282, states that one-fifth of the estate is given to end the support obligation. See also Juan Larrea Holguin, *Manual de Derecho Civil en Ecuador,* 3rd. 3d. (Quito: Corporación de Estudios y Publicaciones, 1989), p. 278. This amount is to be paid to the innocent party.

wide range of matters, such as the children's schooling, the wife shares that right (for example, in Uruguay and Venezuela).[31] In Venezuela, that right extends to the administration of any matrimonial property. That these legal changes have altered the behavior of Latin American husbands by much seems questionable—until the needed research has been carried out.

A second broad characteristic of these decisions about post-divorce arrangements is that Latin American judges have very broad powers, even though the legal systems themselves derive from the Roman tradition. It is very likely that this discretion arose through the decades in which all cases were legal separations, involving a delicate and intimate knowledge of specific families, while the judgments were partly a reflection of political factors determined by family alliances.

A third, and perhaps the most important, general pattern builds on a different historical foundation than that of Protestant countries. The Catholic law is more likely to prefer solutions that urge the responsibility of all family members (not only wives and husbands) for one another. More specifically, in the recent past and in some countries even now, there were more people in the status of "separated" than "divorced," For centuries, separation was the only possible "divorce" for most people: After dissolution, mutual obligations still remained. Thus, it was taken for granted that many responsibilities of the marriage would continue, for, after all, in law the marriage was never fully dissolved. The "normality" of separation meant that the notion of dividing marital property was much more self-evident as well. That is, the marital pair were still a "couple," although they were living apart, and the logic of giving at least some of the family resources to each of the spouses seemed more reasonable. So, similarly, was the ideal of maintaining the children and the former wife in the standard that is at least stated in principle (for example, in Uruguay and Argentina).[32] If adequate historical research is ever carried out in these countries, however, I am certain that it would find that financial neglect was in fact the norm in the past.

Of course, several social understandings shaped those traditional separation arrangements. First, most of these wives were middle class (or higher), and did not hold jobs, for opportunities were rare and society disapproved of that option. Thus it was understood that most women would need to be

31. On the sharing of *patria potestas* in Venezuela, see Jesus Esparza, "Venezuela: A New Approach to Family Law," *J. Family Law* 29:2 (1991), p. 493. A unique Uruguayan law, however, dating from 1913, permits a woman to demand a divorce without citing any grounds, but requires three separate hearings for completion. See "Uruguay: Novel Thoughts on Divorce and Legitimization," ibid., p. 482.

32. See Maria Inés Varela, *Obligación Familiar de Alimentos* (Montevideo: Fundación de Cultura Universitaria, 1984), p. 51, and Julio Lopez del Carril, *Régimen del Matrimonio, Separación Personal y Divorcio* (Buenos Aires: De Palma, 1989), pp. 136ff.

supported after a marital dissolution. They could not, as in modern European countries, expect to receive governmental support, since the broad coverage of the modern welfare state had not come into existence. Moreover, it was taken for granted that in most cases it would be the husband whose derelictions caused the breakup.

On the other hand, the traditional codes of law gave great power to husbands, which was only somewhat diminished by the legal separation. Thus they did not thereby lose all their authority. Perhaps also—here I speculate, but on reasonable grounds—it was not anticipated that court orders for alimony would be strictly enforced, since it would be expected that many or most women would return to their own families after divorce. The Latin American tradition continues to be more familistic than the European. About two-thirds of the children of consensual unions in Mexico and Colombia and about 40 percent of those from legal unions go with their mother to live with her parents. This is true of the children of younger mothers more than of older ones.[33]

When absolute divorce became possible, a widespread set of understandings about sharing marital property and remaining responsible for wives and children through court-ordered support was in place, based on generations of experience with legal separations as the sole form of divorce. Similar provisions exist and have existed in Protestant countries, but they have always been in conflict with the equally widespread attitude that marital dissolution means the end of family responsibilities so that each spouse can and must be free of the other. In the common law tradition of the Protestant countries, the husband was the sole owner of almost all the property the couple built or acquired during the marriage simply because his name was on the deeds—even when his wife had obviously contributed to its accumulation, as on a farm or in a small business. In short, in the Protestant countries marriage was more likely to be seen as a type of contract, with documents and specific laws determining its rights and obligations. When the contract was terminated, the obligations ceased. That harsh Protestant reality has become widely accepted in Western countries, expressed in many court decisions, and it is still an important theme in political debates about divorce.

Fourth, except in Chile, it is now possible in all these countries to get a divorce on traditional severe grounds or on the basis of legal or de facto separation, the length of time varying from nation to nation. If the latter route is chosen, the couple presents to the court a plan stating how the

33. These data are from the World Fertility Survey, analyzed by K. Richter, working paper, University of Wisconsin, 1988–89.

children will be supported, how the matrimonial property will be allocated, whether alimony will be paid, and so on.

A next broad change is the shift in Latin American codes, as occurred earlier in other Western countries, from penalizing the "guilty" party. In the past the court would impose alimony payments on (usually) the guilty husband or refuse them to a guilty wife. In addition, it would require an ex-wife to remain "innocent" after divorce as a condition of continuing to receive support. For example, until the 1983 revisions, Mexican laws favored the innocent spouse in determining whether to award any support at all, and it would continue only if the woman remained "innocent."[34] Such clauses are now less common, or their meaning has softened somewhat. Some decisions (for example, in Uruguay) broaden that category to include even an ex-wife who maintains a stable affective relationship with a man.[35] However, as in the United States, social workers as well as judges are likely to be at best somewhat ambivalent in dealing with such cases, especially when the mother receives welfare. They will assume, as most citizens do, that any "man in the house" is contributing to the support of the household. The 1983 reforms in Mexico eliminated the "good behavior" clause as a condition for alimony.[36]

On the other hand, since there are no charges of fault in a divorce by agreement, the woman must be assumed to be innocent.[37] Perhaps more important, in several countries the criterion of compassion can in some circumstances override that of guilt. For example, the laws of Ecuador, Chile, Peru, and Argentina have the striking provision that even the guilty party may be given support or part of the matrimonial property if he or she absolutely lacks means.[38] Of course, the category of "innocence" continues, but modern laws do not give it so much weight as in the past.

My final broad generalization is, however, of most importance for the adequate functioning of the household after divorce. As in other divorce systems, it is easier to write laws prescribing generous behavior toward children and ex-spouses if there is no machinery to enforce those payments. The laws may amount to little more than exhorting others to be virtuous. In any event, it now seems clear that ex-husbands in Latin America, as in most

34. For the generally egalitarian laws of 1975, see Marisol Martin, *El Divorcio en México* (México: Compañía General de Ediciones, 1979), ch. 4, esp. pp. 124–25.

35. For example, see Varela, *Obligación*, p. 59.

36. Alicia Elena Perez Duarte y Norona, *La Obligación Alimentaria* (Mexico: Editorial Porrúa, 1989), p. 132.

37. Varela, *Obligación*, pp. 51–54.

38. Larrea Holguin, *Manual*, pp. 278–80; Hector Chavez Cornejo, *Derecho Familiar Peruano* (Lima: Librería Studium, 1987), p. 366; Julio Lopez del Carril, *Regimen*, p. 159; and Chile: Código Civil, book I, title 6, article 175.

countries elsewhere, do not welcome the summons to continue support after the marriage has ended.

In support of that conclusion I have found (with one exception) only occasional complaints and comments. For example, in one of the few references to the actual arrangements that become part of the support agreements for a legal separation or divorce in Mexico, Martin makes an impassioned protest against the bargaining weaknesses of the woman in divorce negotiations, who must accept her husband's proposals or simply leave without any agreement. By contrast, under the present conditions a husband does not need an agreement—or a divorce—for he can obtain alternative partners anyway. Martin also notes the general failure of husbands to comply with the agreements and the inability of women to gain a good job once divorced or legally separated, while there is little support of any other kind from other people or agencies.[39]

To what extent do Latin American men comply with support agreements and court orders after divorce? Grosman's research in Argentina provides us with a rare glimpse of what actually happens once the divorce is finalized.[40] It is a useful example because Argentina's provisions for support are similar to those in other Latin American countries, including its incorporation of pre-existing rules that originally applied to separation.

A complete revision of the basic provisions for divorce in Argentina was put into effect in mid-1987. It prescribed support for the innocent party (as noted earlier) at the level the couple enjoyed during the marriage, within the limits of both parties' resources, taking into consideration the age and health of the spouses, their income potential, their respective estates after the division of property, the level of care for the children, and so on.[41] It also anticipates the need to recalculate the value of the support when the currency is devalued—a sometimes spectacular process in Argentina.

As we noted for other countries, a divorce by agreement (no fault is charged) requires the spouses to present to the court a plan that uses the same criteria as in a divorce based on fault. It must provide for visitation rights, and state who is to use the house, and how support for the wife and children is to be assured.[42] The division of matrimonial property—property built during the marriage—is presumed to be equal. That property does not

39. Martin, *El Divorcio* esp. ch. 4, pp. 57–87.

40. Cecilia P. Grosman, *El Proceso de divorcio* (Buenos Aires: Editorial Depalma, 1985). See also "Divorcio: A dos años de la ley," in *La Nación,* Sept. 8, 1989, and "Drama después de la separación: Una responsabilidad postergada," Dec. 20, 1984; as well as Eduardo Jose Cardenas, "Crisis familiares e hijos menores: Está vedada a los jueces la prevención?" *La Ley,* no. 244, tomo 1988-A, Dec. 21, 1987, pp. 709–16; and Cecilia P. Grosman, "Medidas frente al incumplimiento alimentario," *La Ley,* no. 175, tomo 1985-D, Sept. 11, 1985, pp. 936–54.

41. Lopez, 1987, pp. 148ff.

42. Grosman, *El Proceso,* pp. 212ff.

include personal property that either spouse owned before marriage. The required equal division is not altered, moreover, if one spouse (presumably the wife) has not actually invested capital in the property.[43] Rather, it is assumed that the joint efforts of both spouses have contributed to whatever property has been accumulated during the marriage.

The results of these laws cannot be presented in detail, but their general effects can be seen in these broad facts:

First, it is clear that women are economically disadvantaged after divorce. In the 1980s, mother-headed families made up two-thirds of those seeking governmental grants and help, while families with both parents were only 9 percent of the total.

Second, separated and divorced women had the highest labor force participation among women, and that did not diminish much with age.

Third, many husbands who were ordered to pay support do not may it. Most of the men who were charged with failing to obey the court orders for support were not poor—they were white-collar or independent workers, and the highest delinquency rates were among professional men.[44] These data suggest that the provisions for support were not, at best, achieving their supposed aims. Although penal law covers the delinquencies just noted, it was rare for an ex-husband to be jailed for nonpayment because of the general belief that locking up the breadwinner will necessarily stop the flow of support. (This belief was widespread in the United States as well until research proved that the threat—and use—of jail does have considerable effect.) The courts in Uruguay also express that attitude, but Varela asserts that arrests are effective in Chile.[45] One might pause to observe, of course, that in most cases there is no ongoing flow of support to be stopped.

Nor is this problem likely to diminish, as some Argentine analysts suppose, because there will be a drop in the rates of dissolution. There was some reduction from the peak divorce rates of 1987–1988, marked by the introduction of the revised law. In Buenos Aires, however, which is almost certain to reflect what will happen in the future, the number of divorces continued upward in 1988 as well.

Much of this body of law, in Argentina and elsewhere, does not apply to the lower classes because they cannot afford divorce, because so many of them have not legally married, and because the governmental social work agencies furnish them an easy alternative. They work out a de facto separation, in which stipulations for support are negotiated with the spouse.

43. Augusto Belluscio, *Manual de Derecho de Familia* (Buenos Aires: De Palma, 1989), vol. 2, pp. 171–72.
44. Grosman, "Medidas," p. 1.
45. Varela, *Obligación,* pp. 75–77.

Cecilia Grosman's research compared the financial terms of the divorces that were "negotiated" or "by agreement" with those in which fault was charged. She found, as in other Latin American countries (and in most European nations), that in divorces by agreement husbands were able to use their greater financial and legal resources to shape the post-divorce arrangements in their own favor. Thus only 15 percent of the Argentine wives were granted support in negotiated divorces, in contrast to 80 percent of the wives in cases where fault was charged.[46] Support for children was ordered in about four-fifths of all cases (somewhat more for fault divorces).

Again, as in most other countries, the amounts of support awarded are minimal, ignoring the legal standard for support—that is, the general level of living during the marriage. Ninety percent are set at less than the average Argentine income, and 70 percent are at less than half that level. Husbands claim in half of fault divorces that the amounts set are equal to one-third of their incomes.[47] The crucial fact, however, is that the record of actual payment falls far short of that level. Only 36 percent pay with reasonable regularity. Grosman also notes (pp. 235–37) that this level of compliance was about equal to that of the French in the late 1970s, but perhaps lower than in Zurich (27 percent apparently did not pay at all) and in Sweden (40 percent delayed). In these countries as in Argentina, few women go back to the court to secure the payments; either they do not know their ex-husband's address or they do not have the financial resources for a court action or they do not believe they will be successful.

The failure to pay alimony or child support is linked, as in Europe and the Anglo countries, with the father's failure to maintain ties with his children. Mother custody has become the usual pattern in Latin America, although many clauses continue to specify exceptions—the "guilty" party should not get custody in some countries; in Peru a boy of seven or more should go to the husband; in Ecuador a boy at puberty may choose his custodial parent, and so on. The Argentine data suggest what we suppose is widespread in other countries, as in the United States and Europe: divorced fathers, especially those who fail to pay child support, do not generally visit their children.[48]

The factors that generate this pattern seem obvious, even if their exact weight is not known. Fathers resent paying for the support of children whom

46. Grosman, El Proceso, pp. 212–13.
47. Ibid., pp. 227–32.
48. See the interviews with social researchers published in La Nación, Dec. 24, 1984; and Grosman, El Proceso, ch. 7, as well as Grosman, "Es la Suspensión del Régimen de Visitas una Medida Conveniente ante la Falta de los Alimentos?" La Ley, tomo 983-B, May 23, 1983, pp. 1155–66.

they feel they have "lost"; they are angry that their ex-wives might be living idly or wastefully on the money sent to the children; visits generate hostile interactions between spouses; and, moreover, the visits are awkward and inconvenient for both children and parents. Finally, since the fathers do not pay, they do not wish to face their children; and so on.

I believe that where the amount of payments is determined by administrative ruling, and husbands are required to pay by simple bureaucratic enforcement, this tangled web of guilt, anger, and resentment will diminish, as seems to have occurred in Scandinavian countries. Under such arrangements, fathers will be much more likely to take advantage of the visitation rights ordered by the court, and the visits are likely to become less awkward.

Although the high rates of husbands' noncompliance might lead us to question the importance of the formal obligations specified in the law, these rules are nevertheless of interest because they establish the normative framework and the parameters within which the support can be negotiated. It is therefore useful to compare the support obligations that several Latin American countries have codified in their laws. All of them emphasize the responsibility of *both* parents to give adequate support to the children, but very few specify the level of that support. Here is a brief summary:

Argentina: Most divorces are by agreement (separation), and in 85 percent of such cases support is given only for the children. By contrast, in 60 percent of fault divorces support is to be given to both ex-wife and children. As described above, that amount is modest (70 percent of the orders are for less than half the average Argentine wage). In most cases it is also a set figure rather than a percentage of the husband's income. When it *is* a percentage of the income, about 80 percent of the orders in fault cases are for 30 percent or more of his income, and a similar percentage of the orders in no-fault cases are at 30 percent or *less.*[49]

Venezuela: According to one provision, the person at fault pays alimony, but no obligation exists if the divorce is based on five years' separation.[50] As to the reality of support in this country, I have found no study comparable to Grosman's, but similar observations have been made, without precise data. In Venezuela, for example, neither legally nor by custom does the ex-husband continue to pay for the maintenance of the ex-wife; his obligation is to the children. This is a joint and equal duty, but it is understood that in fact it is the father who will assume it, since the children will live with their mother. It is not common for the husband to claim that the mother has income or assets of her own to draw on, although such cases have occurred

49. Grosman, *El Proceso,* pp. 222–27.
50. Ibid., p. 301.

in recent years. Fathers are likely over time to become delinquent in their payments. For the most part, fathers try to avoid giving any money directly to the ex-wife, since she might make her own decisions about spending it. Instead, they try to confine their payments to services or good specifically for the children—for example, medical expenses or insurance, school tuition, and the like. They are even less likely to maintain their children once the ex-wife has remarried or entered a union with another man.[51]

Article 195 of the 1982 law does permit the judge to order alimony payments to the innocent party if she (or he) is unable to make a living or lacks assets. But this provision is invoked rarely for cases in which the marriage has lasted many years and the wife was a homemaker.

Uruguay: The guilty party should maintain the other at the same level as during the marriage to the extent that is possible.[52] Child-support payments will be about one-fifth of the father's income, less if the ex-wife has some income, more if the child is older or if there are several children.

Peru: Alimony should not be more than one-third of the income of the person who pays support.[53]

Ecuador: The innocent person (the language is gender-neutral, even though it is assumed this will be the wife) gets one-fifth of the other spouse's income.[54]

Brazil: The spouse will receive support only if innocent and needy, but the judge has considerable discretion.[55]

Colombia: The needy party will receive alimony, depending on the resources of the other spouse.[56]

These stipulations seem few, but in other countries, too, most support arrangements are made by private negotiations or administrative agencies, based on customary understandings or on the accumulation of case law.

Social security and welfare for divorced mothers and children play a lesser role than in European countries, for historical reasons peculiar to Latin America. Although the total tax burden is very large and many contemporary books refer to the crisis of social security in these countries, the structure

---

51. Personal communication from the Venezualan jurist Carmen Luisa Roche.

52. Varela, *Obligación,* pp. 51, 54–55, 63.

53. Chavez Cornejo, *Derecho,* p. 181.

54. Parraguez, *Manuel,* pp. 279–82.

55. Nogueira, *Alimentos,* articles 19 and 20, pp. 109–11.

56. The fullest account of the development of social security in Latin America is Carmelo Mesa-Lago, *Social Security in Latin America* (Pittsburgh: University of Pittsburgh Press, 1978). References to family allowances of various kinds are found on pp. 26–27, 63, 76, 77, 174, 184, 187, et passim. See also James M. Malloy, *The Politics of Social Security in Brazil* (Pittsburgh: University of Pittsburgh Press, 1979), esp. ch. 6, pp. 146ff.

of governmental assistance is very different.[57] That organization was "cor-
poratist" or "syndicalist"—that is, help in case of death or injury, a need for
funds in case of marriage or death, unemployment, maternal health benefits, or medical aid for a family member was tied to employment in a sector of
the economy. For example, civil servants and the military as groups first
obtained this kind of social support. Railway workers, again as a group, were
covered later. Particular groups with some political power, such as miners,
might obtain these rights. A wife would be covered, but only if she or her
husband was a group member.

The general coverage that has come to be taken for granted in European
countries (and to a lesser extent in the United States) has, in short, not been
the common pattern in Latin America. Thus, the aim was not to cover
everyone and thereby automatically to extend help to divorced mothers and
children with or without membership in one of the stipulated organizations.
Various programs for some kinds of aid do exist, as noted earlier for Argentina, but up to now the restructuring of the system itself toward becoming a
general program is politically difficult.

Conclusion

In this chapter we have pointed out why the analysis of changes in divorce
patterns over the past forty years is especially difficult in Latin America. This
is very likely the first attempt made to weigh these changes for *any* period.
Thus, although I take it for granted that I have committed many errors, I
hope this exploration will open the way for later and sounder efforts.

The most serious limitation is that essential data were never recorded,
while technically adequate research on family change is only in its early
phases. I have tried to work with the available documents, to describe the
observable changes, and to take note of problems that will have to be solved
if an adequate description is to be made. Nevertheless, by utilizing a wide
range of sources, from law codes to surveys, and including much material
from unpublished sources, I have ventured a number of broad conclusions
that I hope at least approximate the reality.

I have considered in some detail the task of analyzing marital dissolution,
as it can be understood through imperfect data, within a widespread pattern
of informal marriage. That system arose under three centuries of domination
by harsh political and Church leaders little interested in improving the lot of

57. Maria Isabel Plata, "Colombia: Discriminating against Women," *J. Family Law* 11 (1987),
p. 86.

the masses and still less interested in fully integrating them within the nation. Church weddings were always an option, but too expensive for most people to choose. As a consequence, I have offered the hypothesis—doubtless to be modified or rejected as better data become available—that in the region as a whole, there have been more dissolutions of informal unions than of legal ones. Those cases are now being increased still more by the spread of cohabitation among classes in which formal weddings were previously the norm.

It is especially in considering what happens after divorce that the discrepancy between the written law and social reality is large (in this as well as other family systems). That gap can be filled only by empirical studies. Nevertheless, I have presented some tentative regularities from various countries, with especially useful data from Argentina, whose system is in many relevant ways like those of other major South American nations.

The older system of formal dissolution was of course the legal separation, permitted by the Church to ease conflict without permitting remarriage. Thus a commonly understood body of law existed, specifying the duties of both spouses after separation. It put special obligations on husbands, since these were mainly middle-class families, and abandonment would have been scandalous. It would also have been politically unwise since the wife's family might be powerful. Since social customs did not smile on respectable mothers living alone, however, most of these women almost certainly returned to their fathers' residence.

Such traditional "solutions" are less possible now. Women do not as willingly seek that kind of protection, and various kinds of state support are available for some categories of divorced mothers. Until recently, however, there have been few attacks on the privileged position of divorced fathers, I believe mainly because there have been almost no studies of their failure to make child support payments.

The most important legal change is that the South American nations such as Argentina, Brazil, and Colombia have moved closer to the conservative European countries in their divorce patterns; that is, divorce is possible, but somewhat difficult. Those in Central America and the Caribbean, such as Panama, Guatemala, Honduras, and Cuba, as noted earlier, have had more permissive divorce laws and higher divorce rates for some decades. The South American countries, which have only recently permitted divorce, have so far kept most of the traditional severe grounds for fault divorce (or separation), but (except for Chile) permit some form of divorce by agreement, on the basis of one to three years of separation. It seems likely that this latter form will be used still more as the divorce rates continue to increase.

Chile, as noted, has continued to use a system that permits relatively easy annulment on various bureaucratic, technical grounds.

I predict that these nations will also move to develop a more adequate means of enforcing support payments as the need for such regulations grows. This prediction, however, is based on the hope that more special studies will be made of the failure of ex-husbands to support their children or former wives. That may not be a false hope if divorce becomes a more popular subject of research as these nations begin to accept the normality of divorce and to confront the magnitude of the problems faced by divorced mothers and their children.

8

Stable High-Divorce-Rate Systems and Their Decline: Japan and Malaysia

In this chapter we explore a pattern that, to my knowledge, has not yet appeared in the literature on divorce—countries with stable family patterns over many generations which nevertheless have consistently high divorce rates. Although some of the specific data I use have been analyzed by others, and although I myself have attempted to analyze the possibility of a decrease in divorce rates under industrialization in Japan, this chapter focuses on an important and unique type of family system—one that generates high divorce rates while itself remaining relatively unchanged over long periods of time. I call these "stable high-divorce-rate systems."

For well over two thousand years social theorists have noted differences between urban and rural regions in social patterns and organizations. Plato observed the differences between port cities and other cities, Ibn Khaldun analyzed the contrast between tribal people and the effete city dwellers in the fourteenth century, and indeed, it is very likely that most social philosophers and analysts have pointed out these differences under one label or another. In 1887, Ferdinand Tönnies wrote a systematic exposition of these differences, and in his title and text applied the labels to them we still use, *Gemeinschaft* and *Gesellschaft*. So pervasive have been the ideas in these concepts that some have asserted caustically that sociology is no more than an extended commentary on Gemeinschaft and Gesellschaft.

Since I do not wish to expatiate on those differences except to note how they have been used in research on divorce, I will confine myself to a brief description of the key elements in each type of social system. Gemeinschaft is usually defined by face-to face social interaction, the uniqueness of persons and relationships, commitments to the local collectivity and the family, homogeneity of the people in the community, similarity of norms and values, and village and rural settings. The Gesellschaft type of society is characterized by the opposite traits: people are more heterogeneous, engage in much interaction with others as types or classes rather than as unique individuals, seek their self-interest more (rather than that of the collectivity), and interact with others only in a narrow area rather than as whole persons. In short, they follow the kinds of patterns that we generally observe in urban social settings. Such social traits are of course variables, not dichotomies; that is, communities exhibit more or less of them.

Complexities abound in these concepts, not the least of which is that we can point to Gesellschaft patterns in almost any tribal society, and, conversely, to community, folk, or Gemeinschaft social patterns in any urban setting; but here our concern is only with the supposed relationship between these two "ideal types" and divorce patterns.

The received view in sociology has been that life is more stable and people invest more in the collectivity of the family in rural areas or villages. Wives and husbands share common values as well as customs and thus conflict with each other less frequently and less intensely. Each needs the other economically (as in any rural setting), and social norms support enduring lifelong commitments. Differences between husband and wife are regarded as normal and are tolerated, and spouses see no reason to dissolve their relationship. Husbands and wives are also integrated into a larger community of elders and kin who also reinforce their staying together.

Family life in cities, it has usually been maintained, contrasts with all this. Life is less stable, faster moving. Traditional norms break down, especially those concerning sexual and family behavior. Since people are self-interested, they dissolve their unions when they believe they can find a better spouse. Spouses fight more, because their norms are more likely to be different, because norms and values are changing, and because other people in their networks or neighborhoods have a lesser commitment to traditional family patterns.

Although the acute reader will easily see gaps in this reasoning, he or she will also recognize it. It is commonly found in sociological textbooks, and widely expressed in sermons, newspaper articles, and speeches. Moreover, hundreds of studies (in the West) support the general notion that divorce rates are higher in urban areas, that divorce rates begin to rise first in cities, that traditional family values and norms first begin to weaken in cities, and so on.

Nevertheless, this pattern is not a constant. More important, the notions of Gemeinschaft and Gesellschaft do not constitute a *theory*; rather, they are a complex, rich set of descriptive ideas. We do not have any general theory in sociology to account for the (presumed) buildup of the *traditional* system— that is, one in which there *is* consensus, fidelity to the norms, marital stability, and so on. The "fall away from virtue" we understand better, since any demanding system is likely to weaken over time; thus the slow dissolution of such systems under urbanization (or other social forces) can often be taken for granted. We may even perceive our own lives as such a fall.

This is not the first time I have discussed this pattern, but it is the first time I have analyzed it systematically. Nearly three decades ago I drew attention to the empirical fact of *declining* divorce rates in some urbanized regions, and to high rates in some rural areas. I noted that whether specific rates (birth, death, or divorce) or typical ages (at marriage or the like) rose or fell under the impact of industrialization would depend on where they stood beforehand, under the *traditional* system. In particular, I pointed to some of the traditional systems (for example, Japan and the Arab countries) that generated high divorce rates.[1] These high rates were also to be found especially among *rural* populations; and more generally, all those societies were largely rural. I also predicted that although those Gemeinschaft societies would exhibit declining divorce rates (because the modernizing forces would begin to undermine the traditional ones that generated high divorce rates), the rates would eventually rise again.

Here I continue the analysis of this broad pattern and in this chapter illustrate it with case studies of two countries that have experienced a declining divorce rate, Japan and Malaysia. In later chapters we consider other countries with similar patterns: modern China (which experienced a decrease, but not because of industrialization), the Arab world, where I suspect there has not been as much industrialization (in our specific sense) as is commonly believed, as well as Taiwan and Indonesia.

Before proceeding to concrete examples, however, let us offer some general conclusions about these societies in their traditional phases, *before* they were affected by the ideas, the culture, or the immediate direct pressures of industrialization.

First, over very long time periods, perhaps hundreds of years, very likely the rates of marital instability in any traditional society (including Western ones) exhibited *no trends at all*. The rates went up and down only modestly, in a form Pitirim Sorokin called "trendless fluctuation." This is true whether we consider only formal divorces, or the more general class of marital dissolutions.

Second, in times of great change, such as revolutions and civil wars, epidemics, famines, or conquests, rates of marital dissolution almost certainly went up in the West, as they did in periods of rapid increases in prosperity.

1. William J. Goode, *World Revolution and Family Patterns* (New York: 1965), pp. 25, 155, 358 ff.

Third, each family system within a more or less trendless socioeconomic organization generated a given level of marital dissolution, or divorce if it was permitted. This general rate was very different from that of other traditional societies in the same epoch.

Fourth, some of these systems *typically* created high rates of dissolution or divorce, while others did not, but the differences bear little relation to such modern phenomena as "modernization," industrialization, commercial capitalism, and the like.

Thus the indigenous Japanese system in the Tokugawa period (and extending into the Meiji period for some decades) almost certainly exhibited high rates of marital dissolution especially in rural areas, and so did some of the societies that form the great Moslem crescent from North Africa to Indonesia (some with rates perhaps even higher than those of Japan). The Chinese and Indian systems and Western nations (under the Catholic Church) did not do so until relatively modern times.

On the other hand, at the beginning of the recent modern period, in the Elizabethan era, the noble families of England were prone to a considerable amount of dissolution (though a true legal divorce was not then possible). What was happening to peasasnt families at that time we do not know,[2] but it is likely that in England at least their dissolution rate was higher.

Finally, though we can take note of these stable differences, in sociology we have no overarching theory that could explain why each of them occurred. We can only give *ad hoc* accounts of the factors that seem to generate each set of rates. It should also be noted that the attempts by economists have also been empty so far, because their assumptions about how marriage systems operate pay so little respect to reality (for example, the failure to see *whose* decision it is; the assumption that in each system everyone is maximizing *monetary* gains and that the divorce is propelled by the individual maximizing decisions of the spouses, not by the elders who dominate the system).[3]

Of course, for some cases I feel our explanations are sound. High rates in matrilineal family systems, for example, seem clear enough. Women and their brothers remained firmly linked even after marriage, since they belonged to the same lineage, and shared material and emotional stakes in

2. Lawrence Stone, *Crisis of the Aristocracy, 1558–1641* (New York: Oxford University Press, 1915), pp. 660–62. He also asserts in *Family, Sex and Marriage in England, 1500–1800* (New York: Harper and Row, 1977), p. 30, that "up to the eleventh century there was easy divorce, and the definition of what was marriage was both loose and not very binding until the 1500s."
3. For an elaborate attempt of this kind, see Gary Becker, *A Treatise on the Family* (Cambridge: Harvard University Press, 1981), esp. ch. 10. See also William J. Goode, "The Economics of Nonmonetary Variables," in T. W. Schultz, ed., *Economics of the Family* (Chicago: University of Chicago Press, 1974), pp. 345–51.

lineage matters. The husband was not a member of his wife's lineage, but his children were, and their mother's brother had jural authority over them. If there was a divorce, the husband moved out, and the children and mother remained together as a unit, still possessed of whatever lineage property there was. In many, perhaps most, such societies, some part of the family subsistence came from the wife's lineage—that is, from her brother. In addition, many of these societies were also horticultural, and thus women were very important in the productive process itself.

The implicit reasoning in the foregoing paragraph seems to be that when women are in a stronger position they do not have to tolerate bad behavior in their husbands—or perhaps they become less tolerant of inadequacies in or slights from their husbands. Modern social analysts in Europe and the United States apply the same principle in asserting that because many women in Western countries now earn good salaries, they feel free to be more independent and thus will not adjust to traditional male demands.

That reasoning would not, however, apply to most traditional Moslem and especially Arab societies. Although the Koran guaranteed some rights to women that Western countries did not offer until much later, these social systems typically fell far short of the Koranic injunctions. Since Moslem women have had relatively lowly positions for centuries, the social analyst is tempted to "explain" high Moslem rates generally by the ease with which *husbands* could divorce their wives. They only needed to say "Talak, Talak, Talak" before two witnesses to be irrevocably divorced. Thus we are tempted to explain the high divorce rate in the Arab world by pointing to women's low status and lack of power to prevent a divorce.

Note that we have just invoked two diametrically opposed explanations of high divorce rates based on women's status. In one case, when we analyzed matrilineal societies or the United States, we concluded that divorce rates are high because women are in a strong position. In the second case, when we analyzed the Arab world, we concluded that divorce rates are high because women's position is weak. For Japan, a still different "explanation" is necessary.

None of these explanations is adequate, however, in the sense that the necessary variables are shown to be correlated with higher or lower divorce rates, across a range of countries over time. They are *ad hoc,* and come dangerously close to being no more than a restatement of the question. Still, we can make a few additional general statements about such systems.

One general emphasis to be kept in mind is that in crucial structural ways a traditional high-divorce family system is not like that of a modern Western society with similarly high rates. In all societies, though more in some than in others, men have more power than women. If men were only husbands and not fathers or brothers, it would be in their interest to shape a family system in which they could marry and discard wives at their own whim. As fathers, brothers, uncles, and cousins, however, it is in their interest to protect their own women. All family systems are in part the outcomes of these (and certain parallel) tensions. Thus all family systems contain numerous provisions for the care and welfare of women, whether before or after marital dissolution.[4]

Stable high-divorce societies also share another important principle with others, that women are a valuable resource for the continuance of the society (and for other pleasures) and should be *used*. Thus the high-divorce society is typically a high-remarriage society. And even where the divorce rate is low, as in Ch'ing China, widows and divorced women "disappear demographically" into the married status. If they are still young they are not usually allowed to languish, to be a burden, or to suffer as castoffs. (Brahmin widows, in a group with low divorce rates, were and are exceptions to this rule.) It is only in modern Western and some Eastern (and Arab) countries that we find a large and growing number of divorced mothers who become single heads of family units, at low wages or on social welfare, and who remain unmarried for increasingly long periods or indefinitely. By contrast, since divorces in a traditional high-divorce society typically occurred early, and almost everyone remarried, the percentage of the population in the status "now divorced" did not increase.

In addition, in stable high-divorce societies, divorce arrangements were *institutionalized*. Whether and what part of the bride price is to be returned, who gets the children at what ages, who is responsible for remarriage— all such matters were determined by accepted custom and rule. By contrast, in modern Western countries the problems caused by divorce are a nexus of individual misunderstanding, conflict, litigation, or decision, whose outcome leaves many needs unfulfilled and requires state intervention.

From these differences, we cannot infer that domestic life was happy in low-divorce societies, or full of conflict in high-divorce societies. Nor can we even infer that women in high-divorce societies led a more miserable life. In tribal matrilineal societies, clearly women enjoyed relatively strong positions, while in Japan (again, a high-divorce society) perhaps they did not. In Japan it was the groom's parents who could send the young wife back. Typically the young woman continued to have a secure place in the community after that, however, and in her natal family until she remarried. Indeed, one could suggest that the marital turnover among young Japanese peasants (and perhaps other traditional high-divorce systems) was an extended

4. For an analysis of a related set of tensions, see Goode, "Why Men Resist," in Barry Thorne and Marilyn Yalom, eds., *Rethinking the Family: Some Feminist Questions* (New York: Longman, 1982), pp. 131–50.

phase of the total courtship and mate choice process.[5] In such societies, the duration of first marriages was short—on the average only a year or two— again unlike Western countries. Since so many divorced, and at young ages, most of those who did divorce also remarried. That is, these young divorcees could usually find a potential spouse among the unmarried or the recently divorced or widowed.

More important, contrary to the Western pattern, later marriages were likely to be more stable than first marriages. In some, perhaps all such societies, those who had been married once were given somewhat more freedom of choice. Divorcees were a bit older and more experienced. People eventually do settle down. The divorced population was not "deviant," especially in societies where so many first marriages did not last. Consequently, there was not a growing population of those divorced but not yet remarried.

Finally, we can predict that, other things being equal, a weakening of the historical forces that *proximately* created high divorce rates in a traditional society might reduce the divorce rate. This is not of course the only alternative historical change may reveal. Tribal societies, for example, may be swallowed up by revolution, war, and social disorganization in a new nation. That is, some of the new and powerful social forces may lead not only to a breakup of matrilineal family patterns (as in Central Africa), but also to a reduction in marital stability and even in the chances of life. History is sometimes cruel and often does considerable destruction as the "new era" unfolds.

Thus a traditional society may have high divorce rates, and these may decline under industrialization, a process I consider in this and succeeding chapters. Let us first, however, look at a nation which reduced divorce rates directly as a political program, rather than only indirectly and as a byproduct of modernizing forces.

Japan

The Meiji Restoration in 1868 aimed at nothing short of a revolution—not a socialist but a conservative one: It sought to keep Japan's ancient ways

5. For the most part, these earlier customs are lost to the Japanese public, and even in the early period of Meiji (after 1868) the Japanese leaders began to speak of the "traditional Japanese way" when they meant a new, modified *samurai* form of marriage, which they wanted all to adopt. See Goode, *World Revolution*, pp. 321–31; Kunio Yanagida, *Japanese Manners and Customs in the Meiji Era*, trans. Charles S. Terry (Tokyo: Obunsha, 1957), esp. chs. 4, 6, 10. See also Richard K. Beardsley, John W. Hall, Robert E. Ward, *Village Japan* (Chicago; University of Chicago Press, 1939); and Robert J. Smith and Ella L. Wiswell, *The Women of Suye Mura* (Chicago: University of Chicago Press, 1982). Concerning mostly the advantaged classes, see L. W. Kuchler, "Marriage in Japan," *Trans. Asiatic Soc. of Japan* 13 (July 1885), pp. 114–37.

intact while becoming the first non-Western nation to industrialize successfully. Its astonishing achievements extended to the family as well.

The new leaders sought, through propaganda, formal education, and new legal codes, to impose the family patterns of the *samurai* on all Japanese and to reject the rural patterns as uneducated and primitive. As a result, Japan was the first high-divorce nation to decrease its divorce rate substantially. To be sure, industrialization contributed to the decades-long drop in the divorce rate, but the foundations of the shift were also deliberate political decisions and legal acts, based on the ideology of the Meiji reformers.

But before we discuss the Meiji reforms, let us look at the dynamics of the traditional high-divorce patterns that were in place prior to the Meiji restoration.

The Traditional High Rate of Divorce in Rural Japan

It is very likely that we shall not grasp the dynamics of the Japanese rural high-divorce pattern more than superficially although my previous generalizations about such systems do apply here as well. Historians have documented the high divorce rates in rural Japan in the Tokugawa period, but their focus has been on the differences among the various social strata in Japan.[6] These analyses can be useful, but—as I have noted at various points in this work—most of them do not have much explanatory weight when applied to other nations.[7]

Aside from collections of folk customs, the Japanese did not carry out systematic anthropological field studies of village life prior to World War II. It is possible that John Embree's work on Suye Mura in the late 1930s was the first such study, but by that time the older system was only a remnant in most regions.[8] We can, however, make a sketch of that earlier pattern.

Under the traditional rural pattern Japanese young men and women, unlike the Chinese, not only knew one another prior to marriage but in rural areas they had some clandestine but widely understood private access to one another. But they married only with the permission of their parents (as in eighteenth-century Sweden). Marriage in early adolescence was neither a Japanese ideal nor a common practice. Young women, who married at an average of 19 years in the nineteenth century, were expected to shoulder the heavy adult burdens of rural tasks. Grooms were about 22 years of age and

6. For example, Noriko Iwai has drawn my attention to the complex analysis done by Yoshihiro and Reiko Tsubouchi, in *Rikon: Hikaku-shakaigakuteki Kenkyu* (Divorce: A Comparative Sociological Study) (Sobunsya, 1970). They point out some of the differences between the upper and lower samurai (the latter with higher rates) and various rural groups (pp. 143–223).

7. But see also the thoughtful analysis of the dynamics of marriage and divorce in Laurel L. Cornell, "Peasant Women and Divorce in Preindustrial Japan," *Signs* 15 (1990), pp. 710–32.

8. John F. Embree, *Suye Mura, A Japanese Village,* (Chicago: University of Chicago Press, 1939). See also Smith and Wiswell, *Women of Suye Mura.*

thus considered adults, but it was the parents of the young man who would decide that it was time for him to marry, and with whom.

Local custom ruled marriage practices, and no state license was (or is) required for marriage. And in earlier Japan it was not typically recorded in the family *koseki* until some time had passed.[9] For this reason, it will never be possible to obtain a correct divorce rate for the period before the Meiji Restoration, or for that matter for several decades thereafter. It was common for the union to be unrecorded for a variable period, perhaps until the parents had decided that the daughter-in-law seemed suitable. If they decided that she was not suitable, they could send her back to her own family. (She could also run away, back to her own family, if she was unhappy.)

Thus many breakups were quite informal, and innumerable dissolutions could occur with no official or even family documents taking note of them. Although in the 1880s there were more than 300 officially recorded divorces per 1,000 marriages—a ratio higher than the United States experienced until recent decades—it is almost certain that the true figures were much higher.[10] Indeed, they continued to rise until 1897, when the official ratio was 340, and dropped only in the following year, when the new Civil Code was put into effect. Keep in mind that in the past these rates were mostly rural; now, by contrast, they are higher in urban than in rural areas.[11]

Why was there such a high incidence of marital dissolution? What were the dynamics of interaction in the early stages of household adjustment? We do not know precisely but it is clear that in most cases it was the in-laws who decided to send back the young bride, for it was they who had to be pleased with her, not the groom. By and large, that happened early in the union, usually before the birth of children. But why were there so many of these "send-back" divorces? And why did the high rate of rejection not lead to squabbles between the families of the bride and the groom in the village or local area? In a private communication, Cornell asserts the reasonable hypothesis that a majority of unions occurred between people from different villages, so that any bad feelings between the families would be less costly anyway.

The young woman was not, however, in the situation of the Chinese bride, separated from village and kin, with no resources of her own. Later descriptions of village life inform us that rural women in Japan were more indepen-

9. Fumie Kumagai reports that about two-thirds of all marriages in 1978 were registered within one month of the event. See her informative article, "Changing Divorce in Japan," in *Family History* (Spring 1983), pp. 85–108.

10. This ratio is not of course a true divorce *rate*, but both go up and down together, and the ratio is one mode of describing the prevalence of divorce. See also Goode, *World Revolution*, p. 359. Edward Norbeck, writing of the period after World War II, says that the unrecorded unions in his village were simply not considered divorces when they were dissolved (*Takashimaya* [Salt Lake City: University of Utah Press, 1954], p. 52).

11. Kumagai, "Changing Divorce," p. 86.

dent than Chinese brides and had not yet become as subservient as Western travelers observed urban women to be.[12] As a productive worker, the Japanese bride was valuable, and she knew that others before her had divorced and still found adequate husbands. The remarriage rate was high, almost total, and thus at any given time until the death of a spouse, almost every adult was in the married state, whatever his or her previous marital adventures. In effect, the traditional rural Japanese bride who was confronted by rejecting in-laws always knew that she had an alternative: she did not *have* to adjust. (Below we shall note the same pattern among brides in Indonesia and Malaysia.)

As noted above, the Japanese leaders made a deliberate effort to change these family patterns. Their aim was to reduce the divorce rates and produce a lower-divorce-rate family system that would be more in harmony with samurai ideals. Their success was a result of several factors, but primarily their conscious efforts to impose the samurai domestic ideals and practices on the population by setting in motion both an ideological and a legal program. For example, in discussions about family provisions for the Civil Code that was eventually put into effect in 1898, the Legal Committee agreed that "the customs of the farmers are not to be made general custom— instead we must go by the practice of *samurai* and noblemen."[13]

The patterns of the samurai were thus codified and came to be seen as the "true Japanese way," as if they had been handed down as a unified cultural heritage to all from distant generations. It should be emphasized here that this reference is only to the upper samurai. In fact, many in this "warrior" status were without power or wealth. The reference was not, furthermore, to some empirically recorded statistical description of upper samurai practice, but to the *ideal* samurai way. In contrast, the rural patterns—which in the past were found among the majority—came to be viewed as uneducated and primitive.[14]

The Impact of the Meiji Reforms

How successful were these efforts? Over time family patterns clearly began to change. The situation of the bride under the new system came closer to that of the Chinese ideal: the young woman was absorbed into the household of the groom's father, expected to remain subordinate to her mother-in-law and to devote herself to domestic duties. She was given little opportunity to develop marketable skills (except for education) that would be a resource in the event of family conflict.

12. See especially Smith and Wiswell, *Women of Suye Mura*. Women in fishing villages were, and remain, much more independent, and such areas continue to exhibit high rates of divorce (Kumagai, "Changing Divorce," p. 104).

13. Yanagida, *Japanese Manners*, p. 119.

14. Norbeck, 1954, p. 175; see also Goode, *World Revolution*, pp. 321–30.

Gradually, more marriages were arranged by go-betweens rather than elders, since the young man and woman were increasingly less likely to know each other prior to marriage. Although by the 1880s many young women worked in factories and came to be educated, elders kept strict control over where they worked as well as over their earnings.

The Japanese elders and leaders were well aware of the threat of industrialization, and for a long period were able to prevent it from eroding their power in the cities. And rural people were gradually trained to accept the new modes of domestic life.

More strongly put, these changes were guided by a political ideology that put high value on service to the state. The Japanese leaders most emphatically did not intend to accept the Western *ideology* of industrialization. They wanted only to learn and apply industrial *technology,* while pressing their subjects to hold fast to the highest ancient ideals. Over the long haul, of course, neither Japan nor any other nation has succeeded in doing that. The ideological elements of industrialization continue to become further embedded in people's attitudes and actions.

Although an adequate analysis of the family changes in the early Meiji period would be beyond the scope of this inquiry, we can note a few of the first steps in moving the systems toward the "true Japanese way." Broadly, the aim was to intensify the family hierarchy and male power and to strengthen family controls over the individual, through dominion over access to land in the countryside and to jobs and training in the cities. Greater power was given to the head of the family line and the rule of primogeniture was imposed on all families wherever possible. A member of the family line could not choose his residence or marry without the permission of the head. Education was extended to the whole population. Women were allowed to take jobs in the new factories, but were not allowed to control their own wages or to work there after marriage, thus making them more dependent on their husbands and in-laws.

These steps as well as much propaganda in favor of the new arrangements were aimed at wiping out the rural customs in which women had more scope for decision and action. Of course, rural women and men continued for decades to follow customs at variance with the domestic patterns of the elite. The 1898 Code required state registration for marriages, and thereafter divorces were not reported unless the marriages had previously been reported. This had the immediate effect of reducing the *official* rate of divorce, but in addition the public stance of leaders was that the unofficial shuffling of mates was crude and countrified. Thus in the early stages of rapid industrialization Japan succeeded in creating more family controls over individual choice in marriage and divorce in order to harness the strength of the family for its own purposes—industrial and national power. These efforts were strengthened in the 1930s by an intensive campaign of nationalist propaganda, as Japan moved into an new expansionist phase (it took over Taiwan in 1895) with its conquest of part of China and later much of southeastern Asia. It was not until 1947 that the new Civil Code was passed, envisioning a "modern" family system, more in harmony with industrialization.

Both the 1898 Code and that of 1947 were far in advance of popular attitudes, so it was not until the 1960s that many of the results of the previous decades of changes had become apparent: the lessened power of the elderly, more elders living in their grown children's household (as contrasted with the older system in which the couple would have been living in the *elder's* house), high levels of education for both men and women, a growing approval of free choice in marriage, low fertility, a growing percentage of women working after marriage, and—more recently—even a modest feminist movement.[15] Thus elders cannot control, as they once could, the inevitable conflicts between husband and wife, and husbands have lost some of their command over their wives. The Japanese divorce rate reached its lowest figure in 1963 and steadily rose thereafter until the mid-1980s.

The Impact of Industrialization on Divorce Rates

How can we summarize what happened to the Japanese rate of divorce during industrialization? As I noted in *World Revolution and Family Patterns* (1963), because the Japanese family system "begins with so high a rate of marital dissolution . . . the long-time trend is *downward* during industrialization, not upward." Industrialization "reduced divorces from traditional causes (elder in-laws sending the bride back) but may *increase* the number of divorces due to individual incompatibility between husband and wife" (p. 363). Indeed, beginning in the 1960s, the divorce rate did start upward again. Although it is unlikely that the rate will match those in Western countries over the next few decades, it is rising.

It is sometimes said that the Meiji Restoration displaced the great *daimyo*, the princes, and took away the privileges of the samurai (who at least thought of themselves as warriors even if they never went to war), while opening advancement to all through education and industrialization. However, it is only partly literary exaggeration to say that the consequence if not the intent of this vast program was to make all Japanese into samurai, devoted to endless efforts to keep the nation great. This consequence is obvious in industry, but it is also apparent in the arena of the family, where

15. For example, employed women have gone to court in order to do away with many forms of discrimination; and the government has even passed an employee equal opportunity law. See Frank E. Upham, *Law and Social Change in Japan* (Cambridge: Harvard University Press, 1987).

the goal was to harness this institution and turn it to the task of industrial development.

Recent Trends in Divorce Rates

Since Japan has better data on some aspects of its marriage and divorce patterns than most other countries do, certain other recent divorce trends are worth noting. However, let us first present the time trends for the modern era. Figure 8.1 shows the divorce curve for the past century. Table 8.1 gives the rates themselves. The decline extends over some decades; the rise is recent.

In both the crude divorce rates and the rates per 1,000 married couples we see a steady decline in divorce rates from 1947 to 1963. For example, divorces per 1000 couples dropped from 5.4 in 1950 to 3.7 in 1960 to 3.5 in 1963. After 1963 the rates began to rise slowly but steadily—to 3.9 in 1970, 4.3 in 1975, 4.9 in 1980, and 5.4 in 1985.

Will they continue to rise, however, as we have predicted? The crude rate reached its highest point in 1986, the rate per thousand couples in 1985. The slight changes since then may mean nothing. After all, such rates can go up or down through the years while the long-term or secular trend moves steadily upward. Nor do we know of any new factors in Japanese family life that might predict a continued decline. As in any unique case, almost any change might be possible.

Japanese rates per thousand couples can be calculated accurately only every five years, when the census yields that base; otherwise they are estimates. Age-specific figures have also been calculated, and they show that the rates for both men and women increased in the period 1987–1988 among younger people but decreased among older ones (men over 33 years, women over 32). Those rates did not, however, decrease to the level of 1980.[16]

Another study estimated the married population through 1987; it apparently increased during 1981–1987, but the study suggests that the apparent decrease in divorce rates was caused by changes in the composition of the population. That is, there may have been (1) a decrease in the married population aged about 25–35, where divorce is more common; (2) the entrance of the first cohorts of baby boomers into the older ages, where divorce is less common; and (3) an increase in the percentage of the married population over fifty years of age, where again the rates are lower.[17] Still

16. Kiyoshi Horishima and Rieko Bando, "Divorce Rates in Japan: 1980–1990," *J. Population Problems* 46 (1990), pp. 56–64.

17. Shigeki Amino, "Rikon no Gensyo ni tsuite: Tsuma no Nenrei betsu ni mita Rikon" (On the Decrease of Divorces: Age-specific Marital Divorce Rate for Women), in *Kosei no Shihyo* 36 (1989), pp. 33–37. Courtesy of Noriko Iwai.

Figure 8.1: Marriage and Divorce Rates in Japan per 1,000 Population, 1882–1979

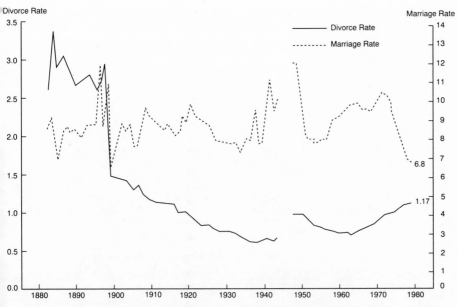

Sources: 1882–1899, *Nihon Teikoku Tōkei Nenkan,* Bureau of the Census, Prime Minister's Office (Tokyo, 1915); 1900–1978, *Vital Statistics, 1978,* vol. 1, Health and Welfare Statistics Dept., Minister Secretariat, Minister of Health and Welfare (Tokyo, 1980); 1989, estimations, Health & Welfare Statistics Association (Tokyo, 1980).

another study of age-specific probabilities of being divorced reports that among younger women the chances continue to increase.[18]

It should be remembered that divorce rates in several European nations were also stable or declining slightly in the late 1980s, perhaps because fewer were in the married state. We do not yet know whether this is a temporary respite.

Although Japan's divorce rate has been rising, it should be repeated that by Western standards it remains low. At its lowest in 1963, it was 3.5 per 1,000 married women. It rose by 25 percent in 1980, to 4.3 per 1,000, and to 5.5 in 1985. Ages at marriage are at about the level of much of modern Europe: in 1980, the average age of grooms was 27.8 years, and that of brides was 25.2 (first marriages); in 1990 they were 28.4 and 25.9.[19] Bride and groom were more similar in age than in the past, as I pointed out earlier,

18. Akira Ishikawa, *Cohort Marriage Tables for Females in Japan, 1950–87: Estimates of Marital Status.* Research Series no. 261, Oct. 1989.
19. *White Report on National Life.* Source: Vital Statistics, Ministry of Health and Welfare, 1983; Marriage and Birth in Japan: The 9th Survey on Fertility, 1987.

Table 8.1: Marriage and Divorce Rates in Japan, 1947–1990

Year	Crude Divorce Rate (per 1,000 population)	Divorce Rates per 1,000 Couples
1947	1.02	
1950	1.01	5.4
1955	0.84	4.5
1960	0.74	3.7
1963	0.73	3.5
1965	0.79	3.6
1970	0.93	3.9
1975	1.07	4.3
1980	1.22	4.9
1986	1.37	5.4 (1985)
1988	1.29	
1990 (est.)	1.31	

Sources: Kumagai, "Changing Divorce," appendix A, 1986; Japan Statistical Yearbook, 1988, and Monthly Abstract of Statistics. Noriko Iwai has sent me a copy of historical data published in 1984, covering the century from 1883 to 1982. Some of the data are revisions of figures published in that period, but they do not vary by much, and the patterns are parallel: *Rikon Tokei: Jinko Dotai Tokei Tokushu Hokoku* (Divorce Statistics: Special Report of Vital Statistics, Ministry of Health and Welfare, Dept. of Statistical Information, 1984) table 1, pp. 34–35.

but even if the decline in the age difference is real enough, it is minute. The change should rather be described as a slight increase in same-age marriages and in unions between a man and an older woman.[20]

A datum that simultaneously reports substantial change and reminds us how different from the West this system remains is the steady decline of "arranged marriages": from 52 percent of the unions of 1950–1954 (1977 Survey) to 23 percent of those married in 1985 and after (1987 Survey);[21] and the increase in the percentage of people who met at the workplace or through friends, or who asserted they had a "love marriage" (from 57 percent of those marrying in 1965–1969 to 75 percent of those who married in 1985 and after).[22]

The Divorce Process: Reaching Agreement

As in the West, women are more likely to be the first "to speak of getting a divorce," and that percentage rose only very slightly (from 51 percent to 55

20. Kumagai, "Changing Divorce," pp. 95–96; but see the more recent data for the period 1978–1988, in *Kosei no Shihyo* (Index of Health and Welfare) 37:5 (May 1990), p. 19. Courtesy of Noriko Iwai. The August 1990 issue, p. 10, reports that in the modal couple of 1965, the husband was three years older than his wife; in 1975 there was only a two-year difference; and by 1988 the modal couple was made up of spouses the same age.

21. *White Report,* 1987, p. 111; and see The 9th Survey, table 2.6 (*Showa 62 nen Nihonjin no Kekkon to Shussan: Dai 9ji Shussanryoku Chosa*). Courtesy of Noriko Iwai.

22. The 9th Survey.

percent) in the period 1968–1978.[23] Of course, who speaks first tells us little or nothing about whose behavior first moves toward breakup. It is nevertheless indicative of great change that Japanese women can take this initiative, as contrasted with the historically distant past in which the young man's parents could send the wife back. It is also noteworthy that in three-fourths of the cases that are *not* "by agreement" it is the wife who first brought up the possibility of divorce.[24] On the other hand, *this is not new.* That figure has been as high, or even higher, since 1900.[25] To be sure, almost all cases are "by agreement"; only one in ten falls into the other categories of mediation (*chotei*), contested cases, or judgment by family court. I do not know what is the changing meaning of "agreement" in a society where women have always had to adjust to informal pressures.

The 1898 Civil Code followed European codes in specifying which offenses justified divorce, but marriage in Japan had never been a sacrament. The new formalization made some changes but, in this arena as in others, the Japanese avoided courts in favor of personal mediation; it was not deemed proper to bring family conflicts to public scrutiny. The Western mind rejects the term " by agreement" as the appropriate label for a result in which people are pressured to agree. But formally the term is accurate: in the past it was "consent," in the sense that the young husband did agree to his elders' decisions by deciding not to challenge them, and the young bride did agree to her dismissal by deciding to return home. The Japanese term may in fact express a deeper truth that the West has come to accept only in the last decade or so: if one ultimately comes to understand that not much can be done about the estrangement, one does "consent" to the divorce. One then "chooses" divorce, against alternatives that seem worse.

If the parties do agree, the divorce procedure will be cheap, quick, and simple. The use of lawyers is uncommon in any disputes, especially in domestic conflict. Going to court suggests that the spouses do not possess adequate sponsors, or a properly functioning family or extended kin, to solve the problem.

In any dispute, respected patrons or sponsors, elders, or kin seek to remove the problem or reduce its scope, and press the warring parties to concede something here and there. Their aim is to achieve a harmonious

23. Women give a higher figure: 65% claimed they made the first initiative, while 55% of the men admitted that women spoke about it first. See *White Report,* table II.2, and *Special Report of Vital Statistics* (Ministry of Health, 1984), fig. 8.2. I noted earlier that such data do not clearly show who "really" moved toward divorce first.

24. See *Special Report,* 1984; in about one-tenth of the cases, it is still the elder generation who "speak first."

25. Source: Annual Report on Judicial Statistics, Supreme Court, in Yasuhiko Yuzawa, *Zusetsu: Gendai Nihon no Kazoku Mondai* (Graphic Illustration of Contemporary Japanese Family Problems) (NHK Publications, 1987), p. 169, fig. 81.1. Courtesy of Noriko Iwai.

unity that the outside world can esteem. If the marriage cannot be patched up, the ideal is simply to file the agreement in the local family registry section. This can be done by personal statement before witnesses, or through a document filed with that section. Yet thousands of women each year claim that they did not give their formal consent. That number has been increasing: there were over 25,000 such complaints in 1985.[26] In the Japanese system of avoiding public conflict that does not mean that these women would go to court to try to repudiate their "agreement."

But despite the rising percentage of cases that went on to mediation or other solutions between 1948 and 1985, the vast majority of divorces, some 90 percent, were formally based on consent. Older women are more likely to go on to court mediation, which reflects the accumulated wealth and pension rights at stake in such unions.[27] And almost certainly more women will take this road in the future, as they learn that they are thus more likely to gain financial advantages and custody of their children.

The Duration of Marriage

The numerical rise in divorce rates has not yet been great enough to reduce the average duration of marriage. Indeed, there was a slow rise during the period 1950–1974, from 5.3 years to 6.9 years. Then, in the period 1975–1983, there was a large jump, to 9.9 years. Perhaps there are two reasons for this. First, the older type of divorce was typically one of short duration, less than a year, and these have declined. For example, 10 percent of all divorces in 1951 lasted less than one year, and that figure had dropped to 7 percent by 1983. Similarly, 49 percent of divorces in 1951 had a duration of 1–5 years, but that dropped to 25 percent in 1981. It should be noted that many of these very short durations would not have been possible in European jurisdictions, for divorce there has required an elaborate court procedure, which often could not be initiated until after a year of marriage.

The second factor is the rise of divorce among marriages of longer duration, and that of course affects the average figure substantially. Its causes are less obvious, although a similar pattern has been occurring in some European nations. In the period 1951–1983, marriages with a duration of 10–

---

26. Nobuyoshi Toshitani and Michiko Ishii have analyzed this problem in *Rikon no Hoshakaigaku: Obei to Nihom* (Tokyo: University of Tokyo Press, 1988). Courtesy of Noriko Iwai.

27. Some of my comments on the post-divorce arrangements are based on the "Background Materials" given by Satoshi Minamikata for the Bellaggio Conference, noted earlier. Some of this material is also published in "Custodial Fathers in Japan," in Lenore Weitzman and Mavis Maclean, eds., *Economic Consequences of Divorce* (Oxford: Oxford University Press, 1992), pp. 383–91. For the relationship between age and mediation, see "Background," tables 3 and 4, and also Teruko Inoue and Yumiko Ehara, eds., *Women's Data Book* (Yuhikaku, 1991), fig. 10.4, p. 21, from *Vital Statistics* (Annual Report on Judicial Statistics), 1987.

20 years rose from 13 percent of the total of divorces to 33 percent.[28] The extent of change may be exaggerated slightly because the older durations are swelled by the postwar baby boom cohort, now middle-aged. Indeed, since 1983 the duration has been relatively constant, and even decreased slightly from 1986 onward. Nevertheless, the change in the divorce patterns among middle-aged and older couples is real enough: in the period 1960–1984, the number of divorces increased eightfold among women 40–49 years of age, and by 7.5 times among women 50–59 years old (but keep in mind that the numbers are small).[29] It is not surprising, then, that the apparent average duration might increase.

Divorce at Retirement

A different dynamic may be at work in explaining divorce among couples in longer marriages, one that is more active than the mere expansion of this age group. It applies to women in longer marriages—especially those married to men who are near or at retirement. (The customary age for retirement in Japan is much earlier than it is in the United States: most men retire from jobs in large corporations at age 55.)

Until recently a woman who was married for 20 or 25 years would not have considered a divorce—even if she was not happy in her marriage— because divorce was widely disapproved of in respectable circles, and women were expected to adjust to their husband's needs. In addition, there were no socially approved roles and little social life for older women outside of marriage (even though Japanese men usually went out socially without their wives). Finally, because few older married women were employed, most women had no income of their own and no prospects of economic security outside of marriage.

There is sporadic but growing evidence to suggest that each of these factors is changing. First, although we do not know whether middle-aged and older Japanese women are changing their standards for happiness or even satisfaction in marriage, we do know that they are now more willing to say that divorce under some circumstances is acceptable.[30] While many are doubtless continuing in unhappy marriages, it is likely that others are being moved by modern rhetoric in the mass media and the ideology of a greater voice and freedom for women.

28. *Kosei no Shihyo* (Index of Health and Welfare) 36:1 (1989,) pp. 164–67, and 37:11 (1990).

29. Ibid., 36:16, (1989), pp. 156–59. Courtesy of Noriko Iwai.

30. As shown in successive attitude surveys 1972–1987, reported in *Jyosei ni Kansuru Yoron Chosa* (Public Opinion Survey on Women) (Tokyo: Prime Minister's Office, 1987), p. 63. Courtesy of Noriko Iwai. See especially table 28, p. 59.

232 JAPAN AND MALAYSIA

Second, the legal system now provides a measure of economic security for longer-married wives: it assures them a share of their husband's pension if they divorce. In fact, I believe that a growing number of Japanese wives are waiting until their husbands are close to retirement to ask for a divorce so that they can claim their share of his pension, wealth, and accumulated goods.[31] (As we noted above, older women are more likely to go on to court mediation today because they are not willing to forgo the accumulated wealth and pension rights to which they are entitled.)

Finally, there are alternative roles developing for these older women. While few of them will live alone, they may choose to live as quasi-dependents in the households of their children. With independent incomes and time available for helping with the grandchildren, they are likely to be, and to be treated as, valuable members of that household.

The poet David Mura offers a Japanese comment on why the middle-aged or older woman would see that as a preferable alternative to staying on as the wife of a retired husband. Mura observes that the older husband must be treated as a lion in his household. That is all very well as long as he works long and late and spends few waking hours at home. However, his wife's anticipation of his being there all the time after retirement leads her to view a separate life with a more receptive eye.[32] If this interpretation is correct, the upward trend in average duration may well continue for some years in the future.

Employed Women

Because more Japanese women are now employed, we would expect a higher—and growing—percentage of divorced women to be employed. We would also expect the rate of divorce among employed women to be higher (and the reverse among men). In Western nations the difference in divorce rates between nonemployed and employed wives is also considerable, for their greater independence makes employed women less willing to tolerate marital dissatisfaction.

Indeed, some analysts (for example, Louis Roussel) have argued that the rise in the employment of women is a major factor in the rise of the divorce rate. As far as I know, no one has actually done a time-based study to see whether women who have been employed regularly have higher divorce rates, and a very precise research design is difficult to achieve (wives who do not work may be very different in many other ways), but the conclusion is at

31. The "old-fashioned" elderly divorce—waiting until their children are married—also persists. See Innovative Multi-information Dictionary, Annual Series (Shueisha, 1991), p. 1085.
32. David Mura, *Turning Japanese* (New York: Atlantic Monthly Press, 1991), pp. 113–14.

least reasonable. Kumagai has cited data to show that the percentage of divorced women who are employed is twice as high as the percentage of women in intact unions, but of course divorced women are also more likely to have to take jobs in order to survive (88 percent of divorced mothers were working in 1988).[33] My colleague Noriko Iwai, however, who has compared several Japanese studies on the possible effect of work status on divorce, concludes that the relationship is still not clear (Personal communication).

The number of children involved in divorce has increased since the low point of about 1960–1963, and so has the percentage of divorces in which there are children. In the period 1950–1988, the percentage of divorcing couples with minor children rose from 57 percent to 65 percent. The percentage of divorces with two children under 20 years old has more than doubled, while a drop has occurred in the percentage of households with one child.[34] The number of children involved, about 200,000, is small by Western standards.

One of the major *changes* in postdivorce arrangements in Japan is the strong trend toward mother custody. In traditional Japan, children belonged to the patriline, and thus to the father. Since he could usually count on important help from his mother or other kin, he could also commonly accept custody. In the much older tradition, it was the young daughter-in-law who was sent away while the children remained in the paternal home, and it was not until 1966 that mother custody rose to above 50 percent. By the early 1980s it had risen to about 70 percent. The figure is about the same if the woman was working before the divorce. It has also risen, but only to 52 percent, among the population still working in agriculture, forestry, or fisheries—pursuits in which children's work contribution would be valuable.[35]

As a consequence, the number of mother-headed families created by divorce has increased tenfold since 1952. Their share of the total number of households has changed but little, since the number of all households has also risen as a result of the continuing trend toward smaller households; Japanese couples are more inclined than in the past to set up independent

33. Kumagai, "Changing Divorce," p. 100. However, see also table 2.5, *Special Report of Vital Statistics* (from Annual Report of the Labor Force Survey 1978, Ministry of Health and Welfare). Over ten years ago, Andrew J. Cherlin noted that family scholars had for some decades suggested the importance of wives' participation in the labor force as a factor in divorce (*Marriage, Divorce, Remarriage* [Cambridge: Harvard University Press, 1981], pp. 53–55). Naohiro Ogawa and John F. Ermisch, "Women's Career Development and Divorce Risk in Japan" (Tokyo: Symposium on Family, 1990), give data to support this thesis.

34. *Kokumin Eisei no Doko* (Trend in Nation's Hygiene), 1990; Vital Statistics, Ministry of Health and Welfare, p. 77. Courtesy of Noriko Iwai.

35. *Rikon Tokei: Jinko Dotai Tokei Tokushu Hokoku* (Divorce Statistics: Special Report of Vital Statistics) (Dept. of Statistical Information, Welfare Statistics Association, 1984), p. 23, Table 6.1, Fig. 6.2, 6.3, Table 13. Courtesy of Noriko Iwai.

dwellings. Nevertheless, mother-headed families form just under 9 percent of all households with children.[36]

Simultaneously, another change has occurred among mother-headed households. In 1952, still in the aftermath of World War II, most mothers who lived alone with their children were widows. (Keep in mind that in Japan, unlike most Western countries, the number of never-married mothers is extremely small.) At that time, only about 15 percent of such households were the result of divorce or separation. Since then, the percentage of mother-headed households caused by widowhood has steadily dropped; by 1988, 70 percent were formed after divorce or separation.[37]

As noted earlier, over nine-tenths of all divorces are bureaucratic events, in which a couple presents to the court an agreement about various post-divorce arrangements, from awarding maintenance to the wife, to custody and child support. Although the basic law asks the courts to examine these agreements, as in other countries it is unlikely that they will actually do so, because the load is too great. On the other hand, this laissez-faire policy, from which Japanese mothers and children suffer, has been criticized. At the beginning of 1991, a government commission began to recognize this fact as well as other problems in contemporary family life.[38]

Divorce Agreements and Financial Provisions

Couples wish to avoid public conflict, but of course women will have less influence in any informal negotiations. The traditional and still approved mode of working through a conflict was to use go-betweens of various kinds, such as respected elders, patrons and sponsors, or kin. However, modern couples cannot so easily call upon such persons as in the past, for often their ties are weaker. In addition, fewer people are now willing to take on this onerous burden, so fraught with the possibility of antagonism. Indeed, they are now less available even for the more honorific and pleasant task of arranging a marriage. Thus lawyers are increasingly used for divorces, even though no court battle is anticipated. In the Anglo countries and in Europe, too, lawyers more often act as intermediaries today (although in some countries couples continue to suspect that they encourage adversarial behavior to increase both their importance and their fees).

36. In the past decade, according to Noriko Iwai, three major national surveys report on these numbers, but (because of different definitions) arrive at somewhat different figures. The numbers from divorce were slightly more than 52,000 in 1952; 529,000 in 1988: "Showa 63 nendo Zenkoku Boshisetai nado Chosa no Gaiyo" (Overall Results of National Survey on Mother-headed Households in 1988) in *Kosei no Shihyo* 37:7 (1990), pp. 49–62, table 1. Courtesy of Noriko Iwai. The 9-percent estimate is based on table 2, no. 37.
37. *Kosei no Shihyo* 37:7 (1990), p. 49, Survey on Mother-headed Households.
38. Personal communication from Noriko Iwai.

The typical Japanese divorce agreement deals with marital assets, maintenance or alimony, pensions, and damages (a kind of reparation award). These items increase in value with the duration of the marriage. The figures have also risen gradually with inflation and with the increasing per capita income in Japan, now among the highest in the industrialized world. As a result the average divorce award for marriages with a duration of 20 years in 1985 was about $45,600 for divorces by mediation or family court.

As might be expected, the monetary awards are much higher in divorces that involve mediation and/or family court than in those that are "by agreement." The average monetary awards for all divorces that were *not* by "consent" or "agreement" more than doubled, from about $10,000 in 1975 to $25,000 in 1985. For cases in which a decision was made about a contract for alimony payment or marital assets (a still smaller category), approximately 55 percent favored such a payment.[39]

In contrast, the wife received nothing in half of the divorces by agreement. In another 17 percent she received only some property. In the 1950s and 1960s, in the ordinary divorce by agreement the husband had no obligation to pay for the maintenance of children. Even as late as 1978, only 22 percent of husbands had to pay for child support alone, and an additional 7 percent shared the expense with the ex-wife.[40] These last figures were higher for divorces that required mediation, as was the amount for the divorce award, if any.

In addition, over these decades husbands have gradually taken over more of the burden of child support. In 59 percent of mediated divorces in 1968, no arrangements were made for child support, but by 1985 that figure had dropped to 38 percent. By 1985, 60 percent of the husbands in such mediated cases were required to pay child support, an increase of almost 20 percent from the 41 percent in 1968. The monthly payment can be as low as $74 per month, but in a small percentage of cases it may rise to over $740.[41] The more typical child-support awards range from about $157 to $313 per month.

As contrasted with these court agreements, a 1988 study revealed that only about 14 percent of divorced fathers currently make any kind of payment for their children, an additional 11 percent have made payments at some time (but not now), and the remaining 75 percent have never made

39. *Shiho Tokei Nenpo* (Annual Report on Judicial Statistics), 1985, table 9 and fig. 89.1.
40. *Rikon Tokei*, 1984, fig. 8.3.
41. *Shiho Tokei Nenpo*, table 11.1. Also Inoue and Yumiko Ehara, *Women's Data Book*. Courtesy of Noriko Iwai.

any payments at all.[42] It is also uncommon for Japanese fathers to make a lump sum payment for child support.

In the 1988 survey just cited, almost three-fourths of the lone mothers (including widows, who are better off) expressed concern about these problems, and four-fifths receive some kind of state support. In a 1990 Survey on National Life, three-fourths of lone mothers said they suffered from economic distress. Some 88 percent of divorced mothers work, over three-fourths of them full time (if we include those who are self-employed or work for the family business).

However, these mothers can take advantage of an array of special benefits now available, many of them through local authorities. If their income is below a certain level, for example, they can claim a child-support benefit, as four-fifths did in 1988. They may also be able to obtain an allowance for child care, currently slightly more than $60 per month per child.[43] In Tokyo City, they can also obtain a loan with which to start a small business or to help pay for a child's school fees. Women who find the double burden too heavy can apply to live in "mother-child dormitories."

Custodial Fathers in Japan

Although the percentage of fathers who get custody is still higher in Japan than in the West, the rise in mother custody continues, and this change brings others with it. The earlier pattern was based on the presumption that the child belonged to the father's family line and that there would be, as in the distant past in Europe and until recently among the Arabs, a household that could take care of young children in the absence of the mother. As the number of people in Japanese households has decreased, that understanding has faded. The father who obtains custody in modern Japan is likely to bear the responsibility himself. He will earn almost twice the income of a divorced mother, but 80 percent of such fathers live in households without other family members to share the burden.

Moreover, as Minamikata points out, fathers with custody face other problems in workaholic Japan. The average per capita income in their households is much less than that of an intact family. They suffer from social disapproval in a society that still does not wholly accept divorce and expects the male head of the family to devote all his energies to his job. Like divorced mothers, they cannot easily work overtime (although that is required in many jobs)—but while that is viewed as understandable for a mother, it is not for a father. In Japan dedicated employees are expected to work long

42. *Showa 63 nendo*, table 7, p. 52. Courtesy of Noriko Iwai.
43. Minamikata, 1992, pp. 389–90.

past official hours, to be ready to take business trips and to work on special assignments. But because the need to care for the child constricts those possibilities, custodial fathers are less likely to be promoted, and indeed almost one-third of them report they have had to change jobs. Agencies that assign home helpers are sometimes reluctant to send a young woman to help in a lone man's household. Local social service groups may even suggest that he alter his plan of maintaining custody. It should be pointed out that most of these statements apply to both divorced and widowed fathers with children, and many of the available numerical data do not distinguish between the two.

Most custodial fathers in the West (and the few social scientists who have looked at their problems) could repeat this litany of concerns and complaints. Perhaps Japanese males are somewhat more dependent on women to begin with and have less competence—almost certainly a cultivated incompetence—in household tasks, but their problems reflect their structural situation, which is shared with custodial fathers in other lands. It is also shared with custodial mothers, who are more likely to take these problems for granted. It cannot be surprising, then, that in a country reputed for the domestic privileges its males enjoy, not only is there a small though effective feminist movement, but men are also joining together in self-help groups and organizations aimed at defending their rights. Very likely this is not an instance of East imitating West; such movements grow from indigenous sources, too.[44] Moreover, national studies and political efforts are producing more help for such men.

Economic Consequences of Divorce

There was a small increase (from 15 to 22 percent) in the percentage of ex-husbands who paid for their children's expenses in the decade 1968–1978 and some decline in the percentage of ex-wives who did so (from 66 to 55 percent, in divorces by consent). It should be emphasized that, as against this small improvement, it is women, not men, for the most part, who bear the burden of supporting their children after divorce. In addition, because Japan makes a much lower contribution to welfare than do Western nations (the United States is also very low), divorced mothers must shoulder the greater financial responsibility alone. Yet they typically have fewer resources than their former husbands. Japanese women also earn far less then men do, get

44. Among the books written on this topic, two may be especially noted: Takayuki Hirano, Tomofumi Oka, Hiroshi Machino and Yukio Akasaka, *Fushi Katei* (Single-Father Families) (Tokyo: Minerva, 1987); and Kisuya Kasuga, *Fushi Katei o Ikiru* (Living in a Single-Father Family) (Keiso, 1989). Courtesy of Noriko Iwai.

few high-level jobs, are used as temporary labor, and have little opportunity for skill development or job advancement. They are therefore concentrated in low-paying jobs.[45]

These facts add up to very different economic circumstances for men and women after divorce. The typical Japanese husband earns about twice as much as his former wife. And he is likely to leave the marriage with the lion's share of their joint property as well. (Recall that in 90 percent of the divorces arranged by agreement the wife receives a minor share [17%] or no property at all [50%]. Thus in over two-thirds of the cases the husband receives most of the property.)

The husband also retains most of his income after divorce. Since he is not likely to have custody of his children, he does not share his household resources with them. Nor does he typically contribute to their financial support. Even though more than half of the men are now required to pay child support, as we have noted, empirical research reveals that 75 percent have never made any payments at all and only 14 percent of the fathers currently make payments.

Divorced women, in contrast, leave the marriage with less income, less property, and lower earning capacities. Since most have children, and since they are likely to have custody, they bear the major responsibility for both the financial support and the care of these children after divorce. Yet, as we have seen, they get very little help from either their former husbands or the state. Even though 75 percent of the divorced mothers claim a child-support benefit (to which they are entitled because their incomes are so low) and even though they may be eligible for a $60-a-month allowance for child care, these welfare benefits are nothing like the extensive system of societal supports provided for lone mothers in the Nordic countries.

It is no wonder that 75 percent of the lone mothers in Japan in a 1991 survey said that they suffered from economic distress. (While custodial fathers—despite the superior financial resources they command—also suffer from economic distress because of the burdens of single parenthood in a nonsupportive society like Japan, we must bear in mind that custodial fathers are much less common and the problems they report are typically even more intense for custodial mothers.) In large part it is women who care for children after divorce and in large part it is these women and their children who are suffering.

Although it may strike some readers as improbable, Cornell's careful study argues that the social and economic status of divorced women in Japan today is worse than before the Meiji Restoration, when divorce rates

45. Samuel Coleman, "Marriage and Childbirth Patterns in Present-Day Japanese Society," *Carolina Population Papers* 12 (Chapel Hill: University of North Carolina, 1980). See esp. p. 8.

were so much higher. She points out that, as compared with peasants in seventeenth-century Tokugawa Japan, women now marry somewhat later but stay married longer (only about one-sixth of divorces occur within two years, one-third within five years). Most have children to care for after divorce. But, in contrast to the almost total remarriage rates for divorced women in the seventeenth century, the pool available for remarriage today is smaller: at age 40 there are only 60 divorced men for each 100 divorced women. Nor are divorced women today easily incorporated into their parents' households. At the end of the 1970s, mother-headed households lived on diminished resources and could command only half the income of father-headed families.[46]

For women, a six-month wait before remarriage is still required. (As in Italy, France, Germany, and the Arab countries, the delay is to make sure there is no pregnancy.) Two recent studies of the chances of eventual remarriage, both seemingly of high technical competence, agree that the gap between men and women has been narrowing, but that men still have higher chances of remarriage than women. They disagree, however, as to how high those chances are. Takahashi reports that in 1965 the chance of eventual remarriage was 89 percent for men and 46 percent for women; by 1985 these figures had dropped to 72 percent for men and risen to 60 percent for women. In Hiroshima and Yamamoto's study the 1985 levels are much lower, 48 percent for men and 44 percent for women, but both figures rise somewhat by 1988.[47] Over the longer period, however, both reports suggest that a lower percentage of women are remarrying.

Over this long period, the Japanese family has moved much more toward a conjugal or nuclear pattern. Increasingly, young people choose their own mates and, where possible, set up their own households. But though many *trends* are like those in the West, the absolute figures remain different and therefore often important. Thus one can report that, when compared to the past, more Japanese families today say that they would like to live separately. Nevertheless, the percentage is still much lower than in other countries and must be contrasted with the very strong and continuing *reality* that about one out of four (adult) children with living parents actually does live with an elderly parent. Even more important, at every age group, from the twenties through the seventies, people still express a preference for living in an extended family over other choices.[48]

46. Cornell, "Peasant Women," pp. 729–31.

47. Shigesato Takahashi, "Effects of the Japanese Mortality Declines on Life Cycle Variables," *J. Population Problems* 45 (1989), pp. 19–33; Kiyoshi Hiroshima and Michiko Yamamoto, "Trend of Marriage in Japan: 1988–89," ibid., 46 (1991), pp. 74–85.

48. Given the high cost of land in the cities, few young people can purchase a home, and living in the parental home may be a comfortable choice. For public opinion data on this

Consequently, without examining a full list of the alterations in the Japanese family, which do at least *move* toward "Western" conjugal patterns, it seems unlikely that the divorce rate of Japan will rise to the level of Western nations over the next few decades. The intense efforts of Japanese leaders in the past to control the erosive effects of industrialization—thus attesting to their power—have, as intended, reduced them below what they would otherwise have been, even while the effects are visible in most areas of family life.

Peninsular Malaysia

Western family theorists have not spent much time developing hypotheses about why the divorce rate of Muslim Malaysians has been falling, since few have ever heard of the fact to begin with. It is a large-scale change, but no important governmental program aimed at it as a central goal.

The striking datum is that the divorce rates in some of the Peninsula substates (Kalantan, Trengganu, and so forth) have been higher than any found in even the United States. In some years the number of divorces has been as high as 70 percent of the number of marriages.[49] Of course, such data do not permit calculation of the eventual chances of divorce over the lifetime of each age cohort, but when divorce rates (however calculated) are high and relatively stable, they will still represent the reality fairly well.

It is almost certain that some states in Malaysia had the highest rates in the world in the late 1940s and the 1950s. For example, in 1950, the crude divorce rate (per 1000 population) was 2.6 in the U.S.; it ranged from 13 to 26 in the three most divorce-prone Malaysian states.[50] The lowest rate in all of Western Malaysia was 3.5 at that time. Decreases occurred in all these states after that time. Although the official figures are not published in the U.N. Demographic Yearbook, Jones has assembled them for the past three decades (see Table 8.2).

---

preference, see *Nihonjin no Kateikan* (Tokyo: Public Information Section, Prime Minister's Office, 1987).

49. The most complete work to date has been done by Gavin W. Jones, "Trends in Marriage and Divorce in Peninsular Malaysia," *Population Studies* 34:2 (July 1980), esp. pp. 287, 289; "Malay Marriage and Divorce in Peninsular Malaysia: Three Decades of Change," *Population and Development* 7:2 (June 1981), p. 260; and Tan Poo Chang and Gavin W. Jones, "Malay Divorce in Peninsular Malaysia: The Near-Disappearance of an Institution," *Southeast Asian J. Soc. Sci.* 178 (1990), pp. 85–114. See also Yoshihiro Tsubouchi, "Marriage and Divorce Among Malay Peasants in Kalantan," *J. Southeast Asian Studies* 6:2 (Sept. 1975), p. 139; and Heather Strange, *Rural Malay Women in Tradition and Transition* (New York: Praeger, 1981), table 6.1, p. 150.

50. Lim Lin Lean, *Population and Development* (Petaling Jaya: International Book Serice, 1983).

Table 8.2: General Divorce Rates
per 1,000 Population Aged 15 Years
and Over, Malaysia

1950	20
1955	15
1960	10
1965	7
1970	6
1975	6
1980	4
1985	3

Source: Calculated by Gavin W. Jones from U.N.
sex and age population distributions and unpublished Malaysian data, in "Divorce in Islamic
Southeast Asia," Demography Department, Australian National University, 1991, table 5.7.

Since 1950 there has been a dramatic decline in the divorce rates. Table
8.2 and Figure 8.2 show this drop over the past generation. The figures are
both linear and sharp: The Malay divorces per 1,000 in the population over
aged 15 went from 20 in 1950 to 3 in 1985. The rates have fallen among
Malays in all Malaysian states as well as those in Singapore.

By 1975 the trend lines of Western divorce rates (rising) and of Malaysian
divorce rates (falling) were coming close together or even crossing.[51] We
predict, however, that in Malaysia the divorce rates will eventually rise again
and, as we shall note later, it is possible that the shift has already begun.
Whether it will continue cannot yet be ascertained.

The family patterns that generated such high rates are very different from
those we have been considering. Although the Malay population is mainly
Moslem, their family patterns derive not from the Koran but from native
custom. Marriages were strictly arranged by parents. Women were married
young (the median age in 1947 was 16.6 years, and only 41 percent were
still single at ages 15–19). Men were an average of six years older.[52] Both
husbands and wives had little education, though of course the husband had
more. Most of the population was rural and agricultural. Polygyny (one
husband with two or more wives) was fairly common. These patterns were
more widespread in the most isolated and poorest regions.

With the exception of polygyny, these family patterns were typical for
much of the world's population until World War II and thus cannot be held
responsible for Malaysia's high divorce rates. Other factors combined to
generate the high instability in these (mainly first) marriages, which were

51. Jones, "Trends," p. 288.
52. Ibid., p. 280.

Figure 8.2: Divorce Rate in Malaysia per 1,000 Population, 1948–1975

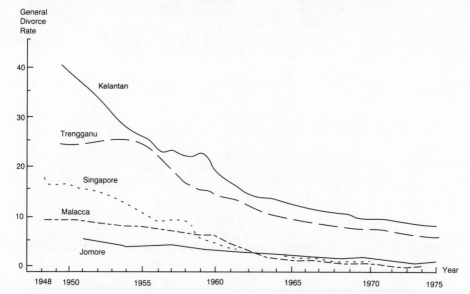

Source: Gavin W. Jones, "Marriage and Divorce in Peninsular Malaysia: Three Decades of Change," *Population and Development Review* (June 1981), p. 266.

different from unions within the other two main ethnic groups in Malaysia, the Chinese and Indians.

The factors that generated the high divorce rates include, first, the normative climate for marriage, especially young marriage. As Wilder notes, Malay marriage was "*normatively* unstable," and Rosemary Firth asserts that "a couple of false starts" are usual for Malaysian marriages.[53] People took it for granted that unions would be brittle. Second, there was little or no social disapproval of divorce, except among the well-educated urban social strata (and needless to say among Chinese and Indian communities in Malaysia).

Third, divorce was legally easy, for Islamic law required only the husband's declaration of *talak*. As is the pattern under Muslim law, couples could, and often did, become reconciled afterward—in some jurisdictions in some years, in up to one-fifth of all divorces—if the husband used the word only once or twice. That is, the husband could revoke his declaration and the

53. William D. Wilder, *Communication, Social Structure and Development in Rural Malaysia,* London School of Economics Monographs on Social Anthropology, no. 56 (London: Athlone Press, 1982), p. 70. Rosemary Firth, *Housekeeping Among Malay Peasants,* 2nd ed., London School of Economics Monographs on Social Anthropology, no. 7 (London: Athlone Press, 1966), p. 34.

spouses might live together again. Stated three times, however, *talak* could not be called back unless the wife had been married and divorced from another man subsequently; only then could a remarriage to her first husband occur. Because such a solution would appeal very little to a couple wanting to reunite, some rather interesting procedures were created to get over the legal hurdle.

Fourth, there were no kinship or legal bars to remarriage. In fact, parents had much less control over their children's marital decisions after their first marriage. Thus most of those who divorced, especially at young ages, entered a second union. For example, of the large sample of ever-married women interviewed in the World Fertility Survey of 1974 (most of whom had married in the 1940s and 1950s), 70 percent of the divorced had married again, about 20 percent had entered a third union, and 10 percent had entered four or more marriages.[54] Successive marriages were more likely to be found among the less educated, younger, and poorer women.

Fifth, remarriage did not demand the costly expenditures of the first marriage. The economic obstacles were also minimal, especially for the wife, who was not then required to have a dowry and was likely to be economically productive, especially in a wet-rice region or in the local markets. If she had any property, she kept it after divorce, and if the couple stayed together long enough to acquire property, it was divided equally.

Although the above fourth and fifth statements of remarriage patterns follow the anthropological reports, some cautions are useful. From a 1981–1982 study of divorced people mainly from high-divorce states, whose marriages had occurred mostly in the decades when these observations were made, it seems that a few qualifications are worth making.[55] First, since many women were very young and their marriages were brief, the legal freedom to choose was limited, as it is everywhere, by other social pressures. For example, 38 percent of these divorced women stated that in their second marriage their parents still made the decision, and almost half got their parents' approval. Men were older and, as usual, more likely to make their own choice (63 percent—again, to be sure, with their parents' approval). And though some stages of the elaborate marriage ceremonies were reduced for women (for example, the engagement ceremonies), more than half of them went through most of them.

54. Calculated from Siti Rohani Yahya, *A Study of Marital Pattern in Peninsular Malaysia,* (Population Study Unit, University of Malaya, 1981), table 3, p. 7.
55. Tan Poo Chang, *The Study of Marriage and Marital Dissolution in Peninsular Malaysia: The Divorced Men and Women* (Report to LPPKN and United Nations Fund for Population Activities, 1987), pp. 76, 79–80.

The sixth factor in explaining the stable high-divorce-rate pattern was the existence of settled customs for taking care of the children if any. Kin would help in socialization, and the children remained with their mother. A divorced mother was likely to keep the house if it was near her relatives but would return to her parents' home if that was more convenient. The husband would also be helped by his kin if he had custody.

Seventh, and equally important for the outcome of inevitable conflicts between spouses both during and after marriage, was the fact that a wife was likely to enjoy a social and economic position nearly equal to that of her husband.[56] She handled the money, and her economic contribution was important. She had a voice in family decisions, and could disagree with her husband. The "ideal" of consistent wifely deference was in conflict with the reality of customary village life, which made husband and wife more nearly equal than Moslem tenets would usually approve.

Finally, and probably the most significant factor in explaining the generation of high-divorce rates, was the Malays' strong wish to avoid personal conflict of any kind. Malays are particularly sensitive to personal affronts and potential assaults on their character or dignity and will go to great lengths to avoid them. They place a high value on harmony and see anger and conflict as a type of pollution in their social environment. This inability and unwillingness to confront others or to carry on disputes are both intense and widespread. There was little privacy, and thus kin (and other villagers) were likely to become involved in marital conflicts. As a consequence, marital fights were experienced not as a mere problem between husband and wife, but (as in Indonesia) as a source of uneasiness and discomfort for kin and possibly the entire village.[57]

In constant interaction with their kin, the spouses could expect them to prefer divorce as a solution to the problem rather than continuing spiritual disharmony. Thus a wife who wanted a divorce against her husband's wishes could engage in public conflict with him or even insult him, knowing that the ensuing humiliation and indignation would very likely lead him to repudiate her, as a way of restoring internal and social tranquility.[58]

As suggested earlier, these social patterns were most extreme in regions that were the least educated, most traditional, most rural, least developed

56. Firth, *Housekeeping*, pp. 37–38.
57. On these dynamics, see Douglas Raybeck, "Kelantanese Divorce: The Price of Kindred and Village Harmony," unpublished paper, Kirkland College, 1976 (?), pp. 10–13; Judith Djamour, *Malay Kinship and Marriage in Singapore* (London: Athlone Press 1959), p. 139; and also Douglas Raybeck, "Social Stress and Social Structure in Kelantan Village Life," in W. R. Roff, ed., *Kelantan: Religion, Society and Politics in a Malay State* (New York: Oxford University Press, 1974), pp. 225–42.
58. Firth, *Housekeeping*, pp. 37–39.

economically, and with the highest rates of polygyny. It was the indigenous social and family patterns, in short, that generated the high divorce rates.

Over the past three decades, however, that system has been much undermined. The Malays have benefited most from the substantial rise in economic growth that has extended over four decades. For example, the government has followed a policy of insisting on jobs and economic opportunities for Malays. The political justification given for this favoritism is that the Chinese and Indian ethnic groups were already more educated and prosperous than the Malays. The state's spectacular economic success ranks with that of other leading Southeast Asian countries such as Korea, Taiwan, Hong Kong, and Singapore.

By the mid-1970s, the age at which young women marry had risen to a median of over 21 years, about that of the United States.[59] By the census of 1980, only 10 percent of the female population aged 15–19 was in the category "ever married."[60] Today almost all girls are being educated, and the gender differential in education is narrowing. A steadily increasing percentage of women are going on to a higher level of schooling. For example, in the late 1980s, they made up about 44 percent of the incoming university students. The female labor-participation rate rose from 37.2 percent in 1970 to 47 percent in 1990. And, as has happened elsewhere in Asia, when female education, employment, and age at marriage all rise, the birth rate has also fallen. By 1980, 34 percent of the currently married and 51 percent of the divorced were in the labor force (including agriculture).[61] These latter figures belie the assertion that jobs for women would not affect marital relations because employment is restricted to single women. In spite of gossip and criticism directed against women who take jobs,[62] they have moved into many sectors in the urban areas, including teaching, nursing, electronics, and factory work.

Variables that increase the age at marriage of course also have other effects, including the reduced power of parents to control whom their children would marry, or their behavior within marriage. Thus women's strong disapproval of their husband's taking a second wife could not be ignored. Technical demographic analyses of the variables that affect the increasing age at marriage in Malaysia (as well as Japan) shows that a key determinant will be the increasing labor participation of women, especially regular full-

59. Jones, "Trends," p. 280.

60. Department of Statistics, Malaysia, *1980 Population and Housing Census of Malaysia, General Report of the Population Census* (Kuala Lumpur), vol. 1, table 4.9, p. 30. This source gives a higher percentage single in 1970 than does Jones.

61. Data courtesy of Kowk Kwan Kit, Chief Statistician, Department of Statistics, Malaysia. Heather Strange, *Rural Malay Women*, p. 27) gives an even higher figure for Trengganu.

62. Jones, "Trends," pp. 284–85.

time employment, and increased schooling. This trend is supported by the lessened disapproval of married women working.[63]

Young people have achieved more freedom of mate choice, and the "Westernization" of some attitudes has had that effect, too. Of course, the age gap between husband and wife has narrowed considerably.[64] Nuclear families have become more usual as more people have moved to the cities. With greater physical and social separation, relatives who in the past felt contaminated by the young couple's spousal conflict and pressed them to restore harmony by divorcing are now less likely to do so. With more freedom of choice, young people are more likely to begin their marriage with at least some attraction and compatibility. Also by marrying at older ages, the spouses are more likely to have accumulated some property, which would now create more complications if there were a divorce.[65]

Perhaps of equal importance is another attitudinal change, very likely in part the spread of the "meaning of modern marriage" in the international culture of our generation. Even in the past, the better educated lower and higher governmental officials as well as professionals had come to feel that divorce was uncouth, "country," backward. Properly reared people have come to feel it is a holdover of the old ways, not "modern" at all.[66] Women's organizations began to campaign against these practices (as also against polygyny), and to press for more restrictive legislation. Thus almost certainly an ideological change has been occurring, toward the attitude that divorce is no longer to be taken for granted, and is perhaps not even proper.

Both semi-official and survey data suggest that earlier reports were correct, which suggested wives were as likely to take steps toward dissolving the union, even if the final step was carried out by the husband. A conciliation procedure is in place, and it is possible that this has had some effect on the decline in rates. Both spouses are likely to use it, the husband talking with a religious official and the wife with a governmental registrar.

Even so, in a 1984 sample, those who divorced did so early in the marriage: 24 percent within the first year and 52 percent within three years.[67] Possibly that has not changed much from the past. In any event, it should be

63. For analyses of family and demographic patterns see Tey Nai Peng, "Demographic Trends and Family Structure in Malaysia," Second National Conference on the Caring Society, Institute of Strategic and International Studies, Kuala Lumpur, 1992, p. 10 et passim; and Kathryn H. Anderson and M. Anne Hill, "Determinants of Age at Marriage in Malaysia and Japan," center discussion paper no. 351, Economic Growth Center, June 1980. This analysis is based on data from the 1960s and 1970s.

64. Jones, "Trends," p. 291. This is a prediction I made in *World Revolution and Family Patterns* about family systems with customary wide age gaps as they are affected by industrialization.

65. Jones, "Malay Marriage," pp. 270–71.

66. Tsubouchi, "Marriage," p. 135. See also Jones, "Malay Marriage," p. 271.

67. Gavin Jones, *Divorce in Islamic Southeast Asia* (Canberra: Australian National University, 1991), p. 23.

noted that even these short durations understate the facts somewhat since from 10 to 20 percent of young marriages were not consummated at all. This pattern of delaying consummation was once fairly widespread in countries where women were married off at an early age, as in India. What is different here is that Malaysian peasant girls could continue in that state, and even manage to get a divorce without consummating the union.

National data on the number of children involved in divorce are not available, but in 60 percent of Tan's small 1981–1982 sample the couple had one or more children. The wife assumed custody, and under Islamic rules the ex-husband was obligated to pay for the support of the children, but about half of the ex-wives said that the husband did not provide maintenance.[68]

The 1984 Family Law Act expresses the broad changes we have been describing.[69] Even though its date of final implementation was postponed, it is mostly now enforced. At a minimum the law expresses one substantial body of elite opinion. For example, it prohibits a married man from taking a second wife unless he has the approval of a *kadi* (a family affairs registrar) or a religious court. If he divorces his wife outside a court he is liable to pay a fine. If she has contributed monetarily at all to the marital assets, she has the right to an equal share, and to some share in any event.[70] The law at least reaffirms the husband's Muslim duty to pay support for his children. If he cannot provide a suitable home for his wife after the divorce, she has the right to stay in the marital home for the traditional period of the *'iddah* (three lunar cycles). On the other hand, the law reaffirms a long list of traditional grounds for divorce (any of them adequate to prove the "irreconcilable breakdown of the marriage"). It also offers twelve bases which a wife can use to ask for a divorce. If, then, the law does not clearly restrict divorce, its goal of creating a court procedure for demanding formal responsibility seems apparent.[71]

Since we can give no exact measure of the forces moving in all these directions, just how far the divorce rate will be reduced cannot be predicted, although in 1980 Jones suggested (p. 292) that the changes may have already run their course. I predict, nevertheless, that the divorce rates will eventually begin to rise somewhat, though not to the traditionally high levels of the past.

Since writing the above paragraph, I can present some more recent data which seem to suggest that the upward movement has already begun. Before presenting them, however, I must express some caution. The time pe-

68. Tan, "Study of Marriage," pp. 49, 66, table 3.8.
69. Tan and Jones, "Malay Divorce," appendix I, II; Tan, "Study of Marriage," pp. 106–17.
70. Tan and Jones, "Malay Divorce," pp. 99–100.
71. For these and other legal provisions, see Tan, "Study of Marriage," pp. 112ff..

riod of this shift seems, in my judgment, very short, and we must wait to see whether subsequent data will confirm the reversal. Jones deserves some praise for calculating these figures since they have not been available (for two years I tried unsuccessfully to obtain them).

In the period 1980–1985, an apparent rise in Malay Muslim divorce rates did occur in several states.[72] By that time, however, they were already below the level in many Western countries. Writing of the increase in Singapore, Kuala Lumpur, and Penang, Jones notes, "the same pressures toward divorce observable in Western societies were also affecting Malays in these booming cities."[73]

Keep in mind that although the change is visible in the ratio of divorces to marriages, it is not yet visible in the crude rate of divorce (that is, divorces per 1000 population aged 15 and over). Nor can it be seen in the percent of males in the divorced status in this period; that hardly changes.[74] But it is clearly observable in the corresponding figures for women: In every age group, and in every state, there is a rise in the percent divorced for this period. It seems reasonable to assert that this is a genuine increase (whether or not it is transient). I also believe that the gender difference is simply caused—as in other countries—by the fact that divorced men "disappear" more quickly from the divorced status than women do. Jones also suggests (1991, p. 5), as we have already observed of other countries, that with rising opportunities Malay women are delaying remarriage, seeing less need for it than in the past.

If that attitude has a large effect, it must be a causal element in the general decrease of marriage rates during this period of several decades, since a delay appeared in both first marriages and remarriages. We noted both trends in the earlier chapters on European countries as well. Under the high divorce rates of the earlier period, which extended into the 1960s, very likely over three-fourths of young divorced women also remarried, and we have already presented data on the prevalence of successive marriages among this group.

The worldwide gender differences in remarriage have also begun to show up in the Malaysian data as well. As a result the ratio of women to men still in the status of divorce grows with each older age cohort.[75] For example, in the women's age group of 40–44 years, which might be paired with the male age group five years older, the ratio was 1.8:1 in 1970, 3.2 in 1980, and 6.2 in 1984. At older age cohorts, the ratios were even higher; that is, there were

72. Tan and Jones, "Malay Divorce," pp. 88–88, table 1.
73. Jones, *Divorce*, p. 16.
74. Tan and Jones, "Malay Divorce," fig. 1; Jones, *Divorce*, table 5.3.
75. Jones, *Divorce*, tables 5.2, 5.3.

more "surplus" women still in the divorced status. Some of these may have gone through more than one marriage, but in any event they were not in a union at that age. The ratios are still higher for widowed women.

This may be simplified and generalized: In any divorce system, doubtless more women than men who divorce, or whose spouses die, will fail to establish a new marriage. I suspect this is even more likely when elders no longer control who marries whom, and especially in a time when the marriage rates are dropping for first and later marriages. One consequence is that even in Peninsular Malaysia there is an increase in the number of female-headed family units.[76]

Conclusion

Changes in the divorce patterns in Japan and among the Muslims of Peninsular Malaysia (about 58 percent of the population) have been dramatic. Both appear to have been what I have called stable high-divorce-rate systems. In this chapter I have given considerable attention to this conception, since it may fit a wide range of societies. I have outlined a substantial list of what seem to be its main characteristics. Whether it will be a fruitful way of analyzing such systems remains to be seen. In both older Japan and Malaysia these systems created a dynamic of "marital sifting," or extended mate selection, through which more compatible marriages were eventually achieved through successive marital unions. We suggested earlier that, in contrast to Western systems, such high rates of divorce are probably not linked with still higher rates of divorce among later marriages. In the West, those who remarry are more likely to divorce than those who marry for the first time. However, the skeptical reader should keep in mind the data for the United States on this point: Since the second marriages that have higher divorce rates in the United States were typically formed by people who were younger at first marriage and divorce, it may be the characteristics of these people (less education, lower SES), not the fact of their remarriage, that is linked to their higher divorce rates. Nevertheless, if we can control for class differences, it seems clear that in Malaysia the same factors that created the first divorce (for example, the elders' very casual attention to mate choices for their children) were weaker in later marriages. Moreover, both in Malaysia and Japan, by contrast, the system that had once generated high rates was weakened by the forces of political, economic, and social "modernization."

76. This is my inference from the age data and calculations from the above tables. See also Tey Nai Peng, "Demographic Trends."

I have suggested that when indigenous, stable family systems generate high divorce rates, we cannot expect that the growth of social patterns common to industrialization will cause them to rise further. Those new social patterns will weaken some or much of the traditional family system, and I have predicted they would therefore lower the divorce rates—at least for some time. I have also asserted that the rates would eventually rise again. (I hardly need add that under conditions of widespread revolution or social chaos, family patterns break down, too, but here we assume a relatively peaceful transition.)

Of course, the highly specific cultures to be encountered in every country will shape such general changes in unique ways. The Japanese have been more assiduous than the Malaysians, for example, in planning not only economic development but social and familial changes on a broad front. They made a radical but successful change in family patterns, trying to move them closer to the samurai way. Perhaps no modern country has been so successful as Japan in avoiding the utilization of its highly educated women in responsible jobs. Malaysians, by contrast, have had to live with three very different, but strongly held, sets of ethnic customs and beliefs about appropriate family behavior—that is, Malay, Chinese, and Indian. Almost certainly, this is the main reason for the slow pace of putting into effect some of the reforms in marriage laws that have been made since 1975. The sacred status of Koranic rules for family life requires some delicacy in any attempts to impose general rules on the population as a whole.

I have presented data in this chapter to confirm the slow rise in divorce rates in Japan, after a long fall, and what seems to be the beginning of an increase among Peninsular Malays. It has also been possible to present at least some of the dynamics of change in other areas of divorce patterns, such as remarriage, the support of children, the repudiation of a divorce, and class. These themes will appear again in succeeding chapters.

9

The Arab World: Internal Changes with Few Clear Trends in Divorce Rates

Arab social analysts have not been so concerned with changes in the divorce rate as have Western analysts. As a consequence far fewer Arabs have carried out serious studies on divorce trends or internal dynamics. The reason is quite simple. In the West, divorce was legally forbidden for centuries, and both theological and moral opinion disapproved of it. That disapprobation continued after divorce became legal, and even when the particular circumstances of a case seemed to justify divorce for the individual couple. Thus the steady rise in divorce among Western countries over many decades and the recent sharp increases have been viewed as an index of the dissolution of the family system, and perhaps even of the moral fabric of society. An upward movement in the divorce rate was viewed as serious and deserving of research attention.

By contrast, divorce was always taken for granted as a possible outcome of marriage in the Arab world. It was a stable high-divorce-rate system. The Koran expresses disapproval of divorce but does not forbid it. For centuries past, both law and custom gave the husband nearly complete freedom to divorce his wife. As in any such system, a wide range of complex social patterns existed to take care of the many problems divorce creates, from the reallocation of bride-price rights to custody and remarriage. Personal and family negotiations could of course be emotional, and the outcome could be determined by power alliances, friendships, money, or prestige, as in any other village conflict. But the legality and normality of divorce did not excite much controversy. Thus divorce was not necessarily seen as a moral failure of the couple or of the system itself, and most divorcees expected to be remarried.

The modern Arab world is different from other regions in another fundamental way. It has generally enjoyed enormously increased wealth and a considerable movement toward modern technology, despite much poverty in several of these countries. It has also experienced the heightened impact of Western political and social forces, at the same time that it confronts a strong, often violent, resurgence of Koranic fundamentalism, which seeks to return its citizens to "traditional" religious behavior and values.

These grand opposing forces are, paradoxically, very close to cause and effect: The increasing strength and power of these states is at least a primary *foundation* for the resurgence of fundamentalism. Arab leaders feel they can finally throw off the yoke of the West, and many want to achieve the power to force others to live by traditional ideals. It remains to be seen whether they will ultimately achieve that second goal, but for both outsiders and insiders the present era is still difficult to understand, and longer-term trends in family and divorce are even harder to assess.

The outcome of fundamentalism, in both the short and the long term, will be of much importance for what happens to divorce patterns. Almost certainly its impact will be great before it slows down, because of several contending forces. Arab intellectuals (both religious and lay) have for generations expressed indignation at being the pawns of Western powers, while the increasing strength of Arab military and nationalist resources has made the Arab challenge to the West more successful. Not only have the Arab countries freed themselves from their colonial status, but those with oil riches have used their wealth politically to begin an elaborate complex of high technology as well as to influence other countries that are partially dependent on them.

Fundamentalists in every Arab country seek control so as to return their fellow citizens to the Koranic tradition and to hold off corrupting influences as well as the threat of the West. In turn, those in office try to use this potential allegiance to Arab ways in order to maintain their power, while restricting, where possible, the internal political dangers of fundamentalist groups, which in every instance prefer to depose them. The danger to present chiefs of states is not merely the possible loss of office but the loss of their lives. Thus the contest is not only between the Koranic tradition and Western influences of all kinds but also among the secular rulers (however pious themselves) and between these rulers and the innumerable sects and political groupings of fundamentalists. The secular-minded Arabs in turn want to enjoy the benefits of consumerism but to hold at bay the social patterns of the West that ordinarily accompany it.

As is clear, these factors are in much tension. Both secular and fundamentalist aspirants seek power, for without it no program can be advanced. Secular leaders, under the general threat of a political takeover and the specific threat of assassination, hope to maintain their leadership position through adroit maneuvering, organized military power, and the benefits of increased wealth and consumer goods. The religious traditionalists hope to arouse the masses against the West and against violations of Koranic doctrine by both terrorism and theological persuasion and thereby to deter secular leaders from giving way any further. Ideally, they hope their followers will be inspired to seize power themselves.

Nevertheless, their followers (both religious-minded and secular) also want the benefits of prosperity. The temptations of austerity are easily resisted and do not move most followers over the longer term, either in the Near East or in the West.

It is risky to claim that there is a *general* position that the many subgroups of fundamentalists hold with respect to divorce, which after all is not itself a large issue. To the extent that there is a general doctrine about the family, it is not that the fundamentalists simply want to place women under a wide array of disadvantages. Rather, they believe that *both* men and women should accept what they view as Koranic responsibilities: men should protect their women, and women should carry out their traditional roles.

With respect to both sexes, however, fundamentalists are likely to label as "Koranic"—that is, mandated by divine revelation—obligations that are actually no more than local or tribal traditions and customs. There is often a contradiction between the social behavior prescribed in the Koran and the local traditions. As acute reformers have argued for generations, much Arab family custom does *not* follow Koranic injunctions. Especially with respect to property, the realities of local tradition, family power, and individual negotiation are likely to override the written law (for example, the woman's rightful share of the family inheritance).

Thus fundamentalists do not approve of many (if any) legal restrictions on a man's right to divorce his wife unilaterally, for that was in fact a right guaranteed in the holy book. On the other hand, they would not want the divorced woman to be abandoned so that she must then establish a one-parent, woman-headed household. But in choosing between these alternatives, because fundamentalists feel strongly that they must fight against the reformers' efforts to obtain more rights for women, they focus their efforts against the general threat of women's emancipation.

Thus the fundamentalists have tried to restrict or remove the right of women to obtain a divorce on their own, the right (through the marriage contract) to prevent their husbands from marrying additional wives, or the right to get jobs independently (for this gives women greater freedom generally). They disapprove of the legal stipulation (in Egypt) that divorced mothers with their children may continue to live in the family dwelling (or one comparable to it) after the divorce until the children are old enough to be in the custody of their fathers. Ideally, they would have girls and women remain under the rule (and protection) of their fathers until marriage, under that of their husbands until divorce, and under that of their fathers again until remarriage. In essence, fundamentalism is concerned with the status of women and with divorce only as new reforms and proposals suggest greater freedom for women.

Because of the centrality of the issue of women's status, it deserves some further comment here. In the nationalist movements after World War II, and perhaps extending to the 1960s, many legal changes were made in the direction of equality or some type of emancipation for women. Fundamentalism as a powerful force throughout much of the Muslim world, however, not the Arab regions alone, has tried to reaffirm the subordinate position of women. But note once again the difference between Arab fundamentalists and those in the West. In the West fundamentalists are more likely to disapprove of divorce itself. In the Arab world their interest is in securing the subordinate position of women. Thus divorce policy—so long as it does not violate the Koran—is only a means to that end. However, it is not clear how much these policy positions would affect the divorce rates themselves. If it simply reaffirms the subordinate position of women, its effect on divorce rates might be ambiguous.

In the Muslim world today the threat of changes in the position of women arouses many fears, while those changes themselves are powered by massive social forces that are perhaps beyond control. The widespread attempt to force women to return to the veil is an indication that many women have been taking it off. Arab political or fundamentalist leaders who wish to generate support by attacking the West can also use the dangers of women's rebellion as a rallying point, for women who seek freedom are viewed as pro-West and anti-Arab. That threat triggers a deep fear about power in the household as well as in the larger political world.

Intellectuals sometimes engage in the donnish, almost grotesque, exercise of arguing that it is not clear that Western women are really "freer" than women in the Arab world. Evidently, Arab men do not really believe this since they attempt to restrict any freedoms they can, and Arab women seem not to believe it either since so many press for "Western" freedoms and rights. These threats to male authority generate a powerful resonance because, as Mernissi points out, male heads of household have been losing authority, not so much to women as to the state.[1] The state has taken over

1. Fatima Mernissi, *Beyond the Veil*, rev. ed. (Indianapolis: Indiana University Press, 1987), pp. 172ff.

many functions, is a major source of salaries, furnishes education, and provides much of whatever economic security may exist. In a period of great change, many analysts assert that men have also lost power to women within the family.

Thus debates about the position of women and the threat to morality that modernism generates are fundamentally debates about power and authority. They have been accompanied by much violence and threats of violence. Even very secular-minded leaders must walk a very careful line in proposing reforms lest they be accused of kowtowing to Western influences.

But though the terrorist activities and violent rhetoric have captured public attention, the defenders of emancipation for Arab women have continued their efforts behind the scenes. Indeed, if their efforts and resistance did not exist, the fundamentalists would feel less impulse to step up their own attack. For example, in spite of threats and real persecution, the physician N. El-Saadawi has continued to shock and outrage Arabs (and Westerners as well) by her exposés of the prevalence of clitoridectomy, infibulation, and other oppressive customs.[2] Scholars and journalists have also documented the widespread attacks against women seeking emancipation.[3]

These attacks would not occur if fundamentalist leaders did not perceive some dissatisfaction and resistance to their repressive posture. Although masters and strong rulers over many centuries in all countries have often explained, patiently or violently, that the oppressed do not want freedom, it has nevertheless remained very attractive to the disadvantaged. The very turmoil of the political arena in Arab states causes many women who would not have questioned their position in normal times to think now about their lack of privileges.

These powerful counterforces make it even more difficult to analyze real trends in family conflict and divorce. We know much more about the intimate lives of Arab women now than we did twenty years ago because more serious field research has been done by intellectuals and academics on the micro-world of women. Those reports suggest substantial inner changes—that is, changes in the hearts and minds of women—that do *not* actively and openly challenge male authority.

    2. See N. El-Saadawi, *The Hidden Face of Eve: Women in the Arab World*, 2nd ed., trans. by Sherif Hetata (London: Zed Press, 1980).
    3. See Andrea Rugh, *The Family in Contemporary Egypt* (Syracuse: University of Syracuse Press, 1984), pp. 150–51; Souad Chater, *La Femme Tunisienne* (Tunis: Maison Tunisienne de l'Edition, 1976–79), pp. 66–105; Attilio Gaudio and Renee Pelletier, *Femmes d'Islam* (Paris: Denoel/Gonthier, 1980), esp. ch. 9. Juliette Minces, "Women in Algeria," in Lois Beck and Nikki Keddie, eds., *Women in the Muslim World* (Cambridge: Harvard University Press, 1978), notes that after gaining its freedom Algeria seemed to take some steps backward. These steps are noted later in this chapter. On Algeria, see also Marnia Lazveg, "Gender and Politics in Algeria: Unraveling the Religious Paradigm," *Signs* 15 (1990), pp. 755–80.

Which will become the dominant reality? It is doubtful that those who claim that women have returned to their duties or that they are reaffirming traditional morals are very astute observers of reality. (They are more likely to be trying to exert social control over women by labeling those who seek freedom as deviants.) Nor does the lack of action and political protest among women suggest that they are satisfied with the status quo (because the costs of taking such action are very large). Thus what might be considered adequate indicators of social change in other contexts are, at best, ambiguous in the Arab context.

We will probably have to wait until this complex set of forces is played out over the next few decades. While it would be risky to claim that we can guess what will happen in the short term, my own prediction is that women's emancipation in the Arab world will continue, in spite of much fundamentalist resistance, because the social and political changes already in motion cannot ultimately be stopped, and one of the most powerful is simply the growing desire to enjoy material benefits. But though it seems very unlikely that fundamentalism will actually achieve "victory" over the long haul, it will have much success before it finally subsides.

How Much Real "Industrialization"?

The period since World War II has witnessed an unprecedented set of global political and social changes. Family patterns—typically more resistant to change than other institutions—have also altered in every part of the world. Although numerous commentators have tried to chart these fundamental changes in order to predict future trends of some worldwide type, current theory does not help us much in charting the *future* of family patterns and particularly of *divorce* trends. Indeed, over the relatively short term—for the family, perhaps a generation or so—the best guess for Arab countries (and many others) is very likely a continuing weakening of traditional values, roles, and obligations, a greater movement toward individual solutions or paths, and an eventual reduction of the pressure toward fundamentalist solutions.

Such an intellectually unsatisfying conclusion seems especially applicable to the Arab world, where turmoil has been nearly endemic over the past quarter-century of revolutions, wars, migration, urbanization, and high-pressure modernization programs, and where extraordinary industrial complexes have been erected on what might seem a physically unstable foundation, a fountain of oil. That widespread effort to "modernize," backed by groups who thought it wise to learn technology from the West as well as by those who wanted to return to Koranic tradition, because both wanted consumer goods, has certainly had a large impact. But whether much real "industrialization" has occurred in day to day family-job relations or attitudes is still open to question.

I cannot examine that question here with the seriousness it deserves, but some important facts merit attention in order to weigh the extent of change in divorce. I shall first comment on the larger question of change and then point out some specific data on modernization generally before going to divorce processes themselves.

Most of these countries have moved toward higher levels of technology. Energy consumption (as a measure of industrial development) doubled or tripled in most Arab states in the period 1960–1980.[4] A few of the oil-rich states have recently achieved per capita incomes far above those of industrialized nations; in fact, Kuwait, Qatar, Saudi Arabia, and the United Arab Emirates (among others) all had per capita incomes of over $5,000 U.S. as long ago as 1981.

Since visitors now observe the trappings of an industrial system in some of these countries, it might be supposed that industrialization theory would be applicable. That is, we should be able to predict many of the changes in family patterns by examining the impact of the social forces and ideology of industrialization on various familial relationships. For example, if the divorce rate had been low, it would be expected to rise; if it had been high, the rate should fall at least temporarily.

We can predict the effects of industrialization only to the degree that this process has actually been occurring. But how much industrialization has occurred in the Arab world? As I have emphasized elsewhere in this volume, the mere existence of a factory or of high technology (for example, in Japan prior to 1910) does not in itself generate the variables through which industrialization has its major impact on the family. The key variable is the degree to which individuals are able to get jobs or promotions and to dispose of their wages independently of their kin or personal and family obligations.[5] That change probably never occurs except under the powerful forces of industrialization and a profit-driven economy, and even then it does not happen quickly. Nor is it a change that most people at the outset even consider desirable (except for its consumer goods). Thus whenever nations in the

4. *World Bank*, vol. 1, *Economic Data*, 3d ed. (Baltimore: Johns Hopkins University Press, 1984), various tables.

5. For an analysis of the theoretical complexity of these relationships, see William J. Goode, *The Family*, 2nd ed. (Englewood Cliffs: Prentice-Hall, 1982), esp. chs. 10, 11.

modern era have moved toward this kind of "modernization," their leaders have made considerable effort to oppose familial independence by law as well as moral exhortation.

Thus it is not a paradox but the result of intention that family position continues to be central in any decisions others make about the individual's economic and occupational fate in the Arab world. They can continue to do so because the Arab family leaders who control the resources do not feel the capitalistic threat of going broke if their enterprises are not efficient and profitable. By contrast, they can impose some standards of efficiency on their foreign workers and severe standards of personal or political behavior as well, for all of them can be expelled arbitrarily at any time.

In the richest states, a majority of those who actually do the work, both ordinary laborers and experts in high technology, are foreigners. The strong control the government exercises over them is illustrated by the expulsions, violence, and summary trials and sentences imposed on foreign workers (almost all Muslims) after the Iraqi war of 1992. The arbitrary government rests, in turn, on the nearly total ownership of economic resources by dominant families. They can equally well coerce any citizens who might wish to resist—for example, the Saudi women who, for one day, drove automobiles. Freedom of choice for individual family members is as elusive as freedom in political matters.

Arab leaders can maintain this system because they are bolstered by their oil sales. As a consequence, holding a job or even participating in the high technology of oil metallurgy or electricity may not give any individual the independence of family controls that is taken for granted in the West. By contrast, a manager in a modern American corporation will not be very much concerned about whether his computer programmer is an excellent wife, mother, or daughter or whether the regional manager of a plant obeys his patriarchal father in choosing a wife.

Of course, the development of a full-scale attempt at industrialization did not quickly undermine traditional family patterns in the West either. The leading Arab families still control all the resources that technical development brings. Thus in Kuwait—which has set in place a most elaborate structure of high technology—income, power, and property allocations are almost exclusively under the control of the ruling families. Control over familial behavior remains in their hands as well. Whether that pattern will now weaken remains to be seen.

During the same period of rapid "industrialization" (1960–1980) the percentage of the labor force in agriculture as well as the dollar value of agriculture dropped, while both rose in industry. As far as we know, analysts have not attempted any probing inquiry into the relations between society and economy in these states to ascertain the social dynamics of a phenomenon hitherto unprecedented (except possibly for Japan) in world history—a high technological system fueled from the top down, in an essentially resource-poor economy (except for oil) that has bypassed the stage of slowly building up the skills, attitudes, and machinery that occurred in other industrialized countries. The great successes in Asia—Japan, Korea, Taiwan, Hong Kong—followed a very different road from that of the Arab countries.

What is certain, as we noted above, is that the usual *social* patterns of increasing technology have not developed to any great degree, for rewards continue to be mostly channeled and determined by highly personalistic, familial links.

On the other hand, both national leaders and the populace of all countries in the modern world are affected by the ideology of the modern nation state and want their country to be recognized as a "modern" nation. This international *ideological* system has a large impact on how people and nations spend their money on socioeconomic allocations (thus the fundamentalist accusation that the West is Satan) and both requires and inspires many social changes. To be a "modern" nation in the world system—that is, if national leaders want others to see the country as modern—the state must set in motion a wide range of social programs.[6] Modern universities must be created, science must be supported, primary schooling must be given to all children, female and male. Nations that want world esteem must create a superstructure like that of the "advanced" nations, and this includes a broad array of organizations and activities, from their own airlines to social security systems. Not all of this may seem sensible even to Western businessmen but it is a social fact.

Thus it is not surprising that literacy rates of both males and females have risen in all Arab countries over the past generation. The percentage of females in primary schools in many Arab nations comes close to that of males. The percentage of females enrolled in secondary schools has actually risen faster than that of males. In Egypt, which has witnessed a large expansion of university education, the ratio of men to women enrolled in the university is now only about 2:1, and the ratio for technical education is about the same.

6. John Meyer and his colleagues have developed their own version of "world system theory" by focusing on ideological changes, fueled by both the mass media and social pressures from world banks, international commissions, diplomatic activities, and demands for development. On the development of nation states, see John Bennet, *The Expansion of Nation-States, 1870–1970*, Ph.D. diss., Stanford University, 1976; on childhood and the state, see John Boli-Bennet and John Meyer, "The Ideology of Childhood and the State: Rules Distinguishing Children in National Constitutions, 1870–1970," *Am. Soc. Rev.* 43 (1978), pp. 797–812. On educational curricula, see Aaron Benavot et al., "Knowledge for the Masses; World Models and National Curricula, 1920–1986," *Am. Soc. Rev.* 56 (1991), pp. 85–100. See also Albert Bergesen, ed., *Studies of the Modern World System* (New York: Academic, 1980).

Such processes set other effects in motion for family patterns and ultimately for divorce. Among them is increasing age at marriage for women, a prediction I made long ago. Allman's rejection of that trend about ten years ago was premature.[7] By now almost all the nations for which data are available show such a rise, and in most the age hovers around 19–21 years.[8] This change reduces the gap between the ages of husbands and wives (another prediction in my earlier work), and it seems likely that the lesser gap in both education and age will have some effect on husband-wife relations over time. I am not asserting that the narrowing gap will make husbands and wives equals, but they will be more nearly equal than in the past.

As Ruth Dixon showed over a decade ago, women's age at marriage, literacy, and gainful employment are all correlated, and each has an independent effect on the others. Education for females became socially acceptable first in Arab countries (although many fundamentalists strongly reject it) not because it led to jobs but because men who had high status wanted wives who were more "modern," more like the models presented in world mass media—and thus fathers came to want education for their daughters. But young women who are more educated are also worth more in the labor market (as well as in marriage) and even in the face of sex discrimination they can obtain some position. The complex interaction among age at marriage, employment, and divorce patterns has been analyzed a great deal in the West. It is not clear at all that the same results are visible in the Arab states.

One further consequence (and evidence of change) is that a differential birth rate by education begins to occur, even though the crude birth rate has changed but little. Mernissi notes for Egypt (on the basis of the World Fertility Survey) that the number of children ever born to women with secondary education is only 2.1, and for those with a university education it is 1.8,[9] much lower than that for women with little or no education. This differential is observable in other Arab countries as well.[10]

Although women's participation in the labor force remains modest—in 1980, only in Lebanon did women make up as much as 20 percent of the labor force (later in the 1980s, Tunisia rose to that level), 16 percent in Morocco—and most women have low-paying menial or rural jobs, the gross

7. James Allman, *Women's Status and Fertility in the Muslim World* (New York: Praeger, 1978), p. xxx.

8. G. Edward Ebanks and Susheela Singh, *Socio-economic Differentials in Age at Marriage*, World Fertility Survey Comparative Studies (Voorburg, Netherlands: International Statistical Institute, 1984); see also U.S. *Population Reports*, series M, no. 4, Nov. 1979, pp. 1–127ff.; Mernissi, *Beyond the Veil*, pp. xxiv–xxv.

9. Mernissi, *Beyond the Veil*, p. xxvi.

10. Allman, *Women's Status*, pp. 3–32, notes fertility declines in several countries.

figures conceal important changes. Because of increasing education some women have moved into better-paying positions. In Morocco they form 28 percent of the civil service employees. They make up 25 percent of the teaching corps of Egyptian universities, and 22 percent even in Saudi Arabia.[11] This trend is viewed by many as pro-Western and anti-Islam. Nevertheless, women are increasingly entering the nontraditional labor force over time.

Contrary to tradition, a sizable portion of the married women are also in the labor force. The World Fertility Survey estimates that as long ago as 1976 the percentage of ever-married females aged 25–49 years who were *currently working* was 21 percent in Syria and around 18 percent in Egypt, Morocco, and Tunisia. The figures for women of the same age group and marital status but with ten or more years of education were two to three times higher. Moreover, the overwhelming majority of those who worked before marriage did so after marriage as well.[12]

One consequence of these relationships is a correlation between being in the divorced status and being in the labor force. Many women must work because they are divorced, and there are more opportunities in the labor force for them to do so than in the past.

More generally, when young women gain more education and earn money, their families have made greater investments in them and are likely to be more concerned with their welfare. Such women increase the earnings in their families and reduce somewhat the burden of the marriage ceremonies because thereby they earn a "dowry," and when married they gain more respect from their own families as well as from others.[13] This is so even if they simultaneously arouse resentment in others. Moreover, their families come to need their continuing income in order to live in ways they view as appropriate.

Divorced women are less restricted in their personal decisions about jobs (as about other things) than are single or married women; thus they can even take factory jobs, and holding a real job reduces the financial burden on their fathers, who are legally responsible for their support.

Our regrettably imperfect understanding of changes in Arab divorce patterns is improved a bit by recalling the system of the past, when marriages

11. Mernissi, *Beyond the Veil,* pp. xxv, xxvii–xxviii.

12. *Women's Employment and Fertility,* U.N. Population Studies, no. 96 (1985), table 2, pp. 16, 34, 43.

13. On part of these processes see Peter MacDonald, "Social Organization and Nuptiality in Developing Societies," in John Cleland and John Hobcraft, eds., *Reproductive Change in Developing Countries* (New York: Oxford University Press, 1985), pp. 99–100. See also Nadia H. Youseff, "The Status and Fertility Patterns of Muslim Women," in Beck and Keddie, eds., *Muslim World,* pp. 69–99, esp. p. 82.

were arranged with much less attention to the wishes of the couple and the groom was likely to be substantially older than the bride. The husband had few restrictions on his power to divorce his wife, for good reason or for none. Of course, the political power of the wife's family might discourage the husband from doing so on the basis of mere whim—and thus divorce was less common among important families, where (patrilateral) cousin marriage was more common. Most divorces occurred earlier in the marriage than in the West—from a few months to two years. One traditional restriction on the husband's right to divorce freely was that by custom most men did not pay the entire "bride-price" at marriage, but the husband was supposed to pay all of it if there was no social justification for the divorce.

That system, as in any high-divorce-rate pattern, generated a high rate of remarriage. The young divorced woman wished to remarry because marriage was the only acceptable status for a woman. There would be a new bride price, though to be sure a smaller one. The family had a stake in her remarriage because otherwise she would be a financial burden and because she had a customary right to part of the family property (half that of her brother) if she remained unmarried. The children if any would be in her custody while young and would later pass to the custody of her ex-husband (when the son was seven years of age, the girl nine, or at puberty) and would not receive support other than maintenance in the husband's house during the 'idda.

Changes in the Law

In Arab countries, proposed changes in the law as well as resistance to them are justified by appeals to the Koran, in an intense and closely textual fashion that is only distantly similar to the occasional quotations from the Bible in, say, Western discussions of family law. In its time, the Koran urged some improvements in the social position of women, yet precisely because vigorous opponents draw so heavily on the same source, as is true in Western political moral debates that draw on the Bible, we can infer that many ambiguities will be encountered there.

The Koran is "a statement of ethical principles" that amounts to law; its injunctions can be interpreted in many ways.[14] Each of the modern traditions of Muslim law (Shi'ite, Sunni, Hanafite, Malekite, and so on) draws different legal conclusions from this sacred text. Moreover, tribal and regional customs have always claimed to be obeying the Koran, while follow-

14. Noel Coulson and Doreen Hinchcliffe, "Women and Law Reform in Contemporary Islam," in Beck and Keddie, eds., *Muslim World*, pp. 37–40.

ing very different rules. Thus for decades some feminist reformers (men and women) argued that the lot of women would be much improved if only the actual laws and customs conformed to the Koranic prescriptions. Any suggestions for change in family law are inevitably discussed in a fervent religious and sectarian atmosphere in which ultimate values seem to be at stake. Most changes in divorce patterns are more likely to come about because of alterations in women's socioeconomic position than because of any sweeping legal revisions of the divorce code, as might occur in the West.

Alterations in divorce law occur both through specific definitions of what may legally be done in a divorce proceeding and through changes in women's status. It is difficult to sketch a general pattern of change in Arab countries because decrees or laws made in one year may be challenged or repealed in subsequent years. For example, in the early flush of enthusiasm, in its first years after its independence, and partly because of the gallant help of its women during the revolution, Algeria moved for a while toward more rights for women. Subsequently, however, it moved in the opposite direction, under the influence of fundamentalist pressures. The national charter of 1976 defines the woman as under the tutelage of the man. The law reinstated polygyny as well as divorce by repudiation, reduced alimony payments, and made it harder for the wife to obtain a divorce.[15] That is not the direction in which other countries have been going, but it is safe to say that "liberal" laws have been under attack in all Arab nations.

A shift of much legal importance, which will doubtless be of greater social importance as time goes on, is the widespread definition of both marriage and divorce as civil actions, not merely private and religious matters. Divorce is generally to take place through a court action rather than as a personal repudiation (for example, Syria, Iraq, South Yemen, Tunisia).[16] Moreover, divorces are to be registered. While there are still many variations from country to country, in general divorce has become more formalized, and courts can more easily intervene in divorce settlements. In Morocco, for example, divorce matters are still handled in a court, but it is a religious court. In an important sense, this change signals a shift in the status of women as persons about whom an outside authority can make legal judgments that (by legal definition) can take precedence over decisions made unilaterally by males within the family.

---

15. Susan E. Marshall, "Paradoxes of Change: Cultural Crisis, Islamic Revival, and the Reactivation of Patriarchy," *J. Asian and African Studies* 19 (1984), p. 8. For an analysis of the resistance that has undermined Tunisian earlier efforts to emancipate, see Chater, *La Femme*. For Algeria, see Helene van de Velde-Dailliare, *Femmes Algeriennes* (Algiers: Office de Publications Universitaires, 1980).

16. Coulson and Hinchcliffe, "Women and Law Reform," p. 44.

It should be emphasized that these are *paper* changes in at least two senses. First, they are bureaucratic procedures, which in themselves alter little or nothing in the conflict leading to divorce or its consequences. Second, not all men comply. In Iraq, for example, the husband can, in some circumstances, register the divorce without really informing his wife or getting her consent. Youssef also points out that male family members appropriate their daughters' or sisters' property holdings, with the justification that the women will eventually get their economic support from the males they marry or those at home if they stay there.[17]

On the other hand, bureaucratic patterns, including the requirement that the case be processed in court, have a tendency to become standard, approved ways of doing things. Thus the state becomes increasingly involved in what was formerly a private religious, familial matter. Some customary patterns seem much more oppressive when reported in a law court. When the laws themselves recognize such conflicts, they are likely to give both parties some real opportunity to state their cases.

Similar changes have been occurring in the marriage arrangements themselves, which affect divorce later on. Most jurisdictions have not forbidden polygyny but some have placed a few restrictions on this relatively uncommon practice. In Iraq, for example, a husband must get the court's permission to marry a second wife.[18] However, wives have increasingly been opposed to such unions, and Tunisia has forbidden them since the new Family Code of 1956.

In some jurisdictions (for example, Morocco, Lebanon) women may stipulate in their marriage contract that they may ask for a divorce if the husband takes another wife. In Egypt a wife has that right even without that specific item in the formal contract. As a step toward the legal recognition of women as persons with some legal rights, Tunisia began to require that the woman sign her marriage contract before a notary. With the rise in women's age at marriage and with the rise in women's education, we assume that far fewer brides today will now sign the marriage contract without being able to read it or with no knowledge of its contents. But requiring a public witness to the woman's signature nevertheless helps to further undermine some of the undesirable customs of the past.

In general it can be said that in most jurisdictions there are *some* circumstances under which women can get a divorce.[19] (Traditionally, under Hanafi law, a woman could not seek a divorce no matter how badly she was

17. Youssef, "Status."
18. Elizabeth H. White, "Legal Reform as an Indicator of Women's Status in Moslem Countries," in Beck and Keddie, eds., *Muslim World*, p. 57.
19. Coulson and Hinchcliffe, "Women and Law Reform," p. 40.

treated.) Under the new dispensations, however, which are viewed as "liberalizing" because they permit women to ask for divorce, when a woman does insist on getting a divorce, she will have to pay compensation to the husband for releasing her—that is, she will be required to pay all or part of the bride price the husband originally paid upon marriage (for example, Tunis, Algeria). In both Syria and Tunisia, if a husband divorces without good cause, he is required to give the wife the equivalent of one year's maintenance. If she resists divorce, in Egypt she is allowed a longer period of support (two years plus the *'idda*).

Algeria has made divorce somewhat harder for women to get, but other states are not likely to follow. Egypt, on the other hand, has been in the forefront of secular laws that at least affirm a standard, public procedure for divorce. Among its provisions are the following: (1) the divorce must be registered before witnesses, and the husband must notify the wife officially; (2) the wife is to get one year's alimony plus two years' maintenance, and the installments are to be paid to her through the Nasser Bank; (3) the husband must guarantee the wife a home while she has custody of his children; (4) the mother has custody until the boy is fifteen and the girl has married; and (5) when the wife seeks a divorce and there are disagreements, court mediation will not be extended beyond nine months; if mediation is unsuccessful, she will be granted the divorce.[20]

The Code of Personal Status, put into Tunisian law in 1956 but amended with substantial revisions in 1981, is much more systematic than the other codes noted so far in its attention to the problem of women's status in marital conflict. Although the initiating legislation expressed, as it is generally wise to do, its allegiance to the Koran and its adherence to the Shari'a (laws drawn from the Koran), it has given more rights to women than may have been envisioned.

Under Koranic law the husband had only to pronounce the formula "Talak" three times before two witnesses in order to achieve a final divorce. A woman could conceivably get a divorce by going to a *kadi*, a judge, and proving that her husband had actually harmed her or her children or had not provided food and shelter for them.

Under the new law, he can no longer repudiate her personally and unilaterally, and he has to go to a civil court. To deal with new cases, a system of national courts was set up. A woman also has the right to ask the court for a divorce. If a spouse (usually the wife) does not desire the divorce, he or she is

20. Eric Mueller, "Revitalizing Old Ideas: Developments in Middle Eastern Law," in Elizabeth W. Fernea, ed., *Women and the Family in the Middle East* (Austin: University of Texas Press, 1985), p. 231.

to be paid some compensation.[21] The legal ideal expressed in these laws would be equal rights.

There are three bases for divorce: mutual consent, proving fault, or a request by one party, who would be required to compensate the other. The court must make an attempt at reconciliation, and there is a waiting period. The compensation was originally to be a lump sum, but in 1981 the possibility of the husband's paying regular sums for a period of time, or even a lifetime (or until remarriage), was begun. Custody was to be decided in the best interests of the children, which has become in effect maternal custody. However, the ex-husband remains the legal guardian of his children and can make most important decisions about them, such as where they will go to school, whether they may get a passport for travel, and so on.

General Divorce Trends

Although Prothro and Diab have asserted that my own earlier predictions of divorce trends in Arab countries were borne out,[22] I myself am skeptical. I wrote that we would expect the Arab countries to exhibit a declining divorce rate as they moved toward industrialization—but that later they would return to somewhat higher rates. However, the genuine industrialization has been so small that we should not expect it to have much impact on the divorce rate. I also noted there that the new ideology of the family might have consequences long before much industrialization occurs, and that in fact has happened.

I am now somewhat more inclined to accept Allman's comment that some of my conclusions cannot yet be quite disproved because the data are simply not good enough.[23] This is in part because determining longer term trends requires a firm *base* figure from which to start—preferably one from several generations ago—as well as good recent figures, and neither requirement can be met as yet. Also, a fairly high percentage of divorces were very likely not recorded at all in the past (since such events were in the realm of the religious courts, and not the state), many occurred in remote villages (for

21. Mounira Charrad's summary of the main points of the Code are especially useful since she has interviewed experienced family lawyers in Tunis to find out how the law worked out and how women have fared under it for the past thirty years. See her "Repudiation *versus* Divorce: Responses to State Policy in the Islamic Context of Tunisia," in Esther Ngan-Ling Chow and Catherine A. Berheide, eds., *Women, the Family and Policy: A Global Perspective* (Stony Brook: SUNY Press, 1991).

22. Edwin C. Prothro and Lutfy Naji Diab, *Changing Family Patterns and the Arab East* (Beirut: American University Press, 1974), p. 6. W. J. Goode, *World Revolution and Family Patterns* (New York: Free Press, 1963), p. 158.

23. Allman, *Women's Status*, p. xxviii.

example, in the Maghreb), and the standards for government record-keeping varied widely. Thus it may not be possible to prove that any robust trend exists at all.

Let us consider the problems of analyzing trends in divorce rates in the Arab world in more detail. Several modes of calculating rates may be used, all of them unsatisfactory in some respects. The most common simply states the number of divorces per 1,000 population aged ten or (more usually) fourteen years of age and older—or even the entire population of any age, as is very common in international compilations (for example, the UN *Demographic Yearbook*, 1990, p. 756). The base figure, then, includes widows, divorcees, and the unmarried as well as the married. But it is only married couples who are at risk of divorce and thus are its proper base group. By including all other marital statuses (especially unmarried children), we dilute the meaning of the divorce rate considerably.

The second measure states the number of divorces in each year per 1,000 marriages *in that same year* (or, in a refinement, a running average of several years together, such as 1985–1987). This technique is unsatisfactory because many of those divorces (to be sure, fewer in Arab countries) occurred not to *those* marriages but to marital unions that took place in previous years.

A third and much more adequate measure states the number of divorces each year per 1,000 couples *currently* in the married status. In perhaps most of the less developed countries, however, it is not possible to obtain a valid count of such couples except in a census year.

We believe that all these methods will yield the same time trend over decades unless extreme demographic processes occur (which may be true of Arab nations). In some circumstances, the second measure—the divorce-to-marriage ratio—may yield a more valid figure than the first, based on the whole population. At least, both sets of events are precisely the acts under scrutiny—that is, marriages and divorces. In Arab countries (as in Latin America), the very high birthrates and the increasing age at marriage mean that the population base to be used for the first measure, crude divorce rates, is heavily skewed toward the *younger* ages, where marriage is now less common than in past years that we would wish to use for comparison. It would be very difficult to calculate the still more sophisticated measure, the percentage of couples who will eventually divorce within any marriage cohort. I have never seen such a figure for any Arab country.

My most important conclusion about changes in divorce rates in the Arab world is, to repeat, that *no strong trend is observable*. This conclusion will be qualified somewhat as we take note of the data in more detail, but in general it fits the available facts. This conservative phrasing also specifically means that I am not certain that the available data report the real facts; but we have no alternative information that would justify a different hypothesis.

It is of course true, as has been noted several times in this book, that robust data on a time scale of at least a generation or more—almost always necessary for analyzing *family* trends—are difficult to obtain for most of the major areas of the world. For example, because of the political boundary changes as well as the political turmoil, good trend data for modern African nations are rare. Although I have presented some figures for Latin American countries, the peculiar nature of marriage in those countries—that is, millions of unformalized unions—means that both "marriages" and "divorces" are often not recorded. In Russia, figures have been published now and then, often for only a single large city such as Moscow, but a firm time series is difficult to construct for the nation as a whole, and of course its meaning is obscured by the wide differences among its various cultures.[24] In the Arab countries still other difficulties are observable. Let us consider them, since they affect the credibility of the data on divorce rates.

Here we face several elementary problems. The first is that the most easily available divorce rates are those published by the United Nations from information supplied by each country, based on the number of divorces per 1,000 population *of all ages and marital statuses.* However, since the data on time changes are republished over several years, we can compare the rates given for a *given* year in one publication, with those published in later years *for exactly the same year.* Unfortunately, these figures sometimes change from one document to another. Usually the changes are small, but sometimes they are substantial, affecting any conclusion.

Second, even when the figures for a given year do not contradict one another in successive publications, they may exhibit substantial changes from one year to the next, going up or down with no apparent trend—a kind of trendless fluctuation. For example, the divorce rate per 1,000 population in Algeria rises nearly 50 percent (from 1.1 to 1.61) in the period 1945–1955, then drops to 0.90 in 1960, then decreases again, to 0.43, in 1965. The rate for Iraq drops nearly 40 percent from 1950 to 1960 (0.52 to 0.30); that for Lebanon rises about 50 percent (0.41 to 0.67) in the period 1950–1955. Calculated by divorce-to-marriage ratios, that of Iraq drops about 70 percent (61 per 1000 marriages to 16) in the years 1975–1980. Such large changes suggest that there are problems in the reliability or validity of the data rather than real changes, but we have no way of proving that. Changes of that magnitude occasionally occur in Western nations with better data, too, but

24. Since the rates for the Asiatic republics, or most of the region east of the Urals, are much lower than for the rest of the nation, many scholars would argue that a rate for "the nation as a whole" has little meaning. Gail Lapidus notes those differences but does present the total numbers for the period 1940–1975 in her *Women in Soviet Society* (Berkeley: University of California Press, 1978). For the late 1930s and most of the 1940s the figures are not firm.

usually when a large-scale event happens, such as a major war or depression.

Third, because of high birthrates, and thus the skew toward younger ages in the Arab populations, and the rising age at marriage, even if the absolute number of divorces remains the same over a few years the crude divorce rate should be dropping (since a smaller percentage of the whole population is now available for divorce). That is, the population base on which the divorce rate is calculated is much younger, larger, and less likely to be married anyway, and discerning a real trend is difficult.

Again, especially in the villages, various observers have claimed that a high percentage of divorces may go unrecorded, and that was especially so in the past. Both initial recording and later reporting to national or international centers may contain gaps. On the other hand, some urban statistics agencies in one nation or another may be very effective. The result is that the differences in rates may reflect simply the different efficiency of several bureaucratic agencies. Indeed, not until this manuscript was in press was I able to obtain any recent official rates for Morocco, which is reported to have higher rates than many other Arab countries, even after writing numerous personal and official letters to both academic scholars and statistical offices. Algeria had a strong demography agency for decades, but recent data on national rates were not available.

But as against this tone of skepticism about the official published data, perhaps we have no good reason to expect any trend. After all, there is no body of adequate theory that would lead one to predict any specific direction to the figures. As already noted, industrialization theory cannot make any firm predictions, since it does not seem likely that these nations have taken many steps toward the fundamental *social* rules of industrialization. Even if we accept what appears to be occurring—a loosening or weakening of traditional rules of family and divorce behavior—that does not specifically predict whether divorce rates will fall or rise over time. Under the older family patterns, it seems likely that those rates were high by comparison with Western rates, but that was not a social *rule*, approved and supported by a norm that approved of divorce. Rather, those rates were an outcome of many social processes, not all of which press toward one particular trend. For example, if men now cannot so arbitrarily cast out their wives as in the past, women on the other hand can more easily demand a divorce. In fact, a common-sense argument might assert that simply because so many new variables of change have come to affect family life, a trendless fluctuation is what we would expect, with perhaps a very long-term rise in the *official* rates.

Let us now consider the divorce rates themselves. Here we present three

Table 9.1: Divorces per 1,000 Population, 1950–1989

	1950	1960	1970	1980	1985–1989
Algeria (Moslems)	1.4 (1959)	.9 (1965)			
Egypt (1989)	3.0	2.5	2.1 (1979)	1.8	1.6
Iraq	0.5	0.3	0.4 (1977)	0.8 (1984)	0.8
Jordan	1.2 (1951)	1.1	.6	.8	1.2 (1989)
Kuwait			1.4	2.6	1.4 (1988)
Lebanon	0.4	0.6 (1961)	0.5 (1974)		
Libya			2.0	1.8	
Morocco Northern Zone	1.6				
Syria	0.8	0.8	0.6	0.6	0.7 (1988)
Tunisia		0.9 (1961)	0.8	1.1	1.6 (1989)

Sources: U.N. Demographic Yearbooks, (the 34th issue has discussion of nuptiality and divorce at pp. 692–99) and other official sources.

different sets of rates and consider them in turn. Table 9.1 shows the number of divorces per 1,000 population. The rates for Algeria (data only to 1965), Egypt, and Syria have dropped somewhat, while those for Iraq and Lebanon (data only to 1974) have risen very slightly. The trends for others seem doubtful. If we look instead at the divorce-to-marriage ratios (Table 9.2), most show no real change, though possibly the rates for Syria, Tunisia, and Kuwait have dropped. If we go back to the turn of the century, the ratios in Algeria dropped by half in the period 1897–1955. However, it is clear that divorce rates must have been higher in the late 1960s than the published rate, since 20 percent of the women aged 35–49 years in a 1972 sample had married a second time, and 4 percent at least a third time.[25]

We also have reason to believe that two decades ago, 15 percent of marriages in Tunisia ended in divorce. For Egypt and Morocco in 1980 the figures were 18 and 28 percent, respectively; for the Yemenite Arab Republic

25. Dominique Tabutin and Jacques Vallin, "Quelques Resultats de L'Enquête Fécondité Algerienne 1970," unpublished paper, Colloque de Demographie Africaine, Rabat, 1972, Oran, 1973.

Table 9.2: Divorces per 1,000 Marriages, 1950–1989

Country	1950	1960	1970	1980	1984–1988
Algeria	167* (1953)	61			
Egypt	331 (167 1953)	230 (1969)	212 (1978)	208	179
Iraq	12	90	93	60 (1975)	
Jordan	169 (1951)	142	127	175	183
Kuwait		385 (1961)	462	250	313 (1987)
Lebanon	64	61	74		
Morocco	288 (1952)				400 (est. 1987)
Qatar					212 (1984–1985)
Syria	97	90	57	56	70 (1986)
Tunisia		155 (1961)	124	149	70 (1980–1988)

*1950 figures inflated because of a social security law requiring civil registration.
Sources: U.N. Demographic Yearbooks and official national yearbooks. National data in Tunisia were not compiled until 1956.

and Algeria in 1970 the figures were 29 and 31 percent, respectively. These figures conform closely to the divorce-to-marriage ratios.[26]

In some of the outlying regions of Morocco in the 1960s the ratio of divorces to marriages ranged from 30 to 50 percent, while many "transitory marriages" without children as well as nonconsummated unions were omitted from the divorce data.[27] I have not been able to obtain official data for the 1970s, but Mernissi asserts that among married women aged 20–24 years, the divorce rate was four times that of the United States.[28] I now have figures for Rabat and Casablanca, with a ratio of slightly more than 40 divorces per

26. Dominique Tabutin, "Nuptiality and Fertility in Maghreb," in Lado T. Ruzicka, ed., *Nuptiality and Fertility* (Liege: Ordina, 1982), pp. 105–06; and Hilda Geertz, "The Meaning of Family Ties," in Clifford Geertz, Hilda Geertz, and L. Rosen, eds., *Meaning and Order in Moroccan Society* (Cambridge: Cambridge University Press, 1979), pp. 386ff..

27. Tabutin, "Nuptiality," pp. 105–06; and Hilda Geertz, "The Meaning of Family Ties," pp. 379ff.

28. Mernissi, in Allman, *Women's Status*, p. 318. For further remarks on the plausibility of high rates in Morocco and their dynamics, see Vanessa Maher, "Divorce and Property in the Middle Atlas of Morocco," *Man* 9 (1974), esp. 108–09; and her "Women and Social Change in Morocco," in Beck and Keddie, eds., *Muslim World*, p. 110.

100 marriages (but no national figure).[29] Such figures do not assert any trend, of course, but they do warn us that the official data may not present a very robust body of information.

Remarriage and Women-Headed Households

The census data clearly reveal one important change in the traditional system of divorce: a *feminization of households.* The trend has two important components: far more divorced women fail to remarry than in the past, or marry after a longer period of being divorced; and more husbands leave their wives behind, temporarily or permanently, to seek jobs elsewhere. Perhaps the customary system is failing to meet the needs of women and their children, or perhaps some women are accepting "independence" when they are forced by circumstances to do so, even if that had not been their intention.

The older system assumed that a woman was not to be the "head" of a family, except because of misfortune. A female was always to be under the protection and rule of a male: in her younger years, her father; then her husband; if she was divorced, she became the dependent of her father again; and then she would be remarried to another husband. If she outlived her husband, she would be a dependent in the house of one of her sons.

We do not have adequate figures to tell us what percentage of women actually remarried. Since the average duration of marriage was short (three to four years), women married young, and their families had good reasons for marrying them off, it is likely that most did enter a second marriage and that they did so quickly. In two Moroccan samples of 1987 (Rabat and Casablanca), 40 percent of those who did remarry did so within a year, 20 percent between one and two years, and 10 percent between two and three years.[30] Partly confirming that report is the fact that in several census distributions from Algeria and Morocco, the actual percentage of women in the divorced status does not rise much by age within the marriageable years.

Censuses show, however, that a higher percentage of divorced women than of men now remain unmarried, and the number of female-headed households is increasing rapidly.[31] Some of the ratios of women to men who are still in the divorced status follows:

29. These ratios were calculated by Housni Arbri, using the World Fertility Study as a base. I have not seen them elsewhere. See his "La Famille Marocaine: Tendance des Dissolutions d'Unions," in *La Famille au Maghreb,* Sixième Colloque de Demographie Maghrebine (Rabat: Association Maghrebine pour l'Etude de la Population, 1986), p. 88.

30. *Menages. Variables socio-demographiques* (Rabat: Centre d'Etudes et de Recherches Demographiques, 1990), pp. 251–52, 280–86.

31. Ibid., table 8, p. 274; and p. 338.

Egypt (1976)   3:1
Algeria (1982)   4:1
Morocco (1982)   4:1
Iraq (1965)   4.7:1

All these ratios apply to the population aged 14 years and up and thus include older female divorcees. The ratios are lower if we focus on the age group 25–40 years:

Morocco (1971) 1.7:1   (1982) 2.5:1
Algeria (1970) 2.2:1   (1984) 3.7:1
Tunisia (1975) 2.2:1

On the other hand, the ratios are higher if we look at urban populations, where we could expect the usual processes of arranging a second marriage for women to be more difficult. Even when the ratios of women to men do not change much from one census to the next, the absolute numbers of women still in the divorced status increase. For example, they increased by 30 percent between 1971 and 1982 in Morocco.

All such figures seem to be underestimates, for Muslim women do not wish to admit that they are in the divorced status. A Tunisian demographer calculated that in the period 1966–1985 about one-half to three-fourths of the divorced women disappeared from that category without having died or remarried.[32] Men disappeared almost as much. Also, census data suggest that women "disappear" into the status of widowed: In the age group 60–64 years in both Tunisia and Algeria, and in successive censuses or official surveys for 1966–1985, 30–47 percent of the women report themselves as widows, but only 3–4 percent of the men.

What are some of the causes of this increase in the number of women without husbands? In the modern world, men leave their wives and migrate to the cities or to other Arab countries in search of employment. Ibrahim argues that one of the effects of labor migration is the feminization of households. He estimates that perhaps half of Egyptian migrants leave their wives and children behind, and of course there is an increasing number of female labor migrants to the capital-rich countries.[33]

Ultimately, the migrant husbands may dissolve the marriage. Such long-term separations, some equivalent to divorce, are of course not recorded. Considerable time may pass before the woman is even free to remarry (although the husband is free to take another wife, and may not bother to divorce the first one). Thus she may become older and less desirable in the

32. Mernissi, in Allman, *Women's Status*, pp. 319–320, asserts that in the decade 1960–71 the percentage of women-headed households increased by 33 percent. The Statistical Yearbook of Egypt notes this change for Egypt as well.
33. Saad Eddin Ibrahim, *The New Arab Social Order* (Boulder, Westview, 1982), p. 92.

marriage market. Also, women are now usually adult when they marry, so their families may feel less responsible for their marital status. With the husband's abandonment, or at least failure to provide support, a woman can ask a governmental official for a divorce. Since 1956, Tunisian wives can initiate a divorce, but judges are somewhat reluctant to grant their petitions. Still, with persistence, it is possible.[34] Moroccan women can do so, and women who are willing and able to compensate their husbands can do so in most countries.

Wives left behind may also migrate (if their husbands are well-to-do, they may take their families with them). Whether they stay or move, most of them will work, and at low-paying or menial jobs. On the other hand, it can be argued that the possibility of getting jobs at all is some improvement over the past, especially in rural areas. Phrased differently, it is now possible for many women to keep a household together, though at an economically depressed level. Saunders and Mahanna analyze these dynamics,[35] although their main focus is on *village* Egypt, and they do not address directly the actual percentage of woman-headed households. They do note that even in the nineteenth century the imposition of forced labor (one-sixth of the total Egyptian population in 1841) created a large-scale migration of male heads of households.

The Arab "patriarch" now has less control over the members of his family and thus has less power to arrange remarriages. Doubtless, too, because more female divorcees now work (a higher percentage than in any other marital status),[36] some may be less enthusiastic about rushing into another marriage with its attendant financial and domestic burdens. Also, women who marry at a later age and are better educated are not so easy to control. As in so many other contemporary polities, men gain much more from remarriage than women do, and the usual bias against age is set primarily against women. Thus more men can and do enter into remarriage.

The important fact is, however, to note the breakdown of the traditional system for taking care of the problems of divorce—in this case, the problem of assuring the woman of a status as a married person. The increase in the

34. Charrad, "Repudiation," p. 12.
35. Lucie W. Saunders and Sohair Mahanna, "Women-Headed Households in Rural Egypt," unpublished paper, Am. Anthrop. Soc. meetings, Philadelphia, 1986, p. 11). For a qualitative analysis of some of the effects of male and female migration on labor force participation (from Jordan, Egypt, Syria, Lebanon, etc.) see H. Azzam, J. Abu Nasr, and I. Lorfing, "An Overview of Arab Women in Population, Employment, and Economic Development," in Julinda Abu Nasr, N. F. Khoury, and Henry T. Azzam, eds., *Women, Employment, and Development in the Arab World* (New York: Mouton, 1985), pp. 27–28.
36. For example, see G. B. S. Mujahid, "Women Labour Force Participation in Jordan," in Fernea, *Women and Family,* p. 116, table 10.

number of "independent" women—that is, women without the support of a
husband—runs counter to fundamentalist attitudes.[37]

Custody and Support

I have been unable to obtain strong numerical reports on the trends in
custody and support, but I shall venture to comment on possible changes on
the basis of other data. The traditional system was clear enough, if sometimes very complex in its interpersonal and interfamilial negotiations. *Jural*
custody was always patriarchal. *Actual* custody was also clear. The male
children were in the care of the mother until the age of seven years, the
female children until the age of nine (or puberty). These ages varied somewhat by region.

Since at divorce the mother and her young children went to her father's
house until she remarried, and the children at the appropriate ages went to
their father's house, there was no issue of either alimony or child support.
That is, the divorced wife received support until the end of the *'idda*, to be
certain she was not pregnant, but no longer. Ideally, the husband would
support his children in the house of their mother's father, though it can be
assumed that her father usually took on this burden.

In any event there was no legal issue about these matters. Both the mother
and the children were cared for by one or the other of the respective families.
They were dependents, and it was never supposed that the mother would
establish an independent household with her children and thus would need
support for a separate existence, as in the West.

Now, however, that situation seems to be changing. The number of
mother-headed households is increasing as the number of families left behind by labor migration rises. The rates of both first marriages and remarriages have fallen. More divorced (and widowed) mothers fail to enter a new
marriage but do not return to their father's households. Their own households, as in the West, are more likely to suffer economic deprivation and
therefore in the mass become a social problem.

Note that, as Youssef remarks, under the customary system the divorced
mother did not have any independent financial or child-care responsibilities, since she and her children were reabsorbed into her paternal
household.[38] She was usually young in any event since most divorces occurred within the first three years of marriage (in Tunisia in the 1980s, 70
percent of those who divorced did so within three years). Nor did the di-

37. Youssef, "Status," p. 82, also affirms this point.
38. Ibid., p. 84.

vorced husband have these responsibilities, since until he claimed custody
the children were cared for by their maternal grandparents. If he remarried,
he was likely to give their care to his own parents or to an older sibling, or to
care for them in his own household.

In Tunisia, Syria, and Egypt the divorced husband may now face a longer
period of support. If he divorces his wife without good cause in Syria or
Tunisia, he must pay one year's support. Under the 1981 Tunisian law,
however, the final discharge of obligation may not be complete, for the wife
may elect to receive alimony instead, which might be a lifelong payment.[39]

In Egypt, if the wife is not willing to be divorced, he must pay two years'
support (plus the traditional period of the 'idda), and in addition she has the
right to stay in the (rented) dwelling unless he arranges another suitable
place for her to live until the end of custody.[40] Such practices may become
more widespread because it is easier administratively to place this financial
responsibility on the husband than to pay huge sums for a national welfare
program to protect divorced mothers and children. Moreover, because of the
spread of education, both female and male children become an increasing
cost for the parents as well as for the grandpaternal households.

The introduction of alimony in Tunisia has not reduced this problem by
much, since the judges still feel uncomfortable with the practice, and family
lawyers view their awards as extremely low.[41] The alimony is supposed to
maintain the level of living the wife enjoyed before the divorce, but of course
as in the West that happens rarely; almost all mothers suffer an economic
loss at divorce. On the other hand, increasingly the new rights of women
become known, and occasional substantial awards to a few women appear
in the newspapers, so that more women are inclined to demand more.

In the rich United Arab Emirates, by contrast, "every divorced woman is
assured of an income if she needs it," and child support is furnished by the
government.[42] Still, perhaps even the OPEC countries (still wealthy in spite
of reduced incomes) would have some difficulty maintaining such a program if faced with large numbers of needy divorced mothers.

It should be emphasized that any legal provisions requiring financial contributions from divorced husbands for their wives and children would be a
large change from the customary pattern. Most fundamentally, it would

39. Charrad, "Repudiation," pp. 7, 14.

40. Charis Waddy, *Women in Muslim History* (New York: Longman Green, 1980), p. 180,
asserts that the law gives her the use of house and furniture, and he must move; if the marriage
has lasted fifteen years, he must pay alimony for life, and he is to pay 40 percent of his salary. I
have seen no independent confirmation that such stringent demands are actually put into
practice.

41. Charrad, "Repudiation," pp. 14–15.

42. Linda Usra Soffan, *The Women of the United Arab Emirates* (London: Croom Helm, 1980),
p. 44.

move the system from purely private, intrafamilial negotiations among and between extended families to procedures imposed by the government. If governmental welfare programs are also used to supplement those steps—as seems likely because state functions continue to expand—it would underscore Mernissi's thesis that the "patriarch" declines in familial power because the state increasingly becomes the source of jobs and other socio-economic allocations.[43]

Such changes would also alter divorce in an important way. In the past, the dissolution of the marriage was, for the husband, a kind of "no-fault divorce"—no fault needed to be asserted, and the divorce contained some penalties, but only a few and they were usually minor. Wives had no power against the decision of their husbands; for example, they could not refuse to accept the divorce. Now the penalties would be potentially more severe.

Equally important, this range of steps would officially recognize another change that I speculate is also occurring: a shift in customary rules of custody. As noted above, the children traditionally belonged to the father's line, a common pattern wherever the influence of the lineage depends on its ability to maintain its fighting strength. This was emphasized in the Arab world by the value placed on the ideal marital union—a parallel-cousin marriage, between a young man and the daughter of his father's brother, which kept any wealth and power within the patrilineage. To be sure, this was most common among higher-status families, but that fact only emphasized the value of the ideal.

However, the system of custody and claims to the children depended on a relatively stable residence so that everyone knew where the children lived during the mother's temporary custody; on the ability and willingness of the paternal and maternal extended family to care for them; and on the assumption that both husband and wife would remarry after divorce. The system also took it for granted that divorced mothers would not be able or required by social and economic circumstances to establish an independent household. These assumptions no longer fit the reality.

The reader should keep in mind that the traditional Arab system has its parallel, though not an exact counterpart, in the West. Until about the middle of the nineteenth century in the United States and later in Western European countries, legal custody was unequivocally paternal. Although I have seen no adequate analysis of the change in this pattern, which is almost never dealt with in standard histories of the Western family, it seems likely that it came about largely by default. That is, men were increasingly involved with large extrafamilial enterprises, with jobs rather than land; geographical

43. In her article, "The Patriarch in the Moroccan Family: Myth or Reality," in Allman, *Status*, pp. 312–22.

mobility was high; and extended kin were less and less able or willing to take on this burden for them.

To put it more bluntly, East or West, men have never been willing to take on the daily tasks of child-care. They wanted—and perhaps still want—to have custody as long as they did not have to take care of the children. They were willing to demand formal custody only as long as the women in their extended kin (aunts, sisters, mothers, sisters-in-law, and so on) would accept the burden. Moreover, since the importance of the *lineage* continues to decline, even the ideological value of custody decreases.

Since the advantages of keeping a tight hold on custody have lessened while the cost has risen, I speculate that even if *legal* provisions for an extension of maternal custody do not become widespread, in the future more children will remain longer in their mothers' care. In the Yemenite Arab Republic, the children typically remain with their mother after the divorce, until they are teenagers, and with their maternal grandmother if their mother remarries.[44] In Egypt, although the expected ages for the end of maternal custody are ten years for boys and twelve for girls,[45] the judge can decide that the children would be better served under continuing maternal custody until the boy is fifteen and the girl is married. The husband also has formal economic responsibility for the children (for the boy, until he is 25 years old). Moreover, the law recognizes a succession of possible *maternal* custodial relatives—female relatives (always before paternal ones) who have the right to custody if the mother is unable to carry out her functions. This suggests once more the growing importance of the mother as custodial parent.

On this matter, the Tunisian experience is instructive. The 1956 code opened the possibility of giving custody to mothers, under the principle that the best interests of the children should be the basis of the decision. By contrast with alimony, this principle did not seem to be much of a violation of tradition, since there had always been circumstances under which the children (especially girls) remained with the mother for longer periods. Thus more judges—in the early years, many of them with little training—seemed to feel that handing the children over to the mother was proper (that occurs now in 90 percent of all cases) especially since the father still remained the legal guardian. He remains so, although the 1981 law has also specified that the mother can become the guardian if he dies. We believe that mother custody will be the trend in other countries, too. To be more cautious, legal

44. Cynthia Myntti, *Women and Development in the YAR,* German Agency for Technical Cooperation, Germany, 1979, pp. 31–32 (although she suggests an earlier age in another sentence).
45. Andrea B. Rugh, *Family in Contemporary Egypt* (Syracuse: Syracuse University Press, 1984), pp. 178–79. Waddy, *Women,* p. 180, gives the ages as nine and eleven years.

custody will remain in the hands of the divorced father, but for most practical purposes de facto custody will be in the hands of the divorced mother. Moroccan women are given custody of their daughters until they are married and of their sons until they reach puberty.[46]

Final Comment: A Decline in Divorce?

Is it possible that any of these developments will change the overall divorce rate in the Arab countries? I am not yet convinced that the data about the past are robust enough to permit a secure test of my conclusion even if real changes were to occur in the near future. Nevertheless, I do not think it likely that a decrease in the rates will occur.

First, it is possible that the greater weight given to freedom of mate choice may increase marital stability somewhat. If women become more nearly equal to their husbands in age, education, and personal status, however, one might also argue that this would lead to greater conflict and *more* divorce.

The Arab divorce rate has generally been higher in villages and rural areas, and higher among the less educated and the poor, so that the traditionally easy, arbitrary repudiation of the wife by the husband may come to be widely viewed (as it is already among the educated) as the behavior of the less cultivated, not in harmony with modern, educated ways. I believe it is likely that easy and arbitrary divorce will be more commonly seen as a vestige of "country customs." On the other hand, the various religious, cultural, military, political, and economic crises of the present and the foreseeable future seem likely to overcome the thrust of this very small set of stabilizing factors in one part of the population. For the shorter term, it seems wiser, if more cynical, to guess that crisis and turmoil will be far stronger, and will weaken family cohesion further.

46. *Menages*, 1990, p. 255.

10

Three Patterns of Declining Divorce Rates in Asia: Under Industrial Growth in Indonesia and Taiwan and under Strong Governmental Intervention in China

In Chapter 8 we analyzed one pattern of declining divorce rates in Japan, a country that once had a stable high-divorce-rate system. That nation put into place an industrializing program as well as strong supports for family control, based on samurai ideals. In this chapter we continue to analyze stable high-divorce-rate systems by considering Indonesia and Taiwan, which followed a different route. We also examine China, though it was not a high-divorce-rate society, because the contrast helps to illuminate the processes of declines in divorce rates.

All three of these countries created elaborate governmental programs aimed at full-scale industrialization. Indonesia's success was not so spectacular as that of Taiwan, perhaps because Taiwan began the 1950s with an advantage: The Japanese had already moved its economy in that direction in the long period between the conquest of 1895 and the end of World War II. In any event, as we note later, the Indonesian achievement was considerable. China's economic program was a failure in major ways in the period between 1950 and the mid-1980s. Yet in all of these countries the socioeconomic transformations during these decades were large.

The inclusion of China here affords several useful comparisons and contrasts. First, China's large-scale, highly ideological mass mobilization aimed at industrialization and a great Communist state could be predicted to cause great upheavals in family life and a sharp rise in the divorce rate. Indeed, that is precisely what happened in the early 1950s. In contrast to the other two countries, the state then embarked on a specific program for reducing the divorce rate. Moreover, unlike almost all other countries, it succeeded.

In Taiwan and Indonesia, the divorce rates were reduced without a plan. They diminished because the socioeconomic development—a real indus-

280

trializing process—undermined the existing family patterns that had been generating high divorce rates. Indeed, unlike Japan, neither country presented or supported a clearly enunciated family model as part of its public rhetoric. It is also fair to say that the Chinese gave lip service to such a model—the "ideal family under socialism"—but no one had ever seen one in real life, and for political reasons they could not create the necessary economic supports for it. In both Indonesia and Taiwan there was so much variation in family patterns during the important years of family change that no serious leader could have imposed any single model on the whole country.

Thus each of these countries has experienced decades of rapid, extensive family change, linked with dramatic political and economic shifts. China serves to remind us that steady bureaucratic pressures can reduce the divorce rate under some circumstances. And all three illustrate the fact that under modern conditions of industrialization it is likely that divorce rates will eventually rise again. They did drop in Taiwan and Indonesia when those socioeconomic processes undermined the family systems that once created higher rates, but the resulting very low rates will not be typical of an industrial society in the modern era. And in fact they have been rising.

Indonesia

Indonesia is a further example of a stable high-divorce-rate system. It is the eastern tip of the great Muslim crescent that begins in northern Africa and extends across Asia. It contains many cultures, languages, and even kinship systems. Almost all its citizens are Muslim, and most live in Java, but its adherence to Muslim principles is also shaped by many indigenous family patterns that may be much older in origin.

Very few family data have been gathered for the nation as a whole, but a number of village studies have reported high rates of divorce. Hildred Geertz, for example, reported that nearly half of all Javanese marriages end in divorce, and people do not suppose that any marriage will last.[1] Singarimbun and Manning's research in Mojolama near Yokyakarta found that almost half the women aged 45 and older had been divorced at least once.[2] Soeradji's analysis of the major national survey of 1973 shows that for

1. Hildred Geertz, *The Javanese Family* (Glencoe, Ill.: Free Press, 1961), p. 69.
2. Masri Singarimbun and Chris Manning, "Marriage and Divorce in Mojolama," *Indonesia*, April 17, 1974, p. 73. See also the extensive bibliography in Geoffrey McNicoll and Masri Singarimbun, *Fertility Decline in Indonesia*, Committee on Population and Demography, report no. 20, (Washington, D.C.: National Academy Press of the National Academy of Science, 1983), pp. 114–30.

certain categories of women as much as 70 percent of first marriages without children and 53 percent of all marriages without sons might end in divorce.[3]

Since almost all the available data come from either village studies done over a limited period or surveys carried out at one time, it is not possible to reconstruct a simple trend in the national divorce rates from the colonial past to the present. More than 150 years ago, however, some observers had remarked on the high rates of divorce in Java.[4] This pattern, therefore, is not an aberration caused by the upheavals of World War II and the revolutionary events afterwards.

Two strong conclusions emerge from the studies now available: first, that divorce rates in Indonesia have been relatively high for a very long time, and second, the divorce rates have been falling. How long they will fall and when or whether they will rise again can be no more than a guess. My hypothesis is that they fell in response to rapid socioeconomic development ("industrialization" in my sense) and that they will rise once more. I shall later present some data, as I did in the case of Peninsular Malaysia, to suggest that the rise might already be in progress.

Grouping all ever-married women aged 15–49 by region, Soeradji shows that the percentage of first marriages ending in divorce in 1973 ranged from only 8 percent in Bali to 32 percent in West Java. As we would expect in a traditional high-divorce society, the rates are higher in rural areas. The Indonesian figures include non-Muslims, whose rates are lower than Muslim rates. Most of the data to follow will focus on Muslims, however, who constitute almost all of the Indonesian population.

What processes generated high divorce rates in Indonesia generally and Java especially? And what has caused the rates to drop? It is somewhat easier to answer the first question.

By custom, Indonesian parents were socially obligated to arrange a marriage for their children and to pay for a lavish ceremony celebrating the union. As in many other societies, the festival seemed to be focused on the social standing of the parents. The choice of mate was not viewed as a solemn or weighty decision, and in turn the lack of serious evaluation could be justified—through an odd but compelling logic—by the widespread expectation that marriages did not last anyway, and that a poor choice would be easily remedied.[5]

Reports differ as to whether marriage often occurred before menstrua-

3. Budi Soeradji Martokeosoemo, *Marriage and Divorce in Indonesia: A Demographic Study* (Chicago: University of Chicago Press, 1970), pp. 164–67. The data from the World Fertility Survey were not yet analyzed at that time. Jakarta was not included in the 1973 survey.

4. Gavin W. Jones, *Divorce in Islamic Southeast Asia* (Canberra: Australian National University, 1991), p. 31, n. 3.

5. The dynamics of the forces that created high marital instability are best analyzed by Geertz, *Javanese Family*, pp. 47ff., 69ff., 137ff.

tion.[6] In any event, those who married at younger ages had less voice in their choice of husband and were more likely to divorce. In the 1973 Indonesian survey the average age of women at marriage for all cohorts was 18 years for nonmigrant urban women and 16.2 for nonmigrant rural women. On average, Muslim women were younger at marriage than members of other religions.

In the most common Indonesian family pattern the wife had a strong position, unlike many other family systems (for example, India, China) in which the young bride without resources of her own entered a household in which she was pressed toward docility by dominant elders. Writing of Java, Geertz notes that she paid formal deference to her husband, but points out that "it is usually she who is dominant . . . families actually dominated by the man are exceedingly rare."[7]

Women could support themselves without much difficulty, in the market, on the land, or (now) increasingly in factories and offices. They could easily return to the households of their parents or sisters. They could marry again, and most did so.[8] Equally important, divorce was both common and socially acceptable. Many older people have been married many times.

Essentially without a courtship period of adjustment, Indonesian couples would discover the difficulties of life together only after marriage. Geertz reports that commonly it was the woman who found the marriage unsatisfactory, and Singarimbun and Manning state that 70 percent of women who gave "dislike of husband" as the reason for divorce did not even consummate the first marriage.[9] Just how they accomplished this seemingly delicate task the authors do not say, but we noted earlier that a delay in the physical union was once fairly common in societies where girls were married at a very young age. Both in Indonesia and in Peninsular Malaysia during the 1950s and 1960s nonconsummation of the marriage was offered as a "reason" for divorce in about one-fifth of the cases for which data are available.

It has always been easy to divorce in Indonesia. The Muslim rule permits the husband to announce the divorce unilaterally,[10] but the woman could always quarrel publicly, or leave him, as a way of precipitating the break. The

6. Singarimbun and Manning, "Marriage," p. 70, report a figure of 23 percent.

7. Geertz, *Javanese Family,* p. 46.

8. Using the World Fertility Survey data of 1976, David P. Smith, E. Carrasco, and P. McDonald report that for early dissolutions, 88 percent remarried; 80 percent of Malays did so. "Marriage, Dissolution and Remarriage," *Comparative Studies,* World Fertility Survey Report, no. 34, (London, 1984), pp. 13ff.

9. Geertz, *Javanese Family,* p. 73; Singarimbun and Manning, "Marriage," p. 80.

10. Hisako Nakamura quarrels with various anthropological reports (especially that of Hildred Geertz) for not seeing how fully the Moslem procedural rules are obeyed (counseling and religious advice, efforts at reconciliation, the many forms of divorce, etc.). See *Divorce in Java* (Indonesia: Godjah Mada University Press, 1983), esp. chs. 7, 8.

financial costs were small, for support was limited to three months or three menstrual periods (the Koranic rule of *'idda*). The woman could take from the marriage any property she owned before the union and one-third of any community property acquired during their domestic life. As a result she was not, and is still not, economically helpless, although it should be kept in mind that most of these people were poor by world standards.

In addition, Indonesians strongly disapproved of conflict and hostility. This cultural pattern, like the one we analyzed in Malaysia, leads both the couple and their neighbors to prefer a divorce to any prolonged antagonism that pollutes their social world. Thus, Indonesian couples avoided quarrels, especially any that others might overhear. Since kin and neighbors felt that spousal conflicts affected their own health and spiritual well-being, they were unlikely to oppose a divorce that would restore social and spiritual harmony. Peter McDonald also suggests that the village spiritualist, the *dukun*, sometimes recommends a divorce to older couples who are facing health or economic problems, because they are not suited to each other "in a mystical sense."[11] Finally, as in any high-divorce system, because the marital turnover was high, and because divorce occurred at an early age, almost anyone who did divorce would find another potential mate among the unmarried or those who had similarly left their marriages. They would also have greater freedom to make their own choice in any later marriages.

Thus in the traditional pattern the predominantly Muslim, rural couples had higher divorce rates. Early, arranged marriages, usually with a man five or six years older, were associated with higher divorce rates. Lower rates were found in patrifilial Bali[12] (Java has a bilateral kinship system; matrilineal systems were more common in Sumatra, and so on). Women who had a high school education were and are more likely to have *lower* divorce rates. So was the urban population. Most of those who divorced did so early in the marriage, usually in the first year or two.

Many changes have affected this traditional system. The four-year war of independence against the Dutch began with the fall of Japan, which occupied Indonesia from 1942 to 1945. The early 1950s was a period of some political stabilization and much investment in economic development, although that period was brief and succeeded by much political muddle. Soeradji's cohort analysis of marriages reveals that the age at marriage was rising by that time (though the rise was small). And 1980 census data confirm that analysis: a steadily decreasing percentage of married men and

11. P. McDonald, private communication.
12. This the term used by Hildred and Clifford Geertz in *Kinship in Bali* (Chicago: University of Chicago Press, 1975), p. 47. Marriage is parallel patri-cousin; the man ideally married his father's brother's daughter, which was the ideal in Arab countries as well.

women at younger ages.[13] The median age at first marriage rose by one full year in the urban areas from the birth cohort of 1936–1944 to that of 1951–1955.

An increasing percentage of both men and women in Indonesia has entered school, and that will further increase the age at marriage for women; both factors reduce the divorce rate, in interaction as well as independently. The median age at first marriage of women with no schooling was 16.9 years in 1980, but 19.3 years for women who had been graduated from junior high school and 21.3 years for high-school graduates and those who had achieved a still higher educational level.[14]

Although it is tempting to assert that the declining divorce rate has been caused by industrialization in my specific sense—new opportunities leading to less control by elders—and the gross data do fit that interpretation, I suspect (without being able to prove it) that another large causal factor has been widespread changes of attitudes about life styles and consumption, much of it ultimately (though not always directly) from Western influences.[15]

The gross data are clear enough. Compared with most other countries in Southeast Asia, Indonesia has been an economic "success." The great depression of the 1930s hit Indonesia very hard, since its major production was in raw materials. The nation then suffered the Japanese occupation and thereafter a colonial war for independence. The postwar economic recovery in the early 1950s (there was a boom during the Korean War) was eventually halted by the inability of the Sukarno administration to make its socialist program work. Even in that period, however, the trends in literacy were upward, child mortality fell, and the age at marriage rose somewhat.

Since the mid-1960s there has been a more sustained improvement. The annual growth rate of the economy since that time has been about 4.9 percent, higher than that of most industrial nations. The growth in industry was 13.4 percent annually during 1965–1973 and 8.3 percent during 1973–1984.[16] If we separate out manufacturing from industry, its growth rate was 9.0 percent annually during 1965–73 and rose to 14.9 percent each year

13. *Biro Pusat Statistik* (Jakarta: Analoisa Ringkas Hasil Sensus Pendukuk, 1980 [1984]), tables 1, 2, 4.

14. Ibid., table 6; see also Soeradji, *Marriage*, p. 140 et passim.

15. McNicoll and Singarimbun, *Fertility Decline*, esp. ch. 2. Focusing mostly on fertility, Gavin W. Jones comments that "all the forces of modern change" have caused the fertility decline, for "modernization of attitudes can occur even in the absence of development as measured by the usual battery of social and economic indicators" (those indicators, however, do exist for Indonesia). See Jones, "Population Growth in Java," in J. J. Fox et al., eds., *Indonesia* (Canberra: Australian National University, 1980), p. 523.

16. World Bank, *World Development Report* (New York: Oxford University Press, 1986), pp. 180, 182.

during 1973–1984. Forty percent of Indonesia's domestic product was in industry by 1984.

During these two decades, the crude birthrate dropped by 24 percent and the death rate dropped by 39 percent. By 1983 almost all children of primary school age, male and female, were in school, and 37 percent of the appropriate age group was in secondary school, though the educational level of Indonesians had already risen even before this period. These changes were most pronounced in Java, but they also occurred in the other islands as well.

Other social changes have accompanied these economic developments. Fewer women are in agricultural production, and more have gone into factory work, teaching, trading, and white-collar occupations. Motor vehicle registration grew annually by 13 percent during the 1960s and 1970s.[17] This has, of course, increased participation in the changes occurring at the national level and reduced the effect of local family customs.

Of course, higher education is linked to lower divorce rates, higher ages at marriage, and more employment in industry or in the government bureaucracy, but it also increases the cultural impact of both consumerism and other outside influences. By 1980, literacy had risen to 86 percent among younger adults. Consumer durables are widely distributed, and the evident desire to buy such material goods is reflected in other changes in family behavior, including a lower birthrate.

The mean age at marriage of the marriage cohort of 1946–1950 ranged between just under 14 years to just above 16, and this rose through the 1971–1975 cohort to between 16.5 and 19.7 in the various states of Indonesia. The age at marriage continued to rise after that, and by 1985 it was between 20.2 and 23.6.[18] This drop reflects a shift away from parentally arranged marriages (which, as noted earlier, are linked with higher divorce rates). Both prolonged breast feeding (a rural pattern associated with lower educational levels) and postpartum sexual abstinence seem to have declined, while a vigorous family-planning program has led to increased use of contraception and a declining birthrate. National civil codes also change family patterns toward "modern" forms.[19]

As to other influences, "the themes of lessened parental control over children, of the increasing primacy of conjugal over other kin relations, and generally the erosion of 'traditional' family values occur repeatedly in films,

17. McNicoll and Singarimbun, *Fertility Decline*, p. 30.
18. Terence H. Hull and Sri Harijati Hatmadji, "Regional Fertility Differentials in Indonesia: Causes and Trends,": Working papers in Demography, no. 22, Research School of Social Sciences, Australian National University, Canberra, 1990, tables 2, 3, 4, pp. 30–31.
19. Ibid., p. 90.

radio, and print."[20] What is "proper" modern behavior is widely discussed, and presented in the mass media. In short, it is not just the introduction of new economic opportunities that undermines traditional family controls and thus the traditional system; those influences must also be accompanied by changes in ideology, values, and attitudes, which actually make it seem desirable to *utilize* those new opportunities to escape the older family customs.

It could be added, for the past decade, that the Marriage Law of 1974 also restricted divorce somewhat,[21] but I suspect that its effects were broader. Precisely because it was fiercely attacked by traditionalist Muslims, its innovations were minor.[22] Many different groups tried to gain public support, however, and family issues were widely discussed. The minimum age at marriage was set at 16 for women, actually below the average at that time. A husband was required to get his wife's permission to take a second wife. More important, perhaps, the law codified the procedures and legally necessary conditions for divorce and other family matters, thus making them more open to public scrutiny.

The data do conform to my thesis that the divorce rate in this high-divorce social system drops with socioeconomic and industrial development. It seems possible, however, that the continued disruption of the society as a result of the Japanese occupation, the colonial war against the Dutch, and the succeeding political troubles also played a part in reducing allegiance to traditional family customs. The strong influence of consumerism and value changes caused by (mainly) Western ideas of a "proper" modern marriage, moreover, may have affected family patterns independently, for these are much in the public eye on television.

We can locate the time period in which the decline in divorce rates begins, with the qualification that any Indonesian data contain technical problems. Soeradji has analyzed the 1973 survey data by birth and by marriage cohorts; these of course overlap in time, but with some looseness. If we consider *birth* cohorts, the first drop in Javanese divorce rates begins in the five-year period from 1940–1944 to 1945–1949 for the marriage duration of 0–2 years as well as for other durations. This is true for rural as well as urban women.[23] If we look instead at *marriage* cohorts, the first drop begins in the period between 1945–1949 to 1950–1954, within the marriage duration 0–2 years, for both rural and urban women. Twenty-one percent of the

20. Personal communication from Dr. Budi Soeradji, Chief of the Indonesian Bureau of Family Planning and Population.

21. McNicoll and Singarimbun, *Fertility Decline*, p. 90.

22. Ibid., p. 93. See also the comments on these matters in G. J. Hugo, Terence H. Hull, Valerie J. Hull, and Gavin W. Jones, *The Demographic Dimension in Indonesian Development* (New York: Oxford University Press, 1987), pp. 162–63.

23. Soeradji, *Marriage*, table 24, p. 149.

marriage cohorts of 1945–1949 were divorced within two years of marriage. In the cohort of 1960–1964 the figure declined to 15.9 percent and by 1965–1973 to 13.8 percent.[24]

As Soeradji notes, the traditional divorce system has come to be considered "very common" and "village people manner." He cites Geertz's view that urban Javanese, especially those in the governmental bureaucracy, disapproved of divorce.[25] Urban residence, less parental control, higher levels of education, and higher age at marriage are all associated with lower and declining rates of divorce.

The importance of age and the critical early stage of marital adjustment between a bride and groom who had not come to know each other well prior to marriage may be seen in one dramatic datum, the relationship between divorce and childlessness.[26] For Indonesia as a whole, a childless woman had a probability of divorce of 34 percent within one year of marriage, but wives with children had a divorce probability of only 3.9 percent for that same short duration. The probability of divorce among childless wives rises to 70 percent by the duration of 11–15 years. It is clear, however, that the relationship has little to do with fertility or with the "integrating effect of children." Rather, many marriages were not consummated at all, or spouses lived together only a short time, and the childlessness was an indicator of the couple's inability or unwillingness to adjust to each other or even to live together.

It should be emphasized that the evidence for short marriages cannot be translated into true divorce rates, but they do tell us something about trends. From the Jones data, we can derive several clear patterns.[27] First, there is little change in the time interval in which the first 10 percent of all marriages ended. This is about ten months for all the marriage cohorts from 1950 to 1976. That seems reasonable, because in the earlier period many young couples did not consummate the marriage but were not in enough conflict to end the union. This delay in consummation has been declining as couples become older at marriage.[28]

Second, rural marriages had higher rates of divorce and ended earlier. Third, the decline in divorce rates is expressed by progressively longer time intervals before a given level of dissolution is reached. For example, 25 percent of the 1950 marriages were dissolved within 31 months, but the 1971–1976 cohort took 40 months to arrive at that level. Finally, confirming my belief that this process of divorce and remarriage is a kind of "marital

24. Ibid., p. 110, table 26, p. 149.

25. Geertz, *Javanese Family,* p. 139. See also Singarimbun and Manning, "Marriage," pp. 74ff.

26. Soeradji, *Marriage,* p. 132, table 39, p. 164.

27. Jones, *Divorce,* pp. 17–19, tables 5.8, 5.9.

28. Terence H. Hull and Valerie J. Hull, "Changing Marriage Behavior in Java: The Role of Timing of Consummation," *Southeast Asia J. Social Science* 15 (1987), pp. 104–19.

sifting," the second or higher-order marriages took much longer to break apart, that is, they seem to have been more stable.

These figures seem to underestimate the rapidity of the dissolution because they are based on *all* marriages, most of which remained intact. If we focus instead on those who actually divorced, we obtain figures for marital duration. It is again clear that the anthropological reports of early dissolution are correct. For the early marriage cohort of 1940–1949, about 20–30 percent of those who divorced did so within the first year and about 60 percent (varying by state) within the first three years.[29] These percentages drop with each successive marriage cohort through that of 1960–1969.

Husbands and wives are often in disagreement about who initiated the divorce. The anthropological data suggest that women take an active role in this process. Legally, almost all divorces occur because the husband has said the operative word, *talak,* but that does not tell us what led to that step. Surveys and registration records, though few and localized, suggest that in the earlier period as well as in the late 1980s, men are at best only slightly more likely than women to press for divorce.

I have not been able to find trend data for remarriage. Anthropological reports suggest that almost all who divorced (at least at younger ages) did remarry. Because marriage rates have been dropping for some time, and so have divorce rates, it seems likely that the rates of remarriage will also decline. About 50 percent of the divorced women in the Fertility Survey of 1973 remarried within two years, and two thirds within three years. Rural women remarried sooner, as did those who were entering their third marriage.[30] (Here we refer to women, not men, because many data come from fertility surveys, which usually focus on women.)

From census reports on the percentage still in the divorced state we can come to a few important conclusions about changes. First, as might be expected, men are less likely to remain in the divorced state, which suggests that they remarry at a somewhat faster rate and perhaps that eventually a higher percentage will remarry. However, the more interesting conclusion is that as late as the 1971 census, among both men and women, there is *no* increase by age in the percentage still divorced. This suggests that most people were remarrying. By the 1980 and 1985 censuses, however, there is in fact an increase in the percentage of the divorced among older women but not yet among men. For example, in the age group 25–29 years 4.2 percent of the women were still divorced; the figure increases to 7.0 percent for the age group 60–64 years.[31]

29. Jones, *Divorce,* table 5.9, p. 22.
30. Ibid., table 5.13.
31. Calculated from table 5.3 in ibid.

In lieu of an official figure for the divorce rate in Indonesia, I have calculated the number of divorced (after subtracting the number of repudiations
[*rujuk*] or negations of the divorce) per 100 marriages over most of this
period. The divorce figures were collected by the Department of Religion. As
I have pointed out before, this is technically not a divorce rate but a ratio, a
comparison between divorces in one year and marriages that occurred in
that same year. The resulting curve or trend upward or downward over time
would, I believe, usually parallel the more correct divorce rate. Fortunately,
Jones has been able to calculate the rate independently for years in which no
official rate was published, and the U.N. has recently begun to include the
figures for the mid-1980s. These data, which are presented in Table 10.1,
show a dramatic decline in the ratio from the 1950s and 1960s (with ratios of
46–53) to 1970 (33), 1980 (16), and 1986 (only 10.3).

Will the rates rise again, as I have suggested, as the influence of industrialization and consumerism increases? The 1990 U.N. Demographic Yearbook
shows a small further drop in 1986. However, between 1976 and 1980 the
percentage of women in the divorced (or separated) status did rise for both
rural and urban populations, and for all age groups.[32] Jones shows a rise in
the percentage of divorced women in every province of Indonesia for the
period 1970–1980.[33] For men, only a few states show a rise. It could be
argued that such figures show no more than that women are much less likely
to remarry or that the divorce rate has in fact already risen somewhat, but
that the percentages of men do not yet reflect that fact since they more
quickly "disappear" into the married state. It is not as yet possible to know.

Taiwan

Taiwan is especially interesting because the decline in its divorce rates
began to occur more than fifty years ago, after an extensive developmental
program had been set in motion whose social forces were much like those of
"industrialization." Taiwan is also the only territory of traditional China for
which precise quantitative trend data on the family have been recorded.

When the Japanese took over the island in 1895 they began an elaborate
system for exploiting it as a colony. Taiwan was closed to immigration. The
administrators began to improve agricultural techniques. Factories were
built to transform raw materials into products needed in Japan. Education
was extended and upgraded to create a more effective working force. Prices
and wages were kept down to achieve a larger excess of surplus over costs. In

32. "Detailed Statistics on the Urban and Rural Population of Indonesia: 1950–2010," Center for International Research, U.S. Bureau of the Census, Washington, D.C., 1984.
33. Jones, *Divorce*, table 5.4.

Table 10.1: Indonesia Ratio of Divorces
to 100 Marriages, 1950–1986*

(R = Divorces − *Rujuk* × 100)
Marriages

Year	Ratio
1950	45.9
1955	53.1
1960	47.8
1970	33.4
1975	25.3
1980	16.4
1984	15.2
1986	10.3

*Rate of Divorce per 1,000 Population***

1985	1.0
1986	0.78

*Calculated from data kindly sent to me by Dr.
Masri Singarimbun, Population Studies Center,
Gadjah Nlede University, Yogyakarta, and from
Indonesian Statistical Yearbook.
**Source: U.N. 1991 Demographic Yearbook.

addition, transportation and shipping facilities were made more efficient. The Japanese intended to stay to reap the harvest of their investments. Indeed, they did remain for half a century, and were expelled only in 1945, upon their defeat in World War II.

The new system strengthened the socioeconomic forces that I think are crucial in the consequences of industrialization: new jobs were created, and people became more dependent on jobs; hiring, promotion, and mobility were much more in the hands of the Japanese and were determined by perceived competence or ability rather than by the power of the Chinese family; and more of the economic rewards went to the individual rather than directly to the family. This transformation, I suggest, weakened the traditional family controls of the Chinese in Taiwan, which had generated a relatively high rate of divorce by comparison with mainland China.

The Japanese were focused on economic exploitation and political control and had no interest at all in improving the life of the local Chinese, but they did create new jobs and skills, new social and economic opportunities, and widespread education. They did not of course wish to strengthen the Chinese clan, which was in any event weaker than in mainland China, or to preserve the traditional power of the elders. Their goal of efficiency led them to use Taiwanese wherever they were needed rather than (as in China) to hire on the basis of family affiliation. Under the traditional system, almost all economic opportunities had been in the hands of family elders. The older men and women continued, as in all family systems, to control as much as they could, but by comparison with the period before these changes they lost some power over the rising generation. The new system weakened the old Taiwanese marriage system as well as the divorce rates it had generated.

Taiwan, then, deserves a separate analysis here because its population experienced an extended, systematic program of economic development while the mainland Chinese people did not; because elaborate and apparently precise data on family events were recorded in the Japanese archives; and because Taiwan's divorce rates were high by comparison with the estimates from China and declined over a lengthy period of time because of changes in the socioeconomic patterns.

It is not now possible to state exactly how much higher the Taiwanese rates were. The research literature seems at first reading to be unequivocal: observers have generally agreed that divorce was very infrequent in traditional China.[34] For example, Lang comments, "Divorces in old China were rather rare." Levy says that a daughter-in-law who found her situation in her husband's family to be intolerable had only two choices, to run away or to commit suicide. Similarly, Freedman reports, "Chinese often answer to casual inquiry that they do not practice divorce." Kulp's survey of rural life in South China during the 1917–1923 period found no case of divorce known to his informants. The category of "divorce" is not even used in the Peking Survey of 1917, although the marital status is recorded. In Ting Hsien, two divorced persons were found in a sample of 515 families. Barclay writes, "The paucity of divorced people has led observers . . . to conclude that divorce itself is all but unknown among Chinese."[35] To be sure, the divorce rates were rising in the cities from the founding of the republic in 1910 onward and were comparable to those in some European nations during the 1920s and 1930s.[36] Nevertheless, the general fact seems firm enough.

By contrast, during the early part of this century, at least 10–20 percent of marriages in Taiwan ended in divorce within five years. The total over the whole duration of all marriages would of course be about one-third higher.

34. This is taken from Goode, *World Revolution*, p. 315. The citations are Olga Lang, *Chinese Family and Society* (New Haven: Yale University Press, 1946), p. 41; Marion J. Levy, *The Family Revolution in Modern China* (Cambridge: Harvard University Press, 1940), p. 186; Maurice Freedman, *Chinese Family and Marriage in Singapore* (London: Her Majesty's Stationery Office, 1957), p. 57; Daniel H. Kulp, *Country Life in South China*, vol. 1 (New York: Teachers College Press, 1925), p. 184; Sidney D. Gamble, *Ting Hsien* (New York: Institute of Pacific Relations, 1954), pp. 6–7.

35. George W. Barclay, *Colonial Development and Population in Taiwan* (Princeton: Princeton University Press, 1954), p. 219.

36. Goode, *World Revolution*, p. 316.

This estimate should be increased still further since one type of common marriage (called here a "minor" marriage) was more fragile *after* the first five years.

On the other hand, where divorce is disapproved, divorced people and their families are reluctant to admit that status, and the apparent number of divorces will be lower. Moreover, on the mainland many dissolutions could occur without that step being officially recorded. As Freedman note, in Fukien and Guandong provinces, "Divorce was practically nonexistent or extremely rare," but marriages were disrupted, wives were sent back to their natal families for support, and so on, just the same.[37] In 1963 I argued that the real rates of marital breakup were higher than the official rates. That thesis now seems even more likely, for now we know that the more fragile forms of the family (discussed below) were far more widespread than was understood before.[38]

It is possible, then, that the efficient Japanese registration procedures recorded as "divorces" many breakups in Taiwan that would not have been so labeled in a family register on the mainland (where no public legal procedure was required). Pasternak concludes, along with Freedman, that there may not have been a great difference between the dissolution rates in Taiwan and the Southeast Chinese provinces from which the Taiwanese mainly emigrated. He expresses his inclination "to attribute it to differences and efficiency of registration." But Wolf and Huang assert that this can be no more than part of the answer, for when they separated out the "standard" or "major" form of marriage in Taiwan, the divorce rates were low, just as they were on the mainland, with no apparent excess due to more meticulous registration.[39]

Why such high rates on Taiwan, then? A common explanation is the sex ratio—that is, the number of males per 100 females. Long distance and overseas migration often creates, especially in the early stages, a large pool of unmarried men (as, for example, in the Far West of the United States or the Chinese settlements in California, where there were more men than women at all marriageable ages). In such a situation, it is alleged, the need for women might lead men to treat them better, and it would also be easier for a disgruntled or unhappy wife to replace a husband, or for another man to

37. Maurice Freedman, *Chinese Lineage and Society* (London: Athlone Press, 1966), p. 60.
38. Arthur P. Wolf and Chieh-Shan Huang have done a remarkable bit of detective work in summarizing these data: see their *Marriage and Adoption in China, 1845–1945* (Stanford: Stanford University Press, 1980), introduction, ch. 26. See also Burton Pasternak, *Guests in the Dragon* (New York: Columbia University Press, 1983), pp. 55–56.
39. Freedman, *Chinese Lineage,* p. 61; Pasternak, *Guests,* p. 80; Wolf and Huang, *Marriage and Adoption,* p. 192.

tempt her away from her husband. Certainly, as we shall see, almost all could remarry, and the data on marital status by age and sex do *not* show—as they do in almost all the nations we have examined—increasingly higher percentages of men than women in the status of "married."

However, that apparent imbalance was also common on the mainland, too. Every population distribution I have seen shows far more males than females at any given age group, but especially at the younger ages. The explanation commonly given is female infanticide and neglect, coupled with a reluctance to report the existence of female children to outsiders. The sex ratios Barclay reports are moderate compared with those found on the mainland. He also asserts that by 1906 there was no trace of infanticide on the island, though there was some evidence of neglect. Specifically, more boys than girls died in the first year of life, but by 10 years of age more boys had survived, throughout the period 1907–1934. This seeming shortage of women was not large, and it steadily dropped during the Japanese occupation, but it may have contributed to the fact that every census during this period shows a higher percentage of women married than of men.[40]

There were several forms of marriage among the Chinese, including one type of "major" marriage and two types of minor marriage. Chinese marriage arrangements were flexible enough to permit a wide array of choices, depending on such factors as class and wealth, whether the family had daughters but no sons, the region, and the amount of control by local descent groups. All of them were legally acceptable, but they varied in their social acceptability and in the internal domestic strains they created. In Taiwan, a substantial number of marriages followed usages that seemed to generate more marital instability.

The first of these forms of marriage is the one most commonly described in traditional accounts of the Chinese family system. In the "standard" or "major" form (Wolf and Huang use the latter term) the young bride is essentially absorbed into her husband's family. Jural rights over the young woman as well as responsibility for her protection and support were transferred from her father's line to that of her husband's father. Specific rituals emphasized this departure and entrance, while many customs underlined her lowly status as a daughter-in-law. A bride price was paid, but usually her family tried to match that amount or more, especially in the form of household effects. These countergifts were a public display of the social rank of the bride-giving family and at the same time an announcement that her family cared about her future treatment. Of course, as travelers have noted many times, these ceremonies were expensive, public, and even ostentatious

40. Barclay, *Colonial Development*, pp. 157, 159, 212–14.

among the wealthy, but they were also followed as much as possible by all those with any claims to social st^nding.

One obvious meaning of these customs was that henceforth the wife was under the authority of her husband's family and had no other place to go, no alternative way of surviving. She would visit her family on ceremonial occasions, and affinal ties could be very important, but divorce was not viewed as a social possibility short of some extreme situation.

However approved the major form was, it coexisted widely with two other forms. One of these was to purchase a daughter for adoption who would then be betrothed, and at a much later date married, to a boy in the family. She was likely to be purchased from a go-between, and thus there was no bride price paid to her family. She would have little or no memory and often no knowledge of her family. The time of marriage was not marked by the public ceremonials of major marriages, and thus much expense was avoided. Mainland Chinese opinion disapproved of such marriages, and though widespread they were by repute confined to the poor. In Taiwan they were also more common among the less well-to-do, but in the communities where they were customary they appear among all classes.[41] It seems likely that they were more common in the north, but they occurred in the south as well.[42]

The third form of marriage was "bringing in" a husband for a daughter. As with the previous two types, there were many variations of this uxorilocal type, differing as to which responsibilities the husband accepted for the support of his parents-in-law, how many of the offspring would be given to the wife's family line, and how many of the husband's rights in his own paternal line he would give up. The union lacked the usual gifts and festivities of a major marriage because in Chinese eyes it violated the central social rule that the son must serve his parents and raise children for that line, ideally within the parental home. Instead, in the usual marriage of this type the groom went to live with his wife's parents. The allocation of children varied, but some would be given to her father's line.

In his analysis of the divorce rates in Taiwan as a whole, Barclay points out that uxorilocal marriages made up about one-fifth of all marriages, and he analyzes the stresses of each unions.[43] Before considering them, we should once more emphasize that the arrangements could vary from the extreme cases in which the man took on all the duties of a son in his wife's father's line. He would leave behind his responsibility for taking care of his own

41. Wolf and Huang, *Marriage and Adoption*, pp. 261–66.
42. Ibid., ch. 26, esp. p. 325; Pasternak, *Guests*; and Burton Pasternak, *Kinship and Community in Two Chinese Villages* (Stanford: Stanford University Press, 1972).
43. Barclay, *Colonial Development*, pp. 226–29.

parents, and of course any rights to family property. He dropped his own name in favor of his father-in-law's and assumed responsibility for the care of his parents-in-law. At the other extreme, he agreed merely to support his in-laws for a specified number of years, but he kept his children in his own family line, and the couple lived in his parents' home. Essentially, these were all matters of contract and agreement, determined by the bargaining positions of the two parties.

Both the "minor" marriage form (raising an adopted daughter to become a later wife) and the uxorilocal union were structurally and psychologically less stable than the major type of union, but for different reasons. However, Pasternak has shown that in at least one Hakka village (Lungtu), the need for male labor kept the divorce rate for uxorilocal marriages as low as that for major unions for some decades before 1930.[44]

Adopting an infant girl who later married a son of the family was a widespread practice, and in some villages there were almost as many such unions as major marriages. The girl was reared as a daughter, though sometimes almost as a servant, and the tie between mother- and daughter-in-law after the union took place remained as it was before, without the friction that was normal in a major marriage. The mother did not have to worry that she would lose her son to the young woman. The girl would not bring an unfamiliar set of practices or wishes into the family or fight with her own (adopted) mother. She had years of experience in adjusting to the authority of the specific elders in her new family. In any event she quite literally had no paternal home as an alternate refuge if a strong conflict broke out. She could not call on her kin and very likely would even harbor some resentment at her (usually unknown) mother, who after all had abandoned her.

The disadvantages were less obvious but nonetheless deep. The most profound was that children reared together as brother and sister did not feel attracted to one another and often did not wish to marry when the appropriate time came. At some level, a Chinese mother would not view that lack of desire as deplorable. Myth and legend in Chinese society supported her wish to hold her son close. The customs of daily living also frowned on any obvious intimacy between husband and wife.

However, the reluctance to marry could be so strong as to defeat the purpose of the adoption. Reared as brother and sister, the couple suffered the humiliation of being teased by other children: they were "betrothed" just as grownups were, but they were little children and also siblings. Wolf and Huang assert that the Westernarck hypothesis is correct, that people who

44. Pasternak, *Guests*.

grow up together feel some kind of psychological aversion in sexual matters.[45] (I shall not enter the ancient debate about why incest is widely
disapproved; the Wolf and Huang data do at least fit that hypothesis.) For
example, they show that if the girl was adopted later in her life the marriage
was more likely to be stable, presumably because the couple were not so
fully "brother and sister."

Nevertheless, in general, adopted-daughter marriages were more prone to
marital conflict and dissolution (a high rate of divorce continued even after
five years of marriage), lowered fertility, and adultery. Another disadvantage
of this form was that it did not create the firm ties with in-law families that
formed part of the economic and political network any family desired for its
security and prosperity.

Uxorilocal marriages were brittle for different and more obvious reasons.
First, what each spouse owed to the other was held in place not by detailed
custom and daily social influences but by explicit contract. Thus many contingencies of fate might move one or the other to renegotiation or conflict.
Most important, of course, the husband was not surrounded by his male kin
and thus lacked that deeply undergirded authority that Chinese males felt
was part of being the head or husband in the household. In some families,
the wife's kin might treat her husband as little more than a servant, though
of course under more pleasant circumstances he might enjoy nearly full
authority. Much folklore contains stories that illustrate how deeply the Chinese mistrusted this "outsider." If, however, he was chosen from the same
village (as in the Hakka case noted above), such a marriage might create
affinal ties. In addition, in at least one case (Pasternak's village of Chungshe),
where there was a continuing need for male labor and less concern about the
maintenance of the woman's father's line, such a marriage might be relatively stable.[46]

Both adopted-daughter, or minor marriages, and uxorilocal unions contributed to the relatively high divorce rates in Taiwan. At a minimum estimate, the divorce rate at about the turn of the century was about 14 percent
(the maximum may be slightly more than 22 percent). About 20–24 percent
of minor marriages and 7–30 percent of uxorilocal marriages ended in
divorce. Major marriages were less stable on Taiwan than on the mainland,
but they were the most stable, at about 7 percent.[47]

The decline in divorce rates was the result of a major shift in the marriage

45. Wolf and Huang, *Marriage and Adoption*, pp. 143ff.
46. Pasternak, *Guests*, pp. 84–85.
47. Wolf and Huang, *Marriage and Adoption*, pp. 183, 185, 190; Pasternak, *Guests*, pp. 78, 81,
83–84.

patterns, away from both the minor and uxorilocal forms to a nearly universal allegiance to major marriages. That is, over the decades the Taiwanese villages in which the two less acceptable types were fairly common moved back to the major marriage pattern that had always been viewed as socially more acceptable.

That statement is actually my interpretation of the current situation and extends beyond the data now available. It can be tested only when detailed archival studies of an adequate sample of all villages have been made. From the information we do have, it is clear that villages varied a great deal in the forms of marriage they preferred, and in some cases we know how local social and economic circumstances shaped the decisions families made. For example, in three Hakka villages the major form of marriage was chosen almost exclusively. This ethnic group felt embattled, and families created a firmer set of affinal links to meet this need.

All the villages were in southern Taiwan. In another southern village, however, settled by people from Fukien, uxorilocal marriages were almost as common as major marriages, and they were relatively stable. Pasternak tells us that there was a shortage of male labor, so that the incoming husbands were needed; there was less conflict about assigning a child to the maternal or paternal line; and most of the men did not come from the "outside" but from the same village.[48] That is, under at least some circumstances the strains that the uxorilocal marriage usually generated were held in check by the more favorable position of such husbands.

What caused this important change in the choice of marriage forms? I believe that Wolf and Huang have accurately described the processes that led to the abandonment of the minor or adopted-daughter marriage, for they would apply to most villages where this form of union was common. During the period 1886–1900, almost 43 percent of all couples in their village married in this fashion, and 11 percent in the uxorilocal form. These percentages were to drop over the decades that followed. What Wolf and Huang call "the revolt of the young" was aimed mostly at the minor marriage.

In the late 1920s and early 1930s, young people became able to resist effectively their parents' arrangements for a minor marriage because "changes initiated by the Japanese undermined parental authority by providing young people with opportunities to make an independent living and also the skills needed to take advantage of these opportunities." This marriage group included the first graduates of the Japanese schools, and many new jobs were opening up in the expanding economy. This must not be

48. Pasternak, *Guests*, pp. 83–84; Pasternak, *Kinship*; Myron L. Cohen, *House United, House Divided: The Chinese Family in Taiwan* (New York: Columbia University Press, 1976).

confused, as the authors warn us, with modern "adolescent rebellion." Open conflict was not the rule, but the elders were aware that their control had diminished. At this time, the percentage of young men for whom an adopted sister was available had not dropped by much, but the number of such marriages actually consummated began to decrease, and continued to decrease through the 1930s. Wolf and Huang argue that 1925 marks a kind of "watershed" in this process.[49] By the 1950s this form of marriage had become uncommon, and a far higher percentage of couples had some voice in the choice of their spouse.

Thus there was a general shift in the composition of marriages in Taiwan; an increasingly high percentage of them were major and thus less prone to divorce. In succeeding pages we present some of the relevant tables that affirm this general decrease.

The uxorilocal marriages were more prone to break up early than the minor form. But why did people shift their choice to major marriages? For the one village in which such unions were fairly stable, Pasternak has an answer. In Chungshe, adult males were needed for field labor by all families at the same time, and thus labor exchanges among local families could not be a satisfactory solution. But by 1930, a new canal system and more effective irrigation made local agriculture less dependent on the immediate availability of labor.[50] The uxorilocal form of union became less attractive after that. From Pasternak's maps, it seems likely that this may have occurred in other villages in the Hakka region.

However, at this time other factors, which apply more generally in Taiwan, were of much importance. First, it must be kept in mind that the particular goals a family sought in arranging a marriage (male labor, a low-cost union, perpetuation of the family line, and so on) within its specific socioeconomic circumstances affected which marriage form the parents chose—that is, the *terms* of the union—but hardly affected the percentage of daughters or sons who eventually married. Here, as in China, the aim was, as far as possible, to get everyone married. We noted earlier the various elements in the uxorilocal union that created stress for the couple and made it a less approved form. Men especially felt that these terms made their male authority ambiguous at best, and they preferred a major marriage if the family could afford it. The men who had to accept those terms were more likely to be later-born sons (first-born sons were supposed to stay with their parents), somewhat older, and poorer, and they enjoyed fewer local opportunities.

With the development of education, the construction of factories and a

49. Wolf and Huang, *Marriage and Adoption*, pp. 198, 199, 201.
50. Pasternak, *Guests*, pp. 6, 71, 72.

better transportation network, new jobs, and general economic expansion, the marriage market shifted somewhat. Public health measures lowered the mortality rate and increased the number of surviving females. Land became scarcer with population growth, but other types of opportunities increased. For example, by 1939 industrial output was slightly higher than agricultural production. Thus more young men could afford to avoid the onerous terms of an uxorilocal marriage and to enter a major marriage more in line with their preference. Consequently, the uxorilocal form of union also decreased over time.

In any system with a stable high divorce rate, the rate of remarriage is also likely to be relatively high. This should have been especially true of Taiwan, where there was some shortage of women. What was the likelihood of remarriage at this time? The patriarchal ideal in China was that the widow did not remarry. Similarly, it was assumed that the stigma of divorce was so great that the divorced woman could not find another man to marry her. Some years ago I stated my belief that "here, as in so many other areas of Chinese family life, there was a considerable difference between ideal and practice." Because few women could afford to live alone, most divorced women (at least those below the upper social strata) "disappeared demographically" from the status of the divorced. Levy remarks that remarriage (for widows) was frequent, and little or nothing was made of it among peasants. Gallin comments (for his Taiwan village) that a young divorcee or widow, unless she was wealthy, could do little but marry.[51]

In Taiwan, divorced spouses did marry, although we have but few exact figures to confirm that hypothesis. In Pasternak's Hakka village of Lungtu, 85 percent of the "younger" divorced men (34 years or less) and 87 percent of the younger women (29 years or less) remarried within five years.[52] Younger men needed a woman to create a family and to take care of domestic and field tasks, while a woman simply could not manage agricultural production on her own.

In Wolf and Huang's village of Haishan, 66 percent of divorced men and 46 percent of divorced women were remarried. This may be an underestimate.[53] As in other countries, divorcees were more likely than widows or widowers to remarry because they were likely to be younger. In addition, if a widow had children, she enjoyed control over her late husband's estate (which belonged to the children) as well as a respected status in the village. In general, whatever the reputed disapproval of remarriage for those who

51. Goode, *World Revolution*, p. 318; Marion J. Levy, *The Family Revolution in China* (New York: Atheneum, 1968 [1940]), p. 46; Bernard Gallin, *Hsin Hsing, Taiwan* (Berkeley: University of California Press, 1966), p. 159.

52. Pasternak, *Guests*, pp. 76–77.

53. Wolf and Huang, *Marriage and Adoption*, p. 227; Pasternak, *Guests*, p. 77.

Table 10.2: Taiwan: Percent of Registered Marriages of Each Year
That Were Dissolved by Divorce Within 5 Years' Duration, 1906–1939

Year	A. Assuming That All Taiwanese Marriages Were at Risk of Divorce	B. Assuming That Divorce Occurred Only to First Marriages
1906	14.4	22.3
1910	9.4	13.8
1915	10.5	14.0
1920	7.9	14.6
1925	7.7	9.4
1930	5.8	6.8
1935	4.7	5.2
1939	3.6	3.9

Source: George W. Barclay, *Colonial Development and Population in Taiwan* (Princeton: Princeton University Press, 1954), p. 221.

had lost their spouses through death or divorce, the behavior itself seems to have been determined by such mundane variables as the economic resources of the candidates and the family's decisions about its needs. Remarriage for a divorced person was a more modest affair than a first major marriage would have been, but for most people in the marriageable ages it was likely to occur eventually.

I have offered the hypothesis that processes of industrialization (in my sense) will very likely reduce the divorce rate in a high-divorce-rate system but that eventually the rate should rise again as socioeconomic development proceeds. As is well known, Taiwan has had a spectacular success with industrialization. It ranks high among the most industrially productive of the Far Eastern nations: Japan, Hong Kong, Korea, Singapore. That transformation should have had an effect on its divorce rate, as it first undermined the old family system to reduce the rates from that source, and eventually to increase the rates in the new family system, as happened in Western nations.

As Tables 10.2, 10.3, and 10.4 show, the decline in the divorce rate continued for some decades. By 1975, the upward movement had begun, and it has continued up to the present.

Table 10.3: Divorces in Taiwan, 1940–1986

Year of Marriage	Number of Divorces	Divorces per 1,000 Married Females
1940	3186	3.1
1950	3348	2.59
1955	4638	2.9
1956	4915	2.9
1960	4630	2.5
1966	4915	2.2

Source: U.S. data.

Table 10.4: Divorce Rates in Taiwan, 1947–1990

Year	Number Divorces per 1,000 Population	Number of Divorces per 1,000 Married Women
1947[a]	0.52	
1955[b]	0.52	
1960	0.43	2.5
1965	0.38	2.2
1970	0.37	2.1
1972	0.37	2.1
1975	0.46	2.5
1980	0.76	3.9
1985	1.1	5.2
1987	1.2	5.5
1990	1.4	6.3

[a]T'ai-Wan-sheng t'ung chi yao lan, 1951.
[b]Taiwan Statistical Abstract, 1956. All other data from relevant issues of this publication (including monthlies). 1990 figures from *Social Indicators in Taiwan Area of the Republic of China*, 1990, Accounting and Statistics (Taipei, 1991), table 5, pp. 40–1.

China

It is too early politically to unravel the complexity of changes in divorce patterns in China since 1949. Divorce remains, for various reasons, a politically sensitive topic, and contemporary Chinese investigations are still guided almost as much by moralistic teachings as by the need to find out what is happening. Archival demographic research requires a greater allegiance to historical objectivity, as well as more technical skill, than will be mustered until a more extended period of tranquility has been achieved.

A simple summary of the pattern of divorce rates between 1950 and 1990 is that divorce rates rose sharply in the early 1950s, then dropped sharply for a few years, and thereafter dropped irregularly until the late 1970s, when they began to rise. Since the restoration of order in 1978 they have been rising steadily. However, the rates were never high by European standards and are not now. Thus China must be included among the modern states with divorce rates on a downward trend, extending over perhaps two decades or slightly more, with an upward trend after that.

The new Chinese leaders interpreted the rise in divorce rates in the early 1950s, just after their accession to power and the introduction of the Marriage Law of 1950, as proof that people who had been living under the feudal conditions abolished by the triumph of Communism were now taking advantage of their new freedom. In spite of the traditional Chinese disapproval of divorce, however, rates had been rising (though less in rural areas) since the original Chinese revolution of 1911.[54] By the 1930s, some local or regional surveys reported rates comparable to those of several European countries. Thus, the increase in divorces in the early 1950s was a continuation of a widespread trend over some decades.

However, the simple set of trends noted above—a sharp rise in the early 1950s, a drop thereafter, and a continued but irregular drop until the late 1970s—is made up of many contrary forces. I shall note some of them but cannot state many of them in quantitative form. After the early 1950s, summary national figures on divorce were rarely published until very recently. Only with the rebirth of sociology at the end of the 1970s were investigations of divorce carried out again. These were based on local, nonrandom samples[55] and were carried out by persons with little training in research methods.

From the 1950s to the 1970s Chinese authorities had several political and administrative reasons for restricting divorce. They may be summarized by saying that the moderate-sized sociopolitical units such as factory committees (danwei), street committees, job-allocation agencies, and so on would prefer stable families living in harmony, because family disruption creates problems for them. For example, because the factory committees (danwei) controlled housing, which was linked to one's job, and because there was and is not enough housing, divorce was, quite simply, an administrative nuisance. A divorce requires another housing unit, and the danwei cannot command it. If both husband and wife work in the same enterprise, the divorce creates problems in social interaction for them and their associates. Where work, housing, and local social controls are so integrated, a divorce makes the administrative burden heavier. It is almost unnecessary to add that when an authoritarian political system must choose between its own administrative convenience and the personal misery and inconvenience of its citizens, it will find good reasons for ranking its own needs as more urgent.

I believe the pressure against divorce from the 1950s to the late 1970s was ideological as well. I believe (and cannot prove) that the new leadership was shocked by the familial tensions that seemed not to diminish even after the Communists established full political control in the early 1950s. (It is not difficult to show that such sentiments were expressed; I cannot, however, prove how widespread they were.) In the new socialism, men and women

---

54. Goode, World Revolution, pp. 316–17.

55. Many of these reports have been published in the Chinese journal Shehui, which began publishing at the Fudan University Branch Campus, Shanghai. Some of these articles have been reprinted in David S. K. Chu, ed., Sociology and Society in Contemporary China, 1979–1983 (Armonk, N.Y.: Sharpe, 1984). Several monographs on the family in Chinese also contain data on divorce.

would ideally marry because of love, live happily together, and be good socialist citizens. Instead, real couples found themselves still saddled with unsatisfactory spouses. While the unhappiness of those who were married before 1949 could be understood because their marriages were vestiges of feudal arrangements and bourgeois culture, those who were married after the Communist takeover in 1950 had no excuse for marital disharmony: they had chosen their mates and were supposed to live in social harmony.

The 1950 Marriage Law permitted divorce if *one* spouse was "resolutely demanding divorce . . . after the mediation of District People's Government and legal organs are ineffective," and the number in this group increased greatly. Even as late as 1955–1956, a report from Tianjin had noted an increase in the number of divorce cases, though without giving any figures (we now have them though).

The Chinese reported over 186,000 divorce cases in 1950, over 409,000 in 1951, and over 398,000 in the first *half* of 1952. When I wrote *World Revolution and Family Patterns*, in the early 1960s, I searched for more recent data but could not find any published figures after that date (again, we can now fill in that gap to some extent). In 1981, a Chinese report states that in 1953, the cases exceeded one million.[56] At first, these huge numbers were used as propaganda, since it proved that under the old system people had been forced into unhappy marriages, parents had followed feudal practices, women had been exploited and so on. Once that bulge had a few years to work through the courts, however, the continuing rise in divorce began to suggest that at the micro level the new socialism was not producing marital affection and harmony. The new system or its citizens must be failing. It is not difficult to predict that a visionary, authoritarian leadership would decide that the real culprits were those who sought a divorce.

The change in official policy after the mid-1950s was justified by the argument that people who had married after 1950—that is, under the new socialism, which permitted "free choice"—should be able to solve the problems of marriage.[57] Seeking a divorce began to be frowned upon not only as an administrative nuisance, but as a self-indulgence: such spouses were not focusing on their obligations to the socialist society.

That summary statement, however, glosses over a continuing ideological conflict about the place of women in the various revolutionary phases in Chinese history after the fall of the Ch'ing dynasty in 1911. A recurring plank in various party programs was the abolition of the ancient "feudal" practices—although in a technical sense China was not feudalistic—

---

56. Renjia Dake, "An Analysis of Divorce Statistics," *Encyclopedia Yearbook of China* (Beijing: Greater Chinese Encyclopedia Publishing House, 1981), p. 543; also Chu, *Sociology*, p. 132.

57. Martin K. Whyte and William L. Parish, *Urban Life in Contemporary China* (Chicago: University of Chicago Press, 1984), p. 188.

including the exploitation and suppression of women. This feminist goal seemed a self-evident need in a society that had bound the feet of its women and offered unhappy young brides the choice of adjustment or suicide. Since many or most political groups were strongly influenced by some ideal form of socialism and democracy, it was also evident that economic development would require its women to be trained citizens, enjoying equal rights.

Equal rights for women have seemed threatening to Western men during the past thirty years. Thus it can evoke no surprise that Chinese men responded with even greater indignation to women's concrete actions toward equality in the 1920s and 1930s. One of the areas of equality was, naturally, divorce. Resistance to women's right to divorce was vigorous after 1924 in Hankow and Heilungfeng, where women's unions and political organizations helped peasant women to claim their rights.[58]

Such struggles also occurred in Kiangsi in the Soviet period, 1929–1934, and were especially intense in the early 1950s, when the new marriage law was given legal force over all China. As in so many other idealistic attempts to impose a new morality from above, it is not merely that the peasants and workers—for whose good the revolution has been wisely proclaimed—reject many of its tenets. In fact, as Plato suggested would happen, the new leaders were themselves steeped in an older tradition of masculine domination.

Resistance to divorce—and to equality for women more generally—was most pronounced among two groups: the rank and file leaders (or cadres) of the community party, and the rural peasants. In the first years after the takeover active Party efforts were focused on the cadres, who resisted the new law and particularly women's right to divorce. The Party was trying to educate women about their new rights and setting up organizations and legal procedures to affirm them while railing at cadres who obstructed them. Simultaneously, peasant resistance was strong from the beginning.[59] However deplorable one may consider the eventual political retreat, it was bound to occur. Equality for women continued to be proclaimed on state and ordinary political occasions (as is now still done in China—indeed, has been done in all countries where it has been a revolutionary political goal), but as a concrete set of goals it was made subordinate to other programs.

The rural resistance deserves special attention, as part of the dynamics of

---

58. Many of the patterns of men's resistance to the rights of women were duplicated in the Soviet Union as well, and are described in Janet Seitzner Salaff and Judith Merkle, "Women and Revolution: The Lessons of the Soviet Union and China," in Marilyn B. Young, ed., *Women in China* (Ann Arbor: University of Michigan Press, 1973), pp. 145–77. For the 1920s as well as the Soviet period in this struggle, see Kay Ann Johnson, *Women, the Family and Peasant Revolution in China* (Chicago: University of Chicago Press, 1983), pp. 45–46, 54, 57 et passim.

59. See Johnson, *Women,* ch. 9 for a description of these conflicting forces, including the intimidation of women who tried to assert their rights.

controlling divorce from the mid-1950s until the early 1980s. The political organizational efforts of Communists, in China and elsewhere, have typically failed in their professed goal of freedom for women, because they judged it to be an automatic by-product of transforming the system of production, not an independent goal requiring an effort in its own right. Bluntly put, freedom for women (including the freedom to divorce) generated turmoil and resistance, which undermined the political appeal of the broader program to a larger, more powerful group, male leaders and followers. Mao pointed out this problem in the 1920s, and the centrist, successful line has followed that pattern of subordinating women's problems to the higher goal of winning power.

In their analysis of rural divorce in the 1970s, Parish and Whyte note why peasants viewed it as especially disruptive.[60] A divorce early in the marriage, before the bride has worked long enough to "pay back" the bride price that the husband or his family has incurred, seemed an obvious injustice. If instead the woman had worked for years and contributed a great deal, peasants objected at least as much, for she threatened to take away much of the common marital property the couple had earned together. In fact, women were not permitted to do so, in spite of their paper rights.

Thus, as these authors describe it, informal and formal mediation was widely used to discourage the attempts of peasant women to leave their marriages, or indeed to bring a suit successfully to the courts. According to a Fukien report of 1953 detailing the efforts begun late in 1952 to reduce family problems and facilitate the harvest, the leadership tried to mediate all such problems. Almost certainly that effort must be seen as a huge success: only 5 percent were judged to be irreconcilable—a success rate that has surely never been equalled among the court-appointed marital counselors and mediators in Western nations.[61] These obstructionist processes, official and unofficial, paralleled those in the cities, although it seems likely that intimidation was somewhat more likely to be used in the countryside, where less police supervision existed.

Consequently, the new socialist government began, ironically, to come embarrassingly close to the traditional Chinese system in its emphasis on the needs of the larger social unit—the older society, the extended family, or the clan. The husband and wife should live in harmony and affection, and if they had difficulties they should *work* to achieve harmony. That relationship should be stable, but not intense, because the state might (as it did) ask one or both to live away from home for years, in the service of socialist goals.

It will also be recalled in this connection that in this early period the Party

60. William Parish and Martin Whyte, *Village and Family in Contemporary China* (Chicago: University of Chicago Press, 1978), pp. 192–99.
61. Salaff and Merkle, "Women and Revolution," p. 168.

often had to repeat its admonition that the new system would *not* permit citizens to abandon the care of older parents. Many wanted to be free of that burden too, but that behavior as well was labeled self-indulgent. It too would have created an administrative nuisance and reflected badly on Chinese socialism. Some twenty-five years ago, tempted into prophecy, I wrote: "It seems likely that in the near future divorce will become somewhat more difficult under the Communist regime than it has been during the past decade, if only because the state has not been able efficiently to take over family activities . . . which must still be given to a fairly *stable* unit. . . . The Communists are searching for a middle ground between the ideologically required "freedom of choice" and the equally important ideological demand that each person be "responsible and not self-indulgent" in his or her private life.[62]

In any event, clamping down on divorce fitted the traditional Chinese disapproval of it very well. This disapproval is still widespread and is expressed in both the research literature and the popular press today.[63] It was also supported because the First Five Year Plan (1953–1957) demanded full economic mobilization, which might be weakened by domestic turmoil.

I have already pointed out how that reduction in divorce rates was carried out. The specific bureaucratic solution is to be found in the second clause of the 1950 Marriage Law, stating that the divorce would be granted after mediation proved ineffective. Street committees could intervene to *make* it "effective," and so could factory or rural committees, and after them the courts, to *press* the couple to reconcile their conflict. The courts came to insist that "legitimate reasons"—serious conflicts and errors (including political errors)—were a requisite for divorce.[64] In fact, during the most repressive period almost no reasons for divorce were accepted as good enough. Now that the Chinese are talking and writing more openly about that period, thousands of stories are told of social and legal efforts to force unhappy couples to stay together. As recently as 1978–1979, most (three-fourths or more) divorce cases ended in a mediated non-divorce.[65]

In 1979, over 200,000 couples were pushed to "reconcile" through mediation, or their cases were transferred to the courts, where they may not have received divorces either.[66] Writing of the 1970s and mainly of village China,

62. *World Revolution*, pp. 317–18.

63. Divorce is frequently in the news, as may be seen in *China Daily*, e.g., Dec. 13, 1985; Jan. 18, 1986; Feb. 3, 1986; Feb. 25, 1986; etc.

64. "What Is the Divorce Situation After the Implementation of the New Marriage Law?—An Investigation of Doncheng District, Beijing." Class of 1977, Marriage Problems Investigation Group, Philosophy Department, Chinese Peoples University, *Shehui* (1982) in Chu, *Sociology*, p. 107.

65. Dake, "Analysis," p. 134.

66. The meaning of some of the numbers that are published in official or semi-official sources is not always clear, since often the phrase "mediated or granted" is used. Thus it is not always certain whether a divorce was in fact ever granted.

Parish and Whyte comment, "the current policy is for local cadres and organizations to try to resolve family disputes and preserve marriages even if both partners desire a divorce."[67]

In 1980 the New Marriage Law, which makes it somewhat easier to get a divorce, was introduced. Article 25 (effective 1981) emphasizes the rupture or break in marital affection, and the courts are now more likely to inquire into the long-term happiness of the parties. There is a more widespread acceptance of the possibility that couples will be happier after a divorce. The new law also abolishes the "crime" of "destroying the family," so that even those who have become involved in a love affair can ask that their marriage be ended because the marital relationship is no longer one of harmony and love.

Judges have accepted the new grounds for divorce, but interpretation of the clause still remains problematic. Some plaintiffs believe that the courts must approve their request, but many judges still believe instead that they must continue to probe the couple's intentions and attitudes and ascertain who is responsible for the rupture. Fox Butterfield, writing in the 1980s, asserts that a number of Chinese women "complained more bitterly about their trouble in getting a divorce than anything else."[68]

It hardly needs to be emphasized that the period 1966–1976 (during the Cultural Revolution) was one of considerable domestic turmoil in China, even though the conflicts were not even typically reflected in the number of divorces granted. Indeed, in 1985 the *Beijing Review* (an official voice) stated that during the Cultural Revolution, "Lower level courts did not even accept divorce cases."[69] Millions of husbands and wives were separated from one another and sent to the countryside for reeducation or punishment. When they returned, some people no longer felt compatible with their spouses. During this period people married hastily for ideological reasons and then later sought divorce because they were in conflict with their spouses after the political climate changes or because they feared that they would be prosecuted because of their spouses' political deviation. Some spouses were "rehabilitated" and brought back to political respectability while their mates were still viewed as deviants or criminals. Young people entering the age of courtship were sent to the countryside for years, where they contracted marriage with people whom their families would not accept later. In short, as in any revolution, a large amount of marital conflict was created during this period, but very little of it was expressed in the divorce data. It should

67. Parish and Whyte, *Village*, p. 194.
68. *Alive in the Bitter Sea* (New York: Times Books, 1982), p. 173.
69. Li Ning, "How Does China Deal with Divorce?" *Beijing Review*, Feb. 4, 1985, p. 18.

also be emphasized that at the present time some analysts of divorce view the recent rise in the rates as caused in part by the turmoil of the recent past.

Keeping in view all these implicit warnings about the meaning of such figures, we present the available official divorce data in Table 10.5. It shows, as we noted above, a sharp rise in the number of divorces in the early years of the Communist regime (from 186,000 in 1950 to 1,170,000 in 1953), followed by a decline as the restrictive bureaucratic measures of the Marriage Law of 1950 began to have an effect. (The number of divorces declines to 710,000 in 1954, and to 170,000 in 1978.) The reversal of this trend and the subsequent rise in the number of divorces in the 1980s are also evident in Table 10.5 (which shows the rise in divorces from 341,000 in 1980 to 752,000 in 1989). In addition, if we look at the divorce rate per 1,000 population, which is the only measure of the divorce rate we have been able to construct, Table 10.5 shows a parallel increase in the 1980s—from .66 in 1979, to .88 in 1985, to 1.2 in 1988.

The skeptical reader will see, however, that there are problems in these data. First, although we now possess some additional figures for the years after the middle of 1952, often our main source is the popular press. It can be argued that almost *any* data that appeared over these decades *must* have been official, since no other data would be permitted. In Communist China as in the former Soviet Union, however, all official figures as well as figures allowed in the press were printed for propaganda purposes as well as the goal of truth. Unfortunately, we do not know which is which. Worse, in many instances neither did those who permitted the data to appear. I personally obtained the numbers for the early 1980s from official sources, when I was in Beijing, but I do not know whether they have been officially printed by now. Moreover, even with the later publication of earlier data, we find few figures for the 1960s and most of the 1970s. However, there are some, and I shall take note of them later.

What is most problematic about the data on divorces granted is that we do not know exactly what percentage of couples who requested a divorce in (I believe) *any* year were ultimately granted. We do know, for example, that in 1978–1979 over three-fourths did *not* get divorces at the first stage of their attempt—and this period supposedly marks the beginning of the "new" period of peace, the end of ideological harshness. Wherever statements are made about efforts at reconciliation, it is clear that the overwhelming majority of applicants failed to get a divorce, either at the first instance or at some later stage of court procedure. That process began in the late 1950s and (judging by the widespread complaints) continued through the long years for which the published data are scanty, until the end of the 1970s.

Moreover, this pattern of rejecting *most* petitions continued into the period

Table 10.5: Divorce Rates in China, 1950–1989

Years	Number of Divorces	Divorce Rate per 1,000 population
1950	186,000	
1951	409,000	
1952	400,000 (1st six months)	
1953	1,170,000	
1954[a]	710,000	
1956	510,000	
1978	170,000	
1979[b]	319,000	0.66
1980	341,000	0.70
1981	389,000	0.78
1982	428,000	0.85
1983	418,000	0.82
1985	458,000	0.88[c]
1986	501,000	0.95
1987	581,000	1.08
1988	655,000	1.20
1989	752,000	

[a]For the years 1954–1956, I have used the figures from the *People's Daily* (*Renmin Ribao*), cited by Erika Platte. She gives no figure for 1978, and her figures for the later years are all smaller than the ones given here, also from official sources.

[b]Whyte and Parish state that in 1979 there were 4.9 divorces per 100 marriages, *Urban Life*, p. 189). With some skepticism, I am following the work of Ming Tsui for the years 1979–1988. Our figures for 1979–1983 are very close, but they do not correspond exactly. However, that statement must be a frequent litany in our analysis of many nations and need not elicit more than the ordinary doubt of the modern reader. Moreover, her figures do correspond with those from Social Statistics of China, 1990.

[c]Social Security Daily, (*Shehui Baozhang Bao*), April 24, 1986, no. 4. *Sources: Statistical Data on Chinese Society* (Beijing: Chinese Statistical Publication Society, 1985), table 20. Earlier figures are from Goode, *World Revolution*, p. 217, and *Renmin Ribao* (People's Daily), April 24, 1957, and April 13, 1957. These data overlap with those given by Erika Platte, "Divorce Trends and Patterns in China: Past and Present," *Pacific Affairs* 61 (1988), p. 431. The figures for 1978–1983—presumably *divorces*, not *cases*—are given in *Statistical Data on Chinese Society* Beijing, 1985), table 20. However, I am here following Ming Tsui, who instead uses data from the *Encyclopedia Yearbook of China* in successive years after 1977. (See Ming Tsui, "Marriage and the Family System in Contemporary Urban China," Ph.D. dissertation, State University of New York, Stony Brook, 1992.) In the years 1978–1982, some divorce cases, and possibly a large number of divorces as well, may be omitted for administrative reasons. On this point, see Ming Tsui, table 1. For 1989 and 1990 I am using *China Statistical Yearbook*, State Statistical Bureau of the People's Republic of China, as well as *Zhonggui Shehui Tongji Ziliao* (Social Statistics of China) (Beijing, 1990), table 19.

of liberalization which begins about 1978. The new marriage law was not put into effect until 1981, which marked a break with this pattern. When divorce figures for Beijing were finally reported in 1979—they had not been generally available for the period 1954–1979—the number is only about the 1954 level. Even in 1981, in the most liberal jurisdiction, Beijing, the official report notes that about one-third of cases were rejected because they were "persuaded" to reconcile, and a bare majority (57 percent) received a divorce.[70] Finally, it is clear that well into the 1980s, many or most courts and civil affairs offices required a letter of permission from the spouses' work unit (*danwei*) before they would process the divorce request, even when the couple was in agreement.[71]

Consequently, by any records, the divorce rates were much lower during the period from the mid-1950s to the early 1980s than in the heady days of the Communist takeover, when the new law was interpreted liberally. In the earliest period, few couples made complaints (in contrast to the survivors of the later period) that suits were being stopped by a long process of attrition which amounted to a kind of social punishment. As Platte remarks, "Presumably the divorce rate reached an all-time low which is suggested by the fact that in 1979 the people's courts at different levels handled only 207,000 petitions."[72]

I believe it is possible to specify the time curve in the divorce rate still further, though of course with a greater risk of error. Ming Tsui's study is focused mainly on a small part of China, but she has made available a fuller body of regional data, from the volumes of *China Population*. These contain successive censuses as well as data and reports from government offices, including the marriage registration offices. Fortunately, many of these contain divorce rates for most of the period 1950–1980.

Consequently, we are better able to confirm at least the gross outline of the time curves for a number of regions. For example, Ming Tsui has given special attention to Tianjin (inner city) and Xuan Wu, a district in Beijing. The data for Tianjin show that the high point was the year 1953, when a rate of 6.8 divorces per 1,000 population was reached—higher by far than the rate in European countries at the time. Then the rate drops by 30 percent the following year; by 1958, more than two-thirds. The rates continued to decrease through the 1960s, but less sharply. Data for the period 1969–1972

---

70. Erika Platte, "Divorce Trends and Patterns in China: Past and Present," *Pacific Affairs* 61 (1988), p. 435.

71. As Li Hanlin shows in detail, the work unit became the basic unit of Chinese social structure, as the clan was in former times. *Die Grundstruktur der Chinesischen Gesellschaft* (Opladen: Westdeutscher Verlag, 1991).

72. Platte, "Divorce Trends," p. 435.

are missing, but the rate was still lower in 1973. For several years the rates stayed at that low level, and began a definite rise only in 1980.[73]

This pattern is paralleled in the data for Xuan Wu, but the low point is 1975, after which the rates rise slowly. Similar curves can be seen in the data published in the regional volumes for Sichuan (1987), Jiangsu (1987), Zhejiang (1987), and Hubei (1987).

The lowest rates seem to be found during the Cultural Revolution, 1966–1976, when ideological attacks were strongest on people who were thought to be following either their private interests or officially branded political deviations. During that period, according to Ming Tsui and in conformity with other sources we have cited, some lower courts did not accept divorce cases. Some did accept them, but often only on the grounds of political disagreements between spouses. After 1977, political cases were less common.[74] In 1990 there was one divorce per 12 marriages in China, a total of 400,000, an increase of 70 percent since 1979.[75] The rate was of course higher in Beijing, one in eight.

It is important to note that there may be significant data missing from the official reports of the number of divorces after 1981 because from that year onward, couples could be divorced in nonjudicial or administrative proceedings. These may best be understood by reviewing the divorce procedures that are currently available, as well as those of the immediate past. Just after the implementation of the 1950 law on marriage, courts seem to have interpreted it broadly to mean (as noted earlier) that if one party really insisted, he or she could be divorced. Thereafter, the qualifying phrase—"after mediation had been unsuccessful"—was instead given greater weight, and much social effort was exerted to force mediation or conciliation on the couple. That is, informal and formal groups made certain that mediation *was* "successful," so that willy-nilly the couple had to continue living together.

After the new law of 1981, that pressure was at least reduced, allowing an increasing flow of dissatisfied couples to leave their marriages. Under its procedures, three routes toward divorce can be followed. One of those was mentioned above: if husband and wife can agree about custody, the division of property, support after the divorce, and the opinion that the marriage has broken down, they can bypass the courts and obtain a divorce without cost through application to a civil affairs department. About 200,000 couples per year went through this procedure in the three years 1981–1983.[76] This is a

73. *China Population. Tianjin Volume,* 1987, p. 309.
74. Ming Tsui, "Marriage and the Family," p. 171.
75. *New York Times,* April 17, 1991.
76. Li Ning, "How Does China," p. 18.

"negotiated" divorce. These cases may not always count among the "court cases" in the official statistics.

When only one of the parties wants a divorce, the spouse can appeal to a people's court, which then tries to bring about a reconciliation. If that effort fails, a "mediated divorce" can be granted. As a third route, the civil court can find that the marriage has broken down and the spouses no longer care for one another, and thus a divorce is granted. Of course, appeals beyond that level are also possible. As noted earlier, in the more liberal Beijing courts, about one-third of the court cases in the years 1981–1983 were dismissed as "reconciled."[77]

Given these figures, the percentage *in* the divorced status remains low: for the population aged fifteen and over, it is only 0.59 percent. For those of older ages, the percentage is higher: 1.2 percent for the age group 45–59, and 1.3 percent for the age group 50–59. Since the mortality figures for China have begun to approach those of European countries, the percentage of those widowed in the younger years remains small, and even smaller than the percentage of divorces until the age group 40–44 years.[78]

Both in the 1950s and recently, women have been the applicants in four-fifths of all divorce cases. It is not clear why this figure is so much higher than in some Western countries.

The personal accounts of people who have complained about the difficulties in getting a divorce do seem to be written mainly about women. And, as noted above, Fox Butterfield reported that women complained more bitterly about their troubles in getting a divorce than anything else. Reading through more journalistic accounts of divorce cases one has the impression of a large number of cases in which the wife has been physically assaulted by her husband. For example, in one informal survey one-third of the women complained that their husbands beat them. If these complaints are representative, it is not surprising that women who are bombarded with ideological pronouncements of their equality would be especially frustrated and outraged by the formal and informal pressures to "reconcile" and continue living with such husbands under the rubric of "living in communist harmony."

More than two-thirds of Chinese women are in the labor force, a level almost as high as that of men, and there may be less occupational segregation than in Western countries. As a consequence, a wife is valuable for more than her household services. Men's reluctance to divorce may also stem from the possibility that a fault divorce may require an ex-husband to pay more support for his children (support is otherwise expected to be equally

77. *Beijing Review,* 1985, p. 20.
78. *Statistical Data on Chinese Society,* 1985, table 5.

shared). He would also lose the domestic services that wives offer to husbands. Here, too, as in the more advanced European countries, there are widespread social services, such as health care, that would continue for the mother and children even if divorced.

Earlier, I suggested that a high-divorce society is a high-remarriage society; societies do not generally allow a large part of the population to go "unused."[79] Correspondingly, the number of remarriages in China almost doubled between 1978 and 1988, from 20,000 to 37,000.[80] Again in conformity with the curves we have been analyzing, the percentage of marriages that were remarriages *dropped* during the period of divorce repression—because fewer people were available for remarriage. So did the percentage of marriages between people once married, or "rejoined marriages." The frequent appearance of this latter datum in public sources may suggest a propaganda aim: the authorities hope to convince citizens that divorce is not after all a solution, and they should stay with their spouses.

However, the trend toward more remarriages has been accompanied by a considerable amount of controversy, of a type that seems peculiarly Chinese. The patriarchal ideal was that the widow would not remarry, and in traditional Chinese society the stigma of divorce would presumably be so great that the divorced woman could not marry. On this point, however, as with reference to divorce generally, the ostensible and the real were not entirely in harmony. Chinese often commented that "the Chinese do not divorce," but some did anyway, even generations ago. Divorced persons certainly "disappeared demographically" from the status of divorcee, for remarriages were somehow arranged just the same.[81]

Men could remarry more easily than women, as is true in European countries, and divorcees who remarried had a narrower (and less desirable) choice of possible mates. In modern China the moral disapproval of divorce remains a considerable obstacle. Another obstacle may be the disapproval of the divorcees' children, especially if they are adults.

There are other barriers to remarriage as well. Even in Europe in the past, young adults sometimes expressed considerable indignation at the discovery that their middle-aged or elderly parents had sexual or romantic interests—and that attitude has not entirely disappeared. In China, those responses remain strong. It is not at all cynical to point out, too, that the older people

79. William J. Goode, "Pressures to Remarry: Institutionalized Patterns Affecting the Divorcees," in Norman W. Bell and Ezra F. Vogel, eds., *Modern Introduction to the Family* (Glencoe, Ill.: Free Press, 1960), pp. 316–26.

80. *Social Statistics of China* (Zhonguo Shehui Tongji Ziliao) (Beijing, 1990), table 19.

81. Goode, *World Revolution*, p. 318. Although this assertion has been challenged, our better knowledge of the variety of Chinese marriage forms in the past and the variation in marital stability suggest that the hypothesis nevertheless may be correct.

are likely to have acquired at least a bit of furniture, some housing rights, even some property, and their children are likely to suspect that they will not be able to share it once a new wife or husband enters the household. Even in the cities some version of an "extended family" is likely to be found, simply because of the housing shortage. A mother who is taking care of some of her adult children, as cook, housekeeper, or babysitter, is a valuable resource, and young adults do not want to lose it to a new husband.

Thus it is that news stories sometimes report domestic conflicts in which young adults have tried to prevent or break up a remarriage, and have even used force to threaten one or both potential spouses. The official position, by contrast, is to encourage remarriages, especially of the elderly, for a married couple is less likely to be a burden on the government. To further that goal, it was announced in 1986 that matchmaking agencies for the elderly were increasing rapidly in urban China.[82]

The same news report also took note of research data concerning the resistance of young people to the remarriage of their elderly parents. Of more than seven thousand applications to a Guangzhou agency after 1984, only 5 percent had married, but "many . . . were stopped by their children from seeking marriage partners." In a separate study, it was reported that on marriage applications almost all the people intending to remarry wrote that they had already obtained the agreement of their children.[83]

Many Chinese have no difficulty perceiving the irony in this situation: a movement *from* the very great power of parents under the old Chinese system, by which they could arrange their children's marriages without consulting them at all and could send a young bride back to her family whether or not she pleased the young groom, *to* a situation in which their young adult children can actually prevent *them* from marrying.[84]

What does this complex portrait of divorce in China suggest about the future? On the one hand there are several trends that might make Chinese marriages more stable. The average age at first marriage for urban women rose from 19.2 years in 1949 to 24.9 in 1982, and the percentage of women under 18 years of age in the status of married dropped continually during

82. *China Daily,* Feb. 5, 1986, p. 3.

83. "An Investigation of the Remarriage Situation in Hong Kou District, Shanghai," Class of 1978, Social Investigation Group, Sociology Department, Fudan University, Branch Campus, *Shehui* (1981), in Chu, *Sociology,* p. 123. See also the plea expressed by Deng Weizhi, "Children Should Not Interfere in the Marriage of Parents," in ibid., pp. 127–29. See also *China Daily,* Feb. 5, 1986, p. 3.

84. Perhaps one can add to the irony by noting that often the children have a good point; the divorce rate among people who remarry *is* of course much higher than that of people who enter first marriages, just as is true in the United States. For a tiny sample supporting this point, see "An Investigation of the Remarriage Situation" in Hong Kou District, Shanghai, Chu, *Sociology,* p. 123.

this period, especially in the period 1970–1975.[85] Men's age at marriage has risen similarly. Although Chinese youth do not typically "date" even now, and do not enjoy "free mate choice," there is a continued drop in the importance of the matchmaker, a rise in the frequency of introductions by friends as a phase in mate choice, and a rise in veto rights by young people. It could be argued that these factors might increase the chances of personal compatibility between spouses in the future.

On the whole, however, it seems more likely that these changes will not override the larger set of social forces—still far less powerful but of a type similar to those in the West—that already make divorce easier and thus more common. One set of factors that generates marital dissolution in China, as in Eastern Europe, but are of less importance in the West is the personal histories of bitter political disagreement. Some married couples stayed together for political reasons, some spouses hid their hostility toward the other's political attitudes or behavior, some were long separated and began other lives, and not all those problems have been worked through over the past decade. However, since those angers cools with age and disappear with death, they are not likely to play a large role. More important will be all the normal tensions between young people, especially in urban settings, who must cope with the complex, expanding industrial life that China is trying to develop in spite of its poverty.

Conclusion

In this chapter we have continued our exploration of stable high-divorce-rate societies with the example of Indonesia, working from both anthropological and official data. Indonesia has considerable success in its moves toward industrialization, though its very great diversity in languages, cultures, and economic development should be kept in mind. Its Muslim heritage legally permits easy divorce, and its traditional social processes supported it as well. But industrialization has undermined several of these traditional forces. Indeed, the contemporary approval of "modern" patterns has replaced acceptance of divorce as normal with the attitude that it is rather uncouth. Contrary to some predictions, the education of women has been widely accepted, and so has their relative independence as workers in factory and office. Thus we would expect the divorce rate to eventually rise again. Possibly that movement has already begun.

Taiwan shares the Indonesian pattern of government-directed economic development. In both Indonesia and Taiwan, the political leaders tried to set

85. *Statistical Data on Chinese Society,* (Beijing: Chinese Statistical Publication Society, 1985), tables 21 and 22.

in motion a full-scale plan of industrialization and largely succeeded. In Taiwan, those leaders were Japanese consolidating their conquest, and they began at a much lower level of economic technology (that is, at the turn of the century). As far as I can ascertain, however, neither set of leaders sought to create a program for development which would reduce the divorce rate.

Nevertheless, it seems plausible that the fall in the divorce rate was at least partially caused by weakening familial controls, which in turn were caused by industrialization. That term, it must be remembered, does not refer to factories but to a new set of social patterns: hiring and promotion by some merit system rather than the performance of family roles; and the right to one's own wages. In Taiwan, the Japanese had little to gain from supporting indigenous Chinese family customs, which would have been difficult anyway, as in Indonesia, because they were so variegated.

I included China is this chapter because it provides an interesting contrast to Taiwan (and Indonesia). Although China and Taiwan share the same cultural and linguistic heritage, the reduction in the Chinese divorce rate was not the byproduct of large-scale economic development. Instead, it was the middle-level bureaucracy that restricted divorce because it caused administrative inconveniences in a shortage economy—and because it was inconsistent with the ideology of the Communist regime. The Chinese case reminds us that some substantial changes can occur that are not simply generated by large-scale industrialization processes. And in contrast with the typical failure of divorce restrictions in the West, China did succeed in stemming the flood of divorces that began in the 1950s.

Note that it did so not by altering the basic divorce law, but simply by *interpreting* it in a particular way. In effect, the social and legal organizations (street committees, factory committees, groups within an apartment house, and so on) agreed that either party had the right to a divorce if indeed their conflict was irreconcilable, but they would accept almost no proof that the marital bond had really ceased to exist. Thus, although hundreds of thousands of suits were filed each year, for a long period most were turned down. The governmental rejection of divorce was "successful." The program was developed because the political and practical objections to divorce were strong, China was too poor to afford enough housing for all, and the factory and office committees controlled all housing. There was no other place for a disaffected wife or husband to go. That process, continued over many years, left an especially bitter legacy in China, which is much talked of to this day.

The crude divorce rate continues to rise in China, but official and unofficial disapproval of divorce remains high. Since I do not believe that the current Chinese leadership will succeed in fully stifling the modern hunger for freedom, both political and marital (even sexual), I am confident that trend will continue for some time.

11

Conclusion and Further Themes

To attain a triumphal note at the end of this study of divorce over the past forty years would require a victory of innocent optimism over good sense. It is clear that divorce rates have been rising in many parts of the world. Some might view this trend as a welcome end to the suffering that people have had to endure under the highly restrictive traditional divorce systems of the past (and the recent past in Spain and Italy and South America) and under repressive regimes like that of China. In most parts of the world, however, the rising divorce rates have brought not only an increase in personal freedom but substantial increases in the number of people—especially women and children—who are suffering economically and need state support to survive. In addition, the details of the processes we have studied suggest that the current high divorce rates represent a fundamental change in family patterns as more people move away from commitments to family obligations.

That is a somber view, shared by many who have done research on family and divorce, not only by those whose job it is to denounce others' family derelictions. If I could offer a serious plan for reversing some of these trends, I would willingly adopt a sanguine tone. Instead, I believe that the family is so intertwined with other social structures that it is not possible to transform it without reversing a multitude of other trends in modern social life, from the economic to the religious. That seems less than likely. I know of no great civilization that at the height of its power and material splendor ever changed its grand onward movement, except by dissolution and military defeat. Certainly none ever did so by conscious social planning.

If there was ever a familial Garden of Eden, in which old and young were pleased or at least contented with their lot, satisfied with their duties as family members, and gratified by their delights, we have no evidence of it. The one official Western account of that state gives us no location or time, or any report of Adam and Eve's feelings about it, and of course they had not yet enjoyed the challenge of trying to control their children's lives. It might be added that as far as we know they never actually married either.

Since that time, our literature has been replete with descriptions of the often tragic or violent outcomes of family relations, from parricide and incest to jealousy and war. Family behavior is probably no better, though possibly no worse, than human action in any other sphere in which high passion molds our behavior.

But for exactly that reason marital dissolution is theoretically interesting. It is one social solution for the inevitable conflicts of marriage. People care deeply about what the members of their family do. Just as living together intimately creates conflict as well as joy, so may any move toward untying the bonds that unite the family. Consequently, how it is held together, or torn apart, is likely to be worth studying.

So it is with the "divorce problem." Few would rejoice that divorce rates have continued to rise, that mothers are left with little support, that children are neglected in one country after another. At the same time, within any nation dozens of groups and organizations take radically different positions as to what should be done about it. And almost all of us support in one way or another the larger, more profound forces that generate high rates. We want others to remain in stable, long-lasting marriages, but we do not always wish to be restricted in our own family lives. We deplore the general self-seeking, materialism, or irresponsibility of others, in public or domestic spheres, but we are unable or unwilling to impose severe restraints on our own contributions to the tone and temper of our era—not even on our own pollution of our country.

To most people, divorce is noteworthy when the rates are high, or when they increase. Implicitly this work asserts instead that divorce processes are worth analyzing even if divorce is uncommon. A family, like a family system, is a social pattern held in place by many contrary tensions, rather than only by a set of firm harmonies. Yet both family and system can be stable, even though they inevitably change or disintegrate over time, as any organic system must. They require continual inputs, which may or may not be made. The system itself can be stable even if the individual units are not. But both possibilities deserve inquiry, for just as stability tells us what is missing in the more fragile arrangement, so breakdown tells us what factors might contribute to sturdiness.

It should be emphasized that we have no reason to believe that when rates are high, or rise, more people are unhappy in their family life. Nor need we believe that people in low-rate systems do not divorce because they are content in marriage. To bring back a striking example, from the late 1950s until the 1980s in China some hundreds of thousands of spouses wanted very much to divorce, but could not break through the wall of bureaucratic refusal. We shall never know the percentage of unhappy marriages in middle-class Victorian England.

This exploration of changes in divorce patterns over the past forty years has focused on the dynamics of those changes, how a wide range of factors interact to produce what we observe. My aim was not to present a simple compilation of the data on divorce among the nations of the world. That goal is worthy enough, for the result would be a useful reference book. Possibly a more practical solution for "looking things up" would be a continually updated computer data base, to be consulted through an easily accessible electronic network.

I have instead sought to present the most fundamental descriptive data, without aspiring to complete coverage. I have also centered the analysis on changes, and thus have omitted literally hundreds of fairly stable correlations. To consider a trivial example, research has generally reported that couples in Western countries who first met socially in the same church were less likely to divorce than those whose religions were different, but that couples who shared the trait of belonging to *no* church had still higher dissolution rates. If there has been a change in that pattern, I know of no studies to prove it. Thus I have usually left out such findings.

In short, my main goals have been intellectual, and my hope has been to convince the reader that a better understanding of changes in divorce patterns is itself worthwhile. At a minimum, for those who intend to redesign these complex processes, surely any new system is more likely to be effective if we know how the system works before we try to repair its faults.

Indeed, there is a profound resonance between a cool empirical analysis of the dynamics of change, made up of both intended and unintended consequences, and a passionate concern with divorce as a social problem. Precisely because these data can describe the results of those changes with relative objectivity, they also yield an unassailable affirmation of the difficulties that nations as well as people face because of divorce. The findings have not been selected to emphasize that problem, but simply to help us understand divorce processes. Equally important, as we comprehend more clearly how those dynamics operate, we may be able to see how to solve some of the problems, or at least to know that some solutions are not likely to be successful.

Even a casual sample of these findings emphasizes the magnitude of the social problems created by large increases in marital dissolutions and the weakening of a commitment to family obligations. In many countries the percentage of divorces involving children is increasing, and so is the absolute number of children affected, even while the birthrate falls. Mother-headed families become a higher percentage of all households with children. The payments of noncustodial parents are usually not enough to support the children, even when those parents can afford them—and some parents cannot. Custodial mothers are much more likely than others to be in the work force. Since for various reasons they command lower wages, and often must work part time (for adequate day-care facilities are lacking), they are more likely to be economically deprived. In most countries, even if they worked full time, they would still be in a precarious financial position. In countries with a genuine welfare system they create a large tax burden. Cohabitation continues to increase, and in several countries a majority of marriages are preceded by cohabitation, which itself is much more prone to dissolution than is legal marriage. The list could easily be extended.

It can be argued that in Western countries some 40 percent of divorces involve no children, that most of those who divorce are relatively young, that a majority of divorcing wives have been or still are in the labor force, and that in most cases neither spouse gains or loses much property after divorce since the couple has but little property. According to this line of argument, such divorces and most dissolutions of cohabiting couples do not constitute a social problem.

At a deeper level, however, even this category of unions contributes to the underlying social forces that increasingly weaken people's commitments to stable family obligations, to any longer-term personal investments in the collectivity of the family, and thus to the society as a whole.

But let us return to the analysis of the dynamics of divorce changes and stability. Our central concern has been to analyze divorce as part of a social system, not to answer the question of why individual persons decide to divorce. Earlier, I presented the various reasons for believing that it may not be possible to answer the general question of why people divorce, and especially how that answer may have changed over time. The common but banal formula is that people divorce when they decide that the pains of marriage are so high, and the comforts so low, that getting out is worth the likely costs. Such an economic answer enlightens us very little about long-term changes or even about sudden large shifts like the rise in Western divorce in the 1970s. It cannot even predict when an individual couple will make that decision.

The differences in the rates themselves are striking. We have given ample evidence that even within a narrow range of nations (from a world perspective) the divorce rate can vary greatly, from literally zero in Ireland to about half of all marriages in Sweden; and Catholic Austria has long had relatively high rates, while rates in Spain and Italy continue to be moderate.

The Role of the Law

It is unlikely that we can "explain" differences in divorce rates by the laws. Sociologists and demographers have asserted or demonstrated for some decades that easier divorce laws have only a small effect on the divorce rates. When such laws are new, there is a spurt in the rates, which quickly subsides. But the secular curve, or the long-term trend, which smooths out any temporary pips or declines (as in a war or depression), will show a steady rise.

I believe, nevertheless, that we can perceive the effects of legal changes even when they are not major. The key relationship is this. Both the rise in divorce rates *and* the laws come from the same source, changing values and norms in the larger society, alterations in economic opportunities, political ideologies, even the models presented by the mass media. Under any legal system, some people try to leave their marriages under the existing laws, but many will also press toward new laws with fewer restrictions. If some barriers are removed, some people get divorced who would not have done so before. But if the deeper social forces that drive both actions become stronger, then still other people will try to dissolve their unions under restrictions they now consider hard, and some will work toward even fewer barriers. At times, the legal barriers hold for rather long periods against much political pressure, but then people become more ingenious in working out ways of breaking out of their unions.

Thus in Chile a full divorce is still not legally possible, but a large traffic in "annulments" continues. In New York State, at a time when only adultery was adequate grounds for divorce, couples traveled to Cuba, Mexico, or Nevada for a divorce. The solution of informal separation and cohabitation can become widespread, as has happened in Brazil, Argentina, and Italy.

Similarly, in Muslim countries, the ecclesiastical law permitted easy divorce, but whether that led to frequent divorce, as in Malaysia, the Moroccan Mahgreb, and Egypt, or to little divorce, as in Afghanistan and Pakistan, was determined by local custom and the strength of social controls. China, too, passed an essentially no-fault law when the new regime came to power, whereupon a sharp rise in divorce occurred in the early 1950s. Then administrative and quasi-judicial measures reduced that flow considerably for over two decades. Legal permission is, then, only one of the factors that affect the level of divorce rates.

These examples also illustrate three time-honored dicta in the sociology of law. The first is that the life of the law lies not in its statutes alone but rather in its administration in practice. Thus the law in action, which includes the large traffic in annulments under the restrictive divorce laws of Chile as well as the harsh administrative restraints under the more liberal divorce law in China, is essential to our understanding of any legal system. Second, the law does have an effect at the margins. Thus those who are not totally determined to divorce are influenced by restrictive laws and administrative hurdles that make divorce more difficult. Finally, it is obvious that legal and administrative restrictions create formidable barriers for the poor. Thus, in the days when adultery was the only ground for divorce in New York State, well-to-do couples could fly to Cuba or Mexico or Nevada to get a divorce, but no such options to circumvent the letter of the law were accessible to the poor.

A Multi-factor Approach

We have pointed out many divorce patterns that are created by the complex interaction of long-term factors. One pattern we have observed in the West is that high divorce rates have been accompanied by an increase in mother-headed families and older women without husbands. This increase cannot be attributed solely to the rise in the divorce rates. Divorce rates as high as those in modern Western countries have occurred before without that effect—for example, in rural Japan until late in the Meiji period and in Malaysia and Indonesia, where almost all divorced women simply remarried.

Other factors have now come into play. In the West both marriage and remarriage rates have dropped among both men and women, though men, with their usual economic advantage, have continued to remarry at a higher rate than women. Moreover, in the marriage market men are "worth more" than women of the same age for almost any age beyond thirty years. In addition, women have added still more years to their life expectancy than have men.

As a consequence, with each passing year, a divorced woman will find fewer men in the marriage pool available to her. Usually she cannot bridge the market gap by money, since her average income will be lower. If she has children, they are likely not to be supported fully by her ex-husband, so that again her market prospects are less rosy.

The Rise and Influence of Cohabitation
The increase in cohabitation has been widespread, and it interacts with divorce processes in myriad ways. In the Nordic countries it was common among rural people, but mainly as a phase of domestic life before a delayed

marriage. In other Western countries it was sometimes a solution, temporary or permanent, for some domestic problem for which the law offered no easy answer. Some of those who entered such a union in the past felt that they were not yet ready economically or emotionally for marriage. In any event, it was not widespread, and was disapproved in respectable society.

It becomes a significant part of the divorce process in our time, however. Most fundamentally, it is an expression of the general and growing un-willingness among both the unmarried and the divorced—and, obviously, among the married as well—to commit themselves fully to a marital union, or to accept the only other alternative available in former generations, sim-ply doing without the pleasures of living together. This generation exhibits little appetite for self-denial or deprivation. Thus the spread of cohabitation is the result of wider social forces that support a general reluctance to bind together in a relatively permanent union.

Cohabiting unions, like legal ones, are of many types, but as a category they exhibit a higher rate of dissolution. Thus, though in lesser degree (be-cause less is usually at stake), they contribute to the social problems that legal divorces create. They also support the progress toward divorce, because they are now socially acceptable and easily observable, so that both the married and the unmarried are reminded that they need not, after all, accept the greater commitments (and higher potential losses) that legal unions still imply. In some countries, as noted earlier, cohabitation "makes up" for the decline in marriage and remarriage, but it should not be forgotten that the types of unions are not the same, and the substitution simply adds to the total sum of dissolutions.

We have considered the Latin American form of cohabitation, the consen-sual union, in some detail for its connection with trends in dissolution processes. In this great region (including the Caribbean non-Hispanic na-tions) this was the customary union in many countries, especially among peasants and the poor. Travelers and anthropologists, especially those who saw the lower classes as comparable to native tribes, often reported that it was as "respectable" as legal marriage was among the middle classes. That judgment was, I think, both condescending (our little brown brothers are different from us) and sentimentalizing (family relations among the poor are warm and harmonious). It was also incorrect. And although cohabitation was customary in rural regions, it was not a remnant of Indian tribal culture. Although it was most common in the Caribbean, its origins did not lie in Africa.

The analysis of divorce processes is especially difficult in this region, not just because so many data are missing, but also because few studies have been made of actual divorce behavior. I came to the conclusion, however, that very likely a majority of *all* marital dissolutions in Latin America as a whole occur to consensual unions. Doubtless that finding will be modified as better data become available, but the calculations do seem to be plausible.

The data do show that the percentage of consensual unions has been rising and that the percentage has been rising among white-collar classes, who can "afford" a legal marriage. Legal divorce has also been on the increase, since all the major South American countries except Chile now permit it. Central American nations have long accepted it.

The Economic Aspects of Divorce

It is clear that some of the support patterns typical of Europe are also common in Latin America—that is, divorced wives do not share equally in the marital property, in spite of a general movement in the civil codes toward the principle of sex equality; income-producing property is more likely to be defined as "his'"; and many women do not receive the child payments or alimony granted to them in the divorce orders. In all these ways it is clear that the Latin American countries maintain firmly their allegiance to the Western cultural system.

Almost all European nations have had, even fifty years ago, some official family policy, often driven by the fear (as their birthrate fell) that other polities would surpass them in the manpower available for war. Over the past twenty years, as divorce increased, they turned to the development of divorce law as part of family policy. They have especially focused on the consequences of marital dissolution. Since most of these unions last an average of ten years or more and involve children, a substantial percentage of the divorces require negotiating the complexities of pension rights, an examination of the agreement brought to the court by a couple through their lawyers, child support by the parents, and state support of various kinds. In particular, state policy with reference to child support has been moving toward the development of administrative rules, or tables, for determining the amounts to be paid, on the basis of the number and ages of children, parental income and level of education, and so on.

The Recent Permission to Divorce

All the Catholic countries of Europe except Ireland now permit divorce, and we noted some of the consequences of opening that door long after hundreds of thousands of couples had already made some informal adjustment to their marital conflict. Thus by 1984 some 400,000 Italian couples were living apart. In each of those countries in which divorce was introduced in recent years (Italy, Spain, Portugal, and several South American nations) a substantial part of the married population was finally able to regularize their domestic life.

The new "candidates" are likely to differ from the normal flow of divorcees in a nation where legal dissolution had long been practiced. Precisely because the new laws were long resisted, they are likely to be rather restrictive by worldly standards. For example, in the first Italian divorce law, unless a couple had been separated for five years they could not qualify. As a consequence, the first cohorts of divorcees in such a system are older, their marriages have endured longer, and a higher percentage of their children are older, even adult, than will be true of cohorts a decade or more later. Because many who in other countries would already have divorced have instead adjusted to life without divorce, many of the separated do not now bother to legalize the end of their dead marriage.

The difficult steps in divorce (for example, a court appearance for *both* the separation and the final divorce) have kept the continuing increase in these two countries from turning into the flood that some commentators predicted. And because women are more likely to feel that they could not oppose their husband's resources at the stage of separation, they have also used the new procedures to return to court later in order to redress their grievances in a more public arena. Relative to a "normal" divorcing population, the first candidates are likely to be better off financially and better educated, because they are the ones who could utilize the new law more effectively. All of those distributions will, of course, shift over time, and some have already done so.

The Role of Custom

Since younger people have a much more secular attitude toward divorce and marriage, they have already come to view divorce as a more or less ordinary part of social life in the Catholic European nations as well as in the South American countries that have recently permitted it.

In almost every nation the official ideology and religion have long engaged in a running but usually quiet series of conflicts with deeper, more ancient customs and understandings in the realms of both religion and the family. We have alluded to that widespread process in Malaysia, in the persistence of old Japanese family customs until World War II, and in the startling looseness of spousal ties among some rural populations of England and Scotland until late in the nineteenth century.

Other probes into history also reveal how old customs may shape family behavior centuries later. In his classic account of marriage and divorce among the pre-Islamic Arabs, William Robertson Smith refers to this persistence of very old patterns.[1] More recent research suggests that if we break

1. William Robertson Smith, *Kinship and Marriage in Early Arabia* (Cambridge: Cambridge

down European nations into smaller, culturally similar units (small provinces or countries), some fertility and family behaviors show much stability over generations.[2] So, similarly, C. K. Rob. Wikman's account of the sexually active courtship and delayed marriage among Swedish farmers and other groups[3] reminds us that, as William Faulkner asserted, the past is not dead; it is not even past.

It is possible that some of these enduring social and family ways have helped to create the diverse styles with which different nations approach the problems of modern family life. Thus the grim Lutheranism in the official morality of the Nordic countries did not, even after several centuries, erase all vestiges of folk usage in family matters. Possibly the tensions between those forces made it more possible for them to attempt to reshape some of their institutions with less moral denunciation and more effective planning. Whether this is more than mere speculation, it is at least possible that, without as much planning, other nations may follow in their footsteps in many ways. The very large changes that have taken place in their marriage and divorce processes seem to presage the future that other countries will experience.

The Nordic Solution: Collective Responsibility

In any event, the Nordic countries have quietly put more energy and money than others into trying to solve the ensuing problems, and less into moral hand-wringing and denunciation. Steadily consulting with one another, Denmark, Norway, Finland, and Sweden are I believe taking a somewhat different course from that of other countries, moving toward accepting collective responsibility for the difficulties created by individual decisions about cohabitation, illegitimacy, and marital dissolution, rather than curbing people's freedom to make those choices.

Although the processes that elsewhere lead to a rise in mother-headed families or in childbirth outside of marriage or in higher divorce rates create similar difficulties here, a smaller percentage of mother-headed families live in poverty, few children born outside wedlock are deprived of support, and ex-husbands are much less likely to escape their financial responsibilities. Many of the subsidies that in other countries may be given (or indeed not given) to those suffering from the consequences of divorce are here given to

---

University Press, 1885; London: Black, 1907), esp. chs. 3, 5, pp. 156ff. Bernard Lewis has warned me, however, that these descriptions can no longer be trusted.

2. Ansley Coale and Susan Cotts Watkins, eds., *Decline of Fertility in Europe* (Princeton: Princeton University Press, 1986).

3. C. K. Rob. Wikman, "Die Einleitung der Ehe," *Acta Academiae Aboensis (Humaniora)*, 11 (1937).

most citizens whether poor or well-to-do. The generosity of the programs varies from one polity to another, as does the extent of the problems occasioned by divorce. I have suggested that the Nordic model may eventually seem more reasonable to other nations—although of course if the older family preferences and practices noted above continue to be expressed, many countries will certainly struggle against it.

The Russian Dilemma: The Inner Dissolution of Marriage

The Russian Revolution proclaimed freedom and justice, but imposed tyranny. At the end of World War II, Soviet leadership brought it to other countries in Eastern Europe. By that time, the Communist authorities had given up the pretense of offering freedom in marriage and divorce, which in fact clashes with the mass mobilization that is needed for quick, basic change. Marriages, divorces, and remarriages all require housing. Illegitimacy creates bureaucratic burdens. Both marriage and divorce may break up old political alliances or strengthen dissident splinter groups. The complexities of trends in divorce processes in these countries over several decades of political turmoil, revolts, and the final resurgence of freedom may never be adequately analyzed. For though family patterns stubbornly resist ideological and military intervention more than other social institutions do, in their very resistance they are altered nonetheless, while both resistance and reshaping are likely not to be recorded for the historian's convenience. Thus it is improbable that my hypothesis can ever be properly tested, that it is not only the temptations of individual opportunity in a successful economy that can move family members to consider their own interests above those of the family as a unit; that response can also arise from a corrupt polity, which teaches its citizens to adjust to whatever its demands may be, since family ties cannot help enough against them, cannot guarantee an adequate reward for selflessly giving to each other over many years.

It is not just that people were imprisoned for small infractions or none and were separated from their families, or that—in a stunning parallel with the experience of lower-class men, Afro-American or white, who are chronically unemployed—men have lost women's respect because they failed to resist or triumph. After all, they did not (because they could not) carry out their obligations as males. What is central is rather the sum of such failures of the system over long years, so that the ideal of a stable family life in which all members can be assured of payoffs for economic competence, political decency, and fulfilling the obligations of wife and husband seemed to many a mockery.

Thus even the increases in the official divorce rates do not adequately describe what may be called the inner dissolution of many marriages. This applies especially to the Russian Republic, as Francine Duplessix Gray[4] has sensitively documented, but to a lesser degree it is also true of other Eastern European countries. If at least some of these countries make a successful transition to a trustworthy polity and a productive economy over the next decade, the divorce rates themselves may or may not drop, but I would predict that relations between the individual and the family unit will yield greater dividends for both.

Lessons from Stable High-divorce-rate Systems

Much attention has been given to change processes in "stable high-divorce-rate systems" because they force us to rethink our standard assumptions about both the differences among various nations and how divorce patterns change as countries move into the modern world. The usual Western view, based on Western history, idealizes the bucolic life, with its adherence to stern, outmoded but admirable values, to stable family units, and to the worth of a strong, protective patriarch. In the city and the court by contrast, decadence and loose family behavior are more likely. Contemporary readers will recognize this view, for a fair number of contemporary social philosophers and journalists continue to agree with it. Some decades ago, referring mainly to the United States, I called it "the classical family of Western nostalgia." This view is also supported to some extent by the fact that innumerable empirical studies prove that divorce rates are higher in urban than in rural populations. It is also affirmed by the fact that countries more advanced in industrialization (in my sense) do, by and large, experience increases in divorce rates. When we broaden our perspective, in time and place, however, other divorce patterns emerge. Considerable historical data even from the West also cast some doubt on those assumptions.

Most important, it is likely that many divorce systems were relatively stable in their levels of marital dissolution, whether high or low. At least a few maintained a stable system with relatively high rates of divorce. Among them were Indonesia, Japan, some of the Arab countries and regions, and (at least relative to mainland China) Taiwan. I suppose there are others, and of course many tribal societies were in this group as well.

Moreover, the modernization that typically erodes people's allegiance to traditional family ways does not then cause increased divorce rates in these systems. To the contrary, since the traditional system itself generated high rates, that erosion actually decreases the rates. I have also offered the hypothesis that eventually the rates will begin to rise again, though not to the original high level.

4. See Francine du Plessix Gray, *Soviet Woman: Walking the Tightrope* (New York: Doubleday, 1990).

Stable high-rate systems enlighten us in several ways. At least on a descriptive level they differ a good deal from one another. To be sure, they do share a handful of traits—for example, the rates are higher among the rural and poor, remarriages are more likely to be stable, and so forth. Very likely, in all of them the costs of divorce were relatively low. But among the Arabs it was the absolute male right of unilateral divorce that seemed to be the key; while in Malaysia (also Muslim) the traditional position of the wife was strong. In Taiwan, the interaction of husband and wife in their earlier years before marriage appeared to be crucial for a large group of divorces, but in Japan I believe it was the in-laws (by legend, specifically the mother-in-law) who sent the bride back to her family.

Much more important—and later we shall take up this theme again when we ask what we can do about divorce in the modern world—in all of these systems divorce was *institutionalized*. This sociological term does not refer to a statistical regularity, or a bureaucratic agency. It points rather to the extent to which a given social pattern is linked to and buttressed by other social institutions, norms and values, and social patterns that people support as simply the right or approved way to do things. Marriage is said to be institutionalized in that sense: surrounded by laws, rituals, local or ethnic customs, expectations and approval of family, friends, and co-workers, a place in history, poetry, and function, and so on.

As so many sociologists have remarked, the Western world has somewhat high rates of divorce, but we have not yet institutionalized divorce: the official act of severance has not yet grown its own surrounding institutional structures.

By contrast, each of the stable high-divorce-rate systems of the past contained a well understood set of obligations and rights associated with that status—for example, the right to custody of the children, the obligation to support the ex-wife or mother and for how long, where the spouse lived after dissolution, and how remarriage was to occur. All such matters were not to be decided anew or *ad hoc* by the couple, but were carried out according to custom. Arguments between families about the divorce were surely acrimonious at times. Whether the bride was at fault, so that the bride-price need not be returned, must have occasionally caused conflicts. Doubtless many spouses suffered the anguish of abandonment, shame, and lost love. Nevertheless, the duties of each party were clearer than in the modern high-divorce society, and each was pressed to carry them out.

Class Position and Proneness to Divorce

One interesting topic of divorce change that I have not addressed is whether the negative correlation between class position and proneness to marital dissolution has decreased—even though this study began with the more modest aspiration of systematically exploring that relationship. I found that my data, gathered from official but sometimes unpublished sources, surveys, and much correspondence were inadequate for the purpose. Nevertheless, the relationship itself is important. It helps to explain many other regularities: for example, the generally poorer performance of divorced children in school, the higher divorce rate of the remarried, the poverty of divorced mothers, the higher income of the married over that of the divorced, the higher divorce rate of those who marry earlier than the usual age, the generally higher divorce rate of Afro-Americans, and so on. As in so many other aspects of family and social life, the factor of class has a strong effect.

I think that I was the first to bring that relationship to theoretical attention, four decades ago.[5] Later I also sought to demonstrate that it was generally applicable in other times and places. Since then others have at least validated it (often, as frequently occurs in sociology, without knowing of my earlier work) but few if any have concerned themselves with its complex significance, or whether it would change.[6]

In my original analysis of why there are higher divorce rates among the poor I pointed out that lower-class women had relatively less to lose economically from divorce because they were more likely to be employed and their wages were more likely to be close to the wages of their husbands. Middle- and upper-class women, in contrast, had a much greater economic stake in the stability of their marriages and much more to lose from a divorce. There was likely to be a much greater discrepancy between their own income (which was often nonexistent since few middle-class women with children were employed in those days) and the income of their husbands.

If the relationship between class position and proneness to divorce has been changing, the change is likely to be the result of a shift in the strongest

5. For the facts and their theoretical meaning, see William J. Goode, "Problems in Postdivorce Adjustment," *Am. Soc. Rev.* 14 (1949), pp. 394–401; "Economic Factors and Marital Stability," *Am. Soc. Rev.* 15 (1951), pp. 802–12; *Women in Divorce* (New York: Free Press, 1956), chs. 4, 5; "Marital Satisfaction and Instability," *Int. Soc. Sci. J.* 14 (1962), pp. 507–26; several analyses in *World Revolution and Family Patterns* (New York: Free Press, 1963); and "Family Disorganization," in Robert K. Merton and Robert Nisbet, eds., *Contemporary Social Problems*, 4th ed. (New York: Harcourt, Brace, Jovanovich, 1976), pp. 531–36.

6. The complexities of trying to use inadequate data for testing this relationship cannot be presented here. The only serious challenge to my finding is presented by the research team led by Louis Roussel and Jacques Commaille in the late 1960s and early 1970s, when divorce was still very difficult and expensive. This study failed to solve some serious methodological problems—for example, most occupations were not recorded—and other French reports have not confirmed this finding in the team's otherwise admirable monographs. See Roussel et al., *Le Divorce et les Français* (Paris: Presses Universitaires de France, 1975), vol. 2, esp. chs. 1, 2.

variable in this pattern: the discrepancy between the husband's and the wife's incomes. Now that more married women from the middle and upper classes are likely to be employed, and more likely to be employed in occupations and professions similar to their husbands, there is less discrepancy between their incomes. With less discrepancy (and with independent incomes), those women now look—sociologically—more like the lower-class women of the past in that they will not experience as great a loss of income if they divorce. The same variable may also account for part of the higher divorce rate among Afro-Americans, since it determines how great a loss the wife would experience if a divorce occurred.

In our time period, in a few countries the average gap between women's and men's wages has narrowed, but the more powerful shift has been an increase in the percentage of middle-class wives who have jobs and who earn a living wage. The family containing a working father and a stay-at-home mother with a child or children is now a statistical minority. Thus there has been a large increase in the percentage of middle-class (or higher-class) families in which the discrepancy between the two incomes is smaller than in the recent past because one of them is no longer zero or close to it. Since people are likely to marry within roughly their own class level, this means that a much higher percentage of middle-class men than in the past are married to similarly trained women (a sampling of *New York Times* wedding announcements of dual-career professional couples is instructive in this respect).

The reasoning in this analysis is borne out by the data. We find that there has been a reduction in the income discrepancy between husbands and wives over time. In addition, there is a surprise in these data—but one that is still congruent with the foregoing analysis. When we look at the relationships between divorce and income we find that the negative association between class or income and divorce rate holds for men, but the relationship seems to be *reversed* for women: the higher their income, the higher the divorce rate.[7] Since most of these women are married to these men, obviously some statistical tensions exist between these two opposing relationships, in a substantial but unknown number of cases. In any event, the net effect is a reduction over time in highly income-discrepant marriages. The

7. I reported this in "Family Disorganization," in *Contemporary Social Problems*, 3d. ed. (New York: Harcourt Brace, Jovanovich, 1971), p. 532, on the basis of U.S. data from the 1970s. In the early 1980s, I obtained unpublished data from the Baden-Würtemberg Microzensus 1978 (courtesy of Prof. Walter Muller) and calculated the propensity to divorce of women and men separately, by income. The result was the same: a negative association among men, and a positive association among women. My calculations from Japanese data in this period (courtesy of Prof. Morioka) show the same regularity. (The pattern holds for Afro-Americans as well.)

consequence of that change should have been a reduction in the stability of marriages among the higher or middle classes relative to the working classes—unless, of course, some as-yet-unreported factors at the same period have raised working-class divorce rates.

That reasoning seems likely, but equally unlikely to be testable at present. Figures on divorce by industrial or occupational *sector* are sometimes available but are irrelevant, since many job levels exist within each sector. Census data on the occupational levels of the divorced are crude, since the category includes recent divorcees but excludes those who have remarried. It is thus not a sample of the occupational distribution of the flow of divorcees, compared with that of the married. Data on the income of that flow are rare, but in any country where agriculturists are numerous they must be separately analyzed. Usually their incomes are on average much lower. Space does not permit a full statement of the difficulties of making an appropriate test of the hypothesis.

I would nevertheless be surprised if adequate data would find *no* differences by class in the proneness to divorce, since class is a strong variable even if it is sometimes a bit slippery. It is often powerful because, however measured, it is a surface factor, beneath which other, more immediate forces are at work—power, prestige, the social pressures on high-level managers to harness their passions to their corporate life, the different life styles of academics at major research universities, the sheer complexities and stress of divorce settlements among the well-to-do, neighborhood and group models, and so on.[8] It is precisely because such measures as income and occupational level capture some of that dense interlock of social costs and pressures, that they consistently reveal strong differences, not so much because spouses in conflict think of their class position.

The Future of Divorce Rates

Having focused so much attention on how various divorce systems actually work, it is customary to address two worldly questions that are in the forefront of public discussion: Will divorce rates continue to go up, or will they drop? And what should we do about the divorce problem?

The first is a question for prophesy, and subsequent events have not dealt kindly with large predictions in social science. The second requires a choice

8. Thus, for example, M. J. Murphy found no association between class and marital breakdown, because he controlled a variety of class factors such as age at marriage and type of housing. In short, he erased the class factors, and then found no relationship between them and divorce. See his "Marital Breakdown and Socio-Economic Status: A Reappraisal of the Evidence from British Sources," *Brit. J. Sociology* 36 (1985), pp. 81–93. However, J. Haskey, "Social Class and Socio-economic Differentials in Divorce in England and Wales," *Population Studies* 38 (1984), pp. 419–38, affirmed the usual patterns.

among means, and very likely ends, too; and such choices are driven by one's own values or ideology. Nevertheless, both questions are challenges not easily resisted.

The immediate changes in divorce patterns in the more developed countries seem simple and clear, and the forces that drive some of them are not mysterious, but the larger trends or directions of these changes are less clear because they are part of the ongoing alterations in family behavior. These in turn are pushed by factors that I believe cannot as yet be weighed adequately. More specifically most of the broad trends over the past century can easily be aligned with the spread of the ideology and practice of industrialization: income from jobs not land; the growing irrelevance of family-role performance for hiring, promotion, wages, and firing; the right to dispose of one's own salary, and so on. But does that set of forces continue to change the family in the same directions indefinitely? If so, the direction would be toward the breakdown of the family, the atomization of the market and society that is a central assumption of microeconomics.

Or, if we are now in "postindustrial" society, what family and divorce patterns will emerge? Theory about this new phase has not focused on the family, and has not linked any presumed traits of postindustrialism with specific trends that we can expect in the near future. For example, a continued movement toward a "tertiary economy" does not foretell much, if anything, about the family system or divorce rates over the next decade.

It is possible, instead, to argue that the industrialization process is not yet complete. After all, tens of millions of people follow rural ways even in parts of Europe and the Anglo world. People in many countries work in factories without accepting the ideology of industrialization for a long period of time. Still deeper social processes continually *recreate* personal and family allegiances, nepotistic bargains, in-group advantages, and gender discrimination, which resist the erosive pressure of the economy. Since those processes seem ubiquitous, even in some sense primordial, perhaps they can serve as a counterweight to the undermining forces from industrialization in its various senses.

By contrast, most social analysts and commentators continue to proclaim that the present historical epoch is witnessing very rapid changes, and on a global scale. Most of them suggest that divorce rates will stabilize (and I have presented some data on this point).

Of course, the worldly philosopher can draw upon ancient wisdom for the two guiding principles of change, when no precise theory is at hand. (1) Current trends will continue, and tomorrow the curve will simply move further up (or down) a bit as it has in the recent past; and (2) organic and social change, however dramatic it may be at present, always occurs within limits, and thus it will slow down. Some would add a third choice, the prediction of cycles, but that is not common sense and is too easy to disprove within short time periods.

The first of these principles asserts that since the divorce rates in the European and Anglo worlds (and some others) have been rising, they will continue to go up. The second asserts that the present rise will level off. So it has been for the number of miles of highways, the rise in incomes, or the number of fruit flies on a banana in an enclosed space. It is possible that one of these principles applies to divorce rates, but neither yields any understanding of the forces that will drive or flatten the same curve.

In the United States an outburst of popular articles at the beginning of the 1990s announced a new era, as though with the turn of the heavenly bodies its leaders were going to put on a different set of behaviors as easily as changing a dress or suit. The "decade of greed" was over, and now people would be more concerned with others' needs. Some political figures asserted that the family would be "the issue of the nineties." If that was correct, then indeed divorce rates might drop, divorced fathers might become assiduous in their support payments, and wives would try harder to live harmoniously with their husbands and children. Or, as in some other countries, perhaps religious fundamentalism would begin to be powerful, and people would move back toward a more traditional disapproval of divorce.

My own prediction is more ambiguous. Most of the scenarios that lead to a diminution of divorce rates are imaginable but implausible. I have suggested that the modern trends in divorce patterns are in a sense "overcaused." Almost any group of modestly educated people can quickly develop a list of important factors that make for widespread marital dissolution and a general unwillingness to sacrifice our own interests for the sake of the family over the long haul, from TV soap operas to the need for two incomes. To change all these forces is about as easy as to convince the world's populations to be content with a modest or austere standard of living. It is not impossible, but no civilization has ever moved in that direction voluntarily.

Moreover, when we consider the truth that all upward organic and social curves do flatten out eventually, we must not forget the harsh basis of that fact: An expanding population of animals or plants does not simply, out of its wisdom, decide to reduce its growth. Instead, predators, disease, and starvation do that for them. And so for great empires: they declined because they were forced to do so, not because their leaders chose to live a simple traditional life.

Thus, although I have no doubt that the curves will eventually fall away from their precipitous upward movement, I do not now see what variables will come into play to make them do so. I have also argued that the current trend toward a lesser investment of people in the collectivity of the family cannot continue indefinitely, because if the family as a social agency fails to function reasonably well, the economy—and the society as a whole— cannot do so either. Consequently, I would assert that there is some point— to be sure, indefinite as to *when*—at which the steady weakening of the family will generate some counterforces and opposing pressures. While we have witnessed many rhetorical calls for increased adherence to family values, concrete programs that really give support to family life have been rare.

Marital dissolution of all kinds might increase so much that few people will bother to set up legalized joint households at all. This, however, may be no more than another way of describing the processes that accompany the upward curve.

Theorizing at this level takes it for granted that moral exhortation will have little effect. What then *can* be done about "the divorce problem"? If by that we mean, how can we make marriage more stable, the solution is about as simple as for any other large-scale social problem of our troubled time, from poverty to war. For example, to paraphrase Crane Brinton's ironic comment, we might make marriage such a delight that people would not wish to divorce at all.

At present, it is unlikely that a return to very restrictive divorce laws would be politically acceptable. Polls in the United States and other countries show that no large segment of the population feels this is a wise route to take. It is now understood that we are more likely to achieve a goal if we plan for it, but decades of experience with a diverse list of social issues also tells us that "solutions" create many unintended and unwelcome consequences. Large-scale attempts to transform dozens of nations since World War I offer evidence that small-scale tinkering with specific problems may be wiser. At a deep level, most people do not have the political will to solve this problem, simply because they do not believe it is important enough to justify changing their society, their family systems, and especially their own lives in any radical way.

Focusing on the Consequences of Divorce

If we rephrase the question, however, and focus on the consequences of the high divorce rates instead of on the rates themselves, then we may find some answers at hand. I believe something can be done about the consequences of divorce. The first step is to face the reality that almost all of the highly developed nations are, or are becoming, high-divorce-rate societies.

Like it or not, divorce will be a firm element in our domestic arrangements for the foreseeable future. Neither through laws nor some sudden switch in our norms and practices will our real family lives be close to the nostalgic dreams of our imaginations.

We can therefore turn our attention to the pragmatic tasks of institutionalizing divorce—that is, transforming it into a social institution—knowing that a high percentage of people, whether or not ever legally married, will at some time be involved in the dissolution of some kind of union. Arrangements for divorce tell us what are the terms of marriage.[9]

It is likely that some form of no-fault divorce will be most prevalent and that marriage will be understood to be terminable by either spouse. In addition, those who enter marriage will know that there is a fair likelihood that their marriage will not last—despite the widespread human talent for convincing ourselves that we are the exception to the statistical norm.

Entering marriage with that understanding will require a parallel awareness and acceptance of the costs of marital disruption. At the present time, the costs continue to be a surprise to many participants because there is no prior set of customs and presuppositions about what should happen after divorce and who should pay for it.

There was such a set of beliefs in the distant past in the United States and more recently in some other countries. Just fifty years ago divorce was still disapproved in the United States. It was possible, but not common. The laws and courts made divorce quite difficult, and spouses tried to avoid a divorce and viewed it as a last resort. According to the norms, divorce would occur only if one of the spouses committed some grievous act. That spouse would then bear as much of the burden as possible: shame, social ostracism, and monetary losses. If, as often happened, the husband committed the grave fault (or connived with lawyers or his spouse so as to *seem* to do so), he would be expected to pay for his failures and the injuries he caused others by receiving less property and being ordered to support his ex-wife and his children after divorce.

Needless to say, most men tried to avoid alimony and to leave the marriage with their property intact. I suspect, however, that most men with moderate to high incomes did have to make some alimony payments. It was expected of them and was part of the legal settlement they signed. (The courts' failure to enforce such orders was generally not known, and most men of means assumed that they had to comply with the law.) In addition, many men had to give up the family home for their ex-wives and children (although they

9. This is the thesis of Lenore J. Weitzman's *The Divorce Revolution: The Unexpected Social and Economic Consequences for Women and Children in America* (New York: Free Press, 1985); see especially pp. xv–xviii and "The Transforming Marriage," pp. 366–78.

typically retained the family business). The net effect of these rules led almost every husband contemplating a divorce to suppose (even if in error) that divorce would be very costly to him in many ways and was to be avoided if at all possible.

By contrast, it would be difficult to sketch a broadly accepted set of pre-suppositions in any country as to what is now likely to happen upon divorce. In addition, few people would claim that either the formal laws or their informal social networks of friends and family and colleagues at work would insist that they follow any particular course of action after divorce—not even that of providing support for their children after divorce. While public opin-ion favors supporting one's children, we all know of individual cases in which someone has been ordered to pay an amount that seems excessive or unduly harsh, and we therefore "understand" his efforts to thwart or escape the court order. The tendency to individualize suggests that there are no clear-cut social norms or customs and there is neither a consensus about what is appropriate behavior—that is, what *should* happen—nor a common understanding about what *will* happen.

As a result, in this historical era, whatever provisions are made for the consequences of divorce will have to be expressed first in formal regulations and laws: they cannot wait for the steady accretion of custom alone. This process does occur in a modern society, but it cannot be powerful unless, as in a tribal society, almost everyone is in close daily contact with other mem-bers, and thus informal social controls are strong. Lacking that, the modern state—and the people in it—must impose some collective controls on the outcome of an intimate and very personal social unit.

The modern polity tries to prevent people or corporations from walking away scot-free from the debris left at the end of a mining or manufacturing venture. So it will (I use this future form, rather than the hortatory "should," for I believe this will happen) require most spouses to take care of as many of the post-divorce problems as they can. To a great extent, such a program will make greater demands on men than have been made in the recent past. That will occur because the data from most countries increasingly show that divorced fathers have, to an astonishing extent, managed to avoid even the responsibilities that courts have imposed on them (aside from those they escaped through clever negotiations or intimidation in the divorce process). Putting the matter in more political terms, in many countries the growing body of research data on this point (such as those compiled by Weitzman and Maclean in *The Economic Consequences of Divorce*) arouses indignation in the taxpayers who must pay for the failures of such fathers. Thus there is, and there will be more, political pressure to develop such a program.

Since instinct is not a sufficient guide, tribal societies enforced their elabo-rate family and kinship rules upon the unwilling as upon the willing. A substantial majority permitted some forms of premarital dalliance, but births outside wedlock were rare, and various devices were used to ensure that result. Societies large and small have not wanted to take over the complex burdens of being a father. People in modern societies still feel that way, and also feel that way about the child-support burdens that divorced fathers escape.

It is usually the mother who will take up that burden, if it is taken up at all. One movement in the direction of ensuring that spouses will share the responsibility for their children—as they are increasingly expected to share their other marital assets—is the slow but growing acceptance of the princi-ple of equal division at divorce. (The Australians sometimes phrase it as the equal division of disadvantage.) I call the trend slow because its *application* has been slow.

The primordial principle of equal division when intimate partnerships break up is widespread as a folk attitude, and in public debate (at least in democracies) it has great political weight. The situation is somewhat differ-ent in practice. As many analysts have noted, courts and lawgivers (mostly men) have been slow to give up the notion that "marital property" is in fact *his* property. In the past the issue was often phrased as, How much of "his" property should be given to her?

Obviously there is a troubling tension between the broad principle of equal sharing and the stubborn feeling that the husband "really earned" the money and built the family resources. This tension is widespread, no less in Latin America than in Europe. Since courts are concerned with the hus-band's ability to make a living, their definitions of what is *not* to be put in the pot for division has in the past exempted businesses, farms, and other income-yielding property, professions, pensions, health insurance (where there is no national system), and so on. Thus, as Weitzman and others have shown, there is often very little left in the category of "marital property" after all those exclusions. The residence is the largest item, and that is mortgaged. When the proceeds of its sale are split, the spouses receive very little. At lower income levels such settlements do not yield enough to be of much help to a divorced mother who needs to establish a new residence with her child or children. To solve that problem, what is now marital property appears to be inadequate.

If settlements at divorce do continue to move toward a wider inclusion of all forms of property (as with pension rights in Germany), perhaps with years of marriage as a standard for how much sharing is required, husbands on balance will lose compared with the present situation, and wives will gain. Very likely, too, the somewhat higher anticipated cost of divorce may persuade some couples to pause a bit before incurring it.

The important element, however, is that if divorce is to be a "normal" process, the rules for taking care of the consequences should be widely understood and widely supported. The principle of equal sharing enjoys at least surface acceptance across a wide spectrum, and if embodied in regulations would become more fully embedded in social norms and daily behavior. Most important, we can move closer to the principle of partnership, and away from the question of "who actually earned the money in the market?" which often undermines that principle.

Earlier I noted Mavis Maclean's judgment that modern discussion of new rules for post-marital support have largely focused on child support, not on alimony. The debates and new rules about child payments are partly a response to much research in several countries. Some general findings have emerged: 1) The number of needy one-parent families continues to grow; 2) Most are mother-headed; 3) The amounts that courts *order* ex-husbands to pay for child support are less than half the costs of rearing a child; but 4) The amounts they *actually* pay are still less, for most pay irregularly, and a substantial minority do not pay at all. In some ways the most striking finding is that there is little or no correlation between the father's income and what is actually paid, and in some countries (for example, Australia) research has actually revealed a negative correlation. That is, even if we accept the guess that very poor fathers can pay only little or nothing, at present the delinquents are mostly fathers who *can* pay.

Public opinion about this general dereliction is strongly negative, for it grows from fundamental notions about the father role. While many people can sympathize with the man who believes that his ex-wife should simply go to work and earn her own keep, there are very few people who feel that divorced fathers have any right to escape their basic responsibility as fathers—that of supporting their children. That feeling extends to the father who does not pay child support as ordered, but then remarries and has still more children. It is simply a final indignity that the burden thus sloughed off is then neatly placed on the taxpayer's shoulders.

It seems easier to work out an acceptable program for the problem of delinquent child-support payments than for the problem of nonsupport of ex-wives. Indeed, several countries have taken firm steps in this direction: the Nordic countries, Belgium and Holland, what was formerly called the Federal Republic of Germany, and Australia. New Zealand as well as some states in Canada have also developed such plans, as have a growing number of states in the United States. These programs typically include effective procedures for tracking down delinquent fathers as well as mechanisms to enforce compliance (such as requiring fathers to make payments to a state agency).

Essentially, such a program has several main elements: 1) The amounts to be paid are not set by judges in an adversarial court case, but by administrative boards or agencies, on the basis of research data on the *actual* costs of rearing a child and specific data on the spouses' incomes, the ages of the children, the level and type of the parents' education, whether the children will continue to occupy the family residence, and so on.

(2) Support is typically collected directly from the source of the father's income, usually through payroll deductions; (3) The custodial parent does not have the burden of locating or pursuing the parent who is delinquent in paying. Instead of lawsuits, crowded legal calendars, and unenforced court orders there are administrative agencies with sufficient personnel to locate absent parents and enforce their compliance.

(4) When the noncustodial parent fails to meet his or her obligation, the state will fill the gap and the delinquent parent will have to reimburse the state. (5) In turn, the state will work out plans to enforce compliance; where necessary it will track down delinquent parents and use state resources to collect the money that is due. This is more difficult in Anglo countries, where there are no systems for the registration of residence and no identity cards. Nevertheless, even in the United States, federal procedures—including the use of Internal Revenue Service and Social Security records—are now available to track down fathers who have tried to escape their parental obligations.

To repeat, although opposition to one or another specific step of this kind will vary, people in general are strongly in favor of not letting fathers escape their parental obligations. Indeed, the situation of widespread delinquency which developed over some decades was definitely not part of some shift in community attitudes. Rather, few people knew it was happening, and most were incensed when it became known.

On the other hand, research of the last five years shows that it is not enough to facilitate payments from the non-custodial parent. Two additional steps are needed. One is to encourage the fullest participation of mothers in the work force. This can be done by providing better child-care arrangements; removing penalties for earning adequate wages; and supplying further education or training to upgrade their skills and hence their wages.

The second step is to provide a wide range of benefits and state assistance to prevent women and children from becoming the economic casualties of divorce. This has been politically more difficult in the Anglo countries but less so in Europe, where the Nordic countries have led the way: by providing state supplements and aid of many kinds, including housing, national medical care, maternity leave, child allowances, support of the incidental costs of child education, and so on. It is politically easier to do this if the benefits are not confined to the poor. The aim is to create supports for many of the basic necessities for children and their caretakers, so that any welfare specifically for the poor is not spent mostly for such elementary needs.

The case is very different for alimony. In the Eastern European and Nordic countries, it is almost a nullity, and few women receive it. In other countries, opinion is divided, and so is practice. I believe that the trend is toward the decline of alimony, but others, such as Weitzman, see a resurgence of alimony awards—often relabeled "compensatory alimony" or "retraining alimony" or "lump sum alimony"—as a means of adjusting postdivorce equities.[10]

In general, feminists have argued for the importance of alimony for three groups of divorced women: older women who have been homemakers and mothers in marriages of long duration; middle-aged women who need to invest in their job skills and enhance their earning capacities so that they can maximize their employment potential after divorce; and women who retain major custodial responsibilities after divorce.[11] They have pointed out that *at present*, women do not enjoy economic equality, and after some years of marriage have handicapped them in the market they should not be discarded without some help. Many men are convinced, contrary to available facts, that women already enjoy equality, if not an unfair advantage, in the job market, and that it is unjust to grant them alimony too.

In each country (even in Japan and the Arab world) women have made spectacular gains here and there, but the overall movement toward equality has been slow. In dozens of occupations, sex segregation persists, and wages are lower in jobs for women. I believe, against much evidence, that the movement toward equality will continue and that one result will be less political pressure in favor of alimony as a general practice, but growing opinion in favor of keeping it for special cases. Again, our guiding principle would be that divorce can occur to any marriage and that the costs of breakup should be accepted as part of the marriage contract—indeed, as part of a widely shared understanding of the meaning of marriage. Correspond-

10. See generally Lenore J. Weitzman, "Alimony: Its Premature Demise and Recent Resurgence in the United States," in Lenore J. Weitzman and Mavis Maclean, eds., *The Economic Consequences of Divorce: The International Perspective* (Oxford: Oxford University Press, 1992), pp. 247–62.
11. Ibid.

ingly, our aim cannot be to restore the advantages each spouse had in marriage but rather for them to share, as in any partnership, the losses that marriage and divorce together have caused.

Most people in the industrialized countries would now agree that wives in short, childless marriages lose little materially through divorce. (Legal arrangements will always be ineffectual against emotional losses.) But even without children, who accentuate the financial loss, many wives in longer marriages do lose in the market. Their careers suffer from the lesser investments they made during the period of their marriage, and if they enter the market anew, they will be much behind their age cohorts in their job levels. After a very long period, they may simply be unable to find an adequate job at all. These losses are much greater for women who have reared children during marriage and those who are still caring for them after divorce.

Thus various types of readjustments should be available as remedies, whether or not these are called alimony. Some wives need only modest subsidies for retraining, others need almost total support for full-time study but for only one or two years, while still others—especially those who have been "career homemakers"—will need support for a longer duration, perhaps for the rest of their lives. Such women have a strong claim on their ex-husband's income, which is usually the most valuable property asset their marital partnership created. In fact, in the state of California, the Senate Task Force on Family Equity, which was established in response to Lenore Weitzman's book on the impact of divorce on women and children, recommended *a presumption of permanent support after a marriage of long duration* "to meet the economic crisis of the displaced homemaker and other dependent spouses . . . [to be] viewed as a form of legal insurance, protection or pension for the spouse who has given priority to the other spouse's career and to child rearing instead of developing his or her own career to marketable skills."[12] That recommendation was adopted by the California legislature in 1987 and is now the law.

The underlying theory of the California legislation is the partnership theory of marriage. The Senate Task Force urged the reformulation of alimony to ensure the sharing of all assets built during the marital partnership, including the enhanced earning capacity of the major wage-earning spouse. As they wrote: "The assumption of 'self-sufficiency' [behind alimony awards] ignores the fact that many of these wives have sacrificed their own career opportunities and earning potential because of tacit or express marital partnership agreements. Adequate support awards . . . reflect societal perceptions of the importance and value of homemaking and child-rearing

12. California Senate, *Final Report of the Task Force on Family Equity* (Sacramento, Calif.: State of California, June 1987), p. V-4.

contributions and sacrifices made during marriage."[13] Again, that is a loss for the ex-husband, but it is a deduction from their common property; it is not simply "his." It could, as in the case of children, be calculated on real actuarial income and cost data. If adequately enforced, as such payments are not now, this might suggest more caution to some couples who are thinking of divorce as well as to those who are considering marriage. It would be a social reminder that the costs of a breakup are part of the responsibility of marriage.

It hardly needs to be pointed out that almost all of the foregoing proposals are only distributional: they shift the burdens somewhat but create no new income or property. Since marital dissolution is more common among the lower classes, where birth rates are also higher, any plan that merely allocates the income and goods of the partnership may in fact have little to distribute. Bluntly, provisions of this kind would make some small inroads on poverty, since a goodly number of mothers and children would be better off. However, many couples were poor during their marriage, too, and sharing those disadvantages will be of only slight comfort. The Nordic states that now show some enthusiasm and competence in tackling this great problem will be of greater help in showing more hesitant nations that it is costly not to engage in it. The society as a whole already pays large costs for the neglect of both the mothers and the poor children of divorce (as also for its other poor children). It is shortsighted to count only the current price of state child support, ignoring the heavy costs over the longer term when we skimp on that support. Better plans, based on what we already know, would add to the total national output if they help women to move to more productive work.

I have hoped to offer intellectual rewards, and thus to persuade the reader to accompany me on this odyssey through time and space. I myself have experienced many surprises as I have explored the complex, often puzzling, dynamics of changes in divorce patterns in many parts of the world over the past forty years. In each subregion, I think, some broad hypothesis has emerged and we have seen some new trends that would not be obvious in a simple registry of the divorce rates in previous decades. A global perspective that treats each area as worthy of attention and also continues to compare different subsystems, uncovers some widespread patterns as well as striking differences that would not easily be seen if we simply looked at each nation separately, one after the other.

As I have emphasized more than once, my aim was not to "solve" the problem of divorce but to move toward understanding its processes. However, I think that suggestions for reducing some of its harsh effects can now

13. Ibid., p. V-5.

be made, based on a considerable body of research information. I have offered a few. They can be summed up, or perhaps a better set created, by using one guiding principle: we should accept the fact that most developed nations can now be seen as high divorce rate systems, and we should *institutionalize* divorce—accept it as we do other institutions, and build adequate safeguards as well as social understandings and pressures to make it work reasonably well.

Even if these proposals are rejected, it is at least necessary to comprehend its causal processes more adequately. I hope this study is a contribution toward that greater understanding.

Index